'At a time when the Four Horsemen of the Apocalypse – War, Famine, Disease, Death – are rampaging around the world, the theme of this work is timely. The *Introduction* sets the tone as it features the unconcealing of the *shadow* of the two editors Christopher Perry and Rupert Tower – grandson of Daphne du Maurier. Perry's own contribution is grounded in the solid work by Gabbard and Celenza on boundary violations that addresses those difficulties. There follow other practice-based clinical pieces and chapters on literature and esoterica. Interspersed with these are weighty entries on the hot topics of today, *viz.*, climate change, gender dysphoria, the metaverse, and modern technology. *Jung's Shadow Concept: the Hidden Light and Darkness Within Ourselves* investigates the darkest recesses of human existence animating one of Jung's major contributions to psychology: the *Shadow* – light and dark.'

Ann Casement, *LP, Professor at the Oriental Academy of Analytical Psychology*

'A most timely reflection by a stellar group of Jungian authors and lay-people shedding light on numerous features of our shadow-rich psyches individual and collective.'

Murray Stein, *editor of* Jung on Evil

I0130954

Jung's Shadow Concept

This insightful volume is designed as a series of invitations towards living attentiveness, examining how we all make the "other", through "projection" (blaming and shaming the other outside ourselves), our enemy with whom we prefer not to dialogue.

All of us are faced daily with individual and collective manifestations of the Shadow – all that we fear, despise and make us feel ashamed. Carl Jung's concept of the Shadow, emerging as it did from his personal confrontation with the realms of his unconscious self, is one of the most important contributions he made to the understanding of humanity and to depth psychology, that realm where the focus is on unconscious processes. The contributors to this book reframe his concept in the context of contemporary Jungian thinking, exploring how the Shadow develops in an individual's infancy and adolescence, and its culmination, where collective manifestations of the Shadow are addressed. The book offers a voyage through a series of fundamental Shadow concepts and themes including couples relationships, disease, organisations, evil, fundamentalism, ecology and boundary violation before ending with a chapter designed to help us integrate the Shadow and hold contra-positions with patience and a tilt towards mutual understanding, rather than being locked in polarities.

This fascinating new book will be of interest to the general public, Jungian analysts, scholars and therapists both in training and practice with an interest in the inner world.

Christopher Perry is a training analyst and supervisor of the Society of Analytical Psychology, of which he is also the former Director of Training. He is the author of *Listen to the Voice Within: A Jungian Approach to Pastoral Care* and several articles on analytical psychology and group analysis. He is interested in the interface between psychotherapy and spirituality. He lives in London.

Rupert Tower is a member of the Society of Analytical Psychology. He studied psychology, worked in the Arts, and was an applied social psychologist and director of an international qualitative cross-cultural research consultancy prior to becoming a Jungian analyst in mid-life. He has published articles on social psychology, market research, and Jung's concept of the Shadow in organisations. He lives and works in Hampstead.

Jung's Shadow Concept

The Hidden Light and Darkness within Ourselves

Edited by Christopher Perry and Rupert Tower

Routledge
Taylor & Francis Group

LONDON AND NEW YORK

Designed cover image: © Bridgeman Images

First published 2023
by Routledge
4 Park Square, Milton Park, Abingdon, Oxon OX14 4RN

and by Routledge
605 Third Avenue, New York, NY 10158

Routledge is an imprint of the Taylor & Francis Group, an informa business

British Library Cataloguing-in-Publication Data
A catalogue record for this book is available from the British Library

ISBN: 978-1-032-18702-0 (hbk)
ISBN: 978-1-032-18700-6 (pbk)
ISBN: 978-1-003-25581-9 (ebk)

DOI: 10.4324/9781003255819

Typeset in Times New Roman
by MPS Limited, Dehradun

To Margaret and to Shawn: with love and gratitude for their solidarity and support through the coming-into-being of this book

Contents

Contributors

Raj Balkaran, Oxford Centre for Hindu Studies, Canada. Raj Balkaran is a prolific author of Indian mythology and a seasoned online educator. He teaches at a number of online platforms, including his own School of Indian Wisdom. He also runs a life coaching practice and hosts the New Books in Indian Religions podcast. See https://rajbalkaran.com for more information.

Wendy J. Bratherton, The Society of Analytical Psychology and The Craniosacral Therapy Association, United Kingdom. Wendy J. Bratherton is a retired Jungian Analyst. She taught Infant Observation, through which she developed an interest in early developmental trauma and the mind–body connection. She trained in BodySoul work with Marian Woodman and as a Biodynamic Craniosacral Therapist. She now works as a Biodynamic Craniosacral Therapist in Norfolk.

Stephen Bushell, IAAP, UKCP, GAP, UK & Spain. Meditation, Tai Chi and mysticism have been life-long sources of wisdom for Stephen Bushell. He is working as a chaplain in psychiatric care. Stephen is trained in London with GAP and set up in private practice. He currently co-runs a small retreat centre in Northern Spain bringing together meditation and Jungian psychology (lesgavatxes.es).

Coline Covington, The Society of Analytical Psychology, The British Psychotherapy Foundation, and The Association of Child Psychotherapists, registered with The British Psychoanalytic Council, United Kingdom. Coline Covington is a Fellow of International Dialogue Initiative (IDI), a think tank formed by Prof. Vamik Volkan, Lord Alderdice and Dr. Robi Friedman in analysing political conflict. Recent publications: *Everyday Evils: A Psychoanalytic View of Evil and Morality* (Routledge, 2017), *For Goodness Sake: Bravery, Patriotism and Identity* (Phoenix Publishing House, 2020) and *Who's to Blame? Collective Guilt on Trial* (forthcoming May 2023).

Alison George, New Scientist, United Kingdom. Alison George is a science writer at New Scientist magazine, who previously worked as a biologist with the British Antarctic Survey. She is the author of *The Brain: A User's Guide* and has edited books on evolution and quantum mechanics.

Sheikh Ahmed Haneef, Islamic Seminary of Hawza, United Kingdom. Sheikh Ahmed Haneef was born in Trinidad and grew up in Toronto. He studied Islamic philosophy, theology, jurisprudence and akhlaq in Qom under notable scholars. He now resides in London with his family and teaches at the Islamic College of Advanced Studies and the Seminary.

Emilija Kiehl, British Jungian Analytic Association in the British Psychotherapy Foundation, United Kingdom. Emilija Kiehl is a Jungian Analyst in private practice in London. She is the Vice President of the International Association for Analytical Psychology, a training analyst and a former Chair of the British Jungian Analytic Association and a senior member of the British Psychotherapy Foundation. She teaches, lectures and supervises in the United Kingdom and abroad.

Clare Landgrebe, The Society of Analytical Psychology, United Kingdom. Clare Landgrebe is a Training Analyst member of the Society of Analytical Psychology. Originally trained as a social worker, she worked as a couples counsellor and supervisor for Relate.

Rowena Mahmoud, IPCAPA and British Jungian Analytic Association in the British Psychotherapy Foundation, United Kingdom. Rowena Mahmoud qualified in 2015 and since then has worked as a Child and Adolescent Psychotherapist for the Bridge Foundation. She has taught and mentored for the British Psychotherapy Foundation and the Tavistock Centre and also contributed to various publications.

David Mathew, PhD, Teams and Leadership, United Kingdom. David Mathew is the Founder of www.teamsandleadership.com, a cloud-based development platform designed to help people and teams increase their effectiveness, fulfilment and resilience, and empower organisational change. Having worked with a number of global and healthcare organisations, he strives to make high-quality research evidence accessible to everyone.

Marilyn A. F. Mathew, British Jungian Analytic Association in the British Psychotherapy Foundation, United Kingdom. Marilyn Mathew is a Jungian training analyst working in south Devon. She has a long-standing interest in dreams, pregnancy, childbirth and infant observation as well as non-verbal communication.

Helen Morgan, British Jungian Analytic Association in the British Psychotherapy Foundation, United Kingdom. Helen Morgan is a Fellow of the British Psychotherapy Foundation and is a training analyst and supervisor for the Jungian Analytic Association within the BPF. Her book, *The Work of Whiteness. A Psychoanalytic Perspective* was published in 2021 by Routledge.

Christopher Perry, The Society of Analytical Psychology, United Kingdom. Christopher Perry is a retired Training Analyst and Supervisor of the SAP, and was formerly its Director of Training. He is the author of *Listen to the Voice Within: A Jungian Approach to Pastoral Care*. He has long been engaged with the application of Jungian ideas outside the consulting room.

Tomasso Priviero, UCL, United Kingdom (Country of Birth: Italy). Tomasso Priviero holds a PhD in History of Psychology from University College London (UCL) and is a trainee Jungian psychotherapist at the SAP. His first monograph was a study of eros and anarchism in the work of Lucretius. His second book is a study of *Jung's Lifelong Confrontation with Dante*, forthcoming with Routledge.

Chris Robertson, UKCP, United Kingdom. Chris Robertson has been a psychotherapist since 1978; is a supervisor, trainer and co-founder of Re-Vision and was chair of the Climate Psychology Alliance with whom he still works. His publications include A *Matter of Life and Death* (2022) (co-author); *Culture Crisis: a loss of Soul in Depth Psychology and Climate Change* (2020), https://www.culture-crisis.net

Ewa Robertson, Re-Vision, London, United Kingdom. Ewa Robertson, UKCP, is a registered psychotherapist, supervisor and trainer. She co-founded Re-Vision in 1988, a transpersonal integrative psychotherapy training centre. She specialises in relational psychotherapy, the mystery of the interplay of body and psyche, and trauma. She is the author of *"Roots and Seeds" and "The Third Body" in Transformation in Troubled Times* (TransPersonal Press, 2018).

Mary-Jayne Rust, The Society of Analytical Psychology, United Kingdom. Mary-Jayne Rust is a Jungian analyst and art therapist. Alongside her therapy practice, she teaches ecopsychology, a growing field of inquiry into our complex relationship with the earth, our home. Her publications include *Towards an Ecopsychotherapy* (Confer Books, 2019). She grew up beside the sea and is wild about swimming.

Malcolm Rushton, The Society of Analytical Psychology, United Kingdom. Malcolm Rushton is a training analyst of the Society of Analytical Psychology and works full-time as an analyst in private practice. He has an interest in shamanism which is expressed in a wide-ranging collection of ancient art. These objects often play a significant part in his analytic work.

Katerina Sarafidou, British Jungian Analytic Association, honorary member, United Kingdom. Katerina Sarafidou is the Head of Research (former Director) at the MSc Psychodynamics of Human Development, run by Birkbeck College and the British Psychotherapy Foundation. She is carrying out academic research at the Warburg Institute and is one of the founders of the Circle of Analytical Psychology.

Laurie Slade, Guild of Psychotherapists, Confederation for Analytical Psychology, Institute for Psychedelic Therapy, International Association for the Study of Dreams, United Kingdom. Laurie Slade practiced for 30 years as a psychoanalytic psychotherapist with a Jungian orientation, and continues to act as a creative consultant. He has been involved in social dreaming since 2001, hosting sessions in a variety of settings in the United Kingdom and internationally.

Rupert Tower, Society of Analytical Psychology, United Kingdom. Rupert Tower is a psychologist, psychotherapist and Jungian Analyst in private practice. Previously, he worked in the Arts and as an Applied Social Psychologist and a Director of an international qualitative research consultancy. He has published articles on Social Psychology, Market Research and Jung's concept of the Shadow in organisations.

Nigel Wellings, Independent Psychoanalytic Psychotherapist, United Kingdom. Nigel Wellings is a psychoanalytic psychotherapist and an author who works within a broadly contemplative perspective. He has been engaged in the relationship between psychotherapy and Buddhism for the last 40 years. His books include *Why Can't I Meditate?* and most recently *Present with Suffering.* He also has a new book due for publication this Spring, *Dzogchen, Who's Who & What's What in the Great Perfection.*

Robert Withers, The Society of Analytical Psychology, United Kingdom. Robert Withers is a training analyst and teacher with the Society of Analytical Psychology and a former senior lecturer in the history and philosophy of medicine at Westminster University. He has written and lectured extensively on transgender issues. He is co-founder of The Rock Clinic in Brighton where he currently works.

Acknowledgements

This book would not have come to life had not the late Jan Lee not introduced us.

Profound gratitude to our authors for mining with courage and devotion the depths of their personal, professional and collective experience of engaging with the Shadow in some of its manifestations.

Endless thanks to Urvi Bhatt, our Administrative Editor, whose constructively critical eye, technical competence and unswerving patience have been mainstays in bringing this book to fruition. We cannot thank her enough.

Our enduring indebtedness to and appreciation of Alice Maher and the team at Routledge for their enthusiasm, encouragement and guidance through the labyrinthine process of publishing, and for bringing this book to the light of day.

Our cherishing of challenging conversations, critical comments, unfailing support and friendship generously offered by Helen Batten, Brian Bradbury, Jenni Convey, Natasha de Grunwald, Joanna Green, Paul Halliday, Christina Harrison, Lucinda Hawkins, Alexis Humphry, Peter Jacobs, Laura LeFeuvre, Martin Schmidt, Ann Shearer, Steve Slann, Katherine Stewart and Susanna Wright. Thank you!

Work with our patients and trainees has heightened our sensitivity to the pain and reward involved in working with the Shadow. They have taught us the importance of humility and patience when confronting and integrating the Shadow, and have helped us to learn to be with them, and to listen to the silence beyond words wherein lies an ever-lasting truth which is beyond time and space. Not this; not that.

The Management and Staff of the Brudenell Hotel, Aldeburgh, supported us during our several sojourns there through various stages of the book and did everything they could do to facilitate our conversations and writing.

The Trickster along the way kept capsizing us at inopportune moments yet kept us honest, ensuring that we remained grounded enough through times of conflict, and able better to face and own Shadow projections between ourselves and towards others.

Acknowledgements –
Permission Credits

A Note on the Paperback Cover Image

Edvard Munch (b. Norway, 1863–1944)
Dancing on a Shore, 1900
Oil on canvas, 95.5 cm by 98.5 cm
Narodni Galerie, Prague, Czech Republic

Originally, The Dance on the Shore of 1900 was part of the collection of 22 paintings entitled *"The Frieze of Life"*. The figures of dancing girls are at the centre of the action being observed by two figures in black – widows. The solitary woman in red symbolises the age of the climax of erotic strength. The cycle of life is rendered in wide colourful lines dividing the space into multi-coloured bands.

Sue Prideaux (2005) describes Munch's shoreline, as seen from his house in Aasgardstrand, and as depicted in *"The Frieze of Life"*, as the landscape against which he set "the secret life of the soul". "Through all there winds the curving shoreline and beyond it the ever-moving sea, while under the trees, life with all its complexities of grief and joy, carries on". In these pictures, Munch expresses his experience of sexual awakening and how he felt after losing his virginity on the shore among the pine trees and later he symbolised the connection between the divided pair with the help of her long, wavy hair like a sort of telephone wire that cannot be cut, as if there were invisible threads connecting them. The frieze essentially portrays the circle of life – the awakening of love, the dance of life, love at its peak, the fading of love, and finally the dance of death (p. 185). This may also reflect his relationship with Tulla Larsen around this time who was inspiring these series of paintings while his close friend Strindberg was writing his play inspired by Munch, *"The Dance of Death"*.

The co-editors were inspired to choose this image as it seemed to echo something of the Shadow dance through life, with its intensities and complexities, forged through the pleasures and rigours of relationship. The figure in red seemed to represent elements of the lifeforce hidden within the Shadow with all its creative potentials that can bring us into a deeper relationship with our whole personality. The creature in the lower left of the canvas perhaps may stand for the instinctual and the psychoid layers of humanity, encouraging us to *"live your animal"* and our otherness (Jung, 2009, pp. 341–342).

References

Jung, G. G. (2009). *"The Red Book Liber Novus Readers Edition"*. Ed. Shamadasani, S. London: W.W. Norton & Company, Philemon Series.

Prideaux, S. (2005). *"Edvard Munch: Behind the Scream"*. New Haven and London: Yale University Press.

Rupert Tower, Hampstead, February 2022.

Introduction

Christopher Perry and Rupert Tower

Our book is an invitation to readers to meet in a spirit of gentle, open and honest curiosity with whatever troubles or unsettles them in their relationships with themselves, their values and aspirations; with partners, families and work-place; with their communities and political allegiance; with the planet and the international community of interdependence. In essence, everything that goes to form the contents of our Shadow: including our hidden potentials, capacities and qualities lying dormant in our unlived life – as well as that which we fear, dislike and despise in ourselves and see in other people.

The germinating seed of this book began through the flourishing of an organic movement from collegiate relationship to deep friendship, in which we found a space over lunch once a month for sharing our mutual passion and vital interest in Jung's concept of the Shadow. In hindsight, we now wonder if we were unconsciously drawn to each other because we are two only children looking for a brother. These experiences contributed to our quest to understand our parents' Shadows as well as to deepen our understanding of our own. One of the things that brought us together was a mutual discovery that we had felt considerable anger at times with organisations which were painful displacements of our anger with our parents. We also shared some exasperation with our Founders' (Freud/Jung/Adler) power drives, father complexes, boundary transgressions and personal flaws that made them incapable of addressing their personal Shadow issues with each other. We determined that we would attempt to address our own Shadow enactments during this creative process with each other in as open an attitude of directness and honesty as we could. These movements between us translated into deeper friendship when we could voice and acknowledge them. We coined a term for this: "Shadow-play", where a lightness of touch brought more connection and reminded us that "*On the seashore of endless worlds … children play*" (Tagore 1912). An example of this was our initial lunch meeting when one of us (C.P.) had come with a whole outline of the chapters of this book only to be met by his trickster co-editor (R.T.), who

DOI: 10.4324/9781003255819-1

flipped the whole thing upside-down, by suggesting that we start taking soundings from the collective – the people's Shadow pre-occupations – rather than imposing an individual schema on the project!! From the outset, we needed to struggle with our different visions and find ways to reach compromise and find convergence. And we wondered how the Shadow might infiltrate the project.

Early on in our creative process, we engaged in a game of generous Shadow jiving where we would freely associate with and to anything and everything that we felt was imbued by Shadow. We noticed that we both have a tendency to enjoy living on the edge of intensity that sometimes could result in making impulsive decisions that then needed reconsidering from a more grounded place. This created a form of reverie in our friendship, like sitting round a campfire at night, watching the sparks rising into the darkness above us.

It seemed important to discover and explore simultaneously what manifestations of the Shadow were lying subliminally in the collective consciousness and in people's unconscious pre-occupations where their existence posed some level of threat to social equilibrium. We devised an exercise in which participants were invited to reveal the three global issues they most did NOT want to think about. Whilst priorities varied between groups and within individuals, a remarkable consistency emerged: the feelings most often shared were collective shame, fear of annihilation and helplessness and alienation in the face of ecological disaster, personal and international transgression of boundaries, inequitable wealth distribution, prejudice and a fear of technology.

We met regularly each month; we kept notes and observed differences between them. What we noticed in this exchange was the usefulness of meandering and allowing for a more associative, spiral rather than linear thinking – what Jung (1956) called "non-directed" rather than directed thinking (CW5, para. 37), in which he outlined that "*whereas directed thinking is an altogether conscious phenomenon, the same cannot be said of fantasy-thinking. Much of it belongs to the conscious sphere, but at least as much goes on in the half-shadow, or entirely in the unconscious, and can therefore be inferred only indirectly. Through fantasy-thinking, directed thinking is brought into contact with the oldest layers of the human mind, long buried beneath the threshold of consciousness*" (para. 39). This allowed us to be influenced by three inter-related processes of "letting happen, considering and facing" (Humbert 1984) what we found.

But, we began to encounter obstacles between us which we avoided by, for example, individually acting impulsively and approaching authors without consulting one another. We realised that we were both involved in some Shadow acting-out. This was fuelled by unconscious rivalry. A Shadow dance evolved between us where one person's restraint increased the other's recklessness, and vice versa, much to our mutual annoyance and exasperation.

Once we began to recognise this, the internal work together enabled us to acknowledge these Shadow impulses and, over time, to trust more in our developing friendship, and therefore anticipate them before they needed to occur. When we were tilted off balance, we were able to recover through the rhythm of the work together – acknowledging doubts about the project, trying to withdraw projections through talking, quietness and constant reflection. This seemed to work well for our creative process.

Another antidote to falling into unconscious Shadow enactments was the ongoing sharing and exploring of our dreams, which brought balance and humour. One such dream: one of us awoke, laughing somewhat wildly. Queen Charlotte of Bohemia (the nickname for one of our favourite meeting places) had come to launch a coracle that both of us had built together. We belonged to a tribe of cavemen, living on the coast of Brittany. It was an unusual vessel, because, once we launched and boarded it, it spun like a whirling dervish over the water, before succumbing to a whirlpool, and singing the plainsong hymn "Veni Creator Spiritus" [Come, creator spirit], which made the Queen of Bohemia convulse with laughter, before she threw herself into the coracle. We all spun down the whirlpool accompanied by a chorus of jellyfish singing discordantly ... We were really made aware of the creative and destructive dynamic between us and reinvigorated our spirit of mutually questioning collaboration.

Deep friendship was forged by sojourns in Aldeburgh, which became our crucible of imagination where increasingly we shared our vulnerabilities with each other beside the beach, the light and sounds of which offered so much to us both through the creative parenting of the Brudenell Hotel, where we stayed, a deeply moving and enabling context for us both. A poem by Rilke (1922–1926) speaks to this:

> Winds of Homecoming.
>
> Ah, not to be cut off,
> Not through the slightest partition
> Shut off from the law of the stars.
> The inner – what is it?
> If not intensified sky,
> Hurled through with birds and deep
> With the winds of homecoming.

What is the Shadow?

What do we mean by the Shadow? It is an invitation to each and every one of us to be curious in a gentle and open way about who and what irks us; and why. We are all aware of suffering, conflict and animosity in our families, personal relationships, in work and in our wider culture and society. For example, the phenomenon of "scapegoating" in families and organisations is common and widespread. All the difficulties of the family or organisation are heaped onto an individual, who is accused of causing misfortune, is blamed for it, persecuted and driven out in the false hope that the expulsion of what was "irking" the remaining members can enable them to deny their responsibility for their own fears and fallibilities.

There are many organisations that are involved in and engaged with issues such as conflict resolution, truth and reconciliation, forgiveness – approaches designed to influence and improve people's conscious behaviour towards each other or their capacity for self-reflection. Our particular interest is in unconscious processes and the different perspective that we, as analytical psychologists, can offer so that a bridge can be made between conscious behaviour and unconscious processes that live within and through us.

Our unconscious contains what is not known and what is not liked as well as the defence mechanisms that keep these out of conscious awareness. We tend to hide what we dislike or are ashamed of in ourselves so that it remains unknown to us but perceptible by others.

Throughout his Collected Works, Jung created many definitions of the Shadow, which he thought of as paradoxical in two senses: (i) that, for example, rotting vegetable rubbish could be transformed into compost; darkness contains light; depression contains the seeds of useful anger; aggression is by its very nature destructive but is also vital for survival and acts as a carrier for the innate potential of creativity; and (ii) that coming consciously to terms with what we repress and project in all the positive and negative manifestations of our nature can intermingle with loving and embracing all of our idiosyncrasies.

Shadow Definitions and Processes

We have chosen five of his definitions that we feel express its essence, meaning and purpose:

> "... that hidden, repressed, for the most part inferior and guilt-laden personality whose ultimate ramifications reach back into the realm of our animal ancestors ... If it has been believed hitherto that the human shadow was the source of all evil, it can now be ascertained on further investigation that the unconscious man, that is his Shadow, does not consist only of morally reprehensible tendencies, but also displays a number of good qualities, such as normal instincts, appropriate reactions, realistic insights, creative impulses etc." (Jung 1959) (CW9 [ii], paras. 422 & 423)

> "The thing a person has no wish to be" (Jung 1954) (CW16, para. 470)

> "The Shadow personifies everything that the subject refuses to acknowledge about himself" (Jung 1959) CW9 [i], para. 513)

"The shadow ... is apt to turn up in the guise of a hostile neighbour, who will inevitably arouse your anger and make you aggressive. It is surely better to know that your worst enemy is right there in your own heart" (Jung 1964) (CW10, para. 456)

"To confront a person with his Shadow is to show him his own light ... Anyone who perceives his Shadow and his light simultaneously sees himself from two sides, and thus gets in the middle" (Jung 1964 (CW10, para. 872)

His simple notions were as follows: (i) We are not friendly with aspects of ourselves that we fear, dislike or despise because (ii) they elicit shades of shame, from which we protect ourselves by (iii) repressing and then projecting and tending to see the unwanted feelings, impulses and instinctual urges in others, whom (iv) we can blame, shame and attack rather than us recognising, accepting and owning these qualities in ourselves. It needs to be emphasised that this whole process is unconscious.

Between (iii) and (iv) we come to a psychic choice: turning one way, we remain unconscious that these aspects belong to us, and we then continue to feed the blame, shame and attack. This results in defensive closure, a lack of flow both within and without, a chronic sense of depletion, and a loss of balance. These can negatively affect individuals, couples, families, groups, organisations, political structures and international relations resulting in anything from a marital spat to a declaration of war. Turning the other way, we choose to take back what belongs to ourselves (the projection) and bring it into consciousness, thus enabling us to see the other as s/he really is and re-connecting with ourselves.

The Personal Shadow

How is the Shadow encountered? It is almost always in projection on some other individual, family member or group. This means that I see in another something I dislike. As projection is such a primitive and powerful unconscious dynamic and defence in our daily lives, it can only be acknowledged once its results have been identified in the other. It requires intensive work and effort to withdraw the projection and to recognise it as an essential quality in us that we prefer not to have to face. As Jung (1959) says, *"It is not the conscious subject but the unconscious that does the projecting. Hence one meets with projections, one does not make them. The effect of projection is to isolate the subject from his environment, since instead of a real relationship to it there is now only an illusory one"* (CW9(ii), para. 17). For those who have been wounded to a greater or lesser extent, recognising, investigating and accepting their disowned qualities and potentials can be both challenging and profoundly healing.

The Shadow's Hidden Potential

What needs to be emphasised very strongly here is that the Shadow contains all sorts of positive qualities, capacities and potential, which if not recognised and owned maintain a state of impoverishment in the personality and deprive the person of sources of energy and bridges of connectedness with others. For example, a person might believe that to be assertive is to be selfish; so he goes through life being pushed around by others and deep down seething with resentment, which in turn makes him feel guilty. In this case, his potential for assertiveness and his resentment both form part of his Shadow. Entering a relational therapeutic process might challenge his value system, track it back to its origins, and help him to become more embodied. This may energise him and thereby enable him to be more in touch with his needs, and open up areas of choice, which would probably lead to his resentment diminishing. Jung also pointed out that whilst we usually think of the Shadow as the dark, negative and destructive sides of our personalities, these aspects of ourselves equally and usually consist of light, positive, loving and creative capacities within us. Typically relegated by our parental upbringing and environment into the realms of the unconscious, they comprise a hidden treasure trove that contains unlived life and a vast reservoir of psychic energy and human potential. This creates an imbalance in the psyche, allowing for a purposive compensatory movement to evolve fed by opportunities in the external world to befriend the contents of the treasure trove, such as instances that require assertiveness. The subjective experience of being with an individual or group in which the Shadow is disavowed and projected is felt keenly as an absence of appropriate vitality.

The Collective Shadow

Thus far we have been focusing on the personal Shadow. But this cannot be separated from the collective Shadow. A metaphor can be used to bring this to life: Imagine that we are swimming together in the sea and that we are treading water. We will work from the head downwards. We share a collective consciousness – the weather, the temperature of the water, our companions. We each have our personal individual consciousness: the sensation of water on my skin, the light and the breeze. Looking down, we can observe that we can see through the water to a certain depth; beyond that area there is insufficient light. This area is called the personal unconscious and it is where the personal Shadow lives. Its depth is unknown, but quite invisibly it meets up with the collective unconscious which is where the collective Shadow lives.

This has at least three inter-linked elements, some of which are buoyed-up by our individual and collective capacity to "turn a blind eye", by which we mean seeing something but also defending against its existence by disavowing its reality: they encompass undercurrents in our society, projections that fuel negative international perceptions, and a negative energy or force in the world. The latter comprises climate warming, the current Covid-19 pandemic, Brexit, the refugee and migration crisis, arms trading, child poverty, sex trafficking, water privatisation, and unethical investment – to name but a few. In addition, we tend to project our fascination with these aspects into the collective Shadow, forgetting that some of them reflect inner dramas. For example, a populist, authoritarian leader inciting a mob to violence; the picture is compelling or repelling, but fascinating.

There is a figure that links the personal and collective Shadow; it is the Trickster. Jung (1959) describes the Trickster as *"the summation of all the inferior traits of character in individuals"* (CW9[i], para. 484). But, the Trickster has a purpose; it is compensatory to the individual's conscious attitude and its integration can transform the meaningless into the meaningful. It can appear in personal accidents, slips of the tongue, parapraxes, dreams and synchronistic events. We all know the experience of wanting to puncture someone else's "inflated" attachment to objects, ideas or obsessions. One of the editors recalls borrowing a car that felt overly precious to its owner to the extent that it had to be returned without a speck of dust. But the Trickster energy bounced in and ensured he crashed the rear into a brick wall.

Shame

We have considered the appearance of the Shadow (through projection onto an "other") and the content (everything we fear, despise and cannot accept in ourselves: that which is underdeveloped, unwanted and disowned as well as the treasure trove of potential capacities). Now, we arrive at the feeling that is most strongly associated with the Shadow: shame, elicited by shaming. This commands a whole repertoire of ways of saying things, tone of voice and associated body language that can make the other want to shrivel up, be swallowed by the earth, and wish that s/he had never been born. This is the experience of a painful sense of exposure, of being seen when one does not want to be seen, or is not ready to be seen, which results in a desperate wish to hide or disappear. What makes shame so crippling is feeling that one's very being is at fault and under serious attack. Emily Dickinson (1830-1886) has this to say about shame:

> Shame is the shawl of pink
> In which we wrap the soul
> To keep it from infesting eyes –
> The elemental veil
> Which helpless nature drops
> When pushed upon a scene
> Repugnant to her probity –
> Shame is the tint divine.

Shame is so withering and inimical to the process of befriending the Shadow that "*At one moment, something else must break through, that laughing insight at the paradox of one's own folly which is also everyman's*" (Hillman 1967, p. 76). We ALL have a Shadow and befriending it is a shared human struggle. When we really "lose it" and reveal something deeply exposing about ourselves to another, what can help to soften and detoxify the searing, shameful feelings is if the other person brings a whisk of humour that helps lead us to self-acceptance. However, we need shame as a corrective. There are those who appear shameless and create anxiety in others by disregarding boundaries and the conventions attached to formal roles. Their behaviour suggests that there is no internal braking system between their impulses and their enactment. These people remind us that the attainment of shame is a necessary developmental achievement attached to social awareness and self-consciousness.

Six days before this book went to press, Russia, under the premiership of Vladimir Putin, invaded Ukraine resulting in several hundred people killed on both sides during the first day. The peace in Europe over the last seventy years seems threatened, as does Western democracy; and many are afraid that the situation could escalate into global conflict on a catastrophic scale. We, the co-editors, believe that this criminal invasion into a neighbouring sovereign state highlights the vitally important psychological challenge of meeting the personal and collective Shadow with attentive awareness. We hold the view that meeting and befriending the Shadow with awareness is a task of the utmost importance that needs addressing both personally and collectively. It demands shifts in orientation: looking inwards rather than outwards; adopting an attitude of curiosity and enquiry towards one's own thoughts, feeling and actions; and taking a stance of constant vigilance and anticipation of our unconscious enactments as a consequence of projection. Rather like walking round a sculpture, this book invites the reader to examine the Shadow's many manifestations from a variety of perspectives and angles in the hope of providing ways to bring Shadow processes into consciousness, and to apply these to personal and social situations.

We have also included in the Appendix a highly unique early monograph on the Shadow by Toni Wolff, originally presented within a collection of papers published in German to celebrate Carl Jung's 60th birthday. This is the first time that Toni Wolff's paper has been translated into English.

We were struck by how resoundingly her words and understanding of the Shadow resonated with much of what we have been struggling to communicate within the book, in particular: how the confrontation with the Shadow is interwoven dynamically with the process of individuation that "*demands the total engagement of the human being*" (Wolff 1935); that the object of our projections, be they inner, Other, or outer, require the ongoing work of integration by the gradual withdrawal of those projections so that we see ourselves more clearly; the importance of the differentiation of the Shadow as "*the dark brother that accompanies the ego everywhere, it is the Other in us that also wants to live with us so that we can be whole*" (ibid.); and compassion for the task of taking responsibility for acknowledging the Shadow within us and its creative potential for wholeness; then such "*realisation does not make me any better, but only a little more aware and honest, and possibly a little more tolerant of what is different and foreign. In so far as I am human towards myself, I can also be human towards others*"(ibid.).

The purpose of this book is to offer ways to understand Carl Jung's concept of the Shadow and to demonstrate its vital relevance to contemporary life. We are aware that inevitably we have had to omit exploration of some crucial areas of Shadow, such as sex trafficking, social media, suicide, culture and film, organisations and work place, addiction, etc.

The book consists of four sections and will begin with a Prologue that places the Shadow in a historical and philosophical context in Western civilisation and outlines the main influences on Jung's thinking.

Prologue: In Liber Novus, Jung embarks on a journey of confrontation with his Shadow, which he describes as a descent into hell. He understands this descent as an initiation and acknowledges that it is the only and necessary road to the inner world – the ultimate redemptive path of the individual. This chapter traces Jung's insights and experiences of working with the Shadow with its historical foundations in Western philosophical, literary and esoteric traditions, all of which sought to grasp something that could not be completely comprehended purely by the intellect, and aimed at elaborating the Self in order to prepare it for union with the Divine. A central part of this process was a descent to those parts of the psyche that were disowned and marginalised, those that were considered evil and were expelled because we were ashamed of them or revolted by them. Jung's initiatory descent in Liber Novus and his confrontation with the Shadow reveal the nature of individuation. It involves a renewed appreciation of the fact that all those inferior animal elements of the psyche compose part of a cosmic wholeness and are indispensable for the recovery of the soul.

Section I: The Personal Shadow

Chapter 1 explores how the Shadow can be created – its firm links to trauma, what affects its density and strength and how this can be worked with clinically. The author tells the story of therapeutic work with a mother and child, which revealed that the mother's journey was engulfed in shadows from even before she was born. These threatened to overwhelm her and her family.

Chapter 2 starts with the premise that every individual is unique, so generalising about trans people is inherently problematic. Nevertheless, some trans people have found it helpful to understand their gender dysphoria as the consequence of a dissociation between mind (subjectively experienced gender identity) and body (objective biological sex). In this chapter, the author combines a Winnicottian approach to mind-body dissociation with a contemporary Jungian approach to the Shadow. He argues that terrifying experiences such as early attachment trauma, ego-alien sexual feelings and sexual abuse can get driven into the Shadow, split-off and projected into the body. This can result in gender dysphoria. If the analyst fails to confront his own Shadow in the countertransference, he is unlikely to be able to help such a gender dysphoric individual re-integrate their own split-off experiences. This may result in premature and unnecessary medical interventions which can themselves constitute unconscious, collective Shadow enactments.

Chapter 3 considers disease as the body's Shadow. Jung maintained that the body and the psyche are inseparable. However, the treatment of each developed into the separate practices of psychotherapy and body work until recently when fresh insights from neuroscience have helped to form a bridge between the two. The body may silently "hold" memories of trauma and emotional problems which have been pushed away out of consciousness, including trauma from infancy resulting in a range of psychosomatic disorders and potentially life-threatening diseases. Examples will be given from analytic and craniosacral therapy to illustrate how engagement with the Shadow of disease may be addressed creatively.

Chapter 4 engages with meaning in facing the process of ageing, with its inevitable losses, decline in health and eventual death. Where the cultural norms suggest ageing as a failing in productivity and increasing obsolescence, the bright Shadow can offer the burnishing of character and resilience in the exposure to life's challenges. What might it mean to consider ageing as an initiation into the deeper questions of oneself, others and the world? Even where initiation confronts failings, these can become the composting that sheds old skins to reveal a place of forgiveness, grace and acceptance.

Chapter 5 explores the Shadow in literature. There are many myths and fairy tales that extend across cultures and civilisations that emphasise the Shadow personality. Touching on one of these *archetypal* motifs, this chapter will explore in depth the *personal* myth of the well-known writer, Daphne du Maurier, as expressed in one of her later works – "The Scapegoat" – in which she may have been delving unconsciously into her own Shadow story as manifested in the various characters that come to life in the novel. The chapter's author also happens to be her grandson and is continuing to mine the family interest in the interplay between conscious and unconscious experience.

We complete this section with Chapter 6 which explores how the opposites of wanting and not wanting intimacy get constellated between couples who are drawn together by an unconscious fit fuelled by projections of unwanted aspects of one partner onto the other. The author uses a case study and revisits the Narcissus myth to illustrate how this dance between couples develops. Early patterns of attachment and loss, trust, dependency, intimacy, loss of self, fear of abandonment and isolation provide the seeds of adult relating.

Section 2: The Collective Shadow

This section embraces cultural and collective challenges within society.

In Chapter 7, the author dreams an atrocity has taken place. It is not clear who is responsible. On waking, he sees this impulse to blame someone else as an example of the Shadow in action. He asks himself what he needs to take responsibility for. But he is not sure whether he is tuning in to his personal Shadow, something in his psyche which he is projecting outwards, or tuning in to something beyond himself with which he needs to engage in one way or another. He takes the dream to a social dreaming matrix, reflecting on how this form of dream sharing contains and gives shapes to the Shadows we struggle with at a social or collective level. He ends up looking at the Shadow as it manifests in the practice of social dreaming. Prompted by this dream, he realises he must take responsibility for a rift which occurred with a friend when both of them were involved in a social dreaming project. This leads to a reconciliation, and so highlights that attending to our dreams can help us identify and integrate our Shadows whether personal or collective.

Chapter 8 begins with the history of whiteness as an emergent phenomenon created to justify exploitation, slavery and colonisation since the 17th century. People with a skin of lighter hue – the Europeans – were linked with the image of "white" as pure and spiritually reinforcing the notion of "white" as good. As white can contain no tincture, "black" had to be created and allocated to those with skin of a darker hue, who were then correlated with the bad, dark and demonic. Jung made some very worrying and blatant statements about the so-called "primitive" that have not been seriously addressed by the Jungian community and which have implications for his theories. A section will refer to how children develop early race awareness, to their parents' blind spots, and to how the process of disavowal ensures that Shadow projection and white privilege is maintained. "Healing" can only occur when "whiteness" recognises and owns the damage done both historically and currently, and we carry out the work of mourning, reparation and, most importantly, the giving up of our white privilege.

In Chapter 9, we explore how the Shadow finds a comfortable home in politics. Its negative aspects are particularly welcome because fear, envy hatred, violence, indifference to the suffering of others (in gender, race, class, species), residing there are easy to exploit and use as fuel for weapons in fights for power.

Section 3: Challenges to Society

Chapter 10 examines the Shadow of ecology and the issues facing humanity involving sustainability, renewability, climate change and global warming. This chapter will show that a journey further into this Shadow territory reveals a long-held worldview that humans are separate from and superior to the rest of nature, seen as a conglomerate of "resources" or objects. Healing anthropocentrism or species arrogance involves a process of taking back our projections onto the non-human world. This process helps to re-vision our animal nature and offers a visceral connection with the oneness of life, leading to a new sense of human identity and belonging. Facing into climate change helps us to rediscover these ancient gifts which have been lost in the process of so-called civilisation.

Climate change is now the greatest threat to our existence on earth. In Chapter 11, we discuss how it confronts us with the fact that we cannot control the most elemental forces of nature nor can we stop the earth from its trajectory towards extinction. Every time the weather surprises us with unseasonal extremes we are reminded of not just our human mortality but the earth's mortality. Paradoxically, the fact that climate change threatens our very existence, makes it harder to take seriously. When Mother Earth becomes unpredictable, our need to maintain the illusion that we can control the world increases.

This leads to extreme reactions of denial that we have a destructive impact on our environment on the one hand and on the other a belief that we are totally responsible for the destruction of our habitat. The existential in-securities that feed these omnipotent reactions also fuel populist leanings towards authoritarianism and our search for all-powerful leaders. The desire to counteract loss and regain an illusion of past security is the shadow cast by profound uncontainable anxiety.

We move on then to Chapter 12 that enquires into the Shadow of tech-nology and likely future indications of change. The Fourth Industrial Revolution, based on a fusion of technologies – physical, digital and biolog-ical – is giving birth to new phenomena, such as Virtual Reality, new forms of social media, instant messaging, online gaming, video games – all of which encourage different ways of relating and potential non-relating. These are analysed from a Shadow perspective, reflecting on the implications for human relationships in the 21st century.

Chapter 13 will differentiate between power and love relationships and show how the former creates a perpetrator–victim dynamic, trapping both parties and severely reducing the capacity for creative thinking.

Such people identify with ideologies and become mindless and terrifying because they are not open to dialogue which they replace with devastating violence which, as martyrs, eventually destroys themselves and, psychically, their families. They tend to create a static polarity from which nothing creative can emerge because neither side can own their Shadows.

Chapter 14 examines the powerfully evocative image of the devil in C. G. Jung's Black Books and the Red Book (Liber Novus). The devil and Satan go to the roots of his "confrontation with the unconscious" as a living image upon which the later formulation of Jung's concept of the Shadow is based. The devil conundrum became a central motif of his psychological model, not as an "idea" or "belief" in a religious sense, but as a psychic reality through images. This lived experience of the *imago diaboli* Jung later developed into his concept of the Shadow.

Chapter 15 will offer a variety of perspectives on evil – a phenomenon about which Jung remained equivocal. Is it the absence of good (*privatio boni*)? Is it a determinant reality? A Buddhist, Christian, Hindu, Judaic and Muslim will offer different ways of looking at the same phenomenon. The chapter invites readers into seeking their own individual definition of evil.

Chapter 16 addresses the thorny subject of sexual boundary violation in therapeutic relationships which almost always leaves the patient–victim betrayed, abandoned and re-traumatised. It looks at some of the dynamics of the Wounded-Healer and offers a profile of therapist–perpetrators as well as exploring institutional responses to transgressions. Advice is offered to patients who become concerned about a therapeutic relationship going off the rails.

Section 4: Ways of Integrating the Shadow

The final chapter – Chapter 17 – provides a "toolkit" of ideas and exercises to help individuals, couples, families, groups and organisations to identify and get to grips with their Shadow. The toolkit will include the necessary requirements of undertaking the task of befriending and integrating the Shadow: compassion, honesty, imagination, courage, vulnerability and stamina before going on to suggest specific tasks for each of the five groups. The exercises will encourage people to use their creativity to explore their Shadow working with guided fantasy, dreams, reflections, artwork, writing, mythology, fairy tales, poetry & literature, film & TV, etc. Some of the exercises may be introduced with an example. Suggestions for self-help will be coupled with an appreciation of how difficult, shameful, humiliating but liberating and life-affirming a task coming to terms with the Shadow can be.

Christopher Perry & Rupert Tower
Aldeburgh, February 2022

References

Dickinson, E. (1830-1886). "Shame is the shawl of Pink". Massachusetts: Amherst Manuscript no. 342, Amherst College Archives and Special Collections.
Hillman, J. (1967). *"Insearch: Psychology and Religion"*. New York: Spring Publications
Humbert, E. (1984). *"C. G. Jung"*. Wilmette, Illinois: Chiron Publications.
Jung, C. G. (1956). "Two Types of Thinking". *CW5*.
Jung, C. G. (1959). "Conscious, Unconscious and Individuation". *CW9i*.
Jung, C. G. (1959). "On the Psychology of the Trickster-Figure". *CW9i*.
Jung, C. G. (1959). "The Shadow". *CW9ii*.
Jung, C. G. (1959). "Conclusion". *CW9ii*.
Jung, C. G. (1964). "The Fight with the Shadow". *CW10*.
Jung, C. G. (1964). "Good and Evil in Analytical Psychology". *CW10*.
Jung, C. G. (1954). "Psychology of the Transference". *CW16*.
Rilke, R. M. (1926). *Ahead of All Parting: Selected Poetry and Prose of Rainer Maria Rilke*. New York: Random House.
Tagore, R. (1912). *Gitanjali*. The India Society in London.
Wolff, T. (1935). "Introduction to the Fundamentals of Complex Psychology". Monograph in *"The Cultural Significance of Complex Psychology"*. Berlin: Julius Springer Publications.

The Descent into the Hell of Self-knowledge

The Shadow in Context

Katerina Sarafidou

Edgar Degas. "Dante and Virgil at the Entrance to Hell". ca. 1857–1858.

DOI: 10.4324/9781003255819-2

Encountering the Shadow: A Descent into One's Own Darkness

The idea of the Shadow plays a key role in Jung's model of the psyche. Jung understands it as that part within each of us that we find most difficult to acknowledge. It is usually the most devalued, inferior, repulsive, animal part of ourselves which remains mostly dark and unknown. The less connected it is to our conscious life, *"the blacker and denser"* it is (CW 11, para. 131). And yet facing the Shadow and assimilating it into conscious awareness and conscious functioning is a fundamental part of the process of individuation. The encounter with the Shadow requires a downward motion through a *"tight passage, a narrow door, whose painful constriction no one is spared who goes down to the deep well"* (CW 9i, para. 45). In other words, it is a "descent into one's own darkness" (CW 14, para. 471).

This descent and its potential transformational effect on the individual are a central theme in Jung's Red Book where it is described as a descent into hell. In the very first entry into the Black Book diaries on 12 November 1913, Jung notes: *"A huge task lay before me - I saw its enormous size - and its value and meaning escaped me. I got into the dark, and I groped along my path. That path led inward and downward"* (BB2, p. 149). The editor of Liber Novus, Sonu Shamdasani, suggested that the entire book could be characterised as Jung's descent into hell (Library of Congress, 2010). This descent is an account of Jung's own process of individuation and a blueprint for individuation as a general psychological framework.

Right before he embarked on the experimentations documented in his Black Books and then transcribed into the calligraphic edition of Liber Novus, Jung was at the pinnacle of his worldly success, but emotionally he felt destitute, and had an unbearable longing to reconnect with his soul. Compelled by the *"spirit of the depths"*, a voice reflective of a deep, unconscious layer of existence beyond the confines of temporality, rational thought or linear understanding, Jung made a heartfelt petition to his soul to return to him.

Once his soul appeared, she guided him into a desert, the desert of his own self, where no heroic ego images could survive and where there was no water, no hope, no thoughts, and no objects where he could direct his desires. In that place of desolation, Jung underwent a process of purification of his ego, shedding his attachments to his previous identity. Following his soul, he then surrendered to an initiatory process that required him to descend into hell, a place of disorder, chaos, torment and hopelessness, where the journey of his individuation began. He elaborates on the concept of hell as follows: *"Hell is when the depths come to you with all that you no longer are or are not yet capable of. Hell is when you can no longer attain what you could attain. Hell is when you must think and feel and do everything that you know you do not want. Hell is when you know that your having to is also a wanting to, and that you yourself are responsible for it"* (RB, pp. 169–170). What Jung describes here is not a Christian hell, but a hellish underworld nevertheless, in the inner recesses of the psyche.

Jung also claims that journeying to hell means *"to become hell oneself"* (RB, p. 156) and concludes that this is the only and necessary road to the inner world, the ultimate redemptive path of the individual. He explains, *"He who does not want evil, will have no chance to save his soul from hell. So long as he remains into the light of the upper world, he will become a shadow of himself, but his soul will languish in the dungeons of the daemons. This will act as a counterbalance that will forever constrain him. The inner world will remain unattainable for him. He remains where he was, indeed, he falls back"* (RB, p. 289). There is a need, therefore, to come to grips with all those aspects of the unconscious that have been excluded, otherwise they will remain *"grotesque and sinister"* (CW 16, para. 388). In this sense, encountering the Shadow also brings up the problem of evil as something that must be dealt with not as an abstract idea, but as a living reality within the individual and within the collective psyche. As Jung notes in the Black Book diaries: *"Evil ... is not to be forgotten. It exists. There is no scientific cover up for it. [T]he word 'evil' is commonplace, but not the thing per se"* (BB3, p. 133).

The Descent as an Initiation

Jung acknowledges the process of the descent as an initiation, with the implication that there is something that needs to be retrieved and re-claimed as an integral part of the personality. It is something that, despite its implicit darkness, is necessary for becoming whole. He writes: *"I am just now through my initiation into the mysteries of the spirit of the depths, about to ... readopt it into my being human, to make my life whole"* (RB, p. 202 fn227).

Historian Mircea Eliade sees initiation as "a basic change in existential condition which liberates man from profane time and history". Eliade suggests that "Initiation recapitulates the sacred history of the world. And through this recapitulation, the whole world is sanctified anew ... [The initiand] can perceive the world as a sacred work, a creation of the Gods" (Eliade 1994).

At the end of his first initiation, Jung is given instructions by the prophet Elijah about his future direction: *"seek untiringly and above all, write exactly what you see"* (RB, p.198). Upon his return from the underworld, he comments: *"I am back again. Something has been completed. It is as if I had brought with me a certainty and a hope"* (BB2, p. 196).

From the above descriptions we can identify some basic components of initiation, which are present in Jung's process:

- It is a transformation of the initiate's sense of "I", realization, death and rebirth into a new identity.
- It provides a connection to a transcendent realm, making the initiate open to spiritual values.
- It results in a revelation of the deep meaning of existence, helping the initiate assume the responsibility of being truly human, and participating fully in society by bringing back new values.
- It is accompanied by a realization of the initiate's limits, and a conviction of a new direction and a new life task.

This idea of descending into hell as an initiatory process, as a psychological experience and a psychological reality that is essential for the development of the individual and for finding one's place in the world has been sustained for millennia in Western philosophical and esoteric traditions, but for the most part it is not to be found in contemporary collective consciousness. Starting more firmly with the protestant reformation in the 16th century, hell was concretised as a geographical location in the earth, and the descent into hell as a mythological image that opened a path to reconnecting with soul and with the inner world became lost. The inner experience of hell as a process of becoming whole was closed off by this conceptual opacity, and the Shadow was projected outwards, persecuting the individual through a distorted image of the "other". Humanity was split into two apparently irreconcilable halves.

As Jung points out, *"when an inner situation is not made conscious, it happens outside as fate … [W]hen the individual remains undivided and does not become conscious of his inner opposite, the world must perforce act out the conflict and be torn into opposing halves"* (CW 9ii, para. 126). Referring to the visions he had during his initiatory descent, he reiterates: *"I want to tell you more about my visions so that you better understand which things the spirit of the depths would like you to see. May those be well who can see these things. Those who cannot, must live them as blind fate, in images"* (RB, p. 154 fn97).

Jung's initiatory descent and his confrontation with the Shadow provide a connecting thread between analytical psychology and major philosophical, literary, religious and esoteric currents in the West: from the post-Enlightenment era and the 18th and 19th-century Romantic movement, to the visionaries of the Middle Ages, through to the esoteric systems of Hermeticism, Neoplatonism and Gnosticism and further back to the Greek pagan mysteries and the practices of the Pre-Socratics. All these traditions and systems involve various practices of descending into hell; in most cases, in individual visionary experiences. Their purpose is spiritual initiation, discovering infinite inner reality and encountering a truth that lies beyond the senses. Jung's Red Book, which is the foundation of all his subsequent works, provides a modern map back into hell, and therefore a way of confronting the Shadow and becoming whole. This is a map that can be traced back to the very beginning of Western civilization.

The History of an Idea

The Classical World

Narratives of descent into the underworld as an imaginal and literary motif abound in classical antiquity in a ritual practice called Katabasis or Nekyia. Several extraordinary persons of that time are said to have embarked on this gruelling journey to the realm of Hades, including Homeric heroes such as Aeneas and Odysseus. This practice enabled them to converse with the dead and gain guidance and knowledge that was essential for their life, their future purpose, and the renewal of their identity. One of the objectives of this practice was to gain insight into the cosmic order, the limits and possibilities of the human being, and the relationship between humans and gods. The etymological root of the Greek word Hades means "invisible", "unseen", "hidden" or "unknown", whereas the Latin equivalent Pluto means "riches".

Jung suggests that the symbol of Nekyia is *"the descent into the unconscious, and the leave-taking from the upper world ... [It] gives intimations of a hidden meaning and is therefore symbolic in character ... The Nekyia is no aimless and purely destructive fall into the abyss, but a meaningful katabasis eis antron, a descent into the cave of initiation and secret knowledge. The journey through the psychic history of mankind has as its object the restoration of the whole man ..."* (CW 15, paras. 210, 213). In the practice of Nekyia therefore, death was understood not as physical finality but rather as an entry to another world and a new beginning, a journey to a new life that required knowledge which could only be attained in the underworld.

Jung stresses the experiential element of this initiatory descent and this is reflected in the ancient Eleusinian Mysteries, one of the highest expressions of Greek religion. The Eleusinian Mysteries represented the myth of the abduction of Persephone by Hades, king of the underworld, and included a ritual descent as one of its secret teachings. Those who were chosen to further their spiritual development through the Mysteries were required to be of high moral calibre and to prepare themselves in specific ways that would allow them to enter the underworld through their own symbolic death.

The precise nature of the central Mysteries remains secret, but we do know (see for example, Foley 1993) that they involved a series of imaginative experiences that afforded the initiate a gateway to a different, heightened existence upon their return to the upper world. During the descent, the initiates were not exposed to theoretical teachings but rather to experiences that induced altered mental states and a change in consciousness that was necessary to become fit for revelation. One interpretation of the possible aims of the Mysteries (see for example, Nilsson 2017) was to elevate man above the human sphere into the divine and to assure his redemption by making him a god, therefore conferring immortality upon him. The realm of the underworld was therefore not just the abode of the dead, but also a liminal place where destiny could intersect with life.

Another notable example of descent is that of the Pre-Socratic philosophers Parmenides and Empedocles. Parmenides in his untitled poem (often referred to as "On Nature"), described a journey to the "halls of Night", a temple where day and night meet and where all opposites resolve into a great oneness. There, he had an encounter with an unnamed goddess who revealed to him the fundamental oneness of reality and the immortality of the soul. It has been noted (Rickert 2014) that Parmenides was associated with a cult of priest healers of Apollo who practised incubation, usually in caves, to receive wisdom and truth. The poem "directly invokes altered states of consciousness, revelations from the goddess and an underworld descent" (Ibid.,). Parmenides argued in his poem that our everyday perception of reality in the physical world of the senses was limited, and that the underlying reality of the world was "One Being" or "Truth". It was an unchanging, un-generated and indestructible whole. What allows someone to experience this reality amidst the ordinary illusion of the senses was not intellectual refinement, but rather the confrontation with one's utter helplessness and incapacity to see or know anything. He understood this practice as learning to die before we die. Kingsley suggests (1999) that the writings of Parmenides but also Empedocles, who outlined an elaborate cosmology that introduced the idea of the four elements, referred to ecstatic mystical visions where they were the recipients of divine revelation about the nature of reality and the recognition of one's own divinity.

Esoteric Systems at the Foundations of Christianity

Similar considerations can be found in the three major philosophical systems of Hermeticism, Gnosticism and Neoplatonism which all flourished in Alexandria in the opening years of the Christian era, at a time when there was rich cross-fertilisation of Greek and Egyptian thought. These doctrines coexisted with the early Christian development and although they express different perspectives, they have significant parallels with each other.

They all sought to grasp something that could not be comprehended by the intellect. They tried to understand ultimate reality and humanity's relation to it, and they offered a programme of spiritual growth that involved self-purification and a series of initiations that led to becoming united with an interior, mystical essence at the centre of things. They practised rituals, invocations and ceremonies, and sought to gain intercession of divine powers for the advancement of spiritual growth. These practices were highly disciplined (particularly in Hermeticism) and involved visionary experiences, including the meeting in vision of a messenger or a master (particularly in Gnosticism) who would provide guidance. The very aim of this spiritual journey was to return to a state of unity with the divine which was considered the great work of humankind.

To achieve this state of unity, initiates first had to confront everything about themselves that was inferior and lowly and to seek balance by embracing all things, superior and inferior. In the hermetic view, the human being has a twofold nature, both divine and earthly. As such, man takes an intermediary position between pure divinity and the earthly realm. It is precisely because of his dual nature that man is a "magnum miraculum", a "great miracle" (Copenhaver 2008) greater even than the gods because he can receive the force of things that are both superior and inferior. Crucially, it is through matter and through humans' lowly, earthly nature that the ultimate reality is revealed, and man is then able to have "the glory of the whole world" (Ibid.,), reconciling the forces of the heavens with those of the underworld. Through this journey, initiates were given the opportunity to recognise the path towards liberation within their earthly life and experience a new birth in the lower world that would allow them to ascent to the heavens.

The cosmology of these systems was emanationist: they posited a totality, an ultimate reality, or (in the case of Neoplatonists) the "One" as a universal divine principle at the root of everything out of which everything arises. According to the Neoplatonist perspective for example, the development of the physical universe is based on a series of emanations from the One, starting with Nous (the divine mind) and Psyche (the world soul) and continuing to various planes of existence and to progressively lower emanations until the concrete manifestations of matter. It is a process of ebb and flow in which spirit gradually unfolds itself in matter, attaining consciousness and then returns to spirit in a higher and more realised form. A critical part of the emanationist cosmology is the understanding that an aspect of the divine penetrates all matter. Nature has "telos" – a final aim and the fulfilment of nature's own desire to reach this aim is embedded into it. Matter is constantly transforming and striving to fulfil itself; it is in constant flux, trying to realise a divine design.

These principles also run through the Western alchemical tradition which reached its heyday in the 6th and 7th centuries AD and continued until the rise of modern chemistry in the middle of the 17th century. Alchemy incorporates the knowledge of both Hermeticism and Gnosticism and includes the idea of engaging with the darker, base elements of one's nature to achieve transformation and spiritual development. Its external (exoteric) goal was the transmutation of base metals such as lead or mercury into gold and the attempt to bring this about was taken literally and seriously. However, alchemists also held that the nature of matter mirrored the workings of the human soul and a practical, experimental engagement with matter led to the transformation of the alchemist himself and to the liberation of his soul from the earthly realm, "*after knowledge and experience of this world have been gained*" (Bernouli 1935, p. 319). Therefore, running parallel with the effort of the transmutation of matter was ultimately a labour of inner work on oneself aimed at giving birth to those elements within that were as unchanging and incorruptible as gold. This was the esoteric, spiritual search for the philosopher's stone (Lapis philosophorum) and the elixir of life, which could afford the alchemist immortality and an integrated vision of Unus Mundus.

Importantly, the very first step to the philosopher's stone was the Black Work of the nigredo, the putrefaction and decomposition of alchemical ingredients so that they can be cleansed and cooked to a uniform black matter. As stated in the alchemical text Rosarium Philosophorum "*When you see your matter going black, rejoice: for that is the beginning of the work*" (Myliu 2011, p. 76). The alchemist's instructions are to "take the foul deposit that remains in the cooking vessel and preserve it, for it is the crown of the heart"(Eirenaeus Philalethes 2011). The transformation process was therefore a building up by tearing down, a putrefying movement of creation, where the corruption of one is the generation of the other and death is the beginning of a new life. In the alchemical text, Splendor Solis (plate 6) the nigredo stage of the work is depicted as Aeneas's descent into hell where chaos and confusion dominate, alongside emotions of despair, doubt, hopelessness, and disgust. This descent, and the ability to recognise and tolerate the raw material of the inner world was essential for the alchemical process to proceed. Jung likened the nigredo stage of the alchemical opus to a confrontation with the Shadow: "*Confrontation with the shadow produces at first a dead balance, a standstill that hampers moral decisions and makes convictions ineffective or even impossible. Everything becomes doubtful, which is why the alchemists called this stage nigredo, tenebrositas, chaos, melancholia. It is right that the magnum opus should begin at this point, for it is indeed a well-nigh unanswerable question how one is to confront reality in this torn and divided state*" (CW 14, para. 708). The integration of these raw, dark aspects of the psyche allows the Shadow to tear down any rigid inner structures, eventually leading to the transformation of the physical body and the ascent of the spirit from the depths of matter (Splendor Solis, plate 7).

It is of course notable that even in the Christian tradition, Christ also descends into hell before turning darkness into light through his resurrection. The harrowing of hell, as this journey is known, receives little attention in the canonical gospels but in the apocryphal gospel of

Nicodemus (2010) we learn that the Christ descended to redeem the dead who occupied the underworld. Paul Bishop notes that in a speech given at the Psychological Club in Zurich in 1916, Jung drew a parallel between the harrowing of hell and human experience: *"In studying Christ's Descent into Hell I was surprised to find how closely the tradition coincides with human experience. This problem is therefore not new, it is a problem of general mankind, and for this reason probably too, symbolised through Christ"* (Bishop 2007, p. 27).

From Medieval Thought to the Romantic Movement

The theme of a visionary descent necessary for spiritual growth can be traced in literary works and esoteric currents without interruption throughout the medieval and renaissance periods from the 13th to 16th centuries (propelled by Marsilio Ficino's translation of the Corpus Hermeticum into Latin in 1463) to the romantic movement in the 18th–19th centuries alongside several influential religious streams and secret societies arising between the 17th and 20th centuries in Europe. Many of these sources served as historical parallels in Jung's thinking for the development of analytical psychology and several of them are referenced by him directly and frequently.

In the early 14th century, in his poem The Divine Comedy, Dante describes the journey of the soul to reunite with God. Jung acknowledges the relevance of Dante's work to his own process by transcribing two verses from the Divine Comedy into his Black Books in December 1913 (BB3, p. 197). Dante's journey begins with a descent into Hell that leads him to a recognition and confrontation with the dark nature of mankind. And although Dante writes in a Christian context, what he writes transcends the narrow Christian/Medieval discourse and expands towards more universal concerns. In his book, Il Convivio (The Banquet), he suggests that his texts can be understood in several different levels, one of which is the "anagogical" level which takes the textual interpretation of the Divine Comedy to a more mystical direction (Alighieri 1998). According to this line of interpretation, Hell is not simply a geographical location but a state of consciousness. And the first step in the journey towards the divine requires one to embrace one's dark side, and to come to terms with one's own capacity to do harm. For Dante, repairing the split between one's conscious self and the part of the psyche that lies in the dark is the prerequisite of becoming whole.

The German theologian Meister Eckhart also understood hell in a psychological way. Jung quotes one of Eckhart's sermons in Psychological Types as follows: *"Therefore do I turn back once more to myself, there do I find the deepest places, deeper than hell itself; for even from there does my wretchedness drive me. Nowhere can I escape myself! Here I will set me down and here I will remain"* (CW 6, para. 427, fn.166). The full experience of one's own psyche is therefore deeper than hell itself and it is a necessary step for the renewal of life.

Later philosophers and romantic poets in the 18th and 19th centuries also saw hell in a psychological way – as a personal redemptive act that demands one's wholehearted participation. Immanuel Kant saw the task of self-knowledge as an experience of hell but also as a moral obligation. In the Metaphysics of Morals, he suggests that moral self-knowledge, which aims to penetrate into the abyss of one's heart, is the beginning of all wisdom. He writes that *"only the descent into the hell of self-knowledge can pave the way to godliness"* (Kant 2017, p. 206). In a similar vein, Schelling suggested that human freedom and the redemption of the soul can only be accomplished when the ground of evil is recognised in positive terms as originating in God himself and residing in the unconscious psyche of each human being. He suggests that evil is not a mere conceptual device nor the mere absence of good (contrary to Augustine's doctrine of privatio boni) but a reality that has substance and needs to be grasped and engaged with in each individual (Rae 2018). Human freedom, therefore, rests on the recognition and the coming to terms with the dark, unconscious parts of the psyche.

Sonu Shamdasani points out that, during the time of writing the Red Book, Jung was also reading William Blake and he draws parallels with some of Jung's entries in the Black Books and Blake's poem Auguries of Innocence (BB7, fn.55). Blake articulated a world of dynamic oppositions necessary for life, including good and evil, heaven and hell. These are not radically dichotomous but rather they are born together and spring from the human psyche. They both need to be engaged with if one is to grasp the liberating unity that lies behind their opposition.

Another important example of a redemptive descent and confrontation with one's own darkness was Goethe's Faust, and Jung found similarities between Faust's process and the descent he himself underwent when writing the Red Book. Goethe presents Faust as a dissatisfied intellectual who feels that his life is empty and yearns for more than earthly pleasures. He becomes willing to barter his soul with the spirit of the Devil in exchange for secret knowledge and power over worldly things. But despite having dirtied his hands with corruption and darkness, this was a necessary part of his quest, which ultimately allowed him to achieve illumination and to be redeemed through an experience of love (Goethe 2008).

A New Understanding of Individuation

Jung recognises that there is a connecting thread between his own experiences and ideas that came before him. In Memories, Dreams Reflections, he writes, *"I had to find evidence for the historical prefiguration of my inner experiences …. If I had not succeeded in finding such evidence, I would never have been able to substantiate my ideas"* (1989, p. 200). By tracing the historical foundations of his insights, he finds himself in direct dialogue with key thinkers in Western philosophy and literature, and in alignment with numerous doctrines and practices of the Western esoteric tradition.

All these practices saw as their ultimate aim the experiential discovery of God within the psyche and the communion with a higher self. They invoked deities and fostered the practice of visions, rites and ceremonies aimed at elaborating and purifying the self to prepare it for the union with the divine. A central part of this process was a descent that allowed the recovery and redemption of those parts of the psyche, of matter and of the cosmos that were disowned and marginalised, the ones that were considered evil and were expelled because one was ashamed of them, fearful or revolted by them. This descent is also the inevitable first step in Jung's own process of individuation. As he writes in the Red Book: "*The way to your beyond leads through Hell and in fact through your own wholly particular Hell. [...] Everything odious and disgusting is your own particular Hell. How can it be otherwise? [...] Your Hell is made up of all the things that you always ejected from your sanctuary with a curse and a kick of the foot. When you step into your own Hell, never think that you come like one suffering in beauty, or as a proud pariah, but you come like a stupid and curious fool and gaze in wonder at the scraps that have fallen from your table*" (RB, p. 231).

Jung's descent into hell and his confrontation with his Shadow as it is described in Liber Novus, reveals the roots and ambition of analytical psychology. It suggests that the nature of individuation is not a mere self-improvement project, aiming at repairing deficiencies from the early relational environment or adapting to external conditions. Rather, it is geared towards the salvation of man which is at the same time the salvation of God.

In his seminar on Nietzsche's Zarathustra, Jung points out that "the thing which we think the least of, that part of ourselves which we repress perhaps the most, or which we despise, is just the part which contains the mystery" (1936/1988, p. 953). It is, in other words, the key to the new God image or to the supreme meaning. This is also the path of Jung's descent; it is a path that recovers that part of ourselves and of the cosmos which contains the mystery and allows a renewed appreciation of the fact that all those inferior, animal parts of existence are not an accident or an error. They are part of the cosmic wholeness and are indispensable for the recovery of the soul. In the dawning of the new Aion, it will no longer be sufficient to be "good". We must aim to become "whole".

References

Alighieri, D. 1998. *Il Convivio*. Salerno Publishing.

Bernouli, R. 1935. Spiritual Development as Reflected in Alchemy and Related Disciplines. In *Spiritual Disciplines: Papers from the Eranos Yearbooks*. Pantheon Books.

Bishop, P. 2007. *Analytical Psychology and German Classical Aesthetics*, Vol. 1. Routledge.

Copenhaver, B. 2008. *Hermetica: The Greek Corpus Hermeticum and the Latin Asclepius*. Cambridge University Press.

Eliade, M. 1994. *Rites and Symbols of Initiation*. Spring Publications.

Fabricius, J. 1976. *Alchemy: The Medieval Alchemists and their Royal Art*. Aquarian Press.

Foley, H., ed. 1993. *The Homeric Hymn to Demeter*. Princeton University Press.

Goethe, J.W. v. 2008. *Faust vols. I & II. Transl by David Luke*. Oxford University Press.

Jung, C.G. 1934. *Archetypes of the Collective Unconscious, in CW 9i*. Princeton University Press.

Jung, C.G. 1934. *Picasso, in CW 15*. Princeton University Press.

Jung, C.G. 1938. *Psychology and Religion, in CW 11*. Princeton University Press.

Jung, C.G. 1946. *The Psychology of the Transference, in CW 16*. Princeton University Press.

Jung, C.G. 1954. *Mysterium Coniunctionis, in CW 14*. Princeton University Press.

Jung, C.G. 1959. *Aion – Researches into the Phenomenology of the Self, in CW 9ii*. Princeton University Press.

Jung. C.G. 1971. *Psychological Types, in CW 6*. Princeton University Press.

Jung, C.G. 1988. *Nietzsche's Zarathustra. Notes of the Seminar Given in 1934–1939*. Princeton University Press.

Jung, C.G. 1989. *Memories, Dreams, Reflections*. Vintage Books.

Jung, C.G. 2012. *The Red Book – Liber Novus: A Reader's Edition*, ed. Sonu Shamdasani. Norton W. W. & Company.

Jung, C.G. 2020. *The Black Books: Facsimile Edition: 1913–1932, Notebooks of Transformation*, ed. Sonu Shamdasani. W. W. Norton & Company.

Kant, I. 2017. *The Metaphysics of Morals*. Cambridge University Press.

Kingsley, P. 1999. *In the Dark Places of Wisdom*. Golden Sufi Centre Press.

Library of Congress. 2010. "The Red Book of Carl G. Jung: Its Origins and Influence", Symposium on 19 June 2010, New York. https://www.loc.gov/item/webcast-4909/.

Martin, S. 2016. *Parmenides' Vision: A Study of Parmenides' Poem*. University Press of America.

Myliu, J. D. 2011. *Rosarium Philosophorum: of the De Alchemia Opuscula*. Theophania Publishing.

Nicodemus. 2010. *The Gospel of Nicodemus, or Acts of Pilate*. Kessinger Publishing.

Nilsson, M. 2017. *Greek Popular Religion*. Pinnacle Press.

Philalethes, E. 2011. *Introitus Apertus Ad Occlusum Regis Palatium*. Edited by J. J. Becher. Nabu Press.

Rae, G. 2018. The Problem of Grounding: Schelling on the Metaphysics of Evil, in *Sophia*, Vol. 57, pp. 233–248.

Rickert, T. 2014. Parmenides, Ontological Enaction, and the Prehistory of Rhetoric. *Philosophy & Rhetoric*, Vol. 47, No. 4, pp. 472–493.

Skinner, S. transl. 2019. *Splendor Solis*. Watkins Publishing.

The Development of the Shadow in Childhood and Adolescence: Shadow Work: Maia's Story

Rowena Mahmoud

> *"The meeting of two personalities is like the contact of two chemical substances: if there is any reaction, both are transformed.*
>
> Jung" (Modern Man in Search of a Soul, 1933, p. 49)

In this chapter, I shall focus on how the Shadow emerged in our work, how we got to know Maia's community of inner figures, and the impact of this on us both. When I met Maia, her psyche was tightly restricted by an overarching persecutory complex, choking any hopeful aspects of her personality. I hope to show how within the crucible of an authentic therapeutic relationship, the flickerings of life could be rekindled. This is not the definitive version of Maia's time with me. A great deal of material is omitted in order to focus on this, and I am aware that other issues were alive throughout. All names have been changed to protect confidentiality.

I met Maia in the Autumn, a few years ago now. She came through a no-fee scheme that provided 14 therapy sessions. Maia was referred by the Perinatal Team, who wanted to close her case. The organisation for which I work accepted Maia, on the basis that her case would stay open to the Perinatal Team also.

Maia identifies as Black British, a different ethnicity to me who identifies as White. Lee, her partner, also identifies as White. Maia was in her early thirties, only a little younger than me. She lived with her family in a high-rise flat on a council estate. When we met, her daughter, Mina, was two years old and her son, Frankie, was six months.

Maia's referral was troubling. She and others were worried about her relationship with her second born, Frankie. She was agoraphobic and wanted to work on issues of trust and abandonment. Underneath those lay deep trauma and multiple losses which Maia was struggling to bear. This was a lot to carry for short-term work.

Maia was brought to sessions by her children's centre worker who cared for Frankie when he was not in sessions with us. I encouraged Maia to bring Frankie into the room, but she quickly grew protective of her space, only

DOI: 10.4324/9781003255819-3

bringing Frankie in once to join us. There may have been other reasons too: was there something she felt was shameful about Frankie? I wondered if she identified Frankie with the vulnerable baby part of herself, that is, her Shadow self, that she had tried to disown for so long.

First Meeting – Shadow Spider

In our first session, she told of how she felt "numb" in her pregnancy with Frankie. As her due date approached, she felt suicidal and wanted Frankie "out of me". He was born prematurely and rushed to intensive care. Following his birth, she did not want to hold him. She did not then see him for three days and in that time felt it was her punishment that he was ill because of "not wanting him". She felt extreme guilt but also longing for him. As she spoke to me, there was a sense that Frankie only became real to her once he was separated from her. This echoes the child psychiatrist Donald Winnicott's thinking that a caregiver only becomes a real person to the baby once they can separate (Winnicott 1960). In this case, it was the mother who felt this. It alerted me to some very early developmental dynamics that can be stirred up in pregnancy and birth: that is, how our own primitive defences and emotions from when we were tiny can appear again at times of transition – the transition to parenthood being one of the most fundamental identity shifts it is possible to experience. Maia felt that she loved Frankie now but that her daughter is her "everything". She described a relationship with Mina which seemed a heavy burden for a toddler to bear. For example, Maia regularly self-harmed and Mina would tell her "Don't scratch Mum, only rub". Throughout the session, Maia picked at the skin on her arms.

She went on to tell me why Autumn was particularly difficult. When she was 15, she was raped in the Autumn. She became pregnant and had an abortion. She wistfully speaks of how, if the baby had lived, s/he would be 13 years old now. At the time, she, and her family, blamed Maia for the attack.

She began to withdraw initially because her attacker lived locally. This intensified until she hardly left the house. We tentatively touched on the grief that she still feels for this potential baby, and how this affects her relationship with Frankie.

At the end of the session, two things stayed with me – when reunited with Frankie they joyfully greeted one another, nestling into each other and pressing their foreheads together. Simultaneously Frankie looked over and gave me a big, beautiful smile. I wonder about this reunion after a separation, particularly in light of their first separation at birth.

When I return to the room, I am shaken to find a huge spider amongst the toys. It was as if something sinister had infiltrated what was meant to be innocent. This could be seen as a symbol of our work. The spider, often identified with a negative maternal complex, but also representing maternal wisdom, as in Jung's terminology of an "Old Chrone" archetype, would spin its web throughout Maia's story. This dual aspect, in it's destructive and healing potential, is very present.

Second Meeting – The Shadow and Trauma

My mood before our meeting was dark. I was exhausted by the demands of a rescue dog I had adopted. I fantasised about how life might be if I was not overwhelmed by this. It was hard to admit I was having these thoughts, as they brought a large measure of guilt and a feeling of utter defeat. I wondered about their possible role as counter-transferential feelings to Maia and her situation. That is, how my feelings may be a reflection of Maia's.

Maia arrives and talks in a flat tone, but picks at her skin significantly less, using more of a smoothing motion. Seeing this I wonder inside if Maia is starting to be able to access a self-soothing rather than persecutory part of herself.

She talks of Frankie's absence. That he is with Lee. She worries Lee does not hold him enough; this is the first time she has left them alone. She sees Lee as critical of her and that he "winds the children up", leaving her to mop up and settle them.

I wonder if Lee is aligned with a "scare-giver" figure (Acquarone 2004, p. 24) that Maia has perhaps internalised; someone who is in the role of a caregiver but does the opposite of this.

Maia then switches tack saying, "I did what you asked me to do". I feel alarmed, wondering what she means. She recounts how she bought a memorial plant for the baby that never was – a peace lily. At this, I feel a huge weight of sadness descend.

She continues that she has now named the baby Ashley, which could be for a girl or boy, as she never knew what gender Ashley was. This "ghost baby" suddenly seems very present, as if s/he had arrived centre stage. With a chill, I look at the toys and blankets I had arranged. I assumed they were for Frankie, but now imagine Ashley with us. The baby that can never grow up.

She then explains that she remembers the rape "like yesterday, every detail". She recounts that it plays like a video in her mind, and is triggered when she is depressed.

We discuss how this diminishes her further rather than strengthening her. I feel we are starting to encounter a persecutory daemon that feeds on Maia's past trauma. This concept has been explored by the Jungian analyst, Donald Kalsched (1996), where he describes how early trauma can trigger an archetypal self-care system in the survivor. We talk about the effects of trauma and how this can manifest. Maia explains that she has all the literature on panic attacks, but it doesn't help. She sadly says that Lee used to help by holding her, but now she has lost all trust as he has cheated on her multiple times.

A pattern is emerging here of a place or person who initially feels safe quickly becoming dangerous. This links in with Maia's "scare-giver" experiences. I wonder inside if I will meet the same fate in Maia's mind.

We discuss approaching what is on the video, if and when she feels ready. I wonder if this might help her lay it to rest, as a horrific thing that happened in the past, but is not happening in the present. She is unsure, convinced the assault was all her fault.

We talk about her mind trying to convince her she had control in an uncontrollable situation. This could be seen as the malevolent daemon figure at work, convincing her she was responsible. The person that she actually was, a victim, was too terrifying to accept. Therefore, we could argue that this victim figure was relegated to become a Shadow child in Maia's psyche – an aspect of her that was denied by her conscious self. This Shadow child was denied by the daemon, convincing Maia she was not this child but had responsibility for her own hurt.

The rape confirmed for Maia her feelings of being unlovable, present since her earliest days. Maia's internal world was incredibly harsh. It was governed by a thorny persecutor that firmly kept her Shadow hidden from awareness. Maia is punished relentlessly for a crime she never committed. This is a coping mechanism that stays with many survivors of trauma.

At the point of trauma, it is activated to protect that person against unbearable feelings of terrifying powerlessness. It holds the promise of regaining control by denying this vulnerable part of the self. This frightened, traumatised figure then becomes part of the Shadow community. Here it dwells disowned, representing who the person does not want to be. We often assume that the Shadow holds only negative aspects of the psyche, but it is a protective system also. Here it holds hostage a potentially valuable part of the self, until it is deemed safe enough to peek out. Kalsched (1996) and Winnicott (1960) both write of this.

We spend the latter part of the session gently bringing Maia back to the present, out of the trauma world. We discuss what is happening for her right now and what she is planning this week. This serves to regulate her psyche and help her leave the session in a way manageable for her.

Afterward, I wonder if the persecutory part of her is holding firm to her lost baby as a punishment, preventing herself from enjoying the children she has in reality. Perhaps naming the lost baby, and the ritual of buying the memorial plant is helping to start a grieving process, which ultimately could let Maia lay Ashley to rest. I think of her own lost baby self that is currently locked away. I wonder about unacknowledged hate and where it lies. As I write, I find I am constantly pressing the save button, trying to catch Maia before she slips through my fingers.

Session 3 – Early Experiences

At our next meeting, Maia's words tumble out so fast I struggle to decipher them. She talks of a violent, unpredictable upbringing. How her grandparents remember her Father threatening to "cut her out" of her Mother's womb. She does not recall much of her childhood, possibly as a protection. She remembers being dragged round by one of her Mum's boyfriends, while he shouted, "Does your Mum love me?" She was five. She remembers being locked outside in the car with her sibling and being kicked out of home at night.

These early experiences in a "scare-giving" environment would have been fundamental in shaping Maia's psyche into one in which vulnerable feelings needed to be hidden to protect her. As we have explored, these feelings could then inhabit her Shadow, being too dangerous to be expressed to the outside world. We could say that Maia suffered cumulative, early childhood trauma (Khan 1963) setting her up as at risk to various dangers, one of which was a predisposition to relegate vulnerable feelings to the unconscious. The acute trauma of the rape then consolidated this and contributed to where she finds herself now.

Maia's experience is one of the complete absence of a protective, predictable caregiver and she is determined her children will not feel the same. She talks of comforting them when they are upset but struggling with her ability to comfort herself. Maia is determined to pass something different on to her children. The one person she feels safe with is her Nana. But this was before Nana got dementia and Maia grieves her premature loss.

I do not see Maia again for a fortnight, she misses the next session due to Frankie being ill. I write to Maia to let her know I am thinking of her.

Session 5 – Lioness

The next time I see Maia changes have occurred. She is wearing lighter clothes, has styled her hair and is wearing an array of charm bracelets. Instead of worrying at her skin, she rearranges her bracelets. I am struck by her rhythmic breathing when we first settle into the session, my association being to a sleeping baby.

After an incident with her Nana and Uncle, in which she was able to draw a boundary and safeguard her children, she is feeling buoyed up, saying incredulously: "I found my roar!"

She recounts how, at the time of Frankie's birth, her Uncle strangled her Mum hard enough to leave bruises. We think of what Frankie has been born into and his physical health now. He has been referred back to the hospital, because of fitting, and there is a question around possible epilepsy. Maia is worried but, interestingly, not blaming herself, and has sought help for Frankie without feeling shamed. I get the sense of her raising her head up and feel very moved by this. She admits that after the incident with her uncle she wanted to self-harm. Instead she called her neighbour. She is now choosing relationship over self-sufficiency.

I am thrilled by this and wonder about the emergence in Maia's mind of a helpful, perhaps maternal figure, who will not shame her. This is the opposite to the malevolent "spider mother" I encountered at the end of our first meeting. Is this a precursor to the long buried, loving mother feeling safe enough to emerge?

She talks of feeling she could contact the police if she wanted. Her internal world seems to be expanding to include figures that have the potential to rescue. I wonder how much this is due to our work here, and perhaps a question of timing. Jung believed that humans are on a spiral of development and, unconsciously, find the situations and people they need to develop at the time that they are ready. This is part of the individuation process of becoming one's self (Jung 1976, p. 295).

She then thanks me for my letter. She seems surprised and touched that I held her in mind. I think about this contributing to Maia's Shadow self gathering the courage to emerge. That is, what had been smothered by her conscious self in order for her to survive, was now coming into awareness. As a baby needs to be held in mind in order to develop, so might our relationship be contributing to Maia's newfound growth.

We explore her experiences with men and how it is not that she "doesn't get on with them" but that multiple men have abused her. Her expectation is that men will hurt her. We think about this in relation to Frankie. She firmly says she does not want to feel that way about him. We think how it can feel to a parent that a baby is being persecutory, when the baby is seeking to get their many needs met. We unpick this, the demands of looking after Frankie and how Maia might feel as he develops; in particular, feelings that might be lingering from the time of his birth, and even earlier. Perhaps in caring for Frankie, Maia may become envious of the care she so lacked when she needed it most. Alternatively, she may identify with Frankie and in caring for him, care for her own baby self (Daws & de Rementaria 2021). Both these processes may be at work here.

We discuss Mina, how she has fallen into the role of caregiver. We carefully think about the age appropriateness of Mina's behaviour. My concern is that as Mina develops, she is absorbing the message that certain feelings cannot be contained by Mum and need to be hidden. That is, we could start to see the formation of a Shadow self that contains all the parts of Mina that are not compatible with being a helpful, compliant big sister.

Maia continues that Mina is outwardly helpful toward Frankie, but I am relieved to hear that she does express her frustration at him and Maia. We wonder about Maia owning an increasing sense of self-worth and perhaps Mina growing in confidence simultaneously.

After the session, I feel amused at myself acting into this "helpful" role by retrieving Maia's hat from the room. Perhaps my own Shadow is not unlike Mina's. It may also be that Maia wanted to leave a piece of her protective covering with me. Perhaps it is a sign that she feels able to shed some of her defences, as they are becoming redundant.

Session 6 – Dream

As I arrange the toys beforehand, I feel again an immense sadness for the baby that never was. I ponder this: whose baby am I mourning? Is it Maia's baby self, or Ashley, or a baby yet to come? Is it all these and more?

Maia appears wearing a t-shirt with "Tired Mum's Club" emblazoned across it. I immediately feel a sense of exclusion, being as yet childless. During the session, I catch a feeling of Maia latching on to me as what Alvarez might call an "enlivening object" (Alvarez 1992). That is a figure that carries hope and life. I try hard to be present with her, wanting to shift her flat, defeated state into something more hopeful. In this way, I am not working in the state of what the psychoanalyst Bion called "without memory or desire" (Bion 1967, p. 279). This is what he felt to be the optimum state in which a therapist conducts a session. Alvarez argues that this is not appropriate for all the people we work with, particularly those who exist in a vacuum of hopelessness. She argues that we must be resonant to this and adapt to what each human being needs (Alvarez 2012).

Part of why Maia is feeling such despair is that she has applied for a job. This in itself is an achievement, but her "internal saboteur", the powerful function of something potentially hopeful and positive being sabotaged by an inner dynamic. (Fairbairn 1954), does not let her see this.

She has applied to be a carer at an elderly person's home. She describes this as wanting to be "seen", not wanting to be a "replaceable" worker. I wonder about her wish in terms of the probable absence of this "seeing" gaze on her as a baby. Does she unconsciously want the whole of her to be seen, even her Shadow, and does she hope that this work might make this possible? Or is she recreating the situation of her childhood, where her Mother's needs often came first?

Now she is struggling with the uncertainty of whether she has got the position or not. To avoid disappointment, she is certain she has failed, and she finds it impossible to dwell in the not knowing.

She then tells me of a re-occurring dream:

> I am on the bus, but it crashes. I'm taken with lots of others to a big house. I phone my mum to tell her I'm OK. In the house they say not to contact anyone but to give them your name and they will contact others to let them know you are safe. Then a woman and two dogs come in and

they start the killing. Others try and fight back. The way out is blocked because people are trying to escape. I wake up really scared.

We explore this in terms of her psyche's established "scare-giver" pattern we encountered earlier. This is of how a safe place or person becomes dangerous very quickly. I wonder aloud if this may happen here. She looks at me blankly. We think about baby Maia, 5-year-old Maia and 15-year-old Maia, who were supposed to be kept safe but were catastrophically let down. I introduce the Jungian concept of everything in the dream being a part of herself. So, both the terrified Maia who feels utterly trapped, and the destructive Maia that can sabotage any glimmer of hope, are both integral to her.

Inside I am interested in how her psyche has taken on this internal work, playing to her in dream form one of her fundamental dilemmas.

A thought here about 15-year-old Maia. Adolescence has the potential to be a fertile period of identity formation. It can offer the opportunity to play within a fluid, liminal space, where sexual identity can be explored. Many developmental challenges first encountered in childhood can be consolidated here. These include starting to integrate the Shadow. For Maia, this process was arrested by the rape trauma which may have effectively frozen 15-year-old Maia into a survival mode. While not feeling safe, play cannot happen, so for Maia adolescence did not offer her these developmental opportunities, and she remained stuck in an unresolved traumatic state.

She tells me she has decided to stop contact with Nana. She does not want her children in danger from her uncle. This is a painful but significant decision. She is protecting both herself and her children from a violent man who sneeringly calls her "little girl". I think she is starting to bar external destructive influences from her life.

I enquire after Frankie, mindful that Maia is much more forthcoming about Mina. She instead references Ashley, that since she bought the peace lily, she does not think of Ashley so much. She does seem more thoughtful and present. Perhaps a potential space is becoming available to contemplate baby Frankie just as he is, rather than identified with her trauma.

Session 7 – Crisis

Maia arrives in a depleted state. She sinks into her chair and stares at me through sunken eyes. Her gaze is direct and urgent, as if trying to tug something from inside me into her.

Throughout the session, I feel she is existing in a fog of undigested, damaging "*beta elements*" (Bion 1962, p.6), or what the alchemists called the "*massa confusa*" (Jung 1953, p. 334); that is, she is persecuted by chaotic and unprocessed fragments of thoughts, emotions and sensory experiences that assault her and of which she cannot make sense. Bion postulated that this is akin to a baby's experience, whose caregiver can then perform what he calls the "maternal function", in order to process these frightening and confusing elements for the baby. Perhaps this was my task here, and what Maia's eyes were trying to tell me.

She says she cannot sleep; when she closes her eyes, she sees her uncle shouting "little girl" and someone tries to shoot her. She has insight that this is not reality, but it terrifies her all the same. She can only sleep with her children, as her mind then goes blank.

Knowing Maia's childhood, I can understand why the words "little girl" would trigger her. But I wonder if there is another layer to this. Maia was only a little girl when she had to encapsulate a part of herself into her Shadow. Does hearing "little girl" echo this and not only bring up feelings of hot shame and traumatic memories, but also a sense of unbearable loss, the loss of Maia herself as a "little girl". She is only able to be comforted when her own children are with her, as if her child self finds safety with other children.

Both children seem to have picked up on Maia's weakened state. Mina is wetting herself and Frankie is hitting himself in the face and ears. Maia is concerned about this, as am I. Combined with this there are also changes in the external world, Mina is starting pre-school and Maia's parent support group is ending.

She talks in a low voice of wanting to be dead, so that she would not be scared of being killed. She feels it is not worth trying to get better, but she is clear these are thoughts and not plans.

We talk about the destructive part of her we identified last week in her dream and how strong it is at the moment. But that we also know there are other parts to her that are just starting to emerge.

We think together about what Maia needs right now. She would like us both to contact her GP. I feel Maia needs a safety net made up of a team, and liaising with the GP is part of this. It does mean breaking confidentiality, but with Maia's permission, I feel this is appropriate, judging by her difficult state of mind. Her health visitor is also due to visit. She talks of the loss of previous health visitors, that they "all get pregnant and leave". She wryly says she must be "giving off testosterone". I am not sure of the significance of this, but log it just the same.

She talks of feeling claustrophobic at home. I get the image of a family with entangled roles; she speaks of Mina as a sister and Lee as another child. I think about how abuse and intergenerational trauma can "flatten" the family roles and boundaries, making for a confusing, airless experience.

Near the end of the session, we reflect on how Maia has made positive changes recently and it may feel like one step forward and two steps back. I say how change is frightening and difficult, it maybe that her old ways of coping are trying to hold on to her. She nods in a defeated way.

Following the session, I speak to the GP and confirm that Maia has an appointment with her that day. A note here about confidentiality: in this situation, I contacted others in Maia's team. One reason for this was the presence of Maia's children and how they are being impacted by her current state. When questions of safety are raised, thinking about the family system as a whole is crucial. I felt Maia valued a drawing together of the team, but I was also aware of how Maia may well have conflicting feelings about confidentiality being broken.

Falling through the gap

Two days later I receive an email saying, "Uncle is stronger, don't know what to do".

Upon reading this my immediate reaction is of white-hot shock; my mind feels obliterated. My thinking capacity is erased for a moment, and I am relieved to be able to call on my clinical team for support. I then call Maia and she tells me how her dreams feel even more physically real; and when she wakes, she feels pain as if she has been shot.

I think again of undigested trauma, or "beta elements" that need another mind to process. I wonder about Maia's own state of mind in these nightmares, that of a very young baby perhaps, where physical and mental experiences are not yet differentiated. With her permission, I contact her GP and the Crisis team, who agree to call her. The perinatal team have closed her case as she is "not risky enough".

As her Shadow starts to emerge, I wonder if the persecutory elements in her are waging a full-scale war against this. Her defence system has been activated to keep at bay what is seen as a threat. It is akin to an autoimmune disease, in which the body mistakenly attacks functional cells.

A few days later I am on the bus and a passenger has an epileptic fit. An ambulance is called. I think of Frankie's fits, Maia's dream of the bus, and my own Father's epilepsy. I wonder about whether these are random events or take place within an interconnected web. Could they be synchronistic as Jung may suggest? That is could they hold meaning rather than being pure coincidence?

Session 8 – Looking After Mummy

I am surprised at the next meeting when Maia offers to bring in Frankie, who is now around eight months. Frankie gurgles and beams at me from Maia's lap. Maia seems more energised than last week, but tells me the week has been "rubbish".

The Crisis team did not call her. With some frustration, I think of how the Shadow can infiltrate a system around a person. In some cases, it can split a team, each colleague identifying with a different part of the person's psyche. In this case, it seems the Shadow child in Maia was to be let down again.

However, help did come in the form of a prescription of anti-psychotic medication. This can be complex as potentially medication could be seen as a "magic cure" and leave the therapy redundant. As we will see this medication did affect Maia strongly, but it also seemed helpful in alleviating the worst of her night terrors.

As Frankie grins at me, Maia murmurs that she feels like giving up. I say how disappointed she must feel about the call that never happened. I could have picked up this comment in the transference, directly linking it to our relationship. I didn't because I sense this is not where Maia is today, I need to acknowledge the pain before I wonder about anything else. I speak to Frankie as he finds my eyes, saying gently that Mummy is very upset. Maia looks as close to tears as I have ever seen her. She says she cannot fight anymore. I softly say how low she is feeling today and has been for some time. Although it is clear Maia is still suffering, I simultaneously wonder about this softer, more vulnerable side she is able to express.

Being on the edge of tears shows a capacity to let the inside out, perhaps grieve for the many losses she has endured. Despite all the odds, perhaps her Shadow child really is beginning to take courage. This perspective is similar to Jung's idea of breakdown or breakthrough: that is, his concept that the most valuable material in life can be found in the darkest places.

Frankie brings me back to the present by banging his hands gleefully on the mat while balancing on his tummy and reaching for a toy. I comment on how curious and outgoing Frankie seems, and, for the first time, Maia smiles. This starts as a small, sad smile, but as she gazes at her son her smile curls upwards and becomes very tender.

Coming out of this short reverie she tells me she has her job interview tomorrow. I talk about her feeling so low today, just when things may change for the better. I exclaim that no wonder she is feeling anxious. Inside I feel a blossom of hope for her. I feel even more that her suffering is a backlash against her Shadow self becoming stronger, and potentially manifesting in the outside world.

She picks Frankie up and he references her before looking back at me. I say he is checking with Mum what kind of person I am, am I safe to look at? I explain to Frankie that Mummy is feeling very worried today, so she has come to think with me about it. Frankie grins and puts his fingers in his mouth. Internally I wonder if this gesture is one of uncertainty, but Maia responds by saying, "Oh, hungry", giving him a breadstick. He eagerly grabs and investigates this with his mouth.

Maia talks of feeling numb, like a shell, how her support group is ending this week, her GP is leaving, and she is worried to start with someone new. I keep my response in the here and now. I remind us that we are halfway through our sessions, and ask how that might feel for her; and I also explore what support she has. I am hoping to construct a maternal, supportive web to hold Maia through this period.

As we talk, I feel myself getting more nervous, concerned about whether I am saying anything remotely helpful, and what sort of impact I am having on Maia. I wonder inside if this is a familiar feeling to Maia, or perhaps it is Mina or Frankie that could feel this? Am I mirroring Maia's encapsulated Shadow child, who perhaps desperately wanted to help her own Mummy, but didn't know how? Or am I connecting with my own Shadow Child, who has had her own trials with maternal figures?

Frankie has finished his breadstick and seems agitated, squirming his body. Maia offers him milk and he happily sucks at the bottle, gazing up at Mum. She gazes back at him and I gaze at her. Within this triangulated area it feels as if a potential thinking space has opened up, and with it the potential for transformation. Frankie suddenly goes to dive forward, but Maia holds him firmly. I say to him: "Mummy is keeping you safe, and she needs some help keeping safe too". Afterwards, I think how Maia deftly caught the baby in danger, but it seems no one was there to catch her at Frankie's age, and what a price she has paid for it, in trying to catch herself.

Maia talks of her children as the only reason she gets up, without them she would not be here. As she says this, Frankie reaches up and grabs at her face, as if to take the words away from her lips. She is impassive and lets him touch. I say he is touching Mummy's face, perhaps to show how close he is to her.

At the end of time, as if on cue, Frankie starts crying. I say how hard it is to leave, perhaps he liked it here and it is hard to go. I talk of Mum feeling sad at the moment and the other adults wanting to help her. I think how, in that moment of tears, he is perhaps expressing Maia's feelings too.

Maia gathers him up and wearily says goodbye.

Session 9 – Persecution

It is two weeks before I see Maia again, due to her transport problems. We meet for the last session before Christmas.

The figure of Uncle has morphed inside into an even more persecutory figure. Although the nightmares have stopped and she is sleeping better, she feels constantly exhausted.

She seems relieved to see me but is adamant she feels nothing at all. She insists it is the meds. I am sure that they do play a part in this. We talk about how stuck she feels at the moment, as if time has stopped. I hold onto the promise of things not always feeling this way, reflecting all the changes she has survived. She is then able to give more eye contact and speaks at less of a pace. I wonder about the effect of the meds, but also the effect of last session, where Frankie was able to gaze at us both so directly. I am also mindful of the break we are approaching and the unplanned break we have just had.

We talk again about safety plans, who I can contact, as she talks again of wanting to "cut myself up" and "hang myself from a tree". The despair and raw aggression she feels is palpable. I am reminded of how her Father said he would cut her out of her Mother's belly. It seems she has internalised this violence toward herself, perhaps as a nuclear option to stop her internal conflict for good.

We think about this violent part of her that can seem overwhelming, where it might have come from, and what other parts of her can keep her safe. We end with the agreement that she will be in contact with the Crisis team and we confirm our return date.

Session 10 – Numb

When we meet again it is with my knowledge that I am carrying a baby. I do not disclose this to Maia. I am mindful of our ending soon and her earlier comment that she must be giving off testosterone because all her health visitors get pregnant and leave. If we were in long-term work, I would definitely be exploring this with her, but as our ending draws close it seems an unnecessary intrusion. However, I am very aware that there are now three of us in the room.

She brings a sense of acute deprivation, and not having access to our sessions compounds this. I am sharply aware we have four sessions left and think with her about this. She talks of severe financial hardship, selling the children's Christmas presents to pay for food.

The session seems jumbled, as if we have lost connection. But there have been hopeful developments. Her relationship with Lee is better and he has started rehab for alcohol addiction. She has been able to go out of the house twice on her own, and she got the job she interviewed for. Of course, she will not let herself feel these achievements.

She feels her emptiness is down to the meds. Again, I urge her to let her GP know about this. I reflect that when she talks, she seems quite angry, does she feel that inside? She shrugs and comes up with "blank". She tells me of self-harming with a light bulb in order to feel something. She shows me the cuts and we talk about her emotional pain being manifested, and seeing the Crisis team again.

When Maia comes to collect Frankie, he is sound asleep. However, his eyes snap open when we approach. He stares at me, looking slightly puzzled. I wonder inside about his experience of being in the room with Mum for one session, and then not. He glances at Mum, and she kisses him tenderly on the ear.

Session 11 – Shifting Roles

Before they arrive, I feel I want to make the reception more welcoming. I put out a soft toy kangaroo with a baby in her pouch. I wonder about my own motives, and my own kangaroo status.

As the ending becomes closer our sessions are filled with thinking about our goodbye and reflecting on all the changes Maia has made in our short time together. But these external achievements are quickly dismissed by her. I wonder out loud if, when she was small, she was acknowledged for her achievements. She responds "No, never". I say how this is understandable; it is so difficult for her to acknowledge achievement, when she has never had that experience. With her sense of pride dismissed to her Shadow self, she has no way of accessing it safely yet.

She talks of Lee being more present and doing more childcare. Simultaneously her role has shifted to being a working Mum. We then think about Frankie as a boy child and how that brings up very difficult feelings from her past, how complex caring for him is for her, but also how strongly she loves him. Frankie continues to be seen regularly at the hospital for scans. Maia worries that she has damaged him somehow, that she has "passed something down". She admits that she feels Frankie is more like her than Mina, and she does not want Frankie to go through what she has. This now makes sense: if Maia's Shadow self includes vulnerability, she may have identified it with Frankie and therefore have very conflicted feelings toward him.

Session 12 – Cut Off

In this session, I am left with dark feelings of despair and pointlessness, whilst Maia leaves looking rather cheerful. I am glad for her and wonder about her being able to leave the persecutory side of herself with me to untangle, rather than carrying it all by herself. This could be an example of projective identification, how one person can receive another's emotional communication, and feel it inside them.

She arrives looking brighter, her face clearer, but by the end her eyes find it hard to focus. As we thought previously, this could be due, in a large part to pure physical exhaustion and the effects of the meds, but it could also be a protective shutting down. By feeling numb she prevents her vulnerable Shadow self from being hurt. It is as if her defence system has shifted from the persecutory Uncle figure, to a numbing out of all emotion.

She tells me she is enjoying her job. I feel excited for her, but it seems I am alone in feeling this. I hold it for her, hoping one day it will be safe enough for her to experience.

I wonder aloud if perhaps her feeling of emptiness is her body protecting her for now. After all the overwhelming emotions she has been through she needs time to reset, then perhaps slowly the feelings will return. She looks sceptical. Inside I feel her Shadow self may be biding her time, almost like an incubation period, or a sense that Maia is pregnant with her baby self.

Session 13 – Protection

In our penultimate session, Maia's message to me is that things are unresolved, I'm abandoning her, and things are not ok. I make this explicit and she talks of having nightmares again of her uncle strangling her. She feels this as a physical experience and wakes in a panic.

Her exhaustion is overwhelming, at one point she gets up to open the window, to stay awake. The exhaustion seems to act as a drug in itself. Its function is to protect her from thinking about our goodbye, and sharpens her focus on practical matters. We talk about feelings that are too painful to feel right now.

We think that Maia's default position is to protect others at all costs – her Mum, her kids, perhaps me too. We try and think of the future, of the Uncle figure as a bullying part of her who tries to stop her speaking, choking her against speaking her own truth.

It transpires that she is now restricting food, surviving on a diet of energy drinks. She seems to be depriving herself of one of the fundamentals of life, food, while the Uncle figure tries to deprive her of breath. Yet still she survives. I note that she is now living on a liquid diet, as a baby would before weaning.

I am left feeling very maternal toward her, wondering if I have played into this role by feeling guilty about the ending. I am careful not to infantilise her, but rather to encourage the separation, her strengths and growing independence, but I am wary of what seems to be her manic flight into over-work.

Session 14 – In the End

On the day I am left with a sense of disappointment and abandonment, as Maia does not arrive and despite my efforts, I am unable to contact her.

It is two months before we are able to meet again. It transpires there were transport problems. I find this out after numerous emails and phone calls, at one point Maia hanging up on me. However, I feel my determination to hold her until the end was helpful for her. This is partly due to how it facilitated an actual goodbye, rather than another disappearance.

On my way to our last session, I feel my baby move for the first time, a little flutter whilst I sit on the bus.

Seeing Maia arrive feels quite momentous – how she has managed to face an ending, particularly as her presenting issues included "abandonment".

We spend the session reflecting on where she was, where she is now, what her triggers are, and what we have learnt about her.

She comes with the news that Nana died, but she feels she "can't cry twice". She felt she said goodbye when she stopped contact with her. Other people's reactions of grief bemuse her.

She has taken Mina out for the day, she has been made "employee of the month", she has stopped self-harming, and she is changing meds to ones that are thought to be less emotionally numbing. Her nightmares of the Uncle figure have stopped, she still has nightmares, but he does not feature.

She talks of her continuing difficulties with fear and anxiety. I reflect how she wants me to know that things are not magically better, even though we are ending. She looks at me intensely and smiles a very small, sad smile.

As the session progresses, I see a side of Maia I have only seen in glimpses before. She is more animated, sarcastic and humorous. She seems enlivened. Perhaps her mischievous Shadow child is feeling safe enough to come out and play.

She reflects that sometimes when she feels down, she feels that death does not even want her. I respond that perhaps life wants her too much. There is a beat after this, and I refer back to her finding her "roar". This seems to land for her. She says, "I'll get there in the end". I reply gently that I think she will. She speaks hopefully about her GP referring her for art therapy and I am relieved that she will be supported.

After our goodbyes, I am left feeling physically very cold, and with a painful, awkward sadness, wondering what I could have missed. I think I am experiencing the effects of projective identification from Maia's persecutory self, where all good is erased and the focus is only on what is absent. This is familiar to me from my own psyche.

I hope, through our work together, this destructive force has become more balanced by Maia's playful, inner child who is cautiously beginning to show herself. I feel this is the very beginning of Maia's journey. I do not know how much of our work was internalised to form a more stable base for her. But at least the work has begun.

As I write this, I am carrying my second child, and as I edit this, I hold her in my arms. Somehow it feels a circle has been completed. Within our work an umbilical cord seemed to twist around Maia's earlier abortion, her previous pregnancy with Frankie, Mina, my pregnancy and the incubation period of her own child self.

Through this writing, I hope I have illustrated how it emerged that Maia's Shadow self contained positive, but fragile, parts of herself that had been hidden from the external world for their own protection. If the Shadow is who we do not want to be, depending on the environment we find ourselves in, we may need to mutilate ourselves internally in order to survive.

Maia's story is of a journey toward reclaiming this Shadow child and allowing her a voice. As you have seen, this was not without its severe hardships and suffering. But I hope it will be the foundation of lasting psychic change for her and her children.

With heartfelt thanks to Maia, for her bravery in our work together and her permission for me to write about it.

For Torin and Namaya

References

Acquarone, S. (2004). *Infant-Parent Psychotherapy: A Handbook*. London: Routledge.

Alvarez, A. (1992). *Live Company: Psychoanalytic Psychotherapy with Autistic, Borderline, Deprived and Abused Children.* London: Routledge.

Alvarez, A. (2012). *The Thinking Heart: Three Levels of Psychoanalytic Therapy with Disturbed Children. London*: Routledge.

Bion, W. (1967). Notes on Memory and Desire. *Psychoanal. Forum*, 2: 272–273, 279–280.

Bion, W. (1962). *Learning From Experience.* London: Karnac.

Daws, D. & de Rementeria, A. *Finding Your Way with Your Baby: The Emotional Life of Parents and Babies*, 2nd Edition. London: Routledge.

Fairbairn, R. (1954). *An Object-Relations Theory of Personality*. New York: Basic Books.

Jung, C. G. (1933). *Modern Man in Search of a Soul. Harcourt*: Brace.

Jung, C. G. (1953). Collected works. Vol. 12. *Psychology and Alchemy*. New York City: Pantheon Books.

Jung, C. G. (1976). *The Visions Seminars: Book Two.* Washington: Spring Publications.

Kalsched, D. (1996). *The Inner Word of Trauma: Archetypal Defences of the Human Spirit. London*: Routledge.

Khan, M. (1963). *The Concept of Cumulative Trauma: The Psychoanalytic Study of the Child.* London: Taylor& Francis.

Winnicott, D. W. (1960). The Theory of the Parent Infant Relationship. *Int. J. Psycho-Anal.*, 41: 585–595.

Chapter 2

Gender Dysphoria, Individuation and the Shadow

Robert Withers

Introduction

Despite our understandable, collective preoccupation with the global pandemic, it has been hard to ignore the clamour generated by the ongoing "gender wars". Are gender dysphoric children and young people being irresponsibly rushed into medical treatment that could irreversibly damage their future well-being? Or are those exercising caution in such matters depriving them of essential medical treatment? What has prompted so many young people's wish to transition? And what is the most helpful attitude for parents, teachers, and therapists to adopt towards them? Should we simply support and affirm them, in the belief that they know best? Should we resist any pressure to act and encourage an attitude of watchful waiting? Or should we attempt to actively explore the origins of their dysphoria in the hope of helping them find a way of resolving it without invasive, irreversible medical treatment? Behind these essentially practical questions lie a series of complex ethical, philosophical, and psychological dilemmas.

In this chapter, I hope to show how Jung's ideas about the Shadow and the process of individuation can help us disentangle some of these knotty problems. Before doing so, however, it would be helpful to try to define what gender dysphoria is.

Gender Dysphoria

Put at its simplest, gender dysphoria (GD) is the discomfort that can arise from a discrepancy between a person's gendered sense of who they are (their gender identity) and their biological sex.[1] Extremists from both sides of the gender wars would probably baulk at this definition. Many queer theorists, trans activists and their allies believe that sex is "assigned at birth" rather than observed. While gender sceptics dismiss the notion of "gender identity" as an unscientific fiction.

This immediately plunges us deep into an age-old philosophical debate about the nature of reality. Those who believe being a man or a woman is a

DOI: 10.4324/9781003255819-4

matter of observed biological fact, and that gender identity is a fiction, are speaking as philosophical materialists. Those who dismiss the objective reality of biological sex and believe that a person's gender identity (observed through a process of introspection) determines whether they are a man or a woman are speaking as philosophical idealists. Both idealism and materialism are "essentialist", "monistic" philosophies. They assert that reality boils down to one essential ingredient – mind or matter. The clash between idealism[2] and materialism is at least as old as Western philosophy itself.

Rene Descartes' (1641) famously attempted to resolve this clash by advocating a kind of dualism that granted a separate reality to both mind and matter. According to Descartes, mind is "un-extended thinking substance", known through introspection; while matter is "extended unthinking substance", known through sense perception and measurement. Separating mind from matter in this way was historically important. It allowed scientists to go on investigating the material world without being accused of blasphemy and excommunicated like Galileo, or burnt at the stake like Giordano Bruno. If science tells us that the earth goes around the sun, but the Bible tells us that the sun goes around the earth – and there is only one kind of truth – then science is blasphemous in the eyes of those who believe the Bible is the word of God. But if religion is concerned with the soul (or mind) and science with the material world (or body) they can coexist. Perhaps reverting to a similar dualistic approach, which grants a separate kind of reality to both gender identity (mind) and biological sex (body), could save us from repeating the worst excesses of this medieval clash between science and religion.

Psychoanalysis

Psychoanalysis, with its belief in an inner world and an outer world, advocates just such a dualistic approach. In his book, "Trauma and the Soul", for instance, Jungian analyst Donald Kalsched (2013, p. 6), talking about an Inuit carving, has this to say:

> With one eye closed, focused on the inner world of dreams and the mytho-poetic images of imagination, and one eye open, focused outwardly on the harder edges of material reality, including the realities of human relationship, it gives dramatic expression to the two worlds that I feel must be kept in view if a genuine and compelling story of human trauma is to be told.

Although accepting a dualistic philosophy entails the loss of a unified world view, it may prove a useful starting point from which to explore some of the questions about gender dysphoria raised in the introduction. But before proceeding, it will be necessary to introduce the concept of the unconscious.

Mind without the unconscious, as envisaged by Descartes, is very different from mind with the unconscious, as envisaged by psychoanalysis.

An Encounter with the Unconscious

My father was an electronic engineer who ran a small business designing and manufacturing apparatus for university psychology laboratories. In 1965, he asked me to help test a new tachistoscope[3] he had just designed and built. I was thirteen years old.

He took me to his workshop and attached two electrodes to the fingers of my left hand. The electrodes were linked to a galvanic skin response meter (GSR); which measures slight changes in skin resistance. A GSR can be used as a lie detector because sweat glands open slightly in response to anxiety, and people get anxious when they lie. This results in detectable changes in their skin resistance. The GSR was linked in turn to a pen recorder which visually recorded any changes in my skin resistance.

My father switched off the lights and sat me in front of the tachistoscope. He told me this experiment would normally be conducted on a student by men in white coats in very formal laboratory conditions so he wasn't sure if it would work. But he asked me to press my face into the tachistoscope's viewing hood and tell him what I could see. At first there was just a uniformly lit background, but then he flicked a switch, and I could see a word that he asked me to read out loud, which I did. He placed a button in my right hand and told me he was going to present me with a series of words for exposure times that would increase incrementally. As soon as I recognised each word, I should read it out to him and press the button, which was linked to the pen recorder. It might take me longer to see some words than others. The pen recorder would mark exactly how long I took to identify each word, while simultaneously recording my skin resistance. Those familiar with it, will probably recognise a more scientifically rigorous version of Jung's famous word association experiment.

The experiment began with a series of neutral words such as "chair" "table" or "car"; each, as far as I recall, taking me almost exactly twelve thousandths of a second to recognise. But as the experiment progressed something remarkable happened. There was a word I simply could not see until finally it was exposed for a full sixty thousandths of a second. Then suddenly there it was: "cunt". It wasn't that I had seen it but thought it could not be true – it had simply not been visible until that moment. Meanwhile, we went back and examined the record of my skin resistance. It clearly demonstrated that long before I had consciously recognised the unexpected word, my skin resistance had dropped drastically. My body had responded with anxiety to something my mind was entirely unconscious of. This experience radically transformed my world view.

Presumably, I reasoned, what is true of a word perceived through the viewing hood of a tachistoscope, is true of the rest of our perceptions. Our knowledge of the world and of ourselves must be powerfully influenced by some sort of censoring mechanism, operating outside conscious awareness, that decides which perceptions to accept and which to reject. But the rejected perceptions must continue to exist in some kind of unconscious state; otherwise, how could their conflict with the censor register in the body as anxiety?

The Girl in the Mirror

Chris's father was a violent alcoholic who attacked his mother, sexually abused his older brother and left the family when Chris was four. Chris's mother was contemptuous and dismissive towards men and used to dress Chris in girl's clothing from an early age. Growing up, Chris was periodically gripped by uncontrollable rages which terrified him because he feared becoming like his father and losing his mother's love. As Chris reached sexual maturity, he developed an urge to dress up in women's clothes and imagine making love to himself in front of a mirror. But giving in to this urge precipitated further bouts of rage and self-loathing. Chris decided to try to rid himself of these unwanted feelings by becoming the girl in the mirror.

Some years later, when he woke up from the operation to remove his penis, the first thing Chris said was "I feel as if all my anger has been cut out". But after nine years on oestrogen, living as a woman, he came to believe that the medical industry had sold him a physical solution to what was really a psychological problem. He decided to go back to living as a man and came to see me for analysis.

Chris's father had failed to provide him with an adequate male role model, and his mother had rejected his male body. This had led Chris to try to distance himself from the rage and sexual feelings he associated with masculinity by identifying as a woman and transitioning. But the relief afforded by this "solution" had only been temporary. Like my perception of the forbidden word in the tachistoscope experiment, his rage and self-loathing persisted outside consciousness. From a Jungian perspective, we could say that he had driven them into his Shadow, but eventually they returned to haunt him.

Individuation

According to Jung, there is a drive within us all that attempts to bring about a state of integration between our conscious (ego) and unconscious (Shadow), our minds and our bodies, the different parts of our psyches, and ourselves and the world. He called this the individuation process. It relates to the religious experience of being at one with oneself and the world and it facilitates being and becoming the unique individual that one is.

Early attachment trauma can disrupt this process and result in a premature awareness of separateness. This can precipitate a precocious split between mind and body as the infant attempts to organise experiences the primary carer (usually the mother) ought to manage (Winnicott 1949).

Perhaps we can conceptualise Chris's experiences from this perspective. Chris felt insecure in his male body from a very early age. His mother could only really love him if he identified as female. This led him to try and distance himself from both his body and the rage and sexual feelings he associated with it. We could say that his male body had come to carry his Shadow and that he attempted to achieve a sense of security by erasing its masculinity and identifying with the girl in the mirror. But it wasn't really Chris's body that was the problem, it was the rage and sexual shame he associated with it. When these feelings began to return, he sought analysis and gradually managed to integrate them. He was certainly aided in this by the understanding and acceptance of his long-term partner, Jane.

From a Jungian perspective, we could say that the individuation process, which had been disrupted by the risk of losing his mother's love and his father's failures, was resumed as he managed to reintegrate the unwanted feelings he had previously driven into his Shadow. If this had happened earlier, he would probably not have felt the need to medically alter his body.

Some Remarks on Being Trans

A word of caution. For Chris it has proved possible to formulate a psychoanalytic understanding of the aetiology of his trans identification. But this is not necessarily the case for everyone. It could well be that some people's trans identification arises spontaneously without being the result of an attempt to evade painful emotions or traumatic experiences. These cases may not normally find their way into a therapist's consulting room, but they remind us of the dangers inherent in generalising about trans people. They also raise some questions; most obviously – do such people need treatment, and if so, why, and what kind?

It seems axiomatic, that if there is nothing wrong, there is no need for treatment. So, why do some trans people demand "essential medical treatment", while simultaneously claiming that their transgender identity has arisen spontaneously and is not a pathology? Presumably, in addition to being trans, (at least) some of them must be suffering from gender dysphoria. In other words, the discrepancy between their transgender identity (their mind) and their biological sex (their body) is causing them pain which they seek to remedy with puberty blockers, cross sex hormones and/or surgery. Many claim that such treatment helps them feel more authentic, as their body aligns more closely with how they feel inside. But this can entail becoming a lifelong medical patient, losing fertility and adult sexual function, increased risk of cancer, osteoporosis, thrombosis, heart attack and mood disruption.

See Malone et al. (2021) and Withers (2021) for a more detailed account of some of the risks of medical treatment. If we conceptualise GD as the consequence of a painful mismatch between mind and body, the following question arises. Wouldn't it be wiser to try to resolve the GD psychotherapeutically before undergoing such risky physical treatment, even if the trans identification itself has arisen spontaneously rather than defensively?

A Word on Composite Cases

Current confidentiality codes, in the United Kingdom at least, make it very difficult to write about real cases because the advent of the internet means patients can easily read about themselves online. Thus, it is no longer considered sufficient to anonymise patients for third parties. Permission to publish must also be sought if a patient could recognise themselves in clinical material. This poses very serious problems for psychoanalysis which has traditionally relied on case studies to develop and communicate its theories and practices. It is not always possible to obtain permission to publish. Seeking permission can disrupt ongoing therapy and being granted permission may depend on agreeing with the patient's view of things which is not always possible or desirable. In addition, certain trans rights extremists are prepared to use any means at their disposal to attempt to discredit and silence those who do not agree with their ideology (see e.g. the cases of Kathleen Stock, Maya Forstater and James Esses in the United Kingdom). Under these circumstances, it may be necessary to construct a composite case. This has the drawback that such "clinical material" could easily be dismissed as the author's fabrication, created to promote their own, potentially prejudiced, position. This is a very real danger, but it does make it possible to condense several clinical experiences into one case. That is the approach I will take with "Alex" and with "Viv".

Alex and the Shadow

"Alex" was a biological female who identified as male. "He" was sixteen and had already socially transitioned by the time he came to see me for psychotherapy. It is my normal practice to meet young people with their parents for their first session, after which I see them alone. I noticed that Alex's parents still called him by his given name and referred to him as "she" and "her". I can understand parents' wish to slow down the rush to medical treatment by resisting social transition. But I respect my patient's wishes when it comes to names and pronouns while keeping one eye firmly on the reality of their biological sex.

Alex had come out as trans eighteen months earlier. His parents said they had seen no signs of him being male identified before then. Six months prior to that he, or she as she then was, had announced that she was a lesbian.

This had upset her parents who were devout Christians and believed homosexuality was a sin. Coming out as lesbian also seemed to precipitate a period of bullying at school. Alex had responded by becoming withdrawn and taking increasingly long periods of time off with a variety of ailments. These included migraines and abdominal pains, which the doctor had diagnosed as irritable bowel syndrome. Both parents worked, so Alex spent these periods off school talking to an international online community of, mainly LGBT, friends, who became increasingly important to her (as she then was). It was during this time that Alex began to identify as male.

Alex's parents felt his online friends were a bad influence, supporting his trans identification and encouraging him to begin the process of medical transition. Alex's doctor had referred him to the Tavistock Gender Identity Development Service (GIDS) but a year later he was still on a waiting list.

Meanwhile, the relationship with his parents was deteriorating. Long periods of withdrawal alternated with short periods of intense hostility. These were generally sparked off by clashes over such issues as the parents' use of pronouns, their reaction to Alex's wish to use a breast binder, and their attempts to control his use of social media. Alex felt these clashes very keenly and following an initial burst of uncontrollable rage, tended to withdraw in deep despair. I tried to help him see that, however clumsily expressed, his parent's interventions were motivated by a desire to protect him from medically altering his body in ways he could later come to regret. But Alex found it hard to accept this and seemed inclined to see himself as the victim of their transphobia – a view that was shared by many of his new online friends. This marked a troubled period in the therapeutic relationship. Alex found it difficult to trust me because I didn't simply side with him against his parents and I had to struggle with my own negative reactions to this mistrust.

As our work progressed, I realised that Alex exhibited several autistic traits, including a difficulty empathising with other people's point of view (coupled with an intense underlying emotional sensitivity to them), a sensitivity to change in general, a tendency to black and white thinking, and a difficulty thinking symbolically. Alex's mother had mentioned in our first session that she had suffered from post-natal depression. Perhaps this had resulted in early attachment trauma which had precipitated these problems. An innate neurodiversity in Alex may have compounded matters. But whether Alex's autistic traits were caused by, or themselves contributed to, early relational trauma; the deep level of despair Alex felt when he fell out with his parents suggested that current conflicts tended to reignite these earlier attachment anxieties.[4]

Discussion

When Alex identified as lesbian, she encountered homophobic bullying at school and rejection by her parents. This seems to have led her to repress her feelings of same sex attraction in the same way as Chris did his rage, and I did my perception of the forbidden word. Identifying as trans reinforced this repression, enabling Alex to think of himself as a straight guy. From a Jungian perspective, we could say that rather than incorporating her feelings of same sex attraction into her individuation process, Alex had dissociated from them and driven them into her Shadow by identifying as male.

As Alex and I began to confront and work through these issues, the pandemic intervened. We continued our work for a while online and Alex did talk about some detransitioners he had spoken to and his fear of having medical treatment he could come to regret. But eventually, citing financial difficulties, he broke off therapy. I worried that, despite our limited progress, Alex would seek out a more "affirmative" therapist who would simply support his wish to medically transition. But six months later, I got an email from him thanking me for our work together and saying that although things were far from perfect, he had been getting on better with his parents (who were now working from home) during lockdown. He went on to ask if I could give him the name of a female, preferably lesbian, therapist for possible use at a later date, which I gladly did.

Viv

Viv was a seventeen-year-old biological male who identified as non-binary, with preferred pronouns "they" and "their". Viv had previously seen a therapist who was a gender specialist, who affirmed them initially as female, but more recently as non-binary. Viv's parents contacted me because they were concerned that Viv was socially withdrawn and suffered from depression. They wanted Viv to see someone who could help with these problems, rather than focus on their gender issues. Viv said they were open to this, so I arranged an initial session to see if we could work together.

In that session I asked what Viv thought was causing the depression. Viv replied that it was because they were non-binary and felt repulsion towards the masculine features of their body. They were confident that taking oestrogen and growing breasts would cure this.

I feared that such thinking would make it very hard for me to work psychotherapeutically with Viv. Any attempt to look at possible psychological aspects of the depression could be construed as an attempt to convert Viv from their non-binary identification. I found myself worrying that if I took Viv on, and the therapeutic relationship subsequently broke down, I could find myself the subject of a complaint or even prosecution. The British government is currently considering legislation to ban "conversion therapy". So, I reluctantly declined to see Viv despite realising that it was quite possible that their disgust with their male body was driven by the same sort of factors that had caused Chris's or Alex's gender dysphoria. I privately consoled myself with the thought that if Viv ended up regretting the decision to take oestrogen and decided to detransition, at least he would be left with a functioning penis; unlike Chris. The long-term effects of oestrogen use in otherwise healthy young males is largely unresearched, but low bone density and increased risk of blood clots are two known dangers and risk of death is increased by 50% 18.5 years after medically transitioning (Asscheman et al. 2011). For these reasons, such treatments remain "off-label" and it seems likely that the practitioners – not the drug companies – will be liable for any eventual compensation claims.

Having described these three cases and outlined a way of conceptualising gender dysphoria in terms of the mind body relationship, it should now be possible to return to the questions raised in the introduction.

Are Gender Dysphoric Children and Young People Being Rushed into Medical Treatment?

The waiting lists in the United Kingdom's gender clinics are so long that it is hard to describe treatment there as rushed. But once patients are seen, clinicians are under pressure to make quick decisions about their suitability for "endocrinology". The Tavistock Clinic in London was once a national centre of excellence for psychotherapy. Now its GIDS is little more than an assessment service. Its safeguarding officer, Sonia Appleby, recently won a compensation claim against the clinic for overriding her concerns about the safety of the children in its care. And ex-patient Keira Bell famously took the clinic to judicial review claiming that she should have been challenged more rather than encouraged to medically transition. Cases such as that of Alex, described above, show how important long-term psychotherapy can be for some clients. But the sheer pressure of numbers makes it very hard for the GIDS to offer long-term psychotherapeutic services.

That leaves clients wanting help with their gender dysphoria with very little option but to turn to private providers. Not everyone can afford this and many of those who can, have (like Viv) already decided that medical treatment is their best option. This is often encouraged by online influencers with little or no medical or therapeutic expertise, many of them effectively in the pay of big pharma. The scientific evidence in favour of such treatment is classed as "poor" or "very poor" by the British National Institute for Clinical Excellence (NICE 2020). A book like this is not the place for a detailed discussion of scientific papers or an assessment of the robustness of the evidence base for current treatment protocols. But it seems to me, that some of those seeking medical transition are "Just victims of the in-house drive by" as Rage Against The Machine (1991) put it. An army of on-line influencers and trans rights extremists has promoted access to "gender affirmative medical treatment" as a trans right, turning these vulnerable, gender questioning young people into life-long big pharma customers. Many therapists and therapeutic organisations, mindful of our profession's former pathologisation of gay people, have unintentionally supported this agenda by effectively denouncing non-affirmative therapy as "conversion therapy". The situation is worse in countries such as the United States without a national health service, where private health care grants quicker access to "gender affirmative" therapy and medical treatment.

Studies consistently show that, without any treatment, most trans children reconcile themselves to their biological sex by the end of puberty (Cantor 2017). A disproportionate number eventually turn out to be gay. It is natural for parents to want to act in their children's best interests. But these studies suggest that, in the long-term, those interests may not be served by facilitating early access to "gender affirmative" therapy and medical treatment.

For those young people who have already decided to medically transition, it may seem as though those counselling caution are in reality simply depriving them of the treatment they need. But the numbers of detransitioners regretting such treatment is increasing exponentially (see r/detrans reddit and Littman 2021). And in her book *Transgender Identities*, psychoanalyst Alessandra Lemma (2022) makes a convincing case for a thorough psychotherapeutic exploration of motivation (including unconscious motivation) as part of a properly informed decision-making process regarding medical transition.

What Has Prompted So Many Young People's Wish to Medically Transition?

The astonishing increase in numbers of trans identifying young people is well documented, as is the switch from a predominance of biological males towards biological females seeking transition. Nobody quite knows for sure what is causing this. But trans woman and former president of the American Professional Association of Transgender Health Erica Anderson (2022) (https://twitter.com/4th_WaveNow/status/1478800491446423560) suggests that social contagion fuelled by loneliness and increased use of social media is an important factor. Anderson notes that the global pandemic has intensified some of these pressures and this coincides with a further rise in transgender identification in the San Francisco area where she works. She goes on to warn that simply supporting their wish to medically transition may be doing these young people a grave disservice.

In Great Britain it seems as though Relationship and Sex Education lessons have also played a part. Children are taught from a very early age about gender identity; often before they have a clear grasp of biological sex. Not only is this confusing for many young people it can lead to them becoming preoccupied with issues around gender identity. To a young person, such as my client Alex, who has autistic traits and struggles with internalised homophobia, adopting a transgender identity may simultaneously appear to offer them a way of explaining their psycho-social difficulties and making them more popular with their peers. Although this can afford them short-term relief, it is not a long-term solution to their problems.

What Is the Best Attitude for Teachers, Parents and Therapists to Adopt?

i   Teachers

Schools are likely to have their own policies, teachers their own views and individual children their own needs. So, it is hard to generalise. But it is important to recognise that, unlike gender identity, which can be mutable, biological sex is fixed. Secondary sexual characteristics may be altered through surgery and hormones, and a person may legally change their gender, but it is not possible to physically change sex. It is quite normal for younger children not to realise this. We do not come into this world with an innate knowledge of biological science; we have to be taught it. One role of a teacher is to do this. I would suggest that another is to help children distinguish between the worlds of mind and body, of gender identity and physical sex; and where these are in conflict, to help them find ways to live with this creatively.

That may involve allowing a child to experiment with gender roles, how they dress and play and what they are called. It may also include referring a child to counselling if gender issues are masking other psychological difficulties. But teachers should be careful not to collude with campaigning organisations and lobby groups (such as Mermaids, Gendered Intelligence and Stonewall in the United Kingdom) if their teaching materials implicitly encourage people like my client Alex to medically transition without addressing underlying psychological problems. In my opinion there should be no place for such teaching material in schools. But if there is, they should be balanced by access to more scientifically based, less ideologically motivated teaching material (see e.g. Transgender Trend and My Body Is Me Publishing).

Teachers can feel under pressure to call trans students by their chosen name and preferred pronouns. This might seem like a basic mark of respect, but parents may quite reasonably worry that doing this moves their child further along the path to medical transition. Such a child may attempt to draw the teacher into viewing their parents as intolerant and transphobic. But rather than accepting such a view at face value, it would probably be more helpful to try to involve the parents in any decision-making process. As some of the above case material shows, clashes over such things as names and pronouns can be the battle ground for conflicts with their origins elsewhere. A teacher who takes sides in such a conflict without understanding its true nature may inadvertently make its' resolution more difficult.

ii   Parents

Parents generally want to do what's best for their children. But having a trans child can make it hard to know what is for the best. Parents are understandably frightened by the threat of suicide though this is often exaggerated by trans activists (see e.g. Transgender Trend 2018); and Dhejne et al. (2011) found that completed suicides are around twenty times more common in post-operative trans people than in a matched control group. So, the much-touted cliché "Would you rather have a dead daughter or a live son?" is not based on sound scientific evidence.

Simply accepting a child's wish to medically transition could facilitate medically induced harm. On the other hand, opposing such a wish too strongly could estrange a child, effectively driving them further into the arms of an LGBTQ community that supports "gender affirmative medical treatment". Of course, it is the parents who are most likely to be the ones left picking up the pieces if things subsequently go wrong.

Once again, it is hard to generalise, as each child is unique. But it is worth bearing in mind that it is quite normal for adolescents to clash with parents as they attempt to separate from their family of origin and establish an independent identity. This clash can take place over virtually any issue, but the important thing is to keep connected by talking as honestly and respectfully as possible. Adolescents are more likely to develop healthy resilience and independence if they know that they are still loved, even if their values and beliefs differ from their parents'.

Such a connection can be hard to maintain, however. When Alex clashed with his parents over breast binders and the use of pronouns, it precipitated catastrophic feelings of rejection and abandonment that probably originated in early attachment experiences. The wish to escape a repetition of these experiences intensified Alex's rage and need to withdraw. Talking this through in therapy made it easier for him to tolerate disagreement with his parents without withdrawing. This may well have contributed to the family being able to get closer during lockdown. The fact that Alex requested contact details for a lesbian therapist suggests that "his" parents may even have begun to accept the possibility that they had a daughter who was a lesbian and needed support with this.

iii   Therapists

Alex's case illustrates some of the therapeutic work that can be done with gender questioning young people whose autistic traits may have contributed to and/or originated in early attachment trauma. My work with Alex was curtailed by the pandemic and financial considerations. But Donald Kalsched (2015) gives a brilliant exposition of his analytic work with a client he calls Mike, who, while not himself transgender, exhibits some of the same autistic traits. Kalsched's case illustrates the strain such clients can place on the therapist, who needs to be able to recognise and utilise elements of his own experience that resonate with his client's disturbance. In particular Kalsched writes about the need for both the therapist and client to be able to re-experience and tolerate the rage and terror of early attachment trauma within the therapeutic relationship (the transference and countertransference) in order for it to be transformed.

But this raises a difficulty. Such feelings can rupture the therapeutic relationship as both therapist and client go through a period of self-doubt and mutual hatred. If the rupture is repaired, and the feelings associated with the original trauma regulated, very early defences can be overcome, and the client can access areas of themselves that were previously unavailable (driven into their Shadow). But there is no guarantee that this will happen. The client may break off treatment, or the therapist may resort to a position of "unconditional positive regard" in order to feel better about himself. Then the work cannot be done. In the normal course of events this would be distressing but my client Viv described above illustrates a particular danger in relation to the transgender client.

Conclusion

To recapitulate: I have distinguished trans identification from gender dysphoria and gender identity from biological sex. I have postulated that trans identification may arise spontaneously for unknown reasons but that it can also arise defensively out of an attempt to resolve psychological conflict. Trans identification may or may not be accompanied by gender dysphoria. I have suggested that gender dysphoria can be regarded as the discomfort that arises when gender identity clashes painfully with biological sex. If there is no gender dysphoria, then there is no suffering and therefore no need for treatment. If there is gender dysphoria, then the question that arises is whether it is best treated psychotherapeutically or medically in the first instance.

I have made my own opinion about this clear. But I hope my readers will feel able to formulate their own answers to this and the other questions I have raised. If this chapter helps them do so in collaboration with their child, teachers, and therapists, it will have achieved its purpose.

Notes

1 It is possible to be trans without suffering from gender dysphoria.
2 The word idealism, in this context, derives from its prioritisation of ideas.
3 A tachistoscope is a machine which displays visual images for precisely timed fractions of a second.
4 See Winnicott (1974) and Ogden (2014) for a psychoanalytic discussion of such issues.

References

Asscheman, H. et al. (2011). A long-term follow-up study of mortality in trans-sexuals receiving treatment with cross sex hormones. *European Journal of Endocrinology*, 164, 636–642.

Cantor, J. (2017). How many trans-gender kids grow up to stay trans? Mental Health. December 30. https://www.psypost.org/2017/12/many-transgender-kids-grow-stay-trans-50499

Descartes, R. (1641). *Meditations on first philosophy* in Wilson (1983).

Dhejne, C. et al. (2011). Long-term follow-up of transsexual persons undergoing sex reassignment surgery: Cohort study in Sweden. *PLoS One*, 6(2), e16885.

Kalsched, D. (2013). *Trauma and the Soul*. Routledge: London and New York.

Kalsched, D. (2015). Revisioning Fordham's 'Defences of the Self' in light of modern relational theory and contemporary neuroscience. *Journal of Analytical Psychology*, 60(4), 477–496.

Lemma, A. (2022). *Transgender Identities*. Routledge: London and New York.

Littman, L. (2021). Individuals treated for gender dysphoria with medical and/or surgical transition who subsequently detransitioned: A survey of 100 detransi-tioners. *Archives of Sexual Behaviour*, 50(8), 3353–3369.

Malone, W. et al. (2021). Puberty blockers for gender dysphoria: The science is far from settled. *Lancet Child Adolescent Health*, 5(9), e33–e34.

NICE. (2020). Evidence review: Gonadotrophin releasing hormone analogues for children and adolescents with gender dysphoria. Arms.nice.org.uk.

Ogden, T. (2014). Fear of breakdown and the unlived life. *International Journal of Psychoanalysis*, 95(2), 205–223.

Rage Against the Machine. (1991). *Lyrics from* Bullet in the Head.

Transgender Trend. (2018). Suicide by trans-identified children in England and Wales. https://www.transgendertrend.com/suicide-by-trans-identified-children-in-england-and-wales/

Winnicott, D. W. (1949). Mind and its relation to the psyche-soma. *British Journal of Medical Psychology*, 27(4), 201–209.

Winnicott, D. (1974). Fear of breakdown. *International Review of Psychoanalysis*, 1, 103.

Withers, R. (2021). Transgender medicalization and the attempt to evade psycho-logical distress. *Journal of Analytical Psychology*, 65(5), 865–889.

Chapter 3

Disease as the Shadow of the Body

Wendy J Bratherton

Jung was one of the first to appreciate the depth of the connection between mind and body. Jung gave a series of seminars between 1934 and 1939 to colleagues on the mind–body link. They were based on Nietzsche's book, *Thus Spoke Zarathustra*. Here he warned of the dangers of becoming too intellectual and ignoring the body, which he felt Zarathustra had done. Jung says:

> The body is merely the visibility of the soul, the psyche: and the soul is the psychological experience of the body. So, it is really one and the same thing.
>
> (Jung 1989: 355)

Working therapeutically with patients, I focus on the language used. Many words used to describe the psychic condition originate from what has been experienced in our bodies. For example, "He turned a deaf ear; I cannot swallow it anymore, she broke my heart". Often the expression tells the story of what is wrong in the body of the person as well as what is rejected in the psyche. Listening carefully, the language used may describe the repressed emotion or part of the Shadow the body is "holding" as disease. Our bodies silently deal with the buffeting of life and this gets lodged in the tissues of our being. This works like the story of the Princess and the Pea. To see if she is a real princess, the Queen makes her sleep on a huge pile of mattresses, under which is a pea. The princess does not sleep. She can feel the pea under a pile of mattresses but does not know what it is. Similarly, we may feel that there is something in us but we do not know what it is; however, it has an effect on us. There are no words but there is some discomfort, pain, or degeneration. This is what I mean by the body "holding" some memory which is experienced but we cannot quite connect to it. Discovering what it is and experiencing what memories and emotions the body is holding may be seen as the way to profound healing. Following Jung's view of

DOI: 10.4324/9781003255819-5

the mind–body link, Dethlefsen and Dahlke comment in their book, *The Healing Power of Illness:*

> It is the shadow that makes us ill – but the encounter with the shadow that makes us well! This is the key to understanding illness and healing. Every symptom is an aspect of the shadow that has precipitated itself into physicality… … Through the medium of the body the symptom makes us whole again. (1997: 40)

My interest in this link of mind and body developed from teaching Infant Observation Seminars for over 20 years. This involved observing infants, usually in their homes, for the first two years of life. The seminar experience provided insights into how infants develop physically and mentally in relation to their caregivers and environments. Subsequently, I became interested in early, developmental trauma, and, as I worked with this in adults, I started to feel the need for more body-focused skills as a therapist. In psychological therapies, we do not touch, but I realised that babies are touched all the time and information passes between the bodies of the baby and caregiver. So, I trained in Biodynamic Craniosacral Therapy where the approach is hands-on, yet non-invasive. Changes in the body are witnessed without any manipulation, enabling a deep listening to the body. Such engagement helps the body to resolve issues at its own pace and in its own time. This holding process is similar to the way the therapist contains the therapeutic space for the psyche to resolve issues. For some people, working with both therapies appeared to give a deeper engagement as both the patient and I could witness the embodied truth of their "dis-ease". This was often deeply healing as it was known in the mind *and* experienced in the body. When a person is taken back gently and slowly to primordial states of mind, an early trauma may be relived and related to in a way that was impossible during infancy. I illustrate examples of this with clinical sketches.

What Do We Mean by Disease as Shadow?

Our conscious and unconscious sides are always together and, like light and shadow, are two sides of the same coin. The two are inseparable, yet opposites. Jung (1968, para. 15) understood the key fact of needing to hold the *opposites of conscious and unconscious* together in our mind–body in order to know ourselves more completely. Only when we can meet and integrate our Shadow – all the aspects of ourselves we do not like – can we become a whole human being. Jung describes vividly his process of integrating his Shadow in *The Red Book* (pp. 356–357).

Traditional cultures, for example, the ancient Chinese Wisdom Traditions, knew about these opposites. Jung writes in his Commentary "On the Secret of the Golden Flower" (1968, para. 7) that the Chinese knew how to hold the two sides together. Their yin-yang symbol, called the monad, encompasses two sides. Here, two complementary opposites, the light and the dark sides, are depicted in a state of constant movement which reflects the dynamic interplay of nature – change being the essence of life. Life continually presents us with fresh opportunities for renewal and healing; the symptoms presented to us by the disease being one. It makes us stop and pay attention to the body.

So, following Jung's ideas, we see that understanding what the body is "saying" through the disease, pain, discomfort, etc., may help us confront aspects of ourselves which we would rather ignore. Nevertheless, if we are courageous enough to look at and into this repressed Shadow side, we may discover unlived life. The physical symptoms of disease may provide a lens by which to understand what our body unconscious is trying to express. Jung suggests that if our conscious mind gets too one sided and out of touch with primordial images, then the other side is announced through the nervous system or disease as a way of rebalancing us.

How Does the Shadow Develop in the Body?

We are born into a culture where we are taught what is right and wrong, what we can and cannot do, what we must achieve and what we cannot allow. To adapt to others as we grow, we usually have to learn to repress parts of ourselves. If the culture and family we live in reflect us and if they "fit" us, there is not a problem. If not, and we have to put on an act, then part of us is hidden and cannot live. It goes into the Shadow. There may be times when this unlived side manifests in illness or disease. When we are born, we have an innate predisposition or instinct for relatedness. If all goes well, a few hours after birth, babies can copy an adult sticking out their tongue, for instance. Babies are sensate and feel everything with their bodies, a fact which is frequently overlooked in our western society.

The brain has two sides. The right hemisphere of the brain is more mature than the left at birth. The right processes the sights, sounds and sensory experiences of touch, smell and taste, and the experience of the primary caregiver and is relational (Wilkinson 2006). Hence, in the very early days, a baby communicates its needs, especially hunger, by crying in order to get mother to feel – *in her body* – what the baby wants. If a mother or caregiver is able to make sense of baby's signals and respond appropriately, her infant will tend to develop a positive sense of self and learn how to make relationships. The left side of the brain matures later, by 2–3 years old, as the infant learns to speak. This enables new experiences of separateness and relating.

What happens if the birth has been difficult and bonding is interfered with, or mother may have received poor mothering herself, or be depressed or ill? Without language to express their needs and, in the absence of a caregiver to interpret the bodily signals, the infant's body may develop a pattern of self-holding. Often this is in the musculature and fascia of the baby's body making it feel stiff to touch. In extremis, the baby may shut down or even stop communicating vocally and become "good". If this happens babies may grow up around these physical holding patterns, which also have a psychic component. Fordham (1976) called these "defences of the self". Although once necessary to support survival, later in life they may cause problems. Sidoli (2000), in *When the Body Speaks*, describes cases of children with whom she worked, some of whom had repeated negative experiences which "*concretely remain in the body and cause physical illnesses*" (p. 38).

Interestingly, such patterns of self-holding can be felt in the body by a craniosacral therapist. Patients have relived a variety of feelings and sensations from their early years as their bodies have released these patterns of holding. These include bewilderment, abject terror, an utter lack of safety and feeling they were floating in space with nothing to contain them. Their tense adult bodies held the early distress, and they never felt safe to relax. Some seemed incapable of calming themselves, or even knowing what this would feel like.

If a person lives continually in an unsafe environment, their nervous system may adapt by becoming hyperalert. Hyperarousal is a normal reaction to danger, for it enables the body to invoke the "fight or flight" response. Since a baby cannot fight or flee, being in a hyperalert state may become a habitual way of being. In this case, the original trauma – for example, the deep pain and distress of separation and abandonment – is held silently in the body. Unless an infant is related to and contained emotionally by a caregiver, the baby's body will continue to hold the traumatic memory. Consequently, the infant (and later the child) may feel "all bad", "dirty", "wrong", "toxic", or think nobody wants to be near them (Clinical Sketch 2). In short, they experience the environment as hostile.

In therapy as adults, these individuals' bodies and psyches begin to release memories and sensations as they re-engage with the buried pain of early trauma such as abandonment, separation and sensing the absence of another there. If the pain, physically and emotionally, is received and re-experienced in a safe environment with a trusted therapist, their bodies begin slowly and gently to relax, often for the first time. As this happens, the ability to relate starts to improve.

Until quite recently, body and psyche have been treated separately. Hence, we go to psychotherapists and counsellors to treat the psyche, and to bodyworkers or doctors to treat the body. Recent findings of neuroscience have rekindled interest in the mind–body connection, throwing light on ways in which early developmental trauma is held silently in the body. Informed by these insights, Levine (2010), Porges (2011) and Dunlea (2019), in particular, have developed new approaches to healing trauma in the body and, correspondingly, in the psyche.

The Polyvagal Theory of Stephen Porges (2011) shows the importance of the vagus nerve to our understanding of different physical and emotional states. It explains why and how our bodies and psyches shut down and why we might be constantly hypervigilant. The vagus nerve receives impulses from the senses – sight, smell, sound and touch – and is connected to the brain stem and main organs of the body. It consists of two aspects: the dorsal vagus (in evolutionary terms the "old" part of this nerve) which supports immobilisation behaviours – rest and digest, and defensive immobilisation or shutdown; and the ventral vagus (a newer evolutionary part) which supports social engagement.

The autonomic system consists of two main branches – the sympathetic and parasympathetic. There are three main pathways of survival which respond to signals and sensations entering the body. The sympathetic branch mobilises us for fight and flight if we sense danger. It is found in the middle part of the spinal cord. Porges suggests that the parasympathetic part of the vagus is divided into two parts. The dorsal vagal pathway is the oldest, primitive part of the nerve. This is connected with immobilisation, shutdown and collapse. It activates when we feel in constant danger and is the place of last resort for survival. Caught in this, a person may feel that they have to hide away and make no sound. The ventral vagal pathway, the more recent part of the nerve, has a pathway which goes under the aorta of the heart and up to the face. It responds to sensations and cues of safety and supports feelings of social connectedness. When we feel safe and warm and held, this part of the nerve helps to regulate our heartbeat, blood pressure and immune system. Then we can engage socially and think more creatively. The sympathetic part which originates in the spinal cord prepares us for flight or fight. It can be altered by the cerebral frontal cortex which might indicate that though we are frightened, actually we do not need to be, or yes, we should move. This is well explained by Deb Dana in *The Polyvagal Theory in Therapy* (2018). She suggests that every day we may move from one state to another, and gives the image of a ladder from the dorsal vagus at the bottom to the ventral vagus at the top. For early trauma, the infant, or infant in the adult, may be stuck in the dorsal vagal response.

When an infant shuts down the reaction is immediate and automatic – a dorsal vagal response not mediated by the cerebral frontal cortex, as an infant is too young for this. The baby's body might feel taut because the baby is trying to self-hold. If the baby cannot recover from this state, never feeling safe enough and sufficiently attuned to, then the baby and, later the child, adolescent and adult, will grow up embedded in physical tension and psychic paralysis. So, if the infant has experienced profound shock and trauma their nervous system may go into freeze. The amygdala in the limbic system lies deep in the brain and fires when there is perceived danger. In an infant, this can be calmed by a caregiver. However, if the infant has not been attuned to, it remains hyperalert. Later, as an adult, if something triggers the early memory and the amygdala fires, that person may suddenly go into the freeze response, (not able to move or speak), and not know why. The response is quick and not mediated by the orbital frontal cortex at the front of the brain. It can also affect the way that infants attach to adults. The fear might make them avoidant or anxious, for instance. Fonagy (2001) in *Attachment Theory and Psychoanalysis*, summarises the work of John Bowlby, who first described in the 1950s and 1960s, the different forms of attachment infants developed and the biological underpinning of these styles of attachment.

The Psychoid Psyche

This most fundamental level of the unconscious Jung (1960: 368, 380) called the psychoid psyche. It is inaccessible to consciousness through words and is closely related to instinct. How, then, can we relate to it?

Jung's key contribution to knowing this "unconscious without words" was through his understanding of archetypes. My own embodied perception of the archetypes came one day when I had been working with clay. I was making a mask, letting it unfold and had no plan of what I was making. In the evening I watched a television programme about the Green Man. I had not heard of the Green Man before but realised that he had emerged from my hands spontaneously! Jung called this synchronicity, when the inside world and outside world meet and create "*a meaningful coincidence of two or more events*" (Jung 1960: 969). I knew, then, that these archetypes live deep within us and can emerge through our bodies or in our dreams. They bring a wealth of meaning, which will be both collective and individual for each person.

Archetypes, then, are shared by all human beings and form part of the "collective unconscious". Jung writes:

> "the archetypes are formal factors responsible for the organisation of unconscious processes: they are patterns of behaviour".
>
> (Jung 1954: 436)

When Jung applied the idea of archetypes to the psychoid unconscious he made a more explicit connection between mind and body. He suggested that each archetype could be envisaged as a spectrum of colour with an infra-red end (the physiological, instinctual pole), and an ultra-violet end (the spiritual or imaginal pole). So, an archetype embraces both ends and everything in between. It may be experienced through either pole. Disease may be seen as the infra-red end of the spectrum and can be engaged with via the body. The mythological or imaginal world, however, can be approached through dreams, poetry and art.

There are two main basic archetypes: masculine and feminine. These are not gendered but represent different qualities we all can have. In patriarchal societies, the masculine traits have been valued over the feminine. This is one reason why the body and what it is "saying", are easily undervalued and not listened to. Remember the monad symbol with two sides always moving from one side to the other? When we get too one-sided, then the other side begins to come back in to rebalance us. If we cut off the body and live in our heads, then the body might get sick. If we can connect with this one-sidedness, we may accept the disease as a symbol of what we need in order to rebalance our lives.

Before considering the clinical sketches, I want to mention an important study by Felitti et al. (1998) in the United States. They studied obesity with over 13,000 participants. All initially lost weight but subsequently many returned to over-eating. Investigating many reasons for this, the study's authors found that some men, for example, those that worked in prisons, liked their extra bulk as it made them feel safer at work. In the case of women participants, 55% had been sexually abused when young. This shocking statistic pointed the way to the link between childhood mal-treatment, illness and attachment problems. Further study has clarified the significant relationship between disease in adulthood following childhood exposure to emotional, verbal, physical and sexual abuse. Also included, are household dysfunction, economic hardship, disappearance of a relative due to divorce, death or incarceration, alcoholism and drug use in the house and having a member of the household with mental illness. As a result, Adverse Childhood Environment (ACE) Programmes have been set up in the United States and Britain which use the ACE measure based on ten types of childhood trauma.

This study confirms the links between trauma and abuse in childhood and later disease.

Most people have a story about their disease. I will now give some clinical sketches of people suffering from a variety of illnesses to show how they made sense of, and found meaning in, their ailments which led to changes in themselves and their lives.

Clinical Sketch 1: Anita's Anorexia Helps Her Claim Herself

A highly intelligent young woman, called Anita, was referred to me. She had been in the hospital for anorexia as a teenager. Anita described how difficult it was to turn her anorexia around as there was so much competition between in-patients not to eat. She made a pact with a friend she met in hospital and they encouraged each other to get well.

In our Western society, there is much importance attached to the way our bodies look. As a consequence of this many people become obsessed with diets and what they eat. Indeed, behaviours around food may become ex-treme leading to diseases such as anorexia nervosa and obesity. Jungian analyst Marion Woodman (1980) came to understand anorexia and obesity as different symptoms manifesting from similar unconscious problems, calling them "counter-poles of one neurosis". For example, the individual who gains weight and cannot lose it may have used food to ease anxiety and emotional emptiness. The instinct is to eat when hungry. If this is interfered with, eating may become an obsession disturbing the whole body–mind system and alienating the person from their body. Woodman shows how it is often hard for individuals to lose weight because the underlying repressed emotions have not been identified and expressed.

As with obesity, anorexia nervosa also alienates the person from their body. However, the symptoms of anorexia are different. In the case of anorexia, there is a refusal to eat, but there is a "high" from the control the person feels they have over food. This control is extreme, and for parents it can be an ongoing torture to watch their child becoming so emaciated they might die.

Both conditions are complex and difficult to overcome as Anita found. In Anita's case, she eventually gained weight and left the hospital. Her recovery was helped by her parents' gradual acceptance that their daughter's needs were different from their own.

As an adolescent, Anita was rebelling against a mother and father who were always hard at work in prestigious occupations and, it seems, unavailable to her emotionally. Her primal anger turned her against food – the one thing she felt she could control. This anger was a non-verbal sign that she did not feel she received the early emotional love and nourishment in the way she had needed as an infant. She had been cared for by a series of nannies who changed frequently, often with very little warning.

Anita returned to education to study drama, not the academic subjects her parents had chosen for her. She completed her education in her own time and at her own pace. Her relationships improved markedly as she started to live her own life and she became very successful in her chosen career.

Clinical Sketch 2: Elizabeth and Raging Eczema

Eczema is a psychosomatic illness. Working with people who somatise used to be unpopular with therapists. People who somatise frequently have difficulty symbolising, instead their affect is held and *express*ed in the body. Psychoanalyst Joyce McDougall in *Theatres of the Body* (1989) considered that physiological states were linked to deep psychic dramas being acted out in the body. She realised that these "silent" expressions of emotion had their roots in infancy. As adults, they could not name their emotions and were cut off from them. She called this state alexithymia (see Clinical Sketch 4). Marion Woodman (1980), based her work on Jung's view of the importance of the body and developed a way of working with physical symptoms as symbols. Her workshops are meticulously described in M. Reinau's book *Love Matters for Psychic Transformation* (2016).

Elizabeth, a woman in her 30s, came to see me. Her hands and parts of her body were covered in weeping, raw, eczema. She was highly intelligent and had a very good job. Her marriage had just broken down because she did *not* want children. In our early work, it transpired that she had been born two months early and for several weeks had been in an incubator. This was at a time when babies in incubators were not touched very much. Through her dreams, where there was intense excitement around instruments of torture, we began to wonder whether, in the absence of mother, she had bonded to the hard objects in the incubator, such as the tubes. Following her birth, her mother had been very depressed and they had not bonded. She showed me a photo of herself, aged four months, which shocked me. She was precariously balanced on her mother's knee – her mother was neither looking at her nor holding her in her arms.

As a result of being in the incubator and having a mother too depressed to relate to her fully, she was left, as an infant, feeling bad and unwanted. She developed a coping persona, but behind this and deep inside her was an unwanted infant-self who was "always screaming". Hence, she could not imagine being a mother.

Initially, she shared her early feelings through paintings of a red-faced, screaming baby called Little One. The feelings from this level of the unconscious, the psychoid level, which had shown themselves through the body, may in therapy be expressed non-verbally through painting, sand play or clay. As she became able to verbalise, she described how "all her tears went inside and hid in a hole in her tummy", her screams becoming like "big black spiders and raging storms". Together we realised that she shut all the storms and screams down and became a good, pretty girl and stepped out of her skin. Elizabeth told her young coping-self that she did not need a mother or father. She thought that she was clever and had left the infant-self behind. But Little One did not die. She kept coming to the surface through the painful, weeping eczema and pains in her body. Elizabeth drew pictures of her adult-self stamping on her infant-self. She gradually became aware that under her bright, coping self, there was a big black hole. She was clever and had to be perfect (which was useful in her work), but if she did anything wrong, her world fell apart, and was swallowed by the hole. She then drew a picture of an infant broken into pieces trying to cling to a mother's head whose eyes were closed and who had no body. The infant's hands were red and raw, like her hands, desperately clawing at mother's face.

We had been working together for a few years and she was slowly feeling more contained by our work, when she brought a painting of a mother holding a screaming baby. Many months later, Elizabeth came with a picture of the body of a woman with a scream *inside* her. Later, as she thought about leaving therapy, Elizabeth came with her carving of a stone child kneeling and covering her face with her hands. Contemplating the stone child with me, she realised she was hiding her terror of separation.

Much had changed in her life by this time and she now had good relationships. Still her powerful feelings of separation were accompanied by
a mantra of "nothing and no one". She felt she should leave but also that
there was more to explore.

When she realised that I was working as a Biodynamic Craniosacral therapist as well as an Analyst she implored me to work with both modalities. I
eventually agreed. The gentle touch enabled her to settle into her body – which
had been difficult with talking therapy alone. The screaming inside subsided
and trust increased. At last, it was ok to feel more relaxed. As her body
calmed, she found she could "take me in" and keep a memory of me alive in
her. Moreover, when I could witness her fear through touch, she began to feel
more real in herself. It was as if I was the mother she never had, who could
sense her feelings and name them for her. As I resonated with her feelings
through touch, Elizabeth felt deeply connected to. As her furious, angry
feelings were held and accepted by me, she began to have an embodied sense of
herself. This was a huge relief to her. Elizabeth's eczema now completely
disappeared. When she left therapy, she commented about the body work:

> In spite of all the words that had passed between us, I could feel that I
> was being heard as my body silently spoke to you. It bought me deeply
> in touch with myself, *being inside my own skin.*

Elizabeth could now use language to express her emotions. Rage no longer
erupted on the surface of her skin as eczema. She could live comfortably in
her own skin and *be* herself and have her *own* life. Elizabeth completely
changed her lifestyle and became who she had dreamt of being as a child.
She no longer had to be the person she thought others wanted her to be,
which had been her innate response since babyhood.

Clinical Sketch 3: Christine, Cancer and the Crows

Christine presented with very low self-esteem. She had a history of birth
trauma – where she and her mother had nearly died. Following her birth, her
mother had been profoundly depressed and agoraphobic. Always feeling
unsafe, Christine had compulsively overworked. She was an apparently
healthy, busy, creative middle-aged woman, with closet artistic tendencies.
One day, after a few years of therapy, she brought the following dream
which turned out to be a warning:

> I am staying in the country in a stone building. It has steps outside where I
> meet an artist friend who is angry with me. She says she will speak with me
> inside the building. When I enter, she has disappeared. I see a device on
> the wall and speak into it. My friend speaks back but is still angry and will
> not speak face to face. I try to placate her, then go outside and walk behind

the house. There I see a wide river with old barges and boats moored along the riverbank. "This was a thriving business which has had its day; it needs to be sold and cleared", I think to myself.

Christine was enjoying her professional life, so it was difficult for her to fully connect to this one possible meaning of the dream – that she needed to stop work and make room for the artist in herself. She was aware that she tended to intellectualise and could see the dream indicated she had to change her life, so she made some adjustments. As her therapist, I had always had a sense that there was a silent part of her who was only rarely able to express herself in words.

Christine had not embodied the dream's full message for, six months later, she discovered a serious cancer which was spreading. Christine stopped everything and focused entirely on her treatment. She began to see that her body, which held her desire to let the artist in herself live, had revealed this to her through the dream. She was left in no doubt now of the meaning of the dream. As a manifestation of her Shadow, even the form of cancer was meaningful as the biopsy revealed a cancer which is not easily detected. We thought how good Christine was at hiding her true desires and subordinating her needs to others. It was not until her body spoke clearly and said "NO" that she could make changes and face this angry side of herself. (In the dream the friend – the angry side of herself – would not speak face to face.) She was caught in a dorsal vagal response.

As cancer treatment began, Christine had another dream warning her not to withdraw from people, her habitual response. She heeded this message and accepted all the help on offer. Christine found time for creative pursuits and accepted intermittent help from a Somatic Experiencing Practitioner trained in the trauma work of Peter Levine. This work tracks the nervous system's responses to events, including trauma responses. She was asked initially to find resources. Resources outside the body, such as an image, object or colour, help us take our attention outside the body in order to enable the nervous system to calm and relax.

The resource she chose was a couple of black crows which had built a nest and were raising a family in view of her window – an image which represented for her the possibility of new life. The synchronicity of the birds appearing outside the window when she most needed something to give her hope, she found very meaningful – particularly when they left as her treatment ended. She felt she was going to survive and could now live her new life. The crows helped her through a personal transformation as everything in herself and in her life had to be re-evaluated.

The experience of cancer treatment and the support Christine received helped her to feel loved for herself and stopped her lifelong feelings of never being good enough. Cancer turned into a profound gift, it made her change her lifestyle and follow the artistic side of herself.

Clearly, the process of engaging with the deepest Shadow through disease can feel messy and profoundly shameful. When people lose their hair through chemotherapy it can feel as if all their identity is stripped away. They are left feeling intensely vulnerable and it is an extremely painful experience, both physically and psychically. One of the most moving and encouraging books about cancer is *Bone* by Jungian Analyst, Marion Woodman (2001). This is a collection of the journal entries Marion wrote in order to engage with her unconscious during the time she was treated for cancer. It resonates with Christine's experience.

Clinical Sketch 4: Richard Finds His Heart Rhythm

Richard was in his 50s when he developed persistent Atrial Fibrillation, where his heart went out of rhythm. He failed to respond to medication and, as a result, endured many cardioversions. This is where his heart was stopped and started again in order to reset the rhythm. He then had a couple of ablations, where a probe is put up an artery into the heart to destroy some "rogue" nodes in his heart. This finally helped his heart rhythm become stable.

Richard realised that he needed to examine the underlying causes of his heart condition. Why was his heart affected rather than any other organ?

Richard worked as an alternative Medical Practitioner. A highly creative man, he had a strong intellect, but his emotional side remained in the Shadow. In therapy, I wondered if he was alexithymic (McDougall 1989). Initially, he thought his problem was connected to his sense of not feeling legitimate in the eyes of the world. Richard's younger brother had been accepted into the prestigious Royal Society. In contrast, he felt he had failed to achieve and thought that doing a PhD was the answer. Richard undertook some research on heart rate variability and how a practitioner's presence may affect it. The aim, through an off-the-body healing practice, was to understand what effect such healing had on both his heart and that of his patient and the relationship between the two. This study earned him a PhD, but while he felt more legitimate in the eyes of the world, his heart continued to fibrillate. His emotions remained in the Shadow. Richard began to see that expressing his feelings would, finally, enable him to experience himself *internally* as a whole and legitimate person.

We eventually realised that, even in therapy, Richard constructed ideas about how the sessions would unfold. This was his way of protecting himself from feeling his intense emotional pain. For several years after obtaining the PhD whenever something deeply emotional happened, his heart went out of rhythm and he was hospitalised. Hospital experiences left him feeling vulnerable and unsafe. Richard started to look back at his life and realised that, in his family, he had never felt able to express his feelings openly. Richard was a sensitive boy, the middle of three, who had had a traumatic start in life, being born six weeks early. This was compounded in being met by a mother who was extremely anxious about caring for a premature baby. She felt unsupported and angry, which made it difficult to attune to him. He shut down and became "good", though hyperalert to other's emotional states. Moreover, at school, he was shunned by his classmates and bullied but he never told anyone. In later life, when Richard's early traumas were triggered and he felt overwhelmed, he would shut down and freeze. He could appear calm outwardly and withdraw into his head, his "safe" place.

As Richard's therapy progressed, he started to remember the events preceding his Atrial Fibrillations. The first fibrillation had followed the highly emotional event of 9/11 in New York. Some years later he had the following dream:

> I was with my wife backpacking from the East to the West coast of Australia. On the first night I stopped at a backpacker's hostel situated in a semi-arid region. The next day I dropped my wife off at a shopping mall and drove to a semi deserted square in the old ruins of a mining town. From the car I took out my black backpack in which were my keys and a first aid pouch from The Body Shop. Whilst trying to retrieve the first aid pouch, it slipped from my grasp and dashed onto the ground where it disintegrated into a cloud of white, floury dust. So did the keys.

The way the contents disintegrated reminded Richard of Ground Zero on 9/11 when the twin towers collapsed. He felt that the key to his healing was feeling in his body the devastation which had prevailed at his own "Ground Zero" on the day that he was born. The embodied "sense" of this connection helped Richard to stop criticising himself and to have compassion and respect for how he had survived as a premature infant with a mother who could not cope. He could now have and communicate his emotions so they did not need to be expressed through his body. His atrial fibrillation did not return. By retrieving this aspect of Shadow, he was able to engage "whole-heartedly" with life.

Covid-19: The Global Shadow

At the time of writing this chapter, the global pandemic of Covid-19 has affected all people across the world. Covid-19, coming out of the blue, has left the world culture on the backfoot, with all the disruption and un-certainties that have been caused at every level of society. Everyone has been affected in some way. Normal rituals around death, such as the gathering of family members at funerals were cancelled and people could not say goodbye to dying relatives. All of which added to their distress. Weddings and holidays were cancelled and postponed. People have had difficulties contacting their doctors, parents had to work from home and home-school children. The list goes on. The outer environment felt very unsafe and these uncertainties caused enormous anxiety and mental stress among all ages of people. Some children, however, who were school refusers, reported that they were pleased that others now experienced the same level of anxiety about going out that they were living with; and it gave them courage! There are always two sides.

From the outset of the pandemic, I was struck by the number of patients who became seriously retraumatised as daily life felt unsafe and frightening. Lockdowns meant they lost aspects of their lives which they had built up in order to support their mental health. I worked with these patients online, drawing on the trauma skills of Peter Levine, to initially calm their nervous systems. Finding new resources to enable them to calm helped them through the emotional trauma into which they had fallen. One commented "I do not think that I could have ever dropped to this level of work unless I had been locked down".

Many medics and nurses who had to work very long shifts working with the dying have been traumatised by it. Those I met in therapy, were very experienced, had worked abroad in deprived areas, and saw themselves as capable and resilient. However, they burnt out and collapsed under the pressure of working with Covid-19. As a result, some were diagnosed with post-traumatic stress disorder. Others found that they also had to engage with early childhood situations lying behind the present trauma. The experience of working with Covid-19 had brought these childhood difficulties and traumas to the surface.

I took the opportunity to converse in depth with several people about their experience of having the virus and being hospitalised. They all recounted their struggles, intense fears and terror with the illness on the edge of life and death. In having to confront death and the fear of death, they realised the preciousness of life. Recovering, they felt compelled to make changes, such as giving more time to family and friends, valuing their own creativity and making time for things they wanted to do. A few made more radical changes, such as leaving a partner or moving to another location. Media coverage of Covid-19 has reflected similar responses in the wider population.

As has been described in this chapter in detail, illness may be a catalyst for change. We have seen how engaging with disease as Shadow can lead to new meaning. As we emerge from the pandemic, we might ask what we have learned and what meaning we can find in it? There is talk of going back to normal. What does this mean? Is it a chance to reset ourselves and also aspects of society or will we emerge from the pandemic the same as we started?

Jungian Analyst Anne Baring, in *Dream of the Cosmos* (2013: 115) describes in detail how we are coming to the end of over 4,000 years of solar mythology which lies behind patriarchal attitudes. Prior to this, lunar mythology dominated and was based on feminine principles. Patriarchal society has valued the archetypal masculine qualities over the feminine ones. Among the more feminine qualities are those of relatedness and care for each other and for the earth. In many ways Covid-19 has helped us to re-experience some of these qualities – such as altruism, caring for others in the community, the importance of our relationships and touch. Covid-19 has also shown the value of stillness in this fast-moving world and of caring for our Earth.

Baring further describes how, at the beginning of solar mythology, patriarchy coincided with climate change, drought and unrest as people moved to areas free of famine. We might see ourselves to be in a similar position, poised on the edge of a new era. We talk about returning to normal or to a "new normal". What is it and is it desirable? Baring suggests the changes we need and the lessons we need to learn, are about re-incorporating more feminine values – for example, working together across the world, relating, dialoguing and caring for each other. Climate change is beckoning us to engage with such values at all levels.

Conclusion

I have attempted to describe in this chapter how disease as Shadow, if fully engaged with, can lead to transformation of the self.

There is one fundamental aspect of Shadow which has consistently been brought to consciousness. At the deepest layer of the unconscious, for all the people I worked with, lay the intense pain of not feeling "seen" or "accepted" as themselves. Disease for these people meant that the body armour broke down and the outer persona was cast aside to reveal their utmost vulnerability. This took the people described in the clinical sketches back to their infancy when they first had to repress difficult feelings of not being attuned to. If these early experiences have had to be repressed for a lifetime, then the disease may be an opportunity for the individual to break the defensive stranglehold on the body-psyche. In the cases described, we have seen how early lack of attunement between caregiver and infant leads to the child and then the adult having no real sense of themselves. It may lead to feelings of toxicity along with a deep sense of shame and guilt if a child feels it is all their fault. Having to face these early repressed feelings can feel like facing the worst of ourselves.

Bodily afflictions often give us no choice but to change. If a way is found to engage with disease as the Shadow side of ourselves, we can retrieve our "authentic self" as the clinical sketches have shown. It is not necessary to "act" when we can accept both sides of our nature without shame, recrimination or blame. Such acceptance can be healing, as Jung discovered from his own transformative experiences. The Self is always wanting us to heal, it seems. We need to have both sides of our being, the light and the dark. If we can accept disease as Shadow in this way, the prompts and warnings inherent in disease symptoms can be genuinely transformative and life-changing.

References

Baring, A. (2013) *The Dream of the Cosmos: A Quest for the Soul.* Dorset, UK: Archive Publishing.

Dana, D. (2018) *The Polyvagal Theory in Therapy: Engaging the Rhythm of Regulation.* London: W.W. Norton & Company Limited.

Dethlefsen, T. and Dahlke, R. (1997) *The Healing Power of Illness: The Meaning of Symptoms and How to Interpret Them.* Shaftesbury, Dorset, UK: Element Books Limited.

Dunlea, M. (2019) *Body Dreaming in the Development of Developmental Trauma: An Embodied Approach.* London: Routledge.

Felitti, A., Noredenberg, W., and Spitz Edwards, M. (1998) *Relationship of Childhood Abuse and Household Dysfunction to Many of the Leading Causes of Death in Adults: The Adverse Childhood Experiences (ACE) Study.* American Journal of Preventive Medicine, 14(4), 245–258.

Fonagy, P. (2001) *Attachment Theory and Psychoanalysis.* New York: Other Press.

Fordham, M. (1976) *The Self and Autism.* London: Karnac.

Jung, C G (1954). *Archetypes and the Collective Unconscious CW9 (i).* London: Routledge and Kegan Paul.

Jung, C.G. (1960) *The Collected Works, Volume 8: The Structure and Dynamics of the Psyche.* London: Routledge and Kegan Paul Ltd.

Jung, C.G. (1968) *The Collected Works, Volume 13: Alchemical Studies.* London: Routledge and Kegan Paul Ltd.

Jung, C.G. (1998, 1989) *Nietzsche's Zarathustra: Notes on the Seminar Given in 1934-9*, James L. Jarrett (ed.) In two volumes, Bollingen Series XCIX. Princeton, NJ: Princeton University Press, 1998; London and New York: Routledge: 1989.

Levine, P.A. (2010) *In an Unspoken Voice: How the Body Releases Trauma and Restores Goodness.* Berkeley, CA: North Atlantic Books.

McDougall, J. (1989) *Theatres of the Body: A Psychoanalytic Approach to Psychosomatic Illness.* London: Free Association Books.

Porges, S.W. (2011) *The Polyvagal Theory, Neurophysiological Foundations of Emotions, Attachment, Communication, Self-Regulation.* London: W.W. Norton and Company Ltd.

Reinau, M. (2016) *Love Matters for Psychic Transformation: A Study of Embodied Psychic Transformation in the Context of Body Soul Rhythms.* Cheyenne, WY: Fisher King Press.

Sidoli, M. (2000) *When the Body Speaks.* London: Routledge.

Wilkinson, M. (2006) *Coming into Mind, The Mind-Brain Relationship: A Jungian Clinical Perspective.* Hove, East Sussex: Routledge.

Woodman, M. (1980) *The Owl Was a Baker's Daughter.* Toronto: Inner City Books.

Woodman, M. (2001) *Bone, Dying into Life, A Journal of Wisdom, Strength and Healing.* London: Penguin Books Ltd.

Chapter 4

On Ageing: Coming Home

Chris and Ewa Robertson

Ageing is no accident. It is part of being human. What we do with the experience is as much what we make of it as what happens to us. Ageing can be a self-fulfilling prophecy of becoming useless and fear of being a burden on friends and family.[1] As such it is often split off from everyday awareness until it suddenly creeps up on us. We may alternatively welcome the possibilities of retirement and the seductive sense of entitlement that can come with seniority. Each of these constructions has a shadowy base that touch into either vulnerability or domination. By attempting to see through these Shadow windows in facing old age, we explore what it takes to navigate the inherent tasks of human ageing and coming home to one's true Self.

Like elsewhere in this book, Jung's notion of the Shadow is recognised as an ever-unfolding source of learning and humbling. It is not simply a cognitive idea; we have to suffer its meaning. This chapter aims to explore some of the psychospiritual challenges of our times for the older generation and what light the Shadow casts on these. Drawing on experience with clients and ourselves, we explore ageing as much as a cultural construct as that of a biological reality. A manic culture is likely to construe ageing as the approach to cessation and death, hence the elderly within it are prone to depression. Traditional cultures, in contrast, have held elders in high esteem as keepers of ancestral wisdom. A way through this binary dichotomy is to approach ageing as a rite of passage into a challengingly different and potentially unique phase of living.

It takes light to create shadow. Shadows can obscure and they can illuminate. In this chapter, we will place ageing in the cultural Shadow of our Modernist society with its inherent drive for progress. Socially the "failures" of the elderly to keep the cogs of economic machinery turning threaten the productive ethos. They may be the shadow that illuminates the fault lines of our culture. These cracks in the cultural fabric offer fresh ways to engage the meaning of growing old.

DOI: 10.4324/9781003255819-6

Archetypal psychologist James Hillman (1999, p. 38) quotes Jung on the ambiguity and complexity of his eighty-year search into knowing himself:

> I am astonished, disappointed, pleased with myself. I am distressed, depressed, rapturous. I'm all these things at once and cannot add up the sum. I am incapable of determining ultimate worth or worthlessness. I have no judgement about myself and my life. There is nothing I am quite sure about ...

This confession gives us a clue about the nature of Shadow; it is not a thing we can grasp, but more a coming closer to Self that reveals a humbling "unknowing". Each phase of life brings with it its own challenge and we will be exploring what is particular to that of ageing. Whereas Jung used the metaphor of the rising and setting sun for stages of life from youth to old age, we see a cyclical process of rising and setting. The classic developmental phases of leaving home, midlife, retirement and death can also become mini-cycles. There are many homes we can leave and return to, many identity crises to undergo. We may change direction and experience dying symbolically at several junctions.

When film star Bette Davis said: "Old age ain't no place for sissies", she was most probably referring to the decline in energy, health, appearance, independence and eventual death that inevitably come with ageing. Coming from the world of Hollywood where youth, vitality and beauty are prized, growing old can make one feel dispensable, unwanted and a burden on others. But it's not just Hollywood where this is true; our modern society echoes the same attitude. At the time of writing this, in the midst of a global pandemic, the shocking lack of adequate provision and safety within Britain's social care sector, has been magnified and brought into sharp focus.

One could argue that this failure mirrors a more general attitude of disregard towards the most vulnerable sections of our society, especially the elderly. It's no surprise that for many ageing is accompanied by fear. From this perspective it takes courage, even a good dose of denial, to face the challenges that come with ageing. But what if the courage that is needed to face the ageing process is of a different kind, not the tough hero full of willpower or mind over matter approach, but something of a different order?

For young people, growing *up* involves developing a personality – putting on the clothes of the social and cultural life which we inhabit. It is concerned with forming an identity and fitting in with others in order to meet norms and expectations. These social masks are what Jung termed the persona. A young person's life is about expansion, stretching one's horizons and living for a future yet to unfold.

Conversely, growing *down* is the challenge for older people; it involves removing these social layers to reveal more of who we truly are. Hillman (1996, p. 43) suggests: "*Until the culture recognizes the legitimacy of growing down, each person in the culture struggles blindly to make sense of the darkness that the soul requires to deepen into life".*

What is this downwards direction? Despite early fantasies of winged careers or ideal partners, gravity gets the better of us. This de-idealisation involves contraction, relinquishing the illusion of a never-ending future, engaging with one's limitations and being confronted with the afflictions of eventual physical and mental decay. It is chequered with losses of all kinds, including health, bodily functions, memory, significant relationships, professional identity, places, sometimes home and loved ones, all of which can leave one feeling outcast, alone and often lonely. And who would want that?

Retreat from the demands of everyday life can provide an opening for solitary reflection on the past. If we don't resort to self-pity, recrimination and other means to console a fragile self, we may open to the privilege of having time to be still and not chase after things. Time for deep and challenging reflections on what it has all been for – including the losses and what we may have forsaken along the way. Such reflections are the work of growing down that require mourning. Where identity has been caught up with others, whether in caring for them or in other attachments, loss can be traumatic.

John was a white man in his mid-70s who had recently suffered two significant bereavements, those of his wife and brother who were his closest relatives. He had worked as a teacher as well as a fundraiser for various international charities supporting disadvantaged communities in developing countries. Other family members and friends lived far away.

Soon after the death of his wife and brother, John became depressed and unable to cope. He spent considerable time in bed, not taking care of herself or eating properly. Grief eventually took its toll on his health. Apart from being diabetic, John had always been a strong, healthy and capable man, but suddenly he suffered one affliction after another. He developed a skin condition that didn't respond to treatment and which kept him awake at night. His immune system was compromised and he had few defences. Sleep deprived, disoriented, anaemic, with unstable sugar levels he grew weaker and consequently had repeated falls that needed urgent medical attention. Fortunately, his doctor not only addressed his physical needs but also heard the underlying cry for help. By the time he came to therapy John's physical health had slowly started to improve but his mood was still low. The only contact he had with his nephews and nieces was when he sent money for a birthday or Christmas, otherwise they made no effort to contact him. Life was meaningless and he couldn't see how therapy could help. He admitted to feeling suicidal.

What is repressed comes back to haunt us later in life. Typically, the midlife crisis is the first sign that all is not well. Often it is experienced as an urgent need to be true to oneself, to no longer be compelled to fulfil others' expectations in order to give a sense of belonging. In later years, this haunting can take many forms as unbidden memories float to the surface; there may be personal slights and harms, family skeletons that need to be laid to rest, regrets that have never been acknowledged. This haunting wants to bear witness to the wrongs or atrocities that have been banished. It is a daunting task. To make room in our psychological home for what has been banished into the Shadow, needs a re-imagining of who we are so that the negative judgements we previously made can dissolve through a process of acceptance.

Growing down includes facing our darker Shadow side, looking back on our lives, our shortcomings, secrets and lies and how we may have hurt others. The reckoning of failure can reorient our direction away from domination, control and living up to expectations towards a more tempered and reflective mode of being. We could imagine this like a process of shedding skins to reveal more of who has lain hidden within.

> In John's darker moments he was aware that there was something he was deeply unhappy about; as if something was draining him of vitality. He began to pay attention to himself, not only to his physical health but also to what the underlying symptoms of malaise were telling him. It was a dream that eventually helped him remember something he had witnessed in childhood that he had done his best all his life to 'forget'. In the dream, John was being pursued by a faceless dark figure from whom there was no escape. He hid inside the basement of a deserted building as the figure drew closer until he was at last confronted by a black man who was bleeding. John woke up with the realisation that far from wanting to harm him, the figure was pleading for help. In recounting the dream to his therapist, he said there was something familiar about this man.

> John was born in Southern Rhodesia and raised on a farm owned by his father with servants and farm workers who were mostly black. The family home was a grand colonial building. He lived a privileged life but had always been afraid of his father who was physically abusive. One evening he heard a man screaming and saw his father brutally beating one of the farm workers pinned to the ground and whose hands were tied. John recognised the guilt that lay behind his support of many charities and his subsequent attempts to make up for past wrongdoings. What was more difficult to face was how cruelly he had treated others, just as his father had. He felt compelled to break the cycle of this intergenerational wound and make amends rather than blame others. The wounded figure in the dream was himself but it was also his father who had endured his own traumas down the generations which he had inflicted on others and most particularly racially.

Strangely, the diminution of our faculties and strengths in ageing, are precisely what allows an opening to hidden treasures. For the Shadow contains not only dark aspects that have been rejected or disowned and projected onto others, but also positive traits such as what we may project onto others whom we admire. These bright qualities may remain hidden. Paul Cezanne might never have been recognised had he not lived long enough to paint his Cubist still life works of art.

Apart from artists, actors, musicians and writers whose talents may take time to mature and come to public appreciation, what gives permission for older people to stand out and reclaim their unique Self? Sometimes circumstances demand risk and the person, whatever age, can surprise themselves as to their capacities. The experience is marked by a sense of familiarity – a coming home to one's Self. To delve into this notion of ageing and potential eldership, we explore specific aspects through sections on theBody, Eldership, Dying to Live, Melancholia and Second Childhood.

The Body

Peter Laslett (1987) coined the term the Third Age to refer to the period after retirement, a time that is often spent enjoying good health, with an active life and a sense of fulfilment. It marks a new stage when one has fewer responsibilities and, depending on personal circumstance, more time for leisurely pursuits and exploration of new endeavours. Life holds the promise of new beginnings. In contrast, the transition to the Fourth Age marks changes in activity, health, frailty and dependency as one approaches the culmination of a life's journey. We explore how both the promise of new beginnings and frailty can combine to making growing old a meaningful rite of passage.

Our society seeks to avoid the downside of ageing and death; we don't want to think about it, let alone see it. Old age and death live in the Shadow of our society, reinforcing an ageist attitude of older people not being of value, not contributing. Youth and beauty are what our narcissistic culture wants to have mirrored. Today's youth culture regards physical appearance as being of key importance in defining one's value. We are bombarded with messages about how our bodies should look and behave. Of course, exercise and physical activity are important to maintain optimal health throughout one's lifespan but some regimes, such as high-intensity workouts or endurance training, are deliberately intended to reduce, even prevent, ageing. A cultural "mind over matter" attitude reinforces a mind-body split, where the ageing body is a problem to be overcome.

The body has become objectified as a product to be fixed with mechanical, pharmaceutical and surgical repairs. Beauty products seek to erase the telltale signs of ageing. Anti-ageing products for women and men claim to reduce lines and wrinkles, dark circles and puffiness, remove dead skin, tone, hydrate and plump up the skin with collagen. Yet wrinkles, lines and scars tell the story of a lifetime; they are the map of one's life. The face particularly reveals the underlying story of what an individual has lived through; we wear our heart on our face, not our sleeve.

We remember meeting a friend after some thirty years of not seeing one another expecting him to look as we had known him in the past. Of course, his age was visible – the way he looked and moved, he was slower, more vulnerable and needed support. Yet something else shone through his radiant eyes; there was a quality of nakedness and openness we had never seen before as if a skin had been shed to reveal something deeper beneath the surface gloss. Despite his evident frailty and comorbidities, there was dignity, joy and a richness of spirit. No wonder we talk of the eyes as the windows to the soul.

Infants and young children are fascinated by faces, this is how they learn to communicate emotion. The way the face, eyes, muscles and skin move corresponds with specific emotions. The older person's face is full of expression and easier to read. Figures such as wizards and witches with wrinkly faces are typically portrayed as older folk and are a source of fascination for children. Procedures to reduce the signs of ageing of the eyes and face with cosmetic surgery, dermal fillers or Botox can eventually result in the appearance of a flat or neutral face. A neutral face is perceived as untrustworthy and even threatening.

Our bodies are changing throughout the lifespan. Whilst the young body may hide secrets behind a skin-deep mask, the ageing body reveals a deeper truth of fundamental character and nature. Increased risk of illness, inflammation and pain, loss of control, will most likely meet us all at some point. How does one look at what life is offering in the face of sickness, fear and pain? Thomas Moore (2017, p. 121) writes:

> But there is a major difference between understanding illness as physical breakdown and seeing it as an opportunity for initiation. In the first case, you are not present to the experience as a person. You are only going through the physical ordeal. Your soul is not engaged. In the second case, the illness has a positive benefit of taking you further along your life course, as you become a real person, a true individual. Illness serves as a vehicle for transformation.

Illness at any age, and especially in later years, is an opportunity to listen and see through the symptoms to the underlying story that is seeking to be told. In the Arthurian story of the quest for the Holy Grail, the old Fisher King lies wounded. He is the keeper of the Grail, said to be the cup used at the Last Supper. His healing depends on the arrival of a knight who must ask the right question. Only then can the Holy Grail be revealed and the old king healed. In Jungian psychology, the symbol of the Grail has been likened to an archetypal image of the Self, an image of wholeness.

The Grail question that Perceval originally fails to ask is not, "What do you need to get well?" In many versions of the story no clear question is given and when one is, it is mysterious. We are helped on this journey into the unknown, with signs and symbols, but never are we provided with the conceptual tools to decode the mystery. For it is not answers that give meaning but rather the questions themselves and to what they open us through the asking.

The obstacle for Perceval is his lack of care, especially in relation to his mother whom he deserted without a second glance to become a knight. According to Von Franz (1986), his task is to restore his feminine side, which he has repressed through victories in which his heroic ego vanquished all opposing knights. It took many years for Perceval to understand that something else was being asked of him; it was not just a matter of the *right* question but a different state of mind, one of humility that allows for transformation to occur. He needed to de-armour to find the soft vulnerability of his own body before he could ask what troubles (or what ails) the king.

Healing is not the same as a cure. The road to Self is not a straight path. We may attempt to take off our armour, let down our guard before we are ready and risk making ourselves too vulnerable. With woundings or illnesses that are potentially life changing, asking, "How do I get better?" or "How do I stop the pain?" are the wrong order of questions and miss an appreciation of the underlying malaise that needs healing. By removing the symptom without regard for that which needs healing is to treat the body as an object to be cured, or fixed. For illness to become a rite of passage, we need to stay with where it takes us. As Perceval discovers, it is a matter of being open and curious, a willingness to listen to the truth or mystery of what is being expressed through the wound, through the suffering. To find the *right* question he must listen through to what is missing in his own nature, the feminine hidden in his Shadow. When he finally asks the Fisher King "What ails thee?", he is not asking how to fix things. It involves seeing into the heart of the wound, restoring a balance that brings wholeness and healing.

Similarly, staying with stories rather than rushing to conclusions, helps the reader to become present to the message. Older people tell their story over and over again. As a society we are kinder towards children who want to hear the same story repeatedly than we are to hearing an older person recount their story for the nth time; yet this pleasure is one that both old and young share in common. In repeating the same story, just as re-reading a favourite book or watching a favourite film, more is revealed than on first impression. There are layers to any story. What may have been missed first time round gets picked up on another occasion; it forms a ritual. We might think of the story as being re-worked each time it is told. With each telling we bring more elements together thereby bringing new meaning and a sense of wholeness, completion.

Telling the same story over and over again is also a way of ensuring something gets passed on and so is not lost. Hillman (1999, p. 64) suggests that: "*It is as if the soul begs for the same stories so that it knows that something will last*". Stories carry their own inherent message. Aside from the teller's personal association with a story, as with fairy tales and myths, there are collective and universal aspects that speak to a bigger picture. The repetition of a myth is a central element in many traditional and religious rituals, and rites of passage. These mark significant transitions, be they creation myths or heroic myths. They mark the end of one phase and the beginning of the next – birth, death and rebirth.

Eldership

In many traditional societies becoming an elder is marked out with custom and ritual. Elders are respected as the custodians of practical knowledge of how to hunt, build shelters, survive droughts, look after children as well as cultural wisdom about how to navigate the challenges of life. Much of this is irrelevant to a fast-changing Modernist society in which the knowledge economy has built in obsolescence and Google substitutes for practical advice. The grandparents may still be useful for childcare but often fail to be valued other than for instrumental use. A general ageist attitude in some of British society during the COVID-19 pandemic resulted in the elderly in nursing homes dying needlessly due to lack of adequate provision as if their lives did not matter.

What might it mean to become an elder in Western society and why might this matter?

To become mature requires passage through several trials of life which leave their mark. As T.S. Eliot (1944) says in *East Coker*, they will have journeyed through cold and empty desolation. The psychological and physical wounding show. For those who suffered and learnt through the experience, become resilient. Their raw character has been burnished by the trials of life which can act as rites of passage. Archetypally these trials can be felt as belonging to the elements of *fire* and *water*. The trials of fire, such as intense family conflicts, illness and tragedy, can burn away cherished illusions, humble pretentious aspirations and turn hubris into ashes. In alchemy the stage of *Nigredo* is marked by this blackening, a calcination to burn away the dross and impurities. It can equate with what the Christian mystic, St John of the Cross, called the dark night of the soul, when hope is extinguished and all seems lost.

Trial by water involves the washing away, the dissolving through grieving, weeping, feeling flooded and overwhelmed by personal crises such as losing a child or in collective crises such as a pandemic, racial injustice, climate change and the sixth great extinction.[2] This dissolution breaks us open and exposes our tender depths. It often involves heartbreak where the heart is tenderised through deep loss and grieving. Rilke (1980) writes of anguish and how we might squander our hours of pain – what a radical notion! In our present escapist Western culture, pain is to be avoided not engaged as a rich inner resource.

Supported by Sufi teaching on heartbreak, we, the authors, have slowly come to know the transformational power of being with this pain. These lessons in heartbreak were for us part of a midlife passage involving trials of both fire and water, rage and anguished weeping. These trials we can, in retrospect, recognise as necessary to curb defences such as arrogance and entitlement. Such descents are not, as they sometimes seem, cruel humiliations but part of a humbling, rather like how steel is made through the alternate tempering of the iron in fire and water.

After thirty years with the psychotherapy training organisation we co-founded, we set about preparing for our retirement. We drew on these previous trials as lessons in relinquishment to let go of powers and responsibilities that had come with being founders. There was huge sadness and grief in this letting go. These were the treasures of our life's work we were entrusting to others, knowing that they would take a different path. The actual process of handing on took longer and was messier than we had hoped but it happened – we left at the appointed hour. The original vision had run its course and now a new vision had been collectively dreamt. This was a rite of passage; a release from an old form and an opening to an unknown future.

At retirement people are often asked, "What will you do?" The answer could be "Less" but seldom is, as the question looks for actions rather than slowing down. To enter a new rhythm of life that is not ruled by the compulsive pressure to achieve or get things done, requires a shift in identity. To do less in a manic culture is an achievement but of a different kind. To not fall into implicit judgement around worth and potential guilt, there need to be resources other than what we do. Otherwise, retirement can bring an existential vacuum and depression.

For those whose work has been important, the nothingness of retirement can be especially confusing. The hollow lack of meaningful work can lead to suicidal ideation and severe depression. It is as if these retirees have already died as life becomes drained of meaning. Past separation traumas can be triggered with feelings of abandonment and isolation. In contrast to the supposed delights of free time, retirement can be a disappointing shock.

Sometimes in ageing the rich memories of the past get frozen in time. The pain of the transformation is too much to bear; there is too much hurt to repair. This is especially the case where trauma in early childhood have elicited impenetrable defences in the person's psyche. Rather than relinquishing and letting go, past trauma and hurt are carried into the present, resulting in bitterness and cruelty. They can occupy the psyche of the older person and maintain a paranoid defence against the felt impingement of reality. Holding onto old memories can become like a compulsive ritual to defend against the unknown of the present moment. Conspiracy theories are an example of this self-referring and self-fuelling process.

Conversely, ageing provides the reflective opportunity to look back, recognise what was cast off and seek to digest what had previously seemed unbearable. Psychoanalyst Melanie Klein (1999) developed the idea of reparation as an intrinsic psychological means of making amends for past wrongs. What makes reparation possible is grieving, as was the case for John; grieving not simply a matter of practical losses of place and persons but of hopes and expectations that were not met. The failure to grieve for the ideal parent or partner we did not have but had hoped to have, means that we can never accept the far-less-than perfect one we did have. When such grieving and letting go can happen, it leads naturally to acceptance of what we did have and why it had to be so. This cycle of grieving, remorse, acceptance and reparation can take place at any phase of life but it is particularly apposite for the ageing.

A rite of passage can be a single event that marks an occasion, or it can be a circulating process that repeats until the transformation from one life phase to another is completed. This shift away from the outer criteria for satisfaction and instead turning attention towards an inner guidance is part of an eldership rite of passage. Jung (2012) being interviewed on his 85th birthday said: "An ever-deepening self-awareness seems to me as probably essential for the continuation of a truly meaningful life in any age, no matter how uncomfortable this self-knowledge may be".

What makes it possible to re-orient inwards despite discomfort, is an inner guidance not dependent on external approval. A rite of passage can support this transition through simple rituals that mark the shift to inner authority. Eldership involves such a shift of identity. It is not simply getting on in life but a release from old beliefs and, through encounters with Shadow, a connection to what we know in our heart of hearts to be a necessity.

Dying to Live

If elders are those who have learnt to die before they literally die, they act as mentors and guides for a culture on the edge of collapse. Rather than giving advice and setting themselves up as experts, they can be attentive listeners. Martin Prechtel (1998), a shaman, healer and spokesperson for Mayan culture, tells of how elders spoke sparingly at village meetings to discuss complaints, "because they knew that most people's problems were just part of life and would never be solved by human intervention". Through such community meetings, they did not fix anything but ensured that the village bore witness and grieved so making life bearable.

Such respect for and trust in the unfolding of life in its own rhythm has been lost in the drive to progress and be in control. Moderns forget that all life is subject to the process of decay and death without which everything would stay the same – there would be no sexual reproduction or genetic variation and no young to learn differently. As history shows (Diamond 2005), all societies, cultures and civilisations are subject to the same processes of growth and decay. The difficulty with our present Western Modernist culture is the cultural complex of progress that puts death and decay in the Shadow.

By cultural complexes, a notion formulated by Singer and Kimbles (2004), we mean that unconscious core within a culture, built on past collective traumas and shame filtered through the generations, that binds groups to perpetuate simplistic and often prejudiced points of view. Such complexes underlie the culture's espoused beliefs, values and principles and resist adaptation to new realities.

The story Westerners in particular tell of progress is one of infinite growth through technological triumph. This story hides the destructive exploitation in its wake, the ruining of indigenous cultures, language and land. In forgetting that human nature is part of nature, we alienate ourselves and fear the loss of control. Freud recognised this existential vulnerability and wrote:

> The principal task of civilisation, its actual raison d'être, is to defend us against nature. We all know that in many ways civilisation does this fairly well already, and clearly as time goes on it will do it much better.
>
> (Freud 1927, pp. 15–16)

The cultural relativity of "progress" is highlighted in contrast with indigenous cultures such as Aboriginal Australians whose purpose is to maintain their ancestral relation to the land. They had no notion of progress and found Europeans' obsession with it bewildering. The treasured notion that our children will have a better life than ours, so central to the complex of progress, feels like an intrusive aberration where maintenance of ancestral wisdom is the key to a fruitful life. This is especially as "progress" here presupposes an extractivist privilege to exploit the environment without any sense of giving back.

We have been attempting to dig for the treasures hidden in the Shadow of ageing and recognise these later phases of life as having meaning and value. This section makes another twist in this tale by re-imagining dying as a psychological rather than a literal process, hence the "dying before they die". Rather than attempting to banish death, we suggest eldership can incorporate the ancient value of dying as a psycho-spiritual practice, a rite of passage to let go of fixed identities and beliefs.

What can facilitate this transformative process are dreams that invoke and envision new possibilities. Sometimes dreams reveal a powerful presence of what is missing in life, a presence of an absence that has yet to be engaged with and for which soul longs. A surrender to this sense of calling or vision can lead to a re-engaging with life from a new perspective – what Jung called transforming bitterness into the salt of wisdom.

> Having re-established meaningful contact with friends and family, John continued to be interested in his dream about the dark figure who pleaded for help and decided he needed to do more to redress the past. In a further dream with a similar motif he once again heard the voice of a man pleading for help. This time he heard the figure say, quite clearly, 'I am waiting for you'. Despite his age and failing health, he made the journey to today's Zimbabwe to the village where he once lived to meet the descendants of the man whom his father had once beaten so badly. He acknowledged the suffering his father had inflicted and apologised. He saw the man's son, a man of a similar age to John, had tears in his eyes, as if this was what he had been waiting for. What came next was totally unexpected and moved John beyond words; the son brought out a photograph he had kept of John as a young child with all the farm workers who lived on the land. This was both a healing for each of them and reparative engagement with ancestral ghosts.

Transforming bitterness into the salt of wisdom involves experiencing the tragic losses split off into the Shadow side of an old sense of self. Examples from the third and fourth phases of life include retirement, death of a partner or loved one and accident or illness. Many of these, such as funerals, are ritually marked. Rituals catalyse transformation both through participating in forms that have ancient heritage and by focusing a community's attention. Where funerals have not been corrupted into meaningless social etiquette, they provide means of listening to stories about the dead and saying final goodbyes as the body is returned to the earth. In preparing for funerals, we may stay with the dead and attend to the process of decay in the cycles of life and death. This can act as a bridge across the implacable divide that death seems to present and offer unexpected gifts from Hades. Death becomes intertwined with life, its deep Shadow is momentarily brought to life.

Through attending to those in the process of dying, we may be brought closer to the symbolic ending of our world as we have known it. The process of dying psychologically is facing the ending to that which we have been accustomed. Correspondingly, the rite of passage can open up fresh ways to live, a renewed sense of vitality and meaning in life. The dying leads to living.

Melancholia

The failure to go through such a rite of passage, leaves the old with no hope and a withering attachment to memories and conceits. Depression among the old is common and our culture does its best to fix this. The fixing, so typical of our technological medicine, takes away the very discomfort that might catalyse change. As Hillman suggests (1977, pp. 98–99):

> Through depression we enter depths and in depths find soul. It moistens the dry soul, and dries the wet. It brings refuge, limitations, focus, gravity, weight and humble powerlessness. It reminds us of death. The true revolution begins in the individual who can be true to his own depression.

In a similar and equally provocative way, Lars von Trier's comments on his apocalyptic film, *Melancholia,* that it is not so much about the end of the world as about a state of mind. We can read the characters in the film as personifications of the director's struggle with depression and ideas of the "end". In the film family tensions provide a distraction from the very real threat of a huge planet called Melancholia, on a collision course with planet Earth. This theme parallels the distractions of social media and the trivial obsessions with fads that distract our present Western culture from the impending planetary crises.

The main character, Justine, is deeply troubled by this threat despite the celebrations of her wedding. She seems to yearn for something true including suffering. This reflects the Greek notion of the tragic, in which truth is recognised through pain. A deep acceptance of the inevitable end, even if coloured by melancholic withdrawal, accentuates how human mortality is tied to the earth. That the film is both terrifying and strangely peaceful is reminiscent of Ortis Hill's research on the fear of nuclear extermination in *Dreaming the End of the World* (2004). He quotes – an anti-nuclear activist:

> It was weird, but in the dream the feeling was – well, this is it. It was not like we were freaking out. It was very 'Zen'. This is it. I feel like in my dreams, I've progressed from panic and denial to accepting that the Bomb is 'in me'. Out of that, I feel empowered to meet it.

This transformational process, like the journey through old age, is not guaranteed. It is full of distractions and attempted shortcuts. The very real terror of a depressive darkness, the unnameable dread that psychoanalyst and paediatrician D.W. Winnicott called "primitive agonies", can be experienced as a descent into a hell that Hieronymus Bosch would have recognised. This descent can trigger previous traumatic experiences of separation anxiety, abandonment and related defences.

Jungian Monte Cedrus (2003) writes of a night sea journey in which:

> Dark moments can strike like a sudden rending eruption from mysterious and subterranean places. Without warning, the crust of a forever-healing wound, or an old insidious trauma is torn open unexpectedly, and we bleed again. We feel that we have entered into the abyss, body and soul. In the darkest of these times, nothing – no word, no prayer, no loving gesture, no therapeutic intervention – reaches the mark. Everything is lost, crumbled and grey, pointless – our life hopelessly flapping in the maw of a terrifying yet welcome annihilation.

Jungian author David Rosen (2005) discusses how artists, poets and clients have negotiated what he terms "the art of darkness". This archetypal darkness can be imagined as a Black Sun – a malignant and merciless force of death. Rosen sees the malignancy of this darkness as due to Modernity's massive repression of the dark side of psychic life. While personal issues of ungrieved losses can be part of the transformational work, Rosen makes clear that the Black Sun of Melancholia is an archetypal force of potential creativity.

The fear is that of dissolution, a regressive loss of self that Freud saw as death. He imagined this dissolution as Thanatos – the Greek god of death. Jungians and post-Jungians have seen this dissolution less literally, more as a symbolic loss of ego that makes possible psychic transformation to-wards wholeness. The darkness that our egos fear as annihilating can be that of the womb as much as that of the tomb, as much a fertile void as a black hole.

It is sometimes claimed that humans are the only animal to know that they will die. Even though this is a problematic claim as we understand so little of other-than-human species, it can be said that the mystery of dying is an initiatory task. Tibetans have made preparing to die skilfully a central life purpose. The mystery of death is something that faces the elderly of what-ever culture. We have explored how facing death can act as a gateway to a deeper life, through the stripping away outer layers of social adaptation and relinquishing attachment to these badges of social esteem.

In summary, we could revision the issue of obsolescence with which we began this chapter. Ironically it may not be the elderly that are obsolete, rather the current fashion for which the elderly have no use. Elders can model what it might mean to retire from the ego competition of bettering your neighbour with a smarter house, garden, car, job, partner. In the larger context of a threatening social and moral collapse, elders can offer a return to ancient customs of frugal consumption, concern for ecological balance and gratitude for the Earth's generosity. To offer this, they need to have faced the final frontier, not space but death.

Second Childhood

In Western cultures, both childhood and old age rest at the margins of an efficient neo-liberal system. Neither phase is primarily productive or contributes to the national economy as measured by the Gross Domestic Product (GDP). If GDP productivity is the face Western nations show to the world, we could imagine childhood and old age as being in the marginal shadows of this bright driven light. They offer the space for play that is somewhat protected from the demands of the work ethic.

The ambiguity towards ageing in our culture is exemplified in the notion of the second childhood. Is this helpless dotage or a reconnection with the wonders of being alive? Shakespearian times (*As You Like It*, 1599) viewed elderly dotage with disdain, describing the *second childishness* as mere oblivion, *sans teeth, sans eyes, sans taste, sans everything*. In contrast this chapter has attempted to revision this apparent "uselessness" or mere play. Gawande (2015, p. 132) reports the success of Newbridge, a retirement community, sharing grounds with a kindergarten and school where residents' and pupils' lives were "deeply intertwined". The mutual delight older people and children can take in each other expresses a relational delight that defies productive usefulness. It opens up that strange mystery where old and young, beginning and end, birth and death are reconnected.

In the meeting between old and young, we have a practical example of this arriving at where we started and knowing it in an entirely different way. Children can be fascinated with death, despite adults' discomfort. Winnicott thought of play as vital for creative functioning and located in the transitional, or marginal space between inner fantasy and outer actions. In *Playing and Reality* (1971, p. 100), he wrote:

> The place where cultural experience is located is in the potential space between the individual and the environment (originally the object). The same can be said of playing. Cultural experience begins with creative living first manifested in play.

Play encourages creative living and dying through the young trying out and processing what they see, hear and feel in their experience of life and death. Where cultural experience of death is shunned, the dying process takes on dark and terrible hues. As in indigenous cultures, elders and grandparents can encourage the young to give a place to dying as part of life.

Ending Reflections

When T.S. Eliot advised that old men ought to be explorers, he may have had in mind the paradoxical intensity of initiation. A still point between what was and what could be, between the past we leave behind and the unknown that is calling us; the courage to allow the falling apart and be with what Buddhists call impermanence.

Rather than consider ageing as a process of enfeeblement, we have explored it as a rite of passage to eldership that invites courage and intensity. Clearly this is not the norm but lies in the Shadow of Western social and cultural customs. As authors, we know this intensity and are often daunted by it, preferring easier ways to duck or bypass the challenge. The bypass is only temporary and the return to engagement is often through being faced with a new and unexpected challenge.

Despite (and because of) our personal differences our own couple relationship has been a profound container for risks we have engaged. In the joint writing of this chapter, awareness of our own ageing has been part of the process and the knowledge that one of us will die first. This will be a fracture of the holding container that will result in that paradoxical threshold of both lonely melancholia and potential liberation; a threshold, as Eliot describes, into another intensity.

Notes

1 Hence the concerns in the Assisted Dying Bill October 2021 that older people may feel socially obliged to die.
2 Mass extinctions are characterised by the loss of at least 75% of species within a short period of time. Our planet is currently undergoing the sixth of such events in its geological history.

References

Cedrus, M. (2003). At the Threshold of Psycho-Genesis: The Mournful Face of God. In Gustafson (ed.), *The Moonlit Path: Reflections on the Dark Feminine*. Wellington: Nicholas-Hays.

Diamond, J. (2005). *Collapse: How Societies Choose to Fail or Survive*. London: Allen Lane, Penguin.

Eliot, T.S. (1944). *Four Quartets*. London: Faber & Faber.

Freud, S. (1927). *The Future of an Illusion*. London: Hogarth Press.

Gawande, A. (2015). *Being Mortal*. London: Profile Books Ltd.

Hillman, J. (1977). *Suicide and the Soul*. New York: Spring Publications.

Hillman, J. (1999). *The Force of Character and the Lasting Life*. New York: Random House.

Hillman, J. (1996). *The Soul's Code: In Search of Character and Calling*. New York: Random House.

Jung, C.J. (2012). *Become What You Are: C.J. Jung's Answer to Ageing*. https://stottilien.com/

Klein, M. (1999). *Love, Guilt and Reparation: And Other Works 1921–1945*. New York: Simon Schuster.

Laslett, P. (1987). *The Emergence of the Third Age in Ageing and Society*, Vol 7.2, pp. 133–160. Cambridge University Press.

Moore, T. (2017). *Ageless Soul: The Lifelong Journey toward Meaning and Joy*. New York: St Martin's Press.

Ortis Hill, M. (2004). *Dreaming the End of the World: Apocalypse As a Rite of Passage*. New York: Spring Publications.

Prechtel, M. (1998). *Secrets of the Talking Tiger: A Shaman's Journey to the Heart of the Indigenous Soul*. New York: Tarcher/Putnam.

Rilke, R.M. (1980). *The Selected Poetry of Rainer Maria Rilke*, edited and translated by Stephen Mitchell. New York: Random House.

Rosen, D. & Stanton, M. (2005) *The Black Sun: The Alchemy and Art of Darkness*. Texas: A & M University Press.

Shakespeare, W. (1599). 'All the World's a Stage'. *As You Like It*. https://en.wikipedia.org/wiki/All_the_world%27s_a_stage

Singer, T. & Kimbles, S. (2004). *The Cultural Complex: Contemporary Jungian Perspectives on Psyche and Society*. London: Routledge.

Von Franz, M.-L. & Jung, E. (1986). *The Grail Legend*. London: Coventure.

Winnicott, D.W. (1971). *Playing and Reality*. London: Tavistock Publications.

Chapter 5

The Shadow in Literature: Daphne du Maurier's "The Scapegoat"

Rupert Tower

> *Only what is really oneself has the power to heal.*
> (Jung, 1953, Two Essays, para. 131)

Overview

In this chapter, I am presenting my reflections and ideas both as a Jungian analyst and as the grandson of the late Daphne du Maurier who wrote the novel entitled "The Scapegoat" in 1957. I have chosen to explore this story as it is my personal favourite and has always spoken to me deeply about my perennial struggle with finding my creative self. Perhaps an over-identification with the remarkable creative output of my grandmother, her father and grandfather have contributed to my own fears and inhibitions about what it means to be creative. Daphne read Jung's work intensively during the 1950s and was deeply influenced by his psychological and philosophical ideas and his reflections on the Shadow of Christianity.

The Scapegoat is a story about someone who feels dead inside and experiences a crisis but who becomes enlivened again as he is confronted by an uncanny encounter with his Shadow. This descent into his depths brings forth unknown and unrealised capacities for relating creatively both with his internal self and with others. It also expresses in creative form a character's struggles to process internally and to engage with two of Carl Jung's signature concepts – the Shadow and the Individuation process.

The chapter explores several areas of the Shadow experience. For ease of digestion, I will separate out the main narrative synopsis of the story into three parts.

In Part One, I will sketch out the central dilemma that the Shadow encounter can bring into consciousness when in crisis at mid-life. And in so doing, I will attempt to delineate the challenges and opportunities that face the central characters of John and Jean and link these with Freud's idea of the Uncanny.

DOI: 10.4324/9781003255819-7

In Part Two, I will go more in-depth into the specific Shadow struggles of each character, eliciting the potential meanings and unconscious processes that are revealed about their internal relationships to themselves and to other characters in the story. I will then move on to the Shadow of scapegoating and the unusual form of scapegoating described in the story that contains multiple scapegoats.

In Part Three, I will explore the unfolding thread and rhythmic movement of the story as a process of the characters' self-enquiry and emerging self-realisations. I discuss this as an example of maturational development and psychological adaptation as expressed by Jung's concept of the Individuation process.

The Shadow in Literature

The phenomenology of the Shadow has been represented in our history and literature for centuries. From Adam's fall in antiquity, the Shadow has been represented as a terror of being possessed by the powers of darkness. Bram Stoker's "Dracula", Oscar Wilde's "The picture of Dorian Gray", Goethe's "Faust" and E.T. Hoffman's "The Devil's Elixir" are compelling tales that continue to fascinate because of the archetypal nature of the problem they constellate. Faust suffered a mid-life crisis and made a pact with the devil owing to a one-sided and over-intellectualised development of his personality. Stephenson's Dr Jekyll, aware of the duality of his nature, over-idealised his intellectual capacities to do good for mankind and lost sight of the tension of the opposites within him. He became increasingly possessed by his unlived Shadow life, as expressed by the desire for the pleasures of the body and the darkest impulses within him, thus becoming the murderous and evil Mr Hyde. Dorian Gray put on an innocent face as mask for the world, while keeping his Shadow qualities concealed in a hidden portrait of himself that gradually depicted the ravages of his murderous secret behaviours. The anxiety that haunts all such stories is not so much the fear of being caught by others as the fear of losing control of oneself and being taken over by dark irrational forces within.

The Story of "The Scapegoat"

Although Du Maurier's story lies within the tradition of the *"demoniac novel"* (Laski, Times literary Supplement, 19 October 1962, p. 808), she deliberately abandons any notions of the supernatural and grounds her premise in the domain of realism and the psychological. Central to her drama is how her main character continually shares and processes his internal struggles and conflicts with the reader in response to what he experiences.

Part One - The Shadow Encounter and Confrontation with the Uncanny

The story is narrated by an English academic, John, holidaying in France and feeling depressed and uncreative on his last day before returning to his work as a university lecturer in mediaeval French history, including Joan of Arc. He realises his sense of alienation, how he has always been an observer rather than a participant in his life. He has lost his bearings. Sitting in an empty church, he finds himself in existential crisis, possibly suicidal. Aware of *"the self who clamoured for release, the man within"* (Du Maurier, 1957, p. 14), he considers a half-formed decision to seek religious confession of his failure to live and to go to a Trappist monastery. The monks might have the answer to the man within. Is this a call for John to know himself?

Prior to departing, he enters a railway station buffet where at the bar he stands next to a man who, reflected in a mirror opposite, appears as his mirror-image – his "double". He is looking at himself. John is shocked by their uncanny resemblance. In contrast to himself, however, the man in the mirror looks urbane, confident and assured – everything John is not. Aroused by a sense of curiosity and a menace which counteracts his usual apathy, John accepts an invitation to dine with his double, who has now introduced himself as the Count Jean de Gue. The next morning John awakes to find he has been drugged by the Count who has switched all their belongings, stolen his identity and exchanged his life for John's own.

The Shadow Encounter at Midlife

A psychological viewpoint to this story might understand that John and Jean (both aged 38) have encountered each other at a point of mid-life crisis when their inner development, what Jung terms as the "individuation process", has come to a respective standstill. Although on the one hand both can be seen in the story as external others and "strangers", on the other hand, they may be seen as one individual whose alter-ego has been projected and whose shadow-self has been split off and repressed into the unconscious. Ultimately this shadow-self has emerged into consciousness and awaits psychological acknowledgement. This can enable the possibility of differentiation, maturation and adaptation.

Carl Jung himself also experienced the midlife transition at age 38 as an intense emotional turning point in his life, calling it *"a confrontation with the unconscious"* (Jung 1963, pp. 170–199).

What does Jung mean by the Shadow? As has been frequently emphasised throughout this book, the Shadow contains everything that we don't want to acknowledge about ourselves, the rejected and inferior person one has always fought becoming. *"The shadow contains all that is vital yet problematic ... represents the wounding of one's nature in the interests of collective social values ... achieving the freedom to feel one's own reality is a necessary step towards healing the inner split"* (Hollis 1993, p. 43).

The Shadow is activated and encountered almost always in unconscious projection on some other individual, family member or group as the object of projection displays characteristics unacceptable to our conscious stance and awareness. Projection is a powerful unconscious dynamic encompassing a natural means to get to know our inner world. It can be used as a defence against anxiety and when pathological, as expressed in the splitting off of aspects of our personality, it can lead to its impoverishment. It requires intensive work and effort to withdraw a projection and to recognise it as an essential quality in us that we prefer not to have to face. A gradual recognition dawns that a differentiation must be made between the other as (s)he "really" is and the projected image so that other people can be seen and respected as separate human beings. As Jung (1959) says:

> It is not the conscious subject but the unconscious that does the projecting. Hence one meets with projections, one does not make them. The effect of projection is to isolate the subject from his environment, since instead of a real relationship to it there is now only an illusory one.
>
> (CW9ii, para. 17)

These ideas build upon psychoanalysis and its object relations theory, which understand intrapsychic processes to be an outcome of interpersonal relations between mother (the mothering other) and child at the beginning of life. If early projections that pass unconsciously between parent and child remain unprocessed, the child's future capacity for differentiation, thus development itself, reverts to early mechanisms of survival which primarily involve black and white, all or nothing thinking – in other words, the extremes of "splitting".

John and Jean can be seen to partake in a developmental split in the opening gambit during their first encounter when Jean says: *"You don't happen to be the devil, by any chance?"* and John replies *"I might ask you the same question"* (Du Maurier, 1957, p. 17). In turn, however, John's capacity for more mature internal differentiation may be also noted when he observes his double, his Shadow, in the mirror and muses to himself, *"it was as though one man stood there"* (ibid., p. 18).

In summary then, the Shadow appears through unconscious projection onto another. When Jean and John refer to the Devil in their interchange, the Shadow's psychic content may be seen more universally to contain everything we fear, despise and cannot accept in ourselves – all that leaves us feeling guilty and shameful.

However, it might not always be thus: Jung in his writing usefully points out that, whilst we often think only of the Shadow as the dark, negative and destructive sides of our personalities, these aspects of ourselves in the

Shadow may equally consist of light, positive, loving and creative capacities within us too. Paradoxically, Jean represents aspects of John's unlived self-expression, and vice versa. As Toni Wolff (1935) writes,

> If we are one thing, the shadow is another, it is half of our basic mirror image that lies in the background. If we are aware of this and allow it to live with us, we are able to tread the middle way and thus do justice to the paradoxical nature of the psyche.

So, if I identify in a differentiated way as a scientist, the undifferentiated Shadow will hold the artist. If reserved in temperament, the Shadow is spontaneous.

Mirrors, Doubling and the Uncanny

"In my end is my beginning" (Eliot, Four Quartets, 1940). Let us go back to John and Jean's initial encounter and the striking image of them looking at themselves in the mirror and seeing each other. It brings in Freud's idea of "The Uncanny" (1919), in which a "double image" is seen that is both familiar and utterly foreign and strange. Freud explores the phenomenon of the double, its connection with reflections in mirrors and shadows, and its defensive function as "*an insurance against the destruction of the ego, an energetic denial of the power of death … and … doubling as a preservation against extinction*" (p. 234). At this opening moment John and Jean seem to inhabit provisional yet unfulfilled lives, unconsciously fragmented and dissociated in a kind of apparent immortality, yet in "*disunion with oneself*" (Jung 1960, CW8, para. 62). Their egos defend from "seeing" something instinctually known and intimate within by projecting that material outward as something alien to themselves. The "double" that they project becomes a source of horror and repulsion[1] similar in nature to the unconscious projection of their Shadow. Freud linked this with an "*inner compulsion to repeat … perceived as uncanny*" (p. 237), a need to return to an old unsolved developmental problem and to go at it again and again in hopes of getting back something that was deprived but needed for growth. As the story progresses and they begin to "live", the "*double' reverses its aspect … it becomes the harbinger of death*" (p. 234). In other words, Freud is saying that the uncanny proceeds from something familiar, such as split-off infantile complexes or affect that have been repressed and concealed from consciousness but are now suddenly revived. With living, then, comes John's/Jean's recognition of mortality, however, and emotional awareness of needs for attachment, love, and the possibility of loss.

And yet, the uncanny may also be expressed not just by the contents of the repressed unconscious, but something non-defensive and infinitely more mysterious residing in the unrepressed unconscious.[2] For the timing of the encounter feels out of time and space. In a way there is a dreamlike quality to the unfolding story, as if Jean had dreamt of "what it could be like" to be a different person (John) within his family in this period of breakdown and found inspiration.

Part Two - The Shadow Ordeal and Engagement with Relationship

Returning now to the middle section of the story of "The Scapegoat", John agrees reluctantly to be driven by Jean's chauffeur to the Count's chateau, protestations unheeded. Unable to resist the devotion in Gaston the chauffeur's eyes John commits to the "Faustian pact" of his new identity as Jean: "*He had given me what I asked, the chance to be accepted. He had lent me his name, his possessions, his identity. I had told him my own life was empty; he had given me his*" (Du Maurier, 1957, p.36). John encounters Jean's family and relatives and immediately experiences how they identify him as Jean. Whatever he says to persuade them otherwise, he is assumed to be him. John begins to get to know his extended family through interactions that reveal how much they all accept him as their husband, lover, son, brother, and father. Nobody but the dog notices the difference.

Over the ensuing days, John becomes exposed to the messy family and financial involvements and their loveless situation. These include a depressed, pregnant wife Francoise; a frustrated and discontented brother Paul with whose wife Renee Jean is having an affair; a bedridden mother (La Comtesse) addicted to morphine; a fanatically religious sister Blanche who does not speak to him, something "*bitter and personal had come between them*" (ibid., p. 122); and an affectionate, lively, ten-year old daughter Marie-Noel who projects herself as a religious visionary and is overly oedipally involved with her father and wishes to atone for his sins. "*I would rather burn in Hell than live in this world without you*" (ibid., p. 70).

Moreover, there is a glass house attached to the chateau – a glass-making family business which is in severe financial difficulties. Jean has failed to secure a new contract in Paris. His family has little faith in his business skills since he has never been interested in his duties as an older brother and heir.

John's curiosity about them develops and in so doing an unmined capacity for relationship comes "alive" in him. No longer the broken, empty, troubled soul prior to his meeting with Jean, he discovers concern, new dimensions to himself, a new person emerging within him and a new meaning in his life.

He becomes motivated to engage with their problems and wants to bring about some form of resolution on his behalf and theirs.

The thread of the story explores in-depth John's internal conflict as he attempts to process the experience of his "new" identity as a relational human being and decides to rectify the situation with the business by renewing the contract despite knowing it continues to run at a loss. A visit to Jean's bank establishes the extent of the family's financial difficulties, including a marriage settlement which ties up his wife's substantial fortune unless she produces a male heir or dies. He now understands why she is anxious about the pregnancy.

He also encounters Jean's lover, Bela, for the first time. *"Jean de Gue had too many women in his life"* (ibid., p. 150). She will become a vital, pivotal figure in the story and disarms him with her warmth, depth of understanding and insight. She wonders aloud to him if his disinterest in the family business was because of what happened to Maurice Duval who died during the Occupation. As the story progresses, the source of the feud between Jean and his sister, Blanche, is revealed to date back fifteen years to the war when Jean and his co-resistance workers murdered Duval, Blanche's fiancé, on the grounds that he was a collaborator.

John is then challenged by the prospect of leading the annual shoot. He cannot shoot whereas Jean is a crack shot. He tosses his watch into a bonfire and deliberately burns himself in retrieving it, thus rendering him disabled. Unbeknownst to him, the watch was a gift from Duval. Marie-Noel sees him thrust his hand into the fire on purpose and fantasises that he did so as a penance for Duval's death. Marie-Noel then disappears until eventually John discovers her in the glass house well, the place of Duval's demise. Marie-Noel had climbed into the well as an act of penitence to absolve her father's sins.

Identity, Trauma and the Shadow of Love and Hate

The story of the "Scapegoat" is "a powerful illustration as to how much of our identity is plastic, and how much of our identity is built on other people's expectations of us, and how others see us" (Covington, Du Maurier Film Showing and Q&A, February 2nd, 2020). It also explores the possibility of assuming another identity and finding freedom and liberation by pretending to be someone else. This brings an aspect of masquerade that involves assuming another's appearance and becoming that persona as a means of developing a new identity (Abi-Ezzi 2003, p. 259).

The identity that we have constructed in the first half of life no longer feels authentic to our inner experience. *"At midlife there is a crossing-over from one psychological identity to another. The self goes through a transformation"* (Stein 1983, p. 3). In "the Scapegoat" both men have "lost their identity and their own connection to themselves"(Covington, Du Maurier Film Showing and Q&A, February 2nd, 2020).

Both men suffered trauma earlier in life (John's loss of his mother aged 10, Jean's war experience and possibly PTSD) and are now suffering from a *"loss of soul"* (Jung 2009, p. 129). Their confrontation with their respective Shadows is constellated at midlife – a stage of transition, adaptation and potential growth. Growth can only occur if both men begin to explore their Shadow. If the Shadow is not confronted truthfully, then an opportunity is lost; the result is to continue to hide and escape defensively from oneself.

John and Jean are faced with a re-constellation of earlier trauma and react to it by defending against anxiety. The specific form of their defences are polar opposites; John defends against the anxiety of love, whereas Jean defends against his anxiety of hate. The story explores two different ways of "coming to terms with the Shadow". "*He was my shadow, or I was his, and we were bound to each other through eternity*"(Du Maurier, 1957, p. 27). Taking a psychoanalytic reading of this, it might be seen that both these men in the beginning of childhood suffered maternal failure.

John's Shadow

John's experience of early abandonment with his mother's death aged ten provides the context for a highly typical Shadow experience at midlife of a deep fear of intimacy, the emptiness of an unlived life, masochism, and exhaustion and depletion physically, emotionally and spiritually.

Shortly after the "exchange", John recognises a "*strange indefinable difference. My own self had become submerged. It **was** the man who called himself Jean de Gue who stood there now ... the change of clothes had brought a change of personality*" (ibid., p. 33). It is as if he has become freed momentarily from his identity, like a "false self" worn as defensive armour, opening the possibility of becoming conscious of an unconscious "true self" hidden within (Winnicott 1960).

Throughout the story the author shares with us, the reader, John's ongoing internal conflict and troubled inner life and his attempts to process the experience of his "new" identity and gradual acknowledgement of his unlived and unknown Shadow qualities. He doubts himself constantly and yet opens himself to unvisited depths of his personality.

He realises that Jean too has "run away from life, ... escaped from the emotions that he himself had created". He too recognises that:

> I was not alone – I was part of the life of other people. Never before had I been concerned with the feelings of anybody but myself, except for the minds and motives of characters in History long since dead. Now I had the chance to do otherwise, through deception.
>
> (Du Maurier, 1957, p75)

He begins to care about the family, the workers.

As he involves himself increasingly in the affairs of the family, he feels that he makes erroneous actions and misjudgements, meaning to heal but causing further misfortune:

I knew that everything I had said or done implicated me further, driven me deeper, bound me more closely still to that man whose body was not my body, whose mind was not my mind, whose thoughts and actions were a world apart, and yet whose inner substance was part of my nature, part of my secret self.

(ibid., p. 132)

In facing his Shadow, John begins to deal with things in his own way and finds a new-found sense of responsibility. He notices how he feels distaste and reluctance to collude with Jean's mother's addictive need for morphine and his daughter's disturbed oedipal anxiety and propensity for self-harm. He then discovers an untapped ruthlessness in refusing to give his blood to save Francoise. From her death, all else flows and finds reparation. He confronts la Comtesse and enables her to recover her agency and dignity. He suggests that Paul take on the contractual side of the business and to travel with Renee to reignite their marriage. Finally, he persuades Blanche to manage the business, and through sincerity and confession of his Shadow's jealousy, envy and eventual murder of her fiancé Duval, he enables her to let go of her loneliness and embittered state.

Throughout the book it is to Bela that John frequently turns to help him process his ambivalence and to seek understanding. It is she who understands that John's repugnance at continued family collusion was "*an advance*" (ibid., p. 231), and she acts as witness and enabler to his developmental growth and emergent capacity to begin to own and integrate his own destructiveness, murderousness and aggression.

Jean's Shadow

Although the reader is less privy to Jean's internal world and processing of events, it becomes clear that he wears negative Shadow qualities (i.e. jealousy, cynicism and hate) on his sleeve, and opposite to John, he is seductively self-assured and charming on the outside.

Early on at their first meeting, he expresses his selfishness and cynicism of others. "*We are every one of us failures. The secret of life is to recognise the fact early on and become reconciled. Then it no longer matters*" (ibid., p. 15).

Jean unconsciously projects many positive Shadow qualities onto others, especially John, such as kindness, compassion, concern. He defends against his experience of an absent mother suffering from depression and addiction not only by projecting his positive Shadow but also by maintaining a myth of apparent self-sufficiency and emotional independence, meeting the world with a cavalier and disarming insouciance. Consciously, he feels overly responsible for his family and projects their need of him as an insatiable hunger. "*The only motive force in human nature is greed ... The thing to do is to minister to the greed, and to give people what they want. The trouble is, they are never satisfied*" (ibid., p. 26). Unconsciously, his passive-aggressive, often sadistic, cruelty towards his family and other relationships betray a deep-seated terror of intimacy, his own neediness, dependency and vulnerability, and most of all intense feelings of guilt. His instigation of Duval's murder reveals his jealousy, envy and rage towards anyone he perceives as a threat to his power, control and dominance of the family. We can wonder if Jean made the "exchange" with John at a time when money, perhaps symbolising his sense of self-sufficiency and power, was running out. He too was running on empty, because absence of money really made him aware of his lack and loss of internal resources.

Jean's disinterest and rejection of the glass house may also act as an alchemical metaphor, as it much resembles an alchemist's "laboratorium" (work in process) without its accompanying "oratorium" (a space for reflection). Jean's refusal to examine his inner relationship to it and his difficult feelings of guilt associated with it has meant that the "opus" has run out of steam.

Speaking obliquely about the "man in charge" within himself, the "Jean" in him believes that the only motive which moves the human race is greed and by ministering to this greed he himself survives. John disagrees: "*The thing is, it isn't greed at all, it's hunger. That's where he's wrong*" (ibid., p. 157).

And yet interestingly, perhaps in part alluding to the "John" part of him that was discovering his capacity for relating, when Jean returns after a week following Francoise's death so now money (internal resources) are available again, he remarks: "*It's a curious thing … I felt myself moved … the chateau … I neglect it, and curse it, and fight against all that it does to me … and yet … I felt I wanted her. In a strange sort of way, I missed her*" (ibid., p. 336). He can it seems recover some ability for concern and the possibility of a more relational engagement with his family.

My own response to the characters' dilemmas is that they are being challenged to reassess their current patterns of being caught up with "doing" obsessively and anxiously and pathologising themselves which acts as a cover-up from exposure to lively embodied feeling, vulnerability and "being". By disconnecting from a potential centredness of feeling, they are unable to value themselves. This is often a core struggle for many analytic patients.

Deepening Shadow Themes: Crisis Leading to Psychological Adaptation and Potential Renewal of Psychic Energy

Further Shadow themes that are explored in "The Scapegoat" story comprise existential crisis and psychic renewal. John and Jean's Shadow encounter can be seen to represent symbolically both an existential, psychological crisis and the call to their individuation process (see later section). The Shadow encounter augurs the beginning of the individuation journey. In everyday life these moments of crisis can precipitate an individual's decision to enter into an analysis and to reconnect with inner life.

John and Jean have reached an impasse in their lives when they meet their incapacity to relate. You could say each is being invited to face diametrically opposite Shadow aspects within themselves (the split), that taken together psychologically constitute a potential transformation of their total personality.

John has no family name. He has no family ties or relationships, no identification or power. He is dead inside and fears living like a dried-out riverbed. He is undergoing a sense of emptiness, depletion, depression and grieves for the felt absence of a life unlived. He is keenly aware of his incapacity to experience intimacy and love, to share himself with others. To work through the moment of crisis, to individuate, he needs to change.

Jean on the other hand has become crystallised into over-identification with his "Persona", by which Jung meant on an outer level our many and varied social roles that comprise differentiated personas that act as a series of bridges between us and the outside world. Jean has been unable to develop beyond his biography. He has a name and an ancient lineage; is the owner of a chateau; a one-time principled hero of the Resistance; director of a failing business; head of a fractious, loveless and embittered family; a keeper of too many secrets, and master of nothing. Increasingly, his murderous past, passive-aggression, sadism and hate has immobilised the family and caught up with him. Either he meets the crisis and changes, or he escapes this opportunity to individuate by leaving. He does the latter.

One of the possible pathways for individuation and potential renewal in which the Shadow acts as harbinger at midlife is as the return of aspects of personality that have been repressed in childhood or adolescence. By analogy, it is as if there is a need to exhume the corpse of unlived childhood self-expression and to bury consciously the dead, i.e. to identify the source of pain and then to put the past to rest by grieving and mourning it. This can also include having the courage to disidentify with an earlier identity or rigid persona pattern. The persona and the Shadow stand in a compensatory position to one another.

And yet this crisis offers a turning point of opportunity that can lead to a new experience of identity (Kast 1987, p. 3). There is hopefulness that creativity and development are possible, for a crisis is *the last passageway to a transformation and the last obstacle to change*" (ibid., p. 7). Something shifts in the life of an individual in which new dimensions of experience or a new identity emerges. That is, if the crisis can be acknowledged and worked with and through consciously.

Part Three - Reparation and Potential Integration of Shadow

In the final part of the story, Francoise has fallen from a bedroom window and been taken to hospital. Accident? Or suicide? She requires a blood transfusion, blood group O, Jean's known blood type. But John is type A and says so. Blanche accuses him of wanting Francoise to die. Eventually she dies with her unborn child.

Francoise's untimely death solves the family's financial problems and John acts assertively in an attempt to facilitate reconciliation and reparation. *"Whatever wrongs there had been in the years that were gone, they could not be righted by a stranger. I could only build the present. But not alone"* (Du Maurier, 1957, p. 269). The commissaire of police leaves the chateau satisfied that her death was an accident. John persuades the Comtesse to resume her position as the head of the family, to give up her addiction to morphine, and to begin making the funeral arrangements. John asks Paul to take over the contractual aspects of the business and to travel with Renee. Paul accepts, realising it to be the only way to save his marriage. John faces Renee; he is not in love with her. He then talks with Blanche about the past and tries to apologise, but she is still angry. *"I could not ask forgiveness for something I had not done. As scapegoat, I could only bear the fault"* (ibid., p. 306). He tells Blanche that he wants her to run the glass business in his place and to live in the master's house.

And then, Jean calls. They agree to meet at the master's house. John considers killing Jean. The family priest intervenes, and dissuades him, fearing he will kill himself. Jean, who is armed, mocks John's efforts to heal the family wounds, although is impressed that he has maintained the masquerade for a week. John says, *"I happen to love your family, that's all"* (ibid., p. 330). Jean is surprised that John discovered the secret of Duval. He tells John that he sold his flat, emptied his accounts and exchanged them for French francs. "The self who had lived in London had gone forever" (ibid., p. 335). Jean admits that in a strange way he missed his family. John tries to tell Jean his family have changed. Jean also expresses openness to re-visiting their shared deception from time to time. *"The exchange of clothes in the darkness was macabre, even terrible. It meant, with every garment shed, a loss of the self I had found"* (ibid., p. 337).

John drives to see Bela. She alone had realised that he was someone else and not the real Jean de Gue. She says that he had a *"tendresse that Jean did not possess"* (ibid., p. 343). She says that because of John the family in the chateau will be different, even if Jean tries to undo the good he has done there. John says that his "sin" of failure turned into love but *"the problem remains the same. What do I do with love?"* (ibid., p. 347). He leaves resolving to follow his original path to the Trappist monastery.

The Shadow of Scapegoating

One interpretation of the story that may have been intended by the author is that John takes on the role of scapegoat uncannily on Jean's behalf in order to bring some form of transformation to the family dynamic. This is close to the idea that *"originally the scapegoat was a human or animal victim chosen for sacrifice to the underworld god to propitiate that god's anger and to heal the community. The scapegoat was a 'pharmakon' or healing agent"* (Brinton Perera 1986, p. 8).

Scapegoating has become rather consciously concretised in contemporary culture to mean finding the one/s who in the moral judgement of any given group, family, or organisation can be identified with perceived "evil" acts or wrong-doing, are blamed for it and cast out from the community for their perceived sins. Those that remain can feel guiltless and relieved of acknowledging their role in the process. Actually, the scapegoat is an archetype expressed by the image of the Messiah, a duality of two archetypal patterns – that of the sacrificial martyr and that of the kingly ruler. In the modern era, its deeper meaning remains unconscious within the collective and frequently becomes inflated and distorted, preventing ego development and the individuation potential inherent in the Messiah archetype (Brinton Perera 1986, p. 74).

The Jewish tradition of the scapegoat sacrifice described in the Bible (Leviticus 16) was a central part of the Yom Kippur ritual. In essence, evil representing all the afflictions, sins and transgressions of a religious community is excised and magically transferred to other persons or animals. On a concrete level, the physical stain or pollutant is cleansed by the casting out of the chosen scapegoat but on a symbolic level, the confession of sins and atonement of guilt by the community allows for a renewal of life and re-connection with the divine guiding spirit of the people. The aim of Atonement (at-one-ment) as a form of ritual activity is to ward off psychic fragmentation, disintegration, the trauma of separation and loss, the devastating consequences of the loss of connectedness, and being at-one with a superior power on whom one feels dependent. Hence Yom Kippur, the Day of Atonement, effects a collective catharsis and restores an equilibrium in the relationship with the divine. This is the context in which the scapegoat appears.

Curiously, the description of the scapegoat ritual in the Mishna Yoma (Chapter 6), involves a doubling effect with two he-goats selected for the day of atonement ("The Scapegoat" Q&A contribution and personal communication from Laurie Slade, 2 February 2020). They had to be of equal appearance and value. it was then determined by lot which he-goat would be sacrificed. The vital aspect in this is that one he-goat is chosen, celebrated and sacrificed and the other is loaded with the sins of the community and cast out. This has resonance with the idea of Christ as the one chosen for sacrifice, and evil as that which must be cast out. Moreover, it was understood that the casting out is in itself an evil act for which forgiveness is necessary.

One reading of the story can be ventured that John is the chosen sacrifice, but in order to fulfil this role, Jean must cast himself out from the family due to his own sense of guilt in order for renewal and reconnection to occur. Superficially they exchange identities but internally a different aspect of the total personality that is the potential integration of John/Jean is required to inaugurate a transformative effect.

What is unusual in "The Scapegoat" is that the traditional process of scapegoating is reversed. Rather than the family "selecting" from within its ranks a likely victim for such a role, it "imports" John to unlock a stuck, immobilised and loveless family system to revitalise the family dynamic so that its members can separate and individuate.

As Brinton Perera asserts, "*In Jungian terms, scapegoating is a form of denying the Shadow of both man and God*" (p. 9). The Shadow problem is facing up to our own weakness, helplessness and vulnerability, the parts that don't fit with our ego ideal or with our moral evaluation of the "goodness of God". These tend to be repressed, denied, split off and made unconscious. The unwanted feelings, impulses and instinctual urges are projected unconsciously onto others who are blamed, shamed and attacked rather than us recognising, accepting and owning these qualities in ourselves. Hence, those that are identified with the scapegoat are identified with our own unacceptable inferior Shadow qualities. This results in defensive closure, a lack of flow both within and without, a chronic sense of depletion, and a loss of balance.

And yet who really is the scapegoat? There are many other contenders for the role. Marie-Noel's eagerness to sacrifice herself for Jean/John perhaps makes her the scapegoat of the novel. Moreover, Francoise can be seen as offering herself as scapegoat as she knows several people wish her death. It becomes clear that the stuckness of the unhappy, failed marriage of Jean and Francoise, for which he despised her and maybe himself for having entered into it, holds everything and everyone together falsely in its thrall. Once Francoise dies, her "sacrifice" offers release and brings a new possibility of life and love.

Clearly there is a spiritual questioning as well as a Christian and Catholic dimension to the concept of the scapegoat in the novel wherein John as the "innocent" man suffers for the sins of his double Jean, much as Marie-Noel is willing to suffer the sins of her father. Her fanatical identification with Joan of Arc as sacrificial scapegoat for France mirrors this, as also the theme of martyrdom through burning, re-enacted by John's deliberate self-harm by burning to avoid exposure as an impostor. There may also be an unconscious identification of self-sacrifice between Marie-Noel and Jean, she as Joan of Arc, and he in the French Resistance.

The Shadow and Individuation

"The Scapegoat" takes as its central theme an existential crisis that acts as the provocative agent to face, acknowledge and integrate the Shadow. It also reflects the call to engage in an individuation process in which there is the possibility for radical psychic change and transformation. The Shadow acts as initiator into the individuation process and so it is to the concept of Individuation that we now turn.

Of all the characters in the book, Bela stands out as the only character that is able to hold an analytic position, mediating the tension between the two opposites of John and Jean and who realises that these are two halves of the same person. She has the capacity to differentiate and discriminate between them. She also can engage in "real" relationship with both aspects and can accept them and be understanding. She represents the integrity and moral centre of the book and the psychic aim of developmental growth and balance. She even provides maternal reparation in a moment in the story where she repairs Marie-Noel's animal figurines and may represent maternal love and concern. Jung (1959) also states that when there is a Shadow crisis a saviour arises. "*In the case of the individual, the problem constellated by the shadow is answered on the plane of the anima, that is, through relatedness*" (CW9i, para. 487). Bela can be viewed as an Anima[3] figure in that she acts as a bridge of re-connection for both John and Jean, enabling them to recover lively attachments to their internal selves and others, to feel the pain of loss, and to engage with reality rather than fantasy.

By individuation I mean the potential for an individual to become himself, whole, indivisible and distinct from other people, and yet maintaining relationship with the collective. In other words, a person can become conscious in what respects he or she is a unique human being and, at the same time, be aware of his or her ordinariness. For Jung, individuation takes place in the second half of life, especially mid-life. It is a time to find one's own way, a coming to self-hood or self-realisation.

Perhaps John expresses something of this awareness in his concern for the other. "*What was happening, then, was that I wanted to preserve Jean de Gue from degradation. I could not bear to see him shamed. This man, who was not worth the saving, must be spared. Why? Because he looked like me?*" (Du Maurier, 1957, p. 110).

It is Bela that makes him aware of his Shadow problem.

The other Jean de Gue, the one who's been hidden for so long beneath the surface gaiety and charm, I've often wondered if he existed. If he's going to emerge, he'd better do so now. Time's getting on ... You aren't the only one with a dual personality. We all have our multiple selves. But no one avoids responsibility that way. The problems remain to be tackled just the same.

(ibid., p. 156)

When Jean returns and arranges a meeting, John reaches the zenith of his ordeal in acknowledging that Jean is his Shadow.

The emotion that filled me now was violent, overwhelming ... I was the possessor now, he the intruder. The chateau was my chateau ... the family were my family, my flesh and blood; they belonged to me and I to them. He could not return and make them his again.

(ibid., p. 318)

And later, "*His scheme would come to nothing. I was the substance now and he the shadow. The shadow was not wanted and could die*" (ibid., p. 322). At this moment the split is most polarised, and John is in grave danger of not wanting to know his Shadow at all and of killing it off, as if it did not exist. By providence, or perhaps from a Jungian perspective we can say as a reconciling symbol emerging from the tension of opposites, the intercession of the priest stays his hand and removes his revolver.

Ultimately it is Bela that stands for development and differentiation and champions the potential integration of John/Jean's Shadow. In their parting John expresses gratitude for her understanding. During it, he integrates something profoundly moving inside.

I knew with urgency, with conviction ... the old self of Le Mans was dead. The shadow of Jean de Gue had also vanished. In their place was something else that as yet had no substance, no flesh, no blood, but was born of feeling, that could not die, and it was like a flame, contained in the body's shell.

I love them ... I'm part of them now forever. That's what I want you to understand. I shall never see them again, but because of them *I live*. I understand", she said, "and it could be the same for them. Because of you they also live".

(ibid., p. 343, bold italics mine)

And finally, John says:

He's a devil ... No, she said, "that's where you're wrong. He's not a devil. He's a human, ordinary man, just like yourself ... you're describing yourself as well".There was the fear. Which one of us was real? Who lived, and who had died? It struck me suddenly that if I should now look at myself in a mirror I should see no reflection.

(ibid., p. 344)

This relational exchange has much in common with "a moment of truth" in analysis (Stern 1998, p. 912), and perhaps as an example of Jung's concept of the Transcendent Function (Jung 1960), in that the quality of relatedness with Bela brings an emergence of meaning and a change in psychological attitude. The Transcendent Function is a psychological bridge of inter-connectedness between consciousness and the unconscious, or living the "symbolic life", which means sensing the archetypal dimensions within the patterns, actions and choices of everyday life. Bela also functions as Anima and Mediatrix of the tensions of opposites and as relational bridge and connectedness to John's unconscious processes (Hillman 1985). Perhaps we can even say that this new-found relational attunement and "aliveness" (Ogden 1997) facilitated a "co-created" state of Grace (Crowther & Schmidt 2015, p. 69). Essentially, there now exists the possibility for transformation and gradual acceptance of his Shadow projections and awareness that these are ongoing.

Nevertheless, the author leaves us with the ambiguity of not knowing what will befall John on entering the monastery. There is a question left in the reader's mind about whether the monastery, La Grande Trappe, will act as a transitional space where he can assimilate and integrate his newly discovered capacities or a regressive space entrapping him in a mindless past.

This is also a reminder that maturational development and integration can only happen with the toleration of ambivalence, particularly the coexistence of love and hate, envy and gratitude, and innumerable other opposites. It is a prerequisite for avoiding splitting and a central quality needed to achieve individuation.

Conclusion

Daphne du Maurier's psychological novel "The Scapegoat" is essentially a deeply personal exploration about a confrontation with the Shadow, describing a man's existential crisis of meeting dual aspects of his personality and his struggle to re-connect with disconnected and lost aspects of the self.[4] A process begins, moving from initial emptiness and deadness to emergent liveliness through a renewed intrapsychic and interpersonal relational engagement to self and others. The story's end is deliberately ambiguous, it may evolve or lead once more to regression and escape,[5] and yet the prognosis for John/Jean's inner psychological journey is broadly hopeful. There is the potential to "come to terms" with the Shadow and engage more fully with an individuation process. Jung's concepts of the Shadow and

Individuation together with his psychological and religious influence on the author are evident in the novel's conceptual framework.

The trajectory of the story also has an underlying spiritual significance, containing as it does the motifs of the scapegoat and sacrifice. It can be read as an initiatory journey and process that has to be undergone, suffered and experienced in order to recover hidden depths to enable the integration of Shadow elements. This is analogous to Jung's initiatory journey in his Red Book Liber Novus, where he regains and recovers his soul through establishing a dialogue with autonomous fantasy figures and integrating their values into consciousness (Jung 2009). Both entail Shadow work and the task of individuation. John's challenging relationships to various dimensions of the feminine within Jean's family are in their way not dissimilar to Jung's series of Active Imaginations in the Red Book, in that both can be seen as attempts to get to know and integrate various aspects of the whole personality.

Suffering the conflict of opposites is an inescapable condition of life. Jung is saying that individuation is not just a personal, individual psychological development but a cosmological development. The recovery of marginalised and disowned parts of our psyche brings new value and an enlargement of the personality (Shadow integration) and with it a renewed attitude of responsibility that can be contributed to the collective. Jung also perceives individuation as an act of redemption, of bringing the divine into being in Time, of *"giving birth to a 'New God'"* in oneself (2009, p. 323). Those parts perceived by us as inferior, despicable or unacceptable have profound value and contain a mystery, the potential for transformation.

The author might also concur with Macdiarmid (2013, foreword, p. xiv) that the ultimate purpose of understanding the unconscious is "to enable us to find our capacity to love". In my mind one of the overriding themes that my grandmother was trying to explore in the story is the importance of valuing human kindness ("tendresse"). Finding a capacity to express kindness and compassion to oneself and to others is an essential aspect of befriending the Shadow.

I am aware that one of the pleasures of writing this chapter has brought me closer to my grandmother's internal struggles with her Shadow sides that mirror some of my own, as well as a shared interest in ancestral patterns and the world of the imagination.

Daphne once shared with her daughter-in-law that her book was about a 'crisis of self' and 'identity breakdown'. She herself expresses beautifully in a letter to a friend both the tension of the necessity of living with ambivalence in befriending the Shadow, and the possibility of redemption in naming it, thus enabling personal growth and psychological adaptation, and so I will end with her words:

> Everyone of us has his, or her, dark side. Which is to overcome the other? This is the purpose of the book. And it ends, as you know, with

the problem unsolved, except that the suggestion is there, when I finished it, was that the two sides of that man's nature had to fuse together to give birth to a third, well balanced, Know Thy Self. The one man went back home having been given a hint that his family, in future, would be different, would be adjusted; the other man went to the monastery, for a space of time, to learn "what to do with love". (Unpublished and private letter dated 4 July 1957 to Maureen Baker-Munton)

Notes

1 Freud's own footnote (1919, p. 247) attests to his own experience of the uncanny effect of encountering his "double": "... it is interesting to observe what the effect is of meeting one's own image unbidden and unexpected ... I can report a similar adventure. I was sitting alone in my wagon-lit compartment when a more than usually violent jolt of the train swung back the door of the adjoining washing-cabinet, and an elderly gentleman in a dressing gown and a travelling cap came in. I assumed that in leaving the washing-cabinet, which lay between the two compartments, he had taken the wrong direction and come into my compartment by mistake. Jumping up with the intention of putting him right, I at once realised to my dismay that the intruder was nothing but my own reflection in the looking-glass on the open door. I can still recollect that I thoroughly disliked his appearance ... is it not possible, though, that my dislike ... was a vestigial trace of the archaic reaction which feels the 'double' to be something uncanny?"
2 Cohen (2018) describes a contemporary understanding of "doubling" as "a heightened clarity in the texture of moment to moment experience".
3 The inner figure of woman held in a man's psyche. As a psychic image it operates in relation to the dominant psychic principle of a man. Anima acts as a guide of soul or "soul-image" (Jung, CW6) that can connect an individual to creative possibilities and finding ways to enliven the process of individuation (Samuels et al. 1986, p. 23). Hillman (1985) describes the anima as the image by which we will be liberated imaginatively.
4 Du Maurier wrote to Oriel Malet on 19 October 1956: "Re: Scapegoat, I know that has been written from a sort of spiritual awareness ... Actually, in 'Scapegoat', I've tried to say too many things at once. How close hunger is to greed, how difficult to tell the difference, how hard not to be confused, how close one's better nature is to one's worst, and finally, how the self must be stripped of everything, and give up everything, before it can understand love" (Malet 1993, pp. 80–81).
5 It is interesting that the French word "trappe" translates as a "snare" or "pitfall".

References

Abi-Ezzi, N. (2003). *The Double in the Fiction of R.L. Stevenson, Wilkie Collins and Daphne du Maurier*. Bern: Peter Lang AG.
Brinton Perera, S. (1986). *The Scapegoat Complex Toward a Mythology of Shadow and Guilt*. Toronto: Inner City Books.
Cohen, J. (2018). *Not Working Why We Have to Stop*. London: Granta Press.

Crowther, C., Schmidt, M. (2015). States of grace: Eureka moments and the recognition of the unthought known. *Journal of Analytical Psychology, 60* (1), 54–74.

Du Maurier, D. (1957). *The Scapegoat.* Philadelphia: University of Philadelphia Press.

Eliot, T. S. (1940). *The Four Quartets.* London: Faber and Faber.

Freud, S. (1919). *"The 'Uncanny'".* The Standard Edition of the Complete Psychological Works of Sigmund Freud, Volume XVII (1917–1919): An Infantile Neurosis and Other Works, 217–256.

Hillman, J. (1985). *Anima: An Anatomy of a Personified Notion.* Woodstock: Spring Publications.

Hollis, J. (1993). *The Middle Passage: From Misery to Meaning in Midlife.* Toronto: Inner City Books.

Jung, C.G. (1959). "On the Psychology of the Trickster" *CW9i.*

Jung, C. G. (1959). "The Shadow". *CW9ii.*

Jung, C. G. (1960). "The Transcendent Function". *CW8.*

Jung, C. G. (1953). "Two Essays in Analytical Psychology". *CW7.*

Jung, C. G. (1963). *Memories, Dreams, Reflections.* London: Collins and Routledge & Kegan Paul.

Jung, C. G. (2009). *The Red Book Liber Novus A Reader's Edition*, S. Shamdasani (ed.). London: Norton.

Kast, V. (1987). *The Creative Leap Psychological Transformation through Crisis.* Wilmette, Illinois: Chiron Publications.

Laski, M. (1962). Archangels ruined. *The Times Literary Supplement, 3,* 164, (19 October), 808.

Macdiarmid, D. (2013). *Century of Insight the Twentieth Century Enlightenment of the Mind.* London: Karnac Books.

Malet, O. (1993). *Daphne Du Maurier Letters from Menabilly: Portrait of a Friendship.* London: Weidenfeld and Nicolson.

Ogden, T. H. (1997). *Reverie and Interpretation, Sensing Something Human.* London: Karnac Books.

Samuels, A., Shorter, B., Plaut, F. (1986). *A Critical Dictionary of Jungian Analysis.* London: Routledge.

Stein, M. (1983). *In Midlife: A Jungian Perspective.* Woodstock: Spring Publications.

Stern, D. N., Sander, L. W., Nahum, J. P., Harrison, A. M., Lyons-Ruth, K., Morgan, A. C., Bruschweiler-Stern, M., & Tronick, E. Z. (1998). Non-interpretive mechanisms in psychoanalytic therapy: The "something more" than interpretation. *International Journal of Psychoanalysis, 79,* 903–921.

Winnicott, D. W. (1960). Ego Distortion in Terms of True and False Self, 140–153. In *The Maturational Processes and the Facilitating Environment.* London: The Hogarth Press.

Wolff, T. (1935). Introduction to the Fundamentals of Complex Psychology. Monograph in *The Cultural Significance of Complex Psychology.* Berlin: Julius Springer Publications.

Chapter 6

Whose Shadow Is It Anyway?: Jung and Opposites[1]

Clare Landgrebe

When I was applying to train as a Jungian analyst, I was often asked by interviewers: "What brought you to Jung?" A reasonable question, but my mind would immediately go blank and I would feel somewhat panicked. However, I regularly found myself talking about opposites, the tensions they bring, their intractability, and how one or other side could fall into the shadow to avoid the awful conflict between them. It felt a relief that Jung didn't seem to be working towards resolving this dilemma; instead, he suggested that it was important to somehow keep going within the uncomfortable struggle. His view of harmony seemed refreshingly different, valuing discord as well as concord. He was convinced that opposites permeate all of our lives and they are at the centre of communications within our inner world as well as with the external world. I feel that this is particularly well demonstrated in the field of adult couple relationships. There is an inescapable and irresolvable conflict between the opposites of closeness and distance which adult loving relationships present: the ambivalence between wanting and not wanting intimacy. It is played out in the dance couples have to negotiate between togetherness and separateness. We come to couple relationships as adults with history, for I believe that our way of relating is profoundly influenced by our first relationship with our parents. By exploring the rhythm and flow of these early years, I aim to bring to light something of the choreography of this dance of love, how both parties often stumble, treading on each other's toes as they struggle to learn the steps and get them into body memory.

Virtually all the couples I have worked with arrived initially with the hope that their difficulties would be removed. I have learned that it is often more practically useful for them to begin to understand themselves and each other more. This can be followed by a shift in perspective which can revitalise their relationship in ways they had not anticipated, or would even have wished for before therapy. Often the increased understanding would turn out to be an exploration of their own shadows, discovering that they were interacting together through projection on an unconscious level, shadow to shadow, as it were. I will present the narratives of two fictional couples – one a composite of people I have worked with, and one from ancient Greek mythology –

DOI: 10.4324/9781003255819-8

Narcissus and Echo, which reveals my Western background. By using an imaginative amplification of their stories, I hope to elucidate how they may demonstrate the themes of closeness and distance in romantic relationships which may spark some thoughts and ideas for you.

How we see ourselves and how we see other people is an intrinsic part of relationships especially when we fall in love, when our initial perceptions are often notoriously rose tinted. We cannot avoid viewing others and ourselves through the perspective of our own mind and body. "Whatever we look at, and however we look at it, we see only through our own eyes" (Jung 1933). The view I am presenting here is inevitably through my eyes, so it does not represent the only one, or the best one, for there are many ways to consider the influences on relationships, such as race, faith, ethnicity, socio economic conditions, politics, intergenerational trauma to name a few.

The Problem of Meeting an "Other"

"Individuation is only with people, through people. You must realise you are a link in a chain, that you are not an electron suspended somewhere in space or aimlessly drifting through the cosmos" (Jung 1934–1939).

We may not feel very sociable or particularly like others but we do need them. Jung placed an emphasis on people being part of a collective in the external and in the inner world, and that sticking with the conflicts that this creates, such as the clash between hatred of being consumed by the group and fear of being alone, can enhance vitality. In the last two centuries, the growth of industrialisation and globalism have led to our dependence on a complex infrastructure for all of our physical needs from nutrition to defecation. Paradoxically, it is also a time when individualism seems to be prized and the individual must have freedom to develop. Obstacles to this become considered to be inimical to proper human development and as a consequence, dependency tends to be despised and consigned to the shadow. However, when we fall in love we also fall into dependency, one which recalls our very first days and the idyllic feeling of having our needs met and of being understood. These infant experiences and memories are largely unconscious and so it can be difficult to get in touch with them, and furthermore they can be locked away in the embarrassing shadow of being a grown-up. Literature is full of tales and examples of how love turns us upside down, of the crazy things we find ourselves doing and the physical and emotional risks we are prepared to take when in love.

> If thou remember'st not the slightest folly
> That ever love did make thee run into,
> Thou hast not loved.
> (Shakespeare 1993, *As You Like It*, 2.4)

Beginnings

Through our first experience of connectedness, we discover our separateness and our individuality, coming to appreciate that there is a "me" and a "not me". The tense space between distance and closeness is central to this. As human infants cannot fend for themselves, it is essential for a baby to have someone to relate to and depend on. This is often the birth mother but it has never been exclusively this way as circumstances can intervene which make it not possible, cultures have different customs, and "mothering" is not solely dependent on gender. A repeated oscillation between distance and closeness, meeting and not meeting, is part of our earliest days and months and creates patterns which become implicit, stored in our bodies, providing a significant, but largely unconscious model for future relationships. These complex and intricate interactions are described in Chapter 1 and I am picking out a particular aspect which I feel influences the emergence of this model: the embodied sensations and patterns of the movement between closeness and distance which build into a boundary between "me" and "not me". I am thinking specifically of very early experiences in the body: pain, hunger and thirst, yes, but also more indefinable experiences such as the rhythm of being held and rocked, the tone and flow of speech, sensations and feelings gradually beginning to coalesce into shapes which can be recognised, re-membered and anticipated.

At birth the world is not entirely new and there are bridges between the womb and the world outside. A fascinating example is the "breast crawl": the ability of a new born to move itself to the breast immediately after birth. For this the neonate uses its stepping reflex and sense of smell, as apparently the areola secretes odours which smell similar to the amniotic fluid, which will remain on the baby's hands if they have not been washed. This process demonstrates a movement from the familiar and safe – the womb – to the gap that birth creates and then to reconnection with the familiar again. Being attached, losing it and then finding it again. During the early days and weeks after birth the nursing dyad is constantly thrust into trying to work out what each other is doing, wanting, needing; getting it wrong and then getting it right-ish for a while and then it starts all over again.

Careful infant observations of these early interactions have been recorded and studied over several decades. Attachment and psychoanalytic theorists have offered frameworks for thinking about them, and neuroscience has offered a wealth of evidence about how the body responds to this cycle of rupture and repair which repeats itself many, many times during the days and nights following a new baby's arrival into a household. It involves turn taking, moving out and pulling back.

The founder of the Society of Analytical Psychology (SAP), Dr Michael Fordham, used the terms deintegration and reintegration to describe this process. One of the meanings of integration is to participate, to fit in.

He was observing the ebb and flow of a baby taking part in new experiences in the external world (deintegration) and then withdrawing (reintegration) into itself to absorb them and allowing them to become part of its growing map of the world and itself (Fordham 1988). At first Fordham thought that the mother needed to find perfection in the fit between need and gratification, for example between the nipple/teat and the baby's suckling. He came to realise that the gap produced what he called "constructive anxiety", which can promote growth and the capacity to think as the infant's primary self is provoked into action and actively helps to create the environment in which it can develop (Astor 1995).

Donald Winnicott (1973)[2] too affirmed the necessity of providing only "good enough" mothering. This is not just about merging; the baby is also active in the process. Both the baby and the parent are different people with their own characteristics and worries, so right from their beginning together they have to struggle with their difference. The baby is not a passive partner in this – not simply shouting from discomfort and pain – but stimulating the mother to care for her and also moulding herself to the individual aspects of this mother. Allowing enough space for turn taking, for example, may be difficult for an anxious parent who finds the quiet a baby needs to assimilate experience (reintegration) confusing, and can interrupt too much. These kinds of memories are concerned with how the bodies around the baby respond both consciously and unconsciously. A mother's gaze helps the child to see themselves in their mother's eye, and to develop self-reflection. Adoring, deep staring into each other's eyes is very much part of lovers' behaviour. But there are other types of information that looks communicate. Disapproval is most effectively conveyed through "that particular shrivelling look" as one client described it, and also in less conscious ways – a reticence, a pulling away by the adult (unaware perhaps of their own unconscious anxiety) from appeals for closeness or dependence from their child.

"Mind the Gap!"

I often travel by train from the south coast of the United Kingdom into London to see my "brick mother",[3] the SAP. As I pass through the many stations, I am frequently exhorted to: "Mind the gap, mind the gap between the train and the platform!" The psychoanalyst Wilfred Bion (1970) was interested in how our minds develop and he felt that the gaps in connection between parent and child played an important part in this. One of his most well-known theories concerns the mother's capacity to receive her child's strong feelings and experiences and then hold them in her mind by having a kind of "reverie" about them, which detoxifies them and gives them meaning. This allows the baby to receive them back in a more manageable form. He believed that important development, including an awareness of being separate, springs from the times when this process does not run smoothly. For example, in the normal course of events, a caregiver cannot always provide instant gratification and so the infant experiences frustration. Bion (1962) suggested that it is through these gaps that our minds can begin to develop as we have the opportunity to become aware of ourselves and also realise that there are others who are separate from us and who are not under our control.

John Bowlby (1980), who developed Attachment Theory, worked with children who were separated from their parents as evacuees during the Second World War, and with those who had to stay in hospital without their parents. He observed the patterns of distress which tend to occur when attachment is lost, severed in some way, leading to a separation, which could be physical, but also could be emotional. This led him to explore the ways in which attachment and loss interweave themselves throughout our lives. Although they might appear to be opposites, attachment and loss are not two separate issues. I would suggest they are inextricably interlinked – the one is only alive when the other is present. For example, attachment can be deadening and suffocating without loss. Furthermore, as I have indicated, our earliest experiences of attachment inevitably have loss entwined within them and through this we learn about our separateness. It is through these terrifying, but ordinary and unavoidable gaps in connection, the rupture before the repair, that we come to realise we are attached to someone other than ourselves.

There was a game I played as a child which you may recognise: I must not step on the joins of the paving stones in a pavement, otherwise something horrid and frightening will happen. I remember it being fun and a physical challenge to walk in this way without stumbling, but it is also one of the ways by which we as children try to have some sense of control in a world which seems to be controlled by adults, and which we are just beginning to understand. A.A. Milne (1924) describes this game in the poem "Whenever I Walk in a London Street"; talking about the bears who lurk at the corners, waiting to eat up careless children. It conjures up the terror in imagination of what might lie in the tiny spaces between the paving stones and the fears lurking in these gaps can fall into the shadowlands of the psyche. However, it is also through the rhythm of connection and disconnection between parent and infant, the rupture and the repair, the gap and the bridge of reconnection, that Bion proposed mind can appear. It is as though these repeated gaps and connections progressively draw together and create a sense of "I". Fordham observed how the random scribbling of a one-year-old boy began to turn into circles. As the boy started to refer to himself as "I", "as if by revelation", he then stopped drawing the circles for a while (Fordham 1957). He suggested this reveals the beginning of a boundary between "me" and "not me" and all parents know that once a child can say "I", it is swiftly followed by "No!" as the child begins to assert its independence and test boundaries.

Shadow and Projection

I have come across many clients who say "I never had tantrums". Tantrums are a normal and necessary part of childhood. "Where the Wild Things Are" by Maurice Sendak (1963) is a brilliant description of a little boy having a tantrum, being sent to bed and furiously filling his bedroom with the angry internal characters in his imagination. He journeys across the sea in his private boat to meet and tame these monsters, becoming their omnipotent King before returning home, in spite of their pleadings for him to stay, to find a hot supper of reconnection with his mother. The "tantrumless" clients have tended to share similar experiences in childhood such as rigid feeding and behaviour regimes, smacking from parents, and their ordinary childhood behaviour and misbehaviour consistently being interpreted as aggressive and malevolent. When young children are not allowed to express their feelings, and the parent cannot receive them; when they are left to cry in their rooms because "they have to learn", they are left to do something beyond their psychosomatic and developmental capacity. In an attempt to survive the overwhelming emotions of fear and bewilderment, children tend to come to believe that they are the wrong ones. This can become fixed into something Jung called a complex. He suggested that this was a cluster of feelings, impulses, fantasies and experiences emerging from the relationship with a primary carer that can get carried over into new relationships and bedevil them. It can take a life time to integrate them. "One of the commonest causes is a moral conflict, which ultimately derives from the apparent impossibility of affirming the whole of one's nature" (Jung 1948).

Most parents naturally become very angry sometimes. If they cannot make amends, soothing themselves as well as the child and so managing to build a bridge between the good and bad aspects of them which the child experiences, the distress remains untouched, unmediated by the outside and becoming easy prey for raw, unprocessed fantasies in the child's inner world. Then the gap gets too wide leading to the child's shadow needing to be a more urgently defended place. Opposites in the child's experience of their parents remain separate; compartmentalised as they cannot be tolerated and then integrated. Children growing up in these circumstances may not be able to argue or to tolerate conflict as adults; they are frequently convinced that such behaviour would be catastrophic. These parts of themselves then fester in their shadow. It often appears to others, and to themselves, that they are obedient, conforming and docile, but beneath there is often fear, rage and distress which can erupt through the boundaries between mind and body, in a variety of symptoms such as eczema, asthma, eating disorders.

Another method of managing the parts of us we cannot bear, or have learned are unbearable to others, is to project these shadow terrors onto another person and then see them outside ourselves. When this has had to happen to a great deal of our personalities, it can be a problem, as too much of us then lives within another, and these parts can seem as if they belong to a stranger. Sometimes when clients bring dreams of aliens, I wonder whether they may be feeling deeply disconnected from parts of their inner world. Then, the boundary between what is me and what is not me is profoundly blurred and we become less aware of our separate selves. "Projections change the world into a replica of one's unknown face" (Jung 1951).

Couple Fit

It is a common view that love is a powerful and indefinable force which takes us over. Cupid's arrow hits us and we are smitten; the chemistry is overwhelming.

> Since first I saw your face I resolv'd
> to honour and reknown thee. (Anonymous)
> In *Musicke of Sundrie Kindes*, Thomas Ford 1607)

There is mystery involved in this, but I suggest there **is** a kind of chemistry, as there is a powerful unconscious response to some character traits we recognise of ourselves in the other, our missing elements. Let's think about what might be going on in a first meeting. Returning to the circle which preceded the little boy discovering "I" (Fordham 1957), Diagram 6.1 shows two separate circles, each one representing a set, a collection of contents which have something in common. In a sense, our psyches could be thought of as similar in that we are made up of the intersections and clashes between "*Ourselves, our Many Selves*" (Redfearn 1985) and our family histories.
In Diagram 6.2, they overlap, creating a new shared space.
This image recalls the edgy dance between togetherness and separateness, I mentioned earlier because, for the overlap to happen, two fairly intact circles have to be present first, indicating we have an awareness of our own shape as distinct from others and that, when the overlap happens, these boundaries are sturdy enough to weather being punctured by the intrusion of the other's circle.

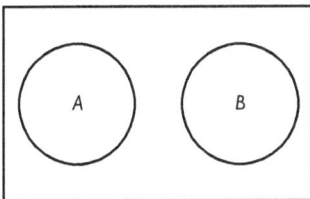

Diagram 6.1

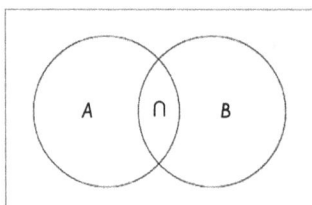

Diagram 6.2

So, why might we be drawn to this particular circle rather that another one? The intersection symbol "∩" indicates the space where there is a mixture of the parts they have in common. We are attracted to these similarities, like the delight in finding our "soul mate". As we notice these features in the other, our boundaries are able to loosen, letting the other in and the conscious and the unconscious mingle. In the unconscious mixing are the characteristics that the other person possesses which "fit" with our shadows. They may express some emotions which have been denied to us, to which we have lost our conscious link as they have been banished to the deep shadow. These alien aspects, which are so terrifying to me (and in me), look as though they are more settled within you and you appear to have an easier relationship with them. Jung felt that it was through connection between people that the meaning and purpose, what he called the "value" of the projection could be revealed, and then these parts which seem so foreign can be integrated, come home as it were, as they feel more manageable. "Only through personal contact do people become able to extract the value which is behind the projection; only in that way can they integrate whatever is their own in the projection" (Jung 1930–1934). Janet Mattison and Ian Sinclair (1979) eloquently describe this process which they term the "unconscious couple fit" in their seminal book *Mate and Stalemate*. Couples who live together need to arrange how to share everyday tasks: "I'll do the dust bins if you do the loo". Feelings can be shared out in a similar way: "I'll do anger if you do vulnerability", suggesting that opposites – what is consciously felt to be opposite – do attract and we find a shadow mate as well as a soul mate. This process often works and it seems to me like the psychological equivalent of a "spooning" embrace. A gentle, loving hug which lovers have enjoyed from antiquity, like the stone age couple found in the ancient burial site at the Alepotrypa cave in Greece. However, these roles can get stuck, fall into stagnation and the shadow remains unconscious.

Sarah and John

If someone who needs a lot of expressions of closeness (insecure/anxious attachment) connects with someone who needs to have a lot of space (avoidant attachment), then they will appear as very different characters. Each can feel in direct opposition to the other as their attachment styles will lead them to having a different view of how relationships work and what is important in them. I haven't met a "typical" couple, but this fictional couple picks up some of the dilemmas I have been writing about. It is a common presentation for one partner, let us call him John, to complain that his partner, Sarah, is distant and will not talk to him about her feelings; she does not want to spend time with him and he feels hurt and rejected. Sarah does not understand why John wants to make life complicated and messy, when things can be summed up very neatly without the risk of misunderstanding so long as he would just follow her logical way. As the therapy proceeds, there evolves an exploration of the communication styles in their families of origin, and it emerges that Sarah describes her childhood as stable and constant. She felt safe: "I had a perfect childhood". But when encouraged by the therapist to think about it more, she found it hard to remember being touched, or cuddled by her parents, recalling that they seemed physically distant from each other. Emotions were not talked about, in fact they were rather scorned as the family looked out at the world of neighbours, friends and colleagues. They prided themselves as a family that didn't get into the messy scrapes they saw around them. It became clearer that they needed to feel secure and they attempted to ensure this by maintaining distance from each other, fostering independence – each following their own interests – keeping disturbing feelings at bay – especially disorganising ones, such as anger, rage, shame and envy. As Sarah began to be able think about the history of her family, it appeared that there were some worrying difficulties in the past such as a fear of expressing anger because there was a conviction that bad things will happen as a result. It was whispered that one grandfather was a violent alcoholic.

Repeating the family's myths and its "party line" can develop into telling the story of the family, allowing space for it to be recollected, thought about, and questioned. Seemingly immutable "truths" can be understood in their context of time and space, and then time can begin to move again, as new perspectives can be considered. Curiosity can replace orthodoxy. This increased conscious knowledge about her past, along with the experience she had of being attended to and heard by the therapist, helped Sarah to open up more, and make contact with aspects of herself which had lingered for so long in her shadow such as her desire for warmth and her shame about this neediness. She asked John for more closeness, perhaps to have a meal in together.

At this point it was John who found that work/sport/stamp-collecting clubs needed him, and he just could not find the time realistically to explore this invitation to deeper intimacy! Then Sarah felt hurt and rejected. John started to talk about his father, Edward. In the culture Edward grew up in, sending a child to boarding school at age 8 was the norm. Although it meant that Edward escaped his parent's furious rows, it was traumatic for him. They divorced during a summer term when he was 14 and he was clear that he didn't want this to happen again with his own children. John came to realise that proximity was very important to his dad; Edward hated leavings, even short separations, and he would stand watching at the window whenever his wife was a bit late from work or shopping etc.

John's mother's family all lived in the same village and they were very involved with each other. He had lots of cousins to play with, aunts and uncles to look after him and he had become used to describing it as idyllic. However, as he talked about it more during therapy, he got in touch with a shadow aspect to this way of living. He realised that it had made him become nervous of new experiences and also that at times he could find it suffocating, but he didn't know how to live differently. Anger was avoided in the family – his father afraid of provoking any kind of rejection and his mother's family privileging closeness and agreement. He became aware that one of the ways that Sarah had been attractive to him was that she didn't seem encumbered by "staying local" – she went travelling for 2 years on her own before university. Together they began to see each other's shame and their families' shame. Both were worried by the tensions of being close and distant and during therapy they began to understand how they swapped roles to manage this ongoing dilemma.

They discovered that they had a shared fear about separation, and difficulties in trusting that intimacy need not mean either engulfment or abandonment. As they became closer, they could find themselves getting increasingly irritated with each other – the concord began to shift towards discord. Character traits which had been ignored consciously or explained away or adapted to became more apparent, and they could start to have spurts of exasperation. The first one took them by surprise as they found themselves in the kitchen shouting about the dishwasher. As they talked about it in the following therapy session, they reported how they stood staring at each other and then burst out laughing. They said that they felt quite exhilarated. They had realised that they had both grown up with fear about disagreement, believing that discord would be catastrophic as it demonstrated difference and this would lead to abandonment. John's family had tried to erase any chance of this surfacing by maintaining proximity to keep those feelings out. Sarah's family used a seemingly opposite tactic by working on the premise that keeping distant and emotionless would preserve their closeness. Both families were fairly insular and were resistant to any change (morphogenesis) and they worked incredibly hard to keep the status quo (homeostasis). Sarah and John found that their relationship could survive the challenge to intimacy that anger expresses: "I don't like this about you". In fact, they felt closer and one result of this was experienced in their sexual relationship which became more relaxed and satisfying.

Trust and Disillusion

"The effect of projection is to isolate the subject from his environment, since instead of a real relationship to it, there is an illusory one" (Jung 1951).

The "honeymoon period" of a relationship can be enchanting and is necessary, but it also is, and needs to be, transitory. Sarah and John managed to face their disillusionment with each other and their concept of marriage and were able to move beyond them. The interplay of illusion and disillusion pricks an unrealistic bubble, as when the circles in the Venn diagram are punctured, and we begin to see that the amazing other has some really annoying and disappointing traits – a major one being that they cannot rescue us from ourselves. The root of the words illusion and disillusion is connected to the Latin "ludere" which means to play. The word also means to mock and to deceive, which are more shadowy concepts and reflect the deluding of ourselves that love can stimulate. The "puncturing" is also one of the ways that distance can be created, allowing the difference of the other to come into focus, bringing with it dis-enchantment that the other is only human; both partners have flaws and limitations, as does the relationship.

The unconscious couple fit creates a container for the relationship. Jung (1931) talks about a particular way this can be lived out in his paper "Marriage as a Psychological Relationship". He describes how one partner (the more "complex" character) may become the container and the other ("the simpler") the contained. Although this may initially be acceptable to both parties, in time the container may start to feel so constrained by this arrangement that they might start "spying out of the window", which may result in an affair. I have found the ideas Jung presents here difficult to get hold of, but Warren Colman's (1995) chapter: "Marriage as a Psychological Container", has helped me to think further about it. He suggests that this pattern serves as an unconscious defensive container for the relationship with its purpose being to stop development. So, the aim of the containment is not to provide a space where the individuals and the relationship might grow and develop, rather it is containing to ensure that no change happens. I think about what might be carried in the shadows of each partner. Complexity may have been banished to the contained's shadow, likewise, simplicity may languish within the container's shadow. When these can be accommodated and integrated more within each partner's own conscious awareness, movement becomes possible. Perhaps the kind of couple which Jung describes find it hard to be two separate people; they need to be so close together that their individual outlines become blurred.

Couples often talk about having lost trust and wanting "complete trust back", especially when there has been the betrayal of an affair. Although this anxiety is understandable, I wonder if "complete trust" is something that is possible or even to be desired in couple relationships? Insisting on complete trust can be restrictive, sometimes having at its core a fear of abandonment. Then it becomes an attempt to control distance in the hope that by keeping you close to me I don't have to worry about you straying or whether you are in danger. It can also arise from a jealous desire to control the other so that their difference is obliterated and they can continue to be the receptacle for our shadow projections. Complete trust perhaps evokes the desire for fusion: then there need be no doubt, for the other's difference does not exist and the gap between is eliminated. Another casualty can be playfulness, for controlling behaviour is often rule bound and confined by projections. Being able to trust perhaps means not taking for granted that the other will always be as trustworthy as we might need them to be. There is always the risk of disaster in a relationship through rejection and betrayal – both of which induce feelings of shame. In loving we cannot escape from the potential for experiencing this shame.

Narcissus and Echo – Shame

Shame is one of the themes in the story of Narcissus and Echo, whose tale has been formative in analytic thinking. It appears that Narcissus does not feel shame himself, but he certainly inflicts it on his lovers, including Echo whom he crushes with his self-centred cruelty. But maybe there is more to the story if we consider the baggage each might bring – the pain trapped in their shadows which they feel so dreadful about and which needs to be projected onto the other. Sarah and John were not so blinded by their projections, that they could not see each other; they were able to increase their ability to tolerate difference and allow the space between them. Narcissus and Echo on the other hand, hardly seem to be a couple at all – they cannot relate but they also cannot separate. They demonstrate stark opposites which are split between them: crippling shame vs brazen self-interest, selfishness vs generosity, desire vs rejection. They seem utterly different to each other. I suggest that their projections cut off large and important swathes of their characters and are set in stone with no possibility of anything being transformed, changed or developed internally, revealing their struggle to know who they are. As with Sarah and John, I will imaginatively explore what they might bring to their meeting, playing with a picture of them as the kind of couple who can neither live together nor be apart, and I will suggest that playing is not possible for Narcissus and Echo.

Narcissus

In the collections of stories *Metamorphoses*, Ovid (8 AD) begins the tale of Narcissus with his mother, Liriope. She is a water nymph, on the margins between the human and the divine. His father, Cephissus, the river god, is absent and may have raped his mother. Liriope seeks out the famous seer,

Tiresias, and asks whether Narcissus will have a long life. The apparently "frivolous" prophecy which Tiresias makes is that he will indeed live long, "if he does not know himself", the antithesis of the motto above the temple at Delphi: "Know thyself". It is not clear why she needs this reassurance. She may be attempting to protect herself from the terrible loss of her son dying before her, an understandable parental fear, and furthermore, as a nymph, although she is not immortal, she would have a long life herself. If she had been raped by Cephissus, she would be traumatised and perhaps this was a way she thought she could protect herself and her son from further suffering. Whatever her reasons, this casual sounding prophecy has sinister implications for her son's future and his development. It implies that Narcissus must not be fully conscious and know who and what he is, for then he would know about mortality and vulnerability. But knowing about the future is double edged. Like Puck in *A Midsummer Night's Dream*, the Trickster is around, and myths and tales throughout the world express how so often something unforeseen turns the understanding and experience of an apparently beneficial prophecy upside down. One of the significant losses for Narcissus is, perhaps, his curiosity and as a consequence he is trapped within concrete thinking. In this way his childhood is stunted. He may appear to act childishly without developing a concern for the other, but there is not a sense that he could be a carefree, innocent child. He is not able to play with the reflection in the water and explore his environment as a baby might with a shape sorter, discovering interiority as well as what might go where, and this inhibits his growth. He could be thought of as a youth who never wants to grow up, but it is also as though he continues to be infantile without being allowed the full experience of his infancy. It seems that there was no space for his mind to develop and he only finds the gap just before his death when he is overwhelmed, with no maternal reverie to help him and he can say at last to his reflection: "I know you now and I know myself" (Ovid 8 AD). Maybe he is so angry with Echo's interruptions because she alerts him to his own fear of rejection and abandonment (a legacy from his mother who was perhaps also terrified of loss) which is firmly lodged in his unconscious.

Echo

After Liriope's visit to Tiresias, Ovid introduces Echo. She is a nymph too and, in this way, she resembles Narcissus's mother. Her habitat, though, is the mountains. She is a great chatterer and it is this character trait which causes her to incur Hera's jealous rage when she realises that Echo has been keeping her occupied with gossip whilst Zeus seduces other nymphs. Sometimes, talking a great deal can be a defence against the silence and the fear of being alone. Echo begins and ends by the rocks; perhaps she comes from and is left in a hard, impassive place without the life and movement of water. Her voice is described as "babbling" and possibly she tries to defend against unresponsiveness by enlivening the other with her endless chatter, like the sound of water in a stream, or like a child who is trying to encourage her withdrawn or depressed parent to respond to her by being endearing and lively. Hera turns against her and in her fury punishes her by making her capable of merely repeating the last few words she has heard. She is deprived of her own voice and can now find it and herself solely in the sound reflection of others. Like bats using echolocation,[4] she is reduced to locating herself, and expressing her individuality, through reflection. When she and Narcissus meet, she cannot communicate her love or her distress independently. It is only by tagging on to his whining that she has to shamefully acknowledge that she gives him power over her. She flees in deep shame to a cave, returning to witness his death. Her excruciating pain reveals our essential dependency, that we need another to reflect us, to hear us, to respond to us and through this we discover our independence.

Self-Reflection and Play

Self-reflection is a part of consciousness which has its foundation in our early experience of being held in our mother's gaze, and we learn about ourselves through developing this capacity. It is one of the keys which opens the door to the mind being able to develop. The implication of Tiresias's prophesy is that Narcissus cannot have this key. Narcissus cannot understand that he is transfixed and in love with his own reflection. Hera takes the key away from Echo too by making her dependent on the reflection of others, and her story tragically illustrates that her life cannot develop any further. They are both arrested in their growth and cannot know themselves and have their own capacity for self-reflection and self-knowledge. It is as though neither of them has managed to reach a sense of themselves as separate, creating enough of a circle to know they are an "I" and then be able to connect creatively with one another. Their experience of reflection is not the healthy, growth-promoting maternal reflection mentioned above. There is no reciprocity, no curiosity and impetus to learn more. There is just sterility, and the result is that they pine away. Narcissus was denied the possibilities of discovering the world for himself, finding out what he could and could not do. Play is one of the keys to entering the richness of learning and tolerating the shame of ignorance is part of learning.

Narcissus does not seem interested in knowing about anyone else; but can Echo appreciate who he is, rather than whom she would like him to be? She refuses to accept his limitations and then move on. One interpretation could be that she is not merely the silenced victim, her one role to be part of the landscape for Narcissus's story. She has her own narcissism, her "anti-relating" (Colman 2014), in that she is utterly gripped by her desire. In this reading, her stalker-like persecution of him is hidden in her position as the victim, like another famous victim, Cinderella, who could be thought about as projecting her greed and envy onto her step sisters, brooding on their charred remains in the cinders in the grate. Echo appears generous with her love, but maybe she projects *her* selfishness into Narcissus?

Ovid ends the story with the only remnant of Narcissus a solitary and beautiful flower. Narcissus is the genus name for daffodils and some of them have a powerful scent, which has been used in perfumery for centuries. One of these species is the Pheasants eye (Narcissus Poeticus var. recurvus) which is a particularly lovely daffodil with pure white petals and a shortened yellow and red corona which for me evokes a vivid sunset. The oil is very expensive and intense and it has a narcotic quality. Perfumers have to be careful not to fall into drowsiness due to its overwhelming effect. The word Narcissus has at its root the Greek word "nárkē", which means numb. Narcissists could be described as being absorbed with themselves but numb to the needs of others and this would fit Narcissus. When projecting one's shadow is perceived as vital for emotional survival, this induces a kind of numbness and lack, dulling the ability to be psychically alive and thus live fully in relationship.

Transformation or Stagnation

"There is no consciousness without discrimination of opposites" (Jung 1938/ 1954).

Jung suggested that sustaining the tension between opposites offers an opportunity for something other and unexpected to emerge which he termed the Transcendent Function. Others have commented that the surface tension of the water in the pool, the boundary between the opposite elements of water and air, is consistently broken as Narcissus struggles to get in contact with the boundary between himself and the other. He is not able to get a grip of his edges as perhaps he couldn't get hold of his mother to help her to really look at him. Both Narcissus and Echo fade away for they have no substance without their shadows and they become arid and desiccated. They may metamorphose but it is a change to enduring, lifeless forms. They are not able to change within themselves.

Our early years are significant and formative, but they do not fix us for ever. Jung believed that there is an urge within us which reaches out throughout our lifetimes in the hope for growth – the urge to individuate. The concept of the unconscious "couple fit" (Mattinson & Sinclair 1979) shows how in adult couple relationships there can be potential for repairing some of the things that didn't work out so well in the primary relationships. The shadows of both people in a relationship can play a part in their ongoing individuation within the partnership, as Sarah and John managed, but they can also compound early damage and leave the players in a worse state, bringing about the downfall of both the relationship and the in-dividuals, like Narcissus and Echo. There is not an easy answer to this conundrum, but if the couple can begin to glimpse what they may be hiding in their shadow and to understand what may be happening for their partner, the defences may weaken as a bit of what has needed to be hidden starts to be allowed out. Then the dynamic can change. Sarah and John were able to do this in therapy but Narcissus and Echo are trapped and cannot grow together and flourish. Perhaps the choreography of relationships is not just about searching for a perfect soulmate partner, but also about finding someone whose shadow can dance with ours.

Notes

1 This chapter is a development of some thoughts I first presented to the IAAP Congress 2019 in Vienna.
2 The psychoanalyst, Dr Donald Winnicott (1896–1971), was a paediatrician at the Paddington Children's hospital for many years and he worked with children who had been evacuated during the Second World War. He trained as a psychoanalyst and was fascinated by children's development. He firmly believed in the influence of early years and was a popular broadcaster and writer for the general public and affirmed that the ordinary "going on being" of mothering was necessary to provide "good enough" mothering.
3 The feelings we had to our caregivers get carried over to other people and sometimes to organisations which reside in bricks and mortar buildings which then can distort our perceptions of such places. Henri Rey (1912–2000), a psychiatrist and psychoanalyst, coined the phrase "brick mother" when he was working in the Maudsley hospital and noticing how important it was for some patients to felt held in a place of refuge by the building.
4 Bats find their way at night by sending out high frequency pulses of sound. These bounce off the solid objects in the environment and gather together to build up a map of "sound reflections" in a highly sophisticated process, thus allowing the bat to orientate itself even in absolute darkness. This is called echolocation.

References

Astor, J. (1995). *Michael Fordham: Innovations in Analytical Psychology*. London: Routledge.
Bion, W. R. (1962). *Learning from Experience*. New York: Basic Books.
Bion, W. R. (1970). *Attention and Interpretation*. London: Tavistock Publications.
Bowlby, J. (1980). *Attachment and Loss*. London: Hogarth.
Colman, W. (1995). Marriage as a Psychological Container. In S. Ruszczynski (ed.), *Psychotherapy with Couples*. London: Routledge.
Colman, W. (2014). The intolerable other: The difficulty of becoming a couple. *Couple and Family Psychoanalysis*, 4(1), 22–41.
Ford, T. (1607). *Musicke of Sundrie Kindes*. London: Stainer & Bell.
Fordham, M. (1957). *New Developments in Analytical Psychology*. London: Routledge.
Fordham, M. (1989). The infant's reach. *Psychological Perspective*, 21, 59–76.
Jung, C. G. (1917). The Problem of the Attitude Type. *CW 7. The First Complete English Edition of the Works of C. G. Jung*. London: Routledge.

Jung, C. G. (1930–1934). In *Visions: Notes of the Seminar Given in 1930–1934 by C. G. Jung (Jung Seminars)* Claire Douglas (ed.). London: Taylor and Francis.

Jung, C. G. (1931). Marriage as a Psychological Relationship. *CW 17*.

Jung, C. G. (1933). Psychological Theory of Types. In *Modern Man in Search of a Soul*. London: Kegan Paul, Trench, Trubner and Co.

Jung, C. G. (1934–1939). *Nietzsche's Zarathustra: Notes on the Seminar Given in 1934–1939*. London: Routledge.

Jung, C. G. (1938/1954). The Psychological Aspects of the Mother Archetype. *CW 9* (i).

Jung, C. G. (1946). The Psychology of the Transference. *CW 16*.

Jung, C. G. (1948). A Review of the Complex Theory. *CW 8*.

Jung, C. G. (1951). Aion. *CW 9* (ii).

Mattinson, J. & Sinclair, I. (1979). *Mate and Stalemate*. London: Blackwell.

Milne, A. A. (1924). *When We Were Very Young*. London: Methuen & Co. Ltd.

Ovid (8 AD). *Metamorphoses*. London: Penguin Classics

Redfearn, J. W. T. (1985). *My Self, My Many Selves*. London: Academic Press.

Sendak, M. (1963). *Where the Wild Things Are*. New York: Harper and Row.

Shakespeare, W. (1993). *As You Like It*. W. J. Craig (ed.). London: Parragon (Original work written 1599).

Winnicott, D. W. (1973). *The Child, the Family, and the Outside World*. London: Penguin.

Chapter 7

The Shadow of Darkness, the Shadow of Light

Perspectives on the Shadow Through Social Dreaming

Laurie Slade

In November 2021, I dreamt:

> In a drawer, two young black children we are looking for are found to have been hidden. This is a relief. But when the drawer is pulled out further, row upon row of dead bodies is laid out – all neatly dressed and for some reason not decomposing or smelling. It is not clear who is responsible for this atrocity, which leaves me and everyone shocked.

> Later, there is discussion about reversing a financial exchange where the original currency has increased in value. I'm shocked again, that a financial value has been put upon this situation. Nothing is being done to investigate the dead bodies, and find out whose they are.

I have found meaning through my dreams for many years. They still have the capacity to surprise and disturb me. Here, the shock is built into the dream.

I don't know who the "we" are. Aspects of myself? Or some wider grouping – economic, cultural, political – which I identify with? And if the bodies are not decomposing, might they be still alive?

The ethnicity of the children is not in doubt. Associations come to me readily, with my birth and upbringing in colonial Kenya, and the heightened consciousness nowadays of white privilege, relative to the disempowerment of black and other ethnic minorities in the United Kingdom, where I have lived for the past 40 years. Reducing the atrocity in the dream to a financial transaction is resonant of the modern materialist mindset, in which "everything has its price". I am reminded that however hard I try to rise above this corrupt value system, I am deeply embedded in it.

Then Trickster energy makes itself felt. I have to laugh. In the dream "it's not clear who is responsible". But I am the dreamer, so clearly I'm responsible! The impulse to put the blame on some nameless party is a giveaway. I have been confronted with my Shadow – something "repressed or neglected or unknown", which Jung suggested our dreams throw up for us

DOI: 10.4324/9781003255819-9

to compensate for the deficiencies of our conscious attitudes (Jung 1985, para. 483, p. 36). Or maybe I have been confronted with the Shadow in me.

What's the difference?

"My Shadow" emphasises the personal dimension of this dream. It has given me a jolt – told me I have work to do on myself. Perhaps this reflects my need – and wish – to continue rooting out the racist tendencies engrained in me through the circumstances of my birth, and the myths of white superiority which I was brought up with, compounded by the advantages these have given me through much of my life. Is the dream laying bare the destructive effects of this way of being? Or is that too obvious? Jung emphasised we should not be too quick to assume we have identified the import of a dream (ibid., para. 533, p. 69). Perhaps the dream is pointing to a more internal dynamic in my psyche, to abuses I have been perpetrating on myself. There's a way to go, down this avenue.

Whereas "the Shadow in me" suggests the dream may not be just about me. Am I tapping into something beyond me? That's not a denial of my responsibility for the dream or for the issues it raises, at a personal level. But it opens up wider possibilities, in terms of where I go with it. I take my dream to a social dreaming matrix.

The Maryon Muse Matrix

I belong to a small group of social dreaming practitioners, who used to meet at a house in Maryon Mews in Hampstead. The first Covid lockdown, in March 2020, forced us to go online. We quickly realised we wanted to make this a monthly meeting, and have named this virtual space of ours "Maryon Muse".

Social dreaming is a practice which involves the sharing of dreams and associations, making connections where possible. We don't try to interpret a dream for the dreamer, or to arrive at any consensus on the significance of the dreams we share. Instead, a dynamic network of images, feelings and thoughts evolves, with multiple meanings and increasing depth, providing fertile ground for new thinking.

What's the point? It depends on the context. For a working group in an organisation, the matrix may facilitate creative development. Elsewhere, it's a tool for research. With artists, it may stimulate new work. At conferences, a matrix may illuminate what is not being talked about, bringing emotional colour and complexity to complement the presentations of the speakers. With a mutual support group such as ours, the sharing of dreams without objectifying, analysing or judging them seems almost an end in itself, enabling us to experience intimacy and connection in a time of heightened anxiety and isolation.

I share my dream. Others run with the images. Someone shares their similar dream, about mass graves. Associations are made with the recent distressing news of young migrants, drowned while trying to cross the English Channel, and of a child brutally murdered by parental carers. I sense a more pervasive, toxic and potentially overwhelming distress than my dream alone could encompass. I'm not alone in this. Julianna Vamos, a participant, comments later:

> From dead bodies to war cemeteries, deserted and wet streets, we were one after another coming up with very dark shadows over our heads and in our dreams.
>
> (Vamos 2022 – quoted with permission)

The matrix gives us a container, a safe-enough space, to engage with these Shadows in the collective. Again, I'm not alone with this thought:

> The fact that you described your experience as being different from when you were alone with it and when you told it in the matrix, showed me (because I am discovering the whole matrix scene) how our listening and associations created the envelope ... a community holding hands, observing the world and thinking about it'.
>
> (ibid.,)

It's our last meeting in 2021. As we face the coming year, the prospects look bleak – socially, pandemically, politically, economically, ecologically. Then Trickster pops up again. Sometimes, in the darkest places, the Shadow holds the light. I share my memory of a sketch from the 1960s satirical show *Beyond the Fringe*. A group of comedians are on a mountain-top, facing the imminent end of the world. The countdown begins, the suspense mounts, the moment comes – and nothing happens. The message goes out: same time tomorrow! We end with a laugh, agreeing on the date of our next meeting.

The Personal and the Collective

The matrix amplifies my dream. But the connections do not stop. Later, while preparing to write this piece, I revisit a passage from Jung's autobiography – *Memories, Dreams, Reflections*. The resonance with my dream and the matrix feels uncanny.

Jung describes a period of inner disturbance, from late 1912 onwards:

> One fantasy kept returning; there was something dead, but it was also still alive. For example, corpses were placed in crematory ovens, but were then discovered to be alive.
>
> (Jung 1983, p. 196)

Eventually, this fantasy found fuller expression in a dream. Jung saw a row of tombs, stone slabs, each with a body lying on it, coming from further and further back in history. The last figure was a 12th-century crusader with clasped hands:

> For a long time I looked at him and thought he was really dead. But suddenly I saw that a finger of his left hand was beginning to stir gently.
>
> (ibid., pp. 196–197)

The disturbance persisted. Jung thought of it as a disturbance within himself, until late in 1913, when he felt a shift – "as though there were something in the air" (Ibid., p. 199). He began to experience apocalyptic dreams and visions, of massive floods – "the drowned bodies of uncounted thousands" (Ibid., p. 199) – and these continued into 1914 with repetitive dreams of a deadly ice age descending on Europe. Then, in August 1914, World War I was declared. Jung felt he had intuitively sensed the approach of this catastrophe:

> Now my task was clear: I had to try to understand what had happened and to what extent my own experience coincided with that of mankind in general.
>
> (ibid., p. 200)

Did my dream and the Maryon Muse matrix indicate the approach of something equally cataclysmic? Or were we simply sharing our end-of-year blues? Time will tell. Meanwhile, Jung's commitment to exploring this interface between the personal and the collective remains inspirational – as it was for W. Gordon Lawrence, who formulated the practice of social dreaming in the 1980s.[1]

The Social Dimension of Dreams

The basic idea with social dreaming is that our dreams may speak of the social realities we are embedded in – as families, as groups, as communities, as cultures, as humanity, as denizens of this planet – much as they speak of the inner life of a dreamer.

This idea would come as no surprise in any of the indigenous dream cultures of the world – whether historic or contemporary – in Africa, Asia, Oceania, in North and Central and South America. But in our contemporary Western culture, I find surprisingly strong resistance to the idea that our dreams can have a social dimension. It seems to come up against an assumption that is deeply entrenched – that dreams are essentially about the dreamer (to the extent that they are granted any significance at all).

In the Shadow of this Western mindset – I suggest – lies a tendency to privilege the insular psyche of the individual, dismissing as primitive groupthink, the inter-connected psyches manifestly involved in traditional practices of dream-sharing. It is we who are out of step. Robin Sheriff, co-editor of *New Directions in the Anthropology of Dreaming*, observes

> Recent work confirms that contemporary hegemonic Western ontologies are virtually alone in their (historically recent) assumption that dreaming is a purely intra-psychic phenomenon'.
>
> (Sheriff 2021, p. 37)

And for those who maintain this singularity of ours is in some way superior:

> Local dream-related ontologies, rather than simply being an object of anthropological analysis, offer, in many cases, more perspicacious conceptualizations of dreaming than are found in western science.
>
> (ibid.,)

Clearly, we have much to learn. *New Directions* gives us papers on the dream cultures of the Asabano in Papua New Guinea, the Tzotzil Maya in Mexico, Muslim dreamers in Egypt, and Tibetan dream yoga, along with research on dream work in contemporary Europe and the United States, and an illuminating survey of the history of Western anthropologies of dreaming. Sheriff's co-editor, Jeanette Mageo, argues that the collection as a whole shows how:

> Dreaming does similar work for us collectively as it does for people individually, helping people to learn, remember and change by integrating daily experience within larger cultural structures that may falter in a particular life confrontation or historical moment – particularly, perhaps, this new global historical moment.
>
> (Mageo 2021, p. 7)

Faltering cultural structures, in a particular historical moment – such thoughts bring to mind the Maryon Muse matrix. Social dreaming, as Lawrence conceived it, is a distinct practice with a particular focus, but I suggest its roots lie in these ancient traditions through which dreams have been shared meaningfully in the community for centuries.

The Shadow of the Holocaust

Jung's fantasy of something dead but still alive comes back to me, as it did to him. His imagery of mass cremations seems to have anticipated not just World War I, but also what would follow, culminating in World War II. His dream of the effigy on a crusader tomb, with a finger that stirs gently, reminds me of the harrowing movie *Son of Saul* (Nemes, 2015).

Saul is a Jewish-Hungarian *sonderkommando*, working in the crematoria of Auschwitz-Birkenau. Clearing corpses from the gas chamber, he sees the body of a young boy begin to move. The boy is swiftly despatched by the Nazis, but Saul becomes obsessed with the idea that this was his son, and he must give the boy a proper burial.

When Death walks unashamedly in plain sight, the Shadow may hold the opposite. The brief flicker of life which he witnesses in the boy puts Saul in touch with his own lost liveliness. His heroic attempt to honour the boy then becomes the story of his own redemption, as he reclaims his entitlement to exist through meaningful action.

Dreamers in Nazi Germany were no less alert than Jung to what was looming. In their case, when a pretence of normality in waking life was a pre-condition for survival, the Shadow emerged in their dreams, speaking to the situation with uncompromising truth.

We know this through the work of Charlotte Beradt, a journalist who was living in Germany in the 1930s. Beradt collected notes on the dreams of ordinary people, more than 300 people altogether, and took these with her, hidden in the spines of books, when she escaped from Germany in 1939. Almost 30 years later, she published this material in *The Third Reich of Dreams*.

The opening pages set the tone:

> Three days after Hitler seized power in Germany, a certain Herr S, a man of about sixty and owner of a middle-sized factory, dreamed he had been crushed, even though no one had actually laid a hand on him …
>
> (Beradt 1966, p. 5)

Herr S's dream involved a humiliating encounter with Goebbels, Hitler's notorious Minister of Propaganda. Herr S struggles to give Goebbels a Nazi salute, which Goebbels rejects, saying "I don't want your salute":

> 'This dream haunted the manufacturer and recurred again and again, each time with new humiliating details. "The effort of lifting my arm was so great that sweat poured down my face like tears …"
>
> On one occasion his dream imagery was devastatingly clear … while struggling to lift his arm, (Herr S's) back – his backbone – breaks'.
>
> (ibid., pp. 5–8)

I'm left wondering, what difference would it have made for Herr S, if there had been a Maryon Muse matrix for him to share his dreams in – for him to realise (as Beradt goes on to demonstrate) that he was not dreaming alone?

Our dream authors, the soon to be totally subjected whose dreams are recorded here, saw it all with greater clarity, "in a dream, a vision of the night."

(ibid., p. 18)

Shadows from the Holocaust

Beradt's book was another major inspiration for Lawrence, in the conception of social dreaming. Perhaps it's no coincidence that the matrix has proved helpful for those struggling with Shadows from the Holocaust, whether through transgenerational suffering or political strife.

Studies have demonstrated the significant influence of the Holocaust on the intractable nature of the Israeli-Palestinian conflict (Levanon 2021). A compelling illustration of what social dreaming can bring to this situation comes from Hanna Biran's paper, "The dreaming soldier" (Biran 2007). Biran describes a collaborative project she led with artist Wolf Werdigier, in the context of an exhibition by Werdigier, which explored how Israelis and Palestinians saw each other. Sessions were held in Jerusalem, with equally mixed Israeli/Palestinian participation, in Tel Aviv, with mostly Israelis, and in Ramallah, with solely Palestinians.

Perhaps surprisingly, certainly movingly, what emerged through the matrix was not the demonisation by each side of the other, the anger and hatred so often constellated in political discourse, but an expression of shared grief and common humanity:

> The dream crosses cultures and reinforces the feeling of a common fate, intimacy and empathy. The "other" seems like a person, like me, with similar fears, desires and pain.

(ibid., pp. 44–45)

Recently, I have been involved in a small project of a similar nature, working with artist Daria Martin. Daria's grandmother Susi was a Holocaust refugee, an artist herself, and an inspirational figure for Daria. She also recorded her dreams, in detail, over many years. Following Susi's death, Daria has been using this massive legacy of dreams as an inspiration for her work.

I met Daria when her installation *Tonight the World* (Martin 2019) was at the Barbican Centre in London. Daria presented five dreams of Susi's, which she had staged and filmed in Brno, where Susi grew up. The pervasive mood was of anxiety, intrusion, alienation and grief – in and around the ancestral home.

I was asked by the Barbican to host three sessions of social dreaming in the exhibition space (jointly with Catherine Cox). These were well-attended and well-received. Daria later approached me to discuss how social dreaming might contribute to the development of a new piece, again based on a dream from Susi's archive – *Nostalgia Ranch* (Martin 2022a).

The mood of this movie was to be different, evoking resilience, a love of life. It would also evoke the next generation, so Daria wanted to engage with others whose families were scarred by the Holocaust. She admits this was partly selfish, in terms of what she hoped to gain from the experience, but she hoped others would gain from it too.

Daria and I worked with Alessandro Bucci, Director at the Holocaust Survivors' Friendship Association in Huddersfield. We developed a programme spread over three sessions. In the first, we would convene the group. Each participant would be invited to share an object associated with their family's Holocaust history and given space to tell a story relating to that object. In the second session, on the following day, we would move to a matrix with space afterwards to reflect on possible links between the material that came up and the objects that had previously been shared. Three weeks later, in the third session, participants would have the opportunity for an individual conversation with Daria, and then to join a gathering of the whole group, to see how everyone was getting on. All participants would be asked to consent to any use Daria proposed to make of material generated in this way and given a veto in respect of anything they felt sensitive about.

We offered these sessions online, in July/August 2021, as Covid still prevented our meeting in person. This meant we could bring in participants from North America and Australia as well as locally from the United Kingdom. It was a small but committed group.

One participant was a friend of mine, Andrew Gellert, whose family suffered horrific losses in the Holocaust – including an uncle, Andrej, known as Bandi, who perished in Auschwitz, and whom Andrew is named after. During the many years of my friendship with Andrew, I have witnessed the burden of transgenerational trauma which he carries; so I was immensely glad he chose to join us. I can share a vignette of his experience of our sessions, from a transcript of the matrix and Andrew's notes (with permission).

The object Andrew brought was a pair of green exit visas issued by the Gestapo. These had enabled Andrew's parents and his infant sister to escape from Czechoslovakia and travel to Kenya in 1939 where Andrew was later born. He went on to share a dream in the matrix. To summarise:

> He was in a small room in his childhood home with a large, locked mahogany cupboard. His nephew showed him where to find the keys needed to open it. They found a secret compartment which Andrew never knew existed. He felt he had missed out, not knowing about these secrets.

Andrew linked the discovery of this secret compartment in his dream with his having found the exit visas after his father died. A further connection was still to come. In our third session – after the matrix, his session with Daria, and through his own reflection – Andrew shared where he had got to:

My uncle Bandi was a wonderful jazz pianist and partly in his memory, my father arranged for me to begin piano lessons when I was 4. Playing the piano remains my soul's chief joy.

When he was alive, Bandi used to visit relatives in the Slovak village of Betlanovce, where (a surviving cousin told me) he would regularly play their grand piano. In the late 1990s I was travelling with family to visit our hometown of Presov. On the way we stopped in Betlanovce. We found the house our relatives had lived in but the piano was no longer there. But villagers knew where it was. We were taken to a small house off the main street. The owners were away but the villagers knew where the key was kept. Just as in my dream, the key unlocked the door and thus the treasure within. Just inside the front door, and to the left, stood the walnut, mid 19th century, Viennese, gold medallion grand piano. Some ivories were missing, it was out of tune, but the tears flowed as my fingers played the same keys that Bandi had played in the 1930s. The same hammers and strings once again sang with the touch of a Gellert family member. What a treasure to unlock …

So, apart from the experience of sustaining one another and sharing our traumatic stories, exploring inherited memory through the social dreaming matrix was especially poignant for me … I am certain I would never have made the connection between that precious memory of playing Bandi's piano and the dream, if not for attending this workshop'.

(Gellert 2021)

I am reminded of Otto Kernberg's realisation, that mourning our lost loved-ones is not just about grief and letting them go; we can re-connect with them as living presences within ourselves (Kernberg 2010).

Daria feels this impulse to re-connect was a pervading theme in our sessions. I quote from her notes (with permission):

Something that strongly emerged was the longing several participants felt for the (European, Jewish) culture that was lost when their forebears migrated. Some learned the old language; others visited artefacts of music or painting that belonged to ancestors. Several were themselves artistic practitioners. It moved me to realise that all of us were perhaps creatively attempting to revive a vibrant cultural life that had been lost. It seems fitting, then, that we should explore that creativity not only as individuals, but collectively – a little microcosm, a seed of a new culture.

(Martin 2022b)

Images that came up have been incorporated in a beautiful song on the soundtrack of the movie, and Daria speaks of other ways in which our sessions affected her work:

> After reviewing raw footage of the film, I realised that an unconscious theme had emerged in the imagery of "carrying" … Among the cast, we had conversations about transgenerational trauma, which is something one carries unconsciously. Here, I felt that each cast member had lifted some of that "baggage" from my shoulders and transformed it into something else. Similarly, the collective process of Social Dreaming allowed a sharing – of hope but also of fear and other feelings – across the group. One group member showed up wearing his (survivor) grandfather's shirt. A similar shirt showed up later in my film. It was as if we were trying on one another's stories. By playing with these histories and images, we made them lighter. That is not to say we "made light" of the histories …
>
> (ibid.,)

The Shadow of Social Dreaming

Such affirming responses might tempt me to idealise the matrix. Where's the Shadow of social dreaming?

A host is meant to facilitate the matrix, not direct it. But George Taxidis maintains that issues of power remain inescapable around the hosting function. It may be difficult for a host to avoid imposing their views and projecting their personal bias, in the matrix or when writing it up (Taxidis 2020).

Other Shadows lurk. The clear focus of the task in the matrix means group dynamics tend not to be addressed there. But Mira Erlich-Ginor suggests they can still affect the choices participants make, such as whether or not they share a dream (Erlich-Ginor 2003, p. 160). And around the margins of the matrix, group dynamics can surface unavoidably. This might be in the reflective space we move into after the matrix to begin processing our experience. Where the function of hosting is shared by a team, there may be unacknowledged tensions between members of the team. Or the internal conflict of a team member may cast a Shadow, as happened once with me.

I met George Taxidis at a matrix in 2015. We discovered we were both keen to start an ongoing matrix for LGBTQIA+ participants. In 2016, we opened a Queer matrix at London Friend near Kings Cross. Our gatherings gained traction. Bi-monthly meetings became monthly. kitt price, a participant, caught the mood:

> I can only speak from my own experience, in which creating a matrix from our dreams has the feeling of coming home., the bridge from

dreaming to waking takes on a completely new aspect in this particular setting. I can feel the image fragments taking on "the feather and muscle of wings" as the speaker and her interlocutor find love can have in Eavan Boland's poem "Love".

(price, 2017)

In due course, George and I invited two others to join us, making a team of hosts so that we could work with a rota. Things moved forward but differences began emerging between us over what we wanted for the project.

My crisis came at a team meeting in February 2020, by which time we were also welcoming two more members. I felt isolated in my view on many of the issues before us. In particular, the rest of the team felt it was inappropriate in future for cis-gendered white gay men to host the matrix together. They wanted the matrix to be visibly more welcoming for people less privileged in the Queer community. I understood the moral imperative in this proposal but was concerned that the new rule would not apply to other identity pairings. I felt this would put cis-gendered white gay men (I'm one) in a separate and lesser category in the matrix, when they too might come as individuals in need of refuge. I struggled to express myself, overtaken by my strength of feeling. Was this simply my discomfort over the prospect of losing my privileged position in a queer context? It felt other than that. With hindsight, I'd say we were grappling with an issue anticipated by price, 3 years earlier:

> Listening to the matrix, I wonder who here and not-yet-here might feel they belong, or not.

(ibid.,)

As I left the meeting, I had a traumatic flashback. In my mid-20s, I was working in a theatre as an Assistant Stage Manager. One of my tasks was to go round the dressing rooms before the show, checking the actors had their props. One day, in an all-male dressing-room, an actor said "Why is it that whenever I see you, I want to tear the shirt off you?" I ignored him.

A few days later, when I was there again, the same man suddenly seized me from behind, held me in a tight embrace and pushed his genitals hard against my buttocks. "I've been waiting to do this", he said. I fought my way free and escaped. I was shaken but assumed no harm was done and kept going.

Why did this come back to me? I took it as an indication that I needed to leave the team immediately and told the others. Beyond that? There was no obvious connection between my distressing memory of a sexual assault and my experience in the meeting.

"*It's not clear who is responsible*". Prompted by my dream of November 2021, I now see that memory-flash as a Trickster moment – a confrontation with my Shadow. Beyond our disagreement, at the meeting, what do I take responsibility for?

I kept going after the dressing room incident. I didn't acknowledge its impact on me. Similarly, in my enthusiasm over the launch and over keeping the Queer matrix going, I didn't acknowledge that elsewhere in me, through my participation, a deep need had been triggered. In price's terms, I had begun feeling that I too wanted to come home. For reasons which I can trace back to a time when gay orientation of any kind was far from privileged, I couldn't quite manage it.

Where was the predator in me? A parting of the ways between founders of a project often happens. I could have shared sooner and more explicitly with George and the team my sense that our views were beginning to diverge significantly on how we saw the Queer matrix developing. Why didn't I do so?

I now feel I was projecting onto the team the abusive dynamics of my own internal conflict. I was forcing myself to stay with the Queer matrix, to gratify both my aspirations for it and my longing for validation in that setting, when my deeper instinct was telling me to go.

I suspect my departure was a relief for the team. I'm pleased to say the Queer matrix has continued to flourish. It went online when Covid lockdown started, and now attracts an international following. As I write, it's coming up for its 6th birthday. I'm proud of what George and I brought into being.

And embracing my Shadow in this way has had an unexpected outcome. Since I'm referring to George here, I send him a draft. He suggests we talk. It's the first time we've done so since I left the team. We still have our differences, but his comments are helpful, and we share our grief over the split. It's healing for both of us.

Conclusion

"In dreams begin responsibility".

(Yeats 1916, p. ix)

Taking Yeats at his word, I suggest that the responsibilities which our dreams bring home to us include acknowledging and integrating the Shadow, individually and collectively. Yeats wrestled with this throughout his life, in what he called "the spiritual intellect's great work":

"Nor can there be work so great

As that which cleans man's dirty slate".

(Yeats 1939)

A late poem by Yeats, *The Man and the Echo*, depicts him lying in bed in the small hours – half-dreaming, half-awake – reviewing the unthought consequences of his actions and the refuge he sought in drink and sex and sleep, until what starts as an old man's navel-gazing becomes an existential cry of anguish for suffering in the world.

Social dreaming provides a space for work of this kind, making poets of us all through the imagery and insight of the dreams we share and the process through which we share them. We focus on the dreams, not the dreamers. It's as if a portal opens. What feels intensely personal speaks with surprising intensity to others. In the patterns of meaning which emerge, we may discern what has been "repressed or neglected or unknown", in ourselves and in the world around. The matrix frees us up in our imaginations and creative potential – not just in what we think but in how we think – transforming how we feel about situations we are dealing with, prompting new thoughts as to where we may go next, alone or in concert. And it bonds and heartens us, to have access to the riches of our dreaming minds in community, a timeless resource, always there for us to draw on.

In this time we're living through, we have many Shadows to face. We surely need to muster every resource we've got.

Epilogue

At the first Maryon Muse matrix of 2022, a young girl in green cartwheels irrepressibly through previously empty streets …

Notes

1 See Lawrence (1998) for his account of the inspirations and genesis of social dreaming.
   I gladly acknowledge my debt to Lawrence in Slade (2019).

References

Beradt, C. (1966) *The Third Reich of Dreams*. Chicago: Quadrangle Books.
Biran, H. (2007) "The dreaming soldier". In W. Gordon Lawrence (ed.), *Infinite Possibilities of Social Dreaming*, 29–45. London: Karnac Books.
Erlich-Ginor, M. (2003) "Sliding houses in the promised land: Unstable reality worked through dreams." In W. Gordon Lawrence (ed.), *Experiences in Social Dreaming*, 157–178. London: Karnac Books.
Gellert, A. (2021) Private communication.
Jung, C.G. (1983) *Memories. Dreams, Reflections*. London: Collins and Routledge & Keegan Paul; (1963) Republished London: Fontana/Flamingo imprint.
Jung, C.G. (1985) "General aspects of dream psychology." In Volume 8, Collected Works of C.G.Jung – *The Structure and Dynamics of the Psyche* (1960). New York: Bollingen. Republished London: Routledge/Ark imprint.

Kernberg, O. (2010) "Some observations on the process of mourning." In *International Journal of Psychoanalysis*, 91(2010–3), 601–619.

Lawrence, W.G. (1998) "Won from the void and formless infinite: Experiences of social dreaming." In W. Gordon Lawrence (ed.), *Social Dreaming @ Work*, 9–41. London: Karmac.

Levanon, O.S. (2021) "Under a constant shadow: The Israeli–Palestinian conflict and the traumatic memory of the Holocaust." In *Peace and Conflict: Journal of Peace Psychology*, 27(1), 58–66.

Mageo, J. (2021) "Defining new directions in the anthropology of dreaming." In Jeanette Mageo and Robin E. Sheriff (eds.), *New Directions in the Anthropology of Dreaming*, 3–22. London and New York: Routledge.

Martin, D. (2019) *Tonight the World* (anamorphic 16-mm film, 35 min).

Martin, D. (2022a) *Nostalgia Ranch* (anamorphic 16-mm film, 8 min).

Martin, D. (2022b) Private communication.

Nemes, L. (2015) *Son of Saul* (motion picture). Camera Film.

price, k. (2017) "Queer social dreaming matrix." In *Studies in Gender and Sexuality*, 2017, 18(1), 86–87.

Sheriff, R.E. (2021) "The anthropology of dreaming in historical perspective." In Jeanette Mageo and Robin E. Sheriff (eds.), *New Directions in the Anthropology of Dreaming*, 23–49. London and New York: Routledge.

Slade, L. (2019) "Renewing the land: The dreaming mind in community." In Susan Long and Julian Manley (eds.), *Social Dreaming: Philosophy, Research, Theory and Practice*, 55–68. Oxford: Routledge.

Taxidis, G. (2020) Review of Susan Long and Julian Manley (eds.), "Social Dreaming: Philosophy, Research, Theory and Practice". In *Transformations – Newsletter of Psychotherapists and Counsellors for Social Responsibility*, Winter 2020 Issue. https://www.pcsr.org.uk

Vamos, J. (2022) Private communication.

Yeats, W.B. (1916) *Responsibilities and Other Poems*. New York: The Macmillan Company.

Yeats, W.B. (1939) "The Man and the Echo." In *W.B Yeats: Poems selected by Seamus Heaney*, S. Heaney (ed.) (2000). London: Faber & Faber.

Chapter 8

The Shadow of Whiteness[1]

Helen Morgan

Introduction

The concept of "Whiteness" as applied to humans is full of paradox and contradiction. We human beings come in all colours from very pale to very dark and most shades of pink, yellow and brown in between. Yet no one, not even the fairest of us, is actually white just as no one is actually black. The binary division between "white" and "black", emerging as it did in the modern era, is both crude and cruel and has divided humanity; in the service of domination, colonialism, slavery and capitalism, it ensured white supremacy.

It is generally accepted that this division came about for political and economic advantage, recorded first in 17th-century Virginia when the first Africans were forcibly brought on slave ships to work the plantations. To prevent the indentured European labour force – mostly Irish and Southern European – from finding common cause with the enslaved Africans, the term "white" was used; transforming the masters, plantation owners and European labourers into one exclusive group. Through a set of laws that privileged whites alone, any class solidarity with the so-called "blacks" was disrupted ensuring that power remained in the hands of the ruling elite.

As Joel Kovel (1988) puts it:

> ... the world is neither black nor white, but hued. A lightly-hued people – aided perhaps by fantasies derived from their skin color – came to dominate the entire world, and in the process defined themselves as white. The process that generated this white power also generated the fear and dread of the black (p. 95).

The Shadow of Whiteness

Bringing all those with lighter-hued skin within the umbrella term "white" allowed the illusion of common privilege but also tapped into our unconscious representations of "white". Such associations are based in the

DOI: 10.4324/9781003255819-10

nature of our bodies and the daily rhythms of our planet. Mother's nourishing milk and father's productive sperm are white. White is associated with daytime, the dove of peace and the pure soul, whereas black belongs to the dark terrors of night, to war and sin. Whereas whiteness clothes the angels, devils inhabit the blackness of Hell. Link those with a lighter hue of skin to "whiteness" and the others to "blackness" and much of the psychological work of justifying domination is done.

The essential element of "white" as a colour (or non-colour) is it can carry no shadow. Whiteness excludes the dark and the damaged so that any stain contaminates its innocence. Once a drop of colour or darkness is added to it, it is no longer white but stained or grey. White symbolises the "pure" the "spiritual" and the "innocent" and, as James Hillman (1986) points out, *"Innocence excludes. 'Innocent' literally denotes an absence of noxiousness; without harm or hurt ..."* (p. 34).

He goes on to conclude: *"Black becomes necessary to whiteness as that co-relative by means of which white takes on its defensive, exclusive definition as im-maculate, un-polluted, in-nocent"* (p. 34). Thus, that which *is* noxious and harmful, damaged and damaging – indeed all that might be included in the notion of "Shadow" – cannot, by definition, be included under the umbrella of "whiteness". "Blackness" is required, therefore, to contain all that is rejected by "whiteness" – the impure, the polluted, the noxious, the profane.

Europeans with fair skin, wishing to conquer and rule indigenous peoples of a darker hue, hitched their paleness to the purity and innocence of the colour white. By doing so the unacceptable, unconscious of the white shadow had to be rejected and projected into those who were now deemed to be "black". Thus, the "blackened" indigenous inhabitants of conquered territories were regarded at best as child-like and ignorant with no culture of their own, or "savage" and dangerous. Either way these so-called "primitive" peoples required the "civilising" influences of the Christian Europeans.

Even before the black/white binary emerged in the modern era, the nature of that European Christianity contained within it the justification – indeed the requirement – of domination. Celia Brickman (2018) notes that:

> When Columbus set sail for the Indies and found himself instead in the New Worlds, already in place were two distinct frameworks for comprehending outsiders. The first was a medieval literary and popular discourse about outsiders as barbarians, wild men and noble savages, while the second was a religious-legal discourse, consolidated during the Crusades, concerning the treatment of infidels and the lawful right of Christians to the confiscation of uninhabited and non-Christian lands (pp. 19–20).

The "Wild Man" was a frightening object who, unrestrained by "civilised" laws, could give full rein to his passions. The "Noble Savage", on the other hand, still lived in the Garden of Eden and represented a lost paradise of innocence and peace which existed before Europeans were burdened with the demands of civilisation. *"The contrasting images of the Wild Man and the Noble Savage ... contributed to a contradictory discourse which represented non-Europeans as both idealized and depraved, fulfilled in their simplicity yet lacking in their humanity"* (ibid., p. 21).

Already the projective framework of division between the "civilised" European and the "wild" or "savage" "barbarian" was well established not only justifying the colonisation and slavery of the latter by the former, but implying a duty, a responsibility for the Christian to bring their religion, their systems of order and culture to these so-called "primitives".

As Kipling wrote in 1899:

> Take up the White Man's burden –
> Send forth the best ye breed –
> Go bind your sons to exile
> To serve your captives' need;
> To wait in heavy harness
> On fluttered folk and wild –
> Your new-caught sullen peoples,
> Half devil and half child

The transatlantic slave trade began in the 15th century with the Portuguese the main plyers in early explorations. The British entered the trade in 1562 when John Hawkyns sailed from England, captured several hundred Africans off the coast of Sierra Leone and took them to what is now known as the Dominican Republic. He returned with a cargo of ivory, hides and sugar. By the 19th century, Britain dominated the trade.

There are no certain statistics of how many individuals were taken from Africa in the centuries since the first ship set sail from Portugal, but the number is estimated to be well over 10 million, about a quarter of whom were children. This figure does not include the many who died on the journey – estimated to be about three in ten. Deaths were also inflicted in the process of capture as well as through disease brought by the Europeans, and the destruction of the existing economic basis for living. Nor does the number take account of all the generations born into slavery who never knew freedom throughout their entire lifetime.

It seemed to be evident to all in Europe in the 16th to 19th centuries that there were real divisions between "races" based on fixed, immutable factors and fundamental differences within humanity forming a natural hierarchy with black Africans at the bottom and white Europeans at the top. This led to the inevitable conclusion that it was the European's right – indeed their duty – to rule and manage those of "lesser" breed.

Religion, biology, anthropology and other sciences were used to "prove" the reality of this belief. The roots of the need to do so lie less in the values of scientific curiosity, and more in a socio/political/economic pressure which lay behind the search for profit and slaves in Africa, Asia and the Americas.

For white Christians, the Bible story that justified colonisation and the slave trade and placed the blame on Africans for their plight, was that of Noah's son Ham who, failing to cover his eyes, saw his father naked and drunk. As a punishment he and his descendants were cursed by Noah and thus were all future generations of Ham's line condemned to serve the children of the "good son" Japheth.

As Farhad Dalal (2002) points out:

> What is crucial to this story is the name Ham. Ham is a vulgarization of Cham. In Hebrew *ch'm* means black, hot, burnt, dark … This linkage allows the story to be used as giving Biblical authority for 19th century slavery: to be black is to be cursed to be a servant (p. 142).

I came across an alternative, African narrative (Boyd 1991) on the origins of difference: "All men were originally black. But when Cain killed his brother, Abel, and God shouted at him, Cain was so frightened that he turned white and his features shrunk up, making him the first white man" (p. 15).

Perhaps this tale of fratricide, murder, God's wrath and Cain's guilt offers a more fitting metaphor for what white Christian Europeans have done to people of colour down the centuries. It refers to a darkness behind the very conception of the notion of whiteness as applied to humans. For looking back, albeit with a different moral emphasis and with our modern concept of human rights, the tragic irony is that what was done in the colonised territories in the name of "civilisation" and "whiteness" is where we find barbarism and savagery and some of the most egregious aspects of the human Shadow.

The Shadow of Whiteness Today

Michael Vannoy Adams (1996) argues that those who are identified as having black skin serve for those who see themselves as white:

> … as a convenient objective correlative – an object relation that is, in effect, not so much an object representation as an object mis-representation, because it is really a self-representation … The alien is the other within the self – that 'inner other' from which the self is most alienated, that stranger from which the self is most estranged (p. 136).

As Frantz Fanon (1986) puts it:

> Satan is black, one talks of shadows, when one is dirty one is black – whether one is thinking of physical dirtiness or of moral dirtiness. It would be astonishing if the trouble were taken to bring them all together, to see the vast number of expressions that make the black man the equivalent of sin (p. 189).

When a light shines upon an object, the details and intricacies of its appearance are illuminated and brought into focus. We can see its features and specific characteristics. A shadow is cast from the base of the object, its darkness dependent on the nature of the light that shines. What we see is a flattened two-dimensional shadow, an outline of the object casting the shadow, but no detail. Just undifferentiated darkness.

When Shadow aspects of the self are projected onto the other in the dynamic of racism, the person "casting" the shadow is allowed a three-dimensional complexity and richness of personal detail which affords them a sense of identity and individuality. The racialised "other" however, is de-personalised and flattened into a grouping where individual character is indistinguishable and made invisible. What is seen by others is the skin colour only, rendering invisible the idea of an individual with an internal life. The implication for the black individual on the receiving end of this dehumanising blanketing is psychologically damaging and disturbing as Fakhry Davids (2011) vividly describes:

> To be black in a white world is an agony. This is because the white world is racist – if you are black, you are seldom allowed to be an ordinary, regular human being. Instead, at every turn you are confronted by hidden stereotypes that can spring to life in a flash, push violently into you, destabilize you and make you think, feel and act in ways that are wholly determined from the outside, as if you yourself had no say in the matter. This can turn even the most innocuous of situations utterly fraught (p. 1).

The Shadow of the White Liberal

From the evidence that has emerged from the analysis of DNA, it is now clear that the term "race" is a constructed concept with no objective basis in biology. The division of the races, created for economic and political purposes, is a deep, entrenched, social structure which creates and promotes white privilege and is one within which we all live. No one can be free from it. The statement "I am not a racist" is meaningless in such a system.

The racist self is an ugly creature and one to which the white liberal wishes to give no house room. This ugliness has expression in such gatherings as white supremacist groups in Europe and the USA and in actions such as genocide, apartheid, etc. where extreme forms of overt racist attack, slavery and exploitation does untold harm to the black "Other" who is the recipient of the evacuation of the hated parts of the racist and who then is hated and attacked. However, the existence of these overtly racist groups may, in themselves, provide a container into which the white liberal can project our racist Shadow. Thus, those of us who do not engage in such extreme acts of hatred and who abhor such groups can retreat to a fairly comfortable position of disassociating ourselves from the whole process. This is denial and another sort of defence – a defence against something ugly we fear in ourselves. Whilst extreme forms of overt racism may be publicly denounced by the liberal white individual, the internal racist will express itself in more covert and subtle ways.

An awareness of the deeply embedded aspect of the racist structure is essential if we are to get anywhere with understanding and changing it. We have *all* been racialised by this system. However, the systemic aspect of the creation and perpetuation of "whiteness" tends to be rejected by its participants. Linda Alcoff (2015) writes: "Whiteness is lived and not merely represented. It is a prominent feature of one's way of being in the world, of how one navigates that world, and of how one is navigated around by others" (p. 9). She goes on to suggest that we tend to reject group concepts in order to maintain the idea that we have control over our identity. She writes:

Being identified in a way that lies beyond our individual control conflicts with individualist ideas, and illusions, about our autonomy. The real concern with race may be less the faulty presumptions about genetic difference than the fact that this is a social fact about us, with social meanings and implications over which we have limited agency. People of colour have largely come to accept this; for whites, the forcible interpellations of their racial identity are more often a new experience (p. 21).

As Adrienne Harris (2012) puts it:

To turn to a deconstruction of whiteness is to make the unremarkable remarkable, to force unexamined assumptions, to open up a set of questions. The goal, of course, is to see whiteness as a social construction, to see that whiteness is the unmarked category and in that particular way accrues and hoards power. (p. 200)

This refusal to see whiteness as a social construction which we inhabit allows us to divide the white world between those who are deemed to be racist and those who are not. The fact that there are overt white supremacists in the world provides a container for the projection of the Shadow of white liberals who can then separate ourselves from the racist system, deny or minimise our own racist thoughts and actions and thus preserving a sense of ourselves as good.

Learning Whiteness

The evidence from recent research carried out in the USA and in Europe suggests that a child born into a Western society recognises racial differences and the advantages of being born with a white skin. The white child sees many people who look like them and their family members on TV, in films, adverts, etc., enforcing the idea that "whiteness" is the norm. As opposed to those who are children of avowed white supremacists, the children in a white liberal household are unlikely to hear anything explicit or overt about superiority/inferiority, yet they will be taking on a sense of privilege that comes with their skin colour. They will also be learning this is a subject not to be discussed.

Van Ausdale and Feagin (2001) studied 3- to 6-year olds in an American nursery school and found that children learnt to identify racial and ethnic markers and use them to gain social control, although these activities were restrained when adults were present. When they presented their findings to the white adults concerned they experienced some hostility. They say: "When most adults are confronted with evidence that three-year-olds are masters at managing racial-ethnic relations, they often become disturbed, try to rationalize the evidence away or dismiss our evidence as unique" (p. 159). They go on to say:

> This failure to acknowledge the importance of racial groups in children's lives arises from the twin adult convictions that children are naïve and that colour blindness is not only desirable but achievable … Frankly put, many white adults insist that racial distinctions do not matter, while all around them children see ample and compelling evidence that they do matter, and matter very much indeed. One practical response to this ideological contradiction by white children is to conceal the creation of their own racial understandings and relationships, at least while the prying eyes of adults are on them. This enables them to reproduce the racial-ethnic hierarchy in their own relationships without interference from adults. (pp. 190–191)

When the child, curious to understand this world into which they have been born, repeats or comments on the differences in power and position they see all around them, they frequently meet discomfort and denial in the white adults around them.

In most other aspects of her or his life, the white child in a modern liberal family can take their curiosity regarding the social milieu they seek to understand and place themselves in to the significant adults in their life. When they raise the matter of differences concerning race and ethnicity and they are responded to with the sterility of a blanket colour-blind position, the lively, engaged presence they had known previously disappears, and they are faced with a blankness, a shutting down and a silencing. The "deadness" evoked by exploring this topic quickly teaches the child it is not welcome for discussion. Their curiosity and developing concern for others, their pre-occupation with the troubled matter of social fairness is shut down and the vertical split of disavowal develops within the psyche.

In *The Work of Whiteness. A Psychoanalytic Perspective,* I discuss how the concept of disavowal operates within the psyche and the collective to maintain *both* white privilege *and* an acceptable view of the self. Whereas the defences such as repression and denial operate as horizontal splits, disavowal develops within the ego when it is faced with two conflicting realities, causing a vertical split.

I suggest this vertical split as it relates to racism is not merely a single line dividing two parts of the psyche with the investment in white privilege and the racist thought on one side, and the condemnation and rejection of racism in the other. On both sides, there remains a capacity for symbolisation which is lacking in certain moments when we are reminded of our racism. The internal psychic structure can be imagined as made up of two vertical layers between which there is a gap, a silent, empty place devoid of symbols in which it is impossible to play or grieve.

In the dead space between the vertical layers of the split of disavowal of the Shadow of whiteness, symbolisation and therefore the capacity to play and to mourn are suspended. The hole is patched over with the response that "we are all equal, all the same" – an assertion the child knows is untrue. The message is conveyed that it is the *recognition* of difference that is the cause of racism rather than the fact that the child has been born into a social system that discriminates against certain groups; they need help to acknowledge, understand and begin to think through how they might respond to this.

The Shadow of Psychoanalysis

Born at the end of the 19th century when Europe dominated much of the world and the trade in African slaves had not long been abolished, psy-choanalysis, with its key concepts of the unconscious, the id, infantile sex-uality, etc., placed the "heart of darkness" deep within the psyche of all humans, including the coloniser. In so doing, Freud potentially challenged the accepted division between the "civilised" white European and the so-called "primitive" indigenous populations.

On the one hand, by demonstrating the tenuousness of the power of the rational ego, it subverts the European Enlightenment view with its emphasis on science, rationality and control. Such a view legitimised binary, oppositional thinking which became incorporated into the structuring of the social and political system, heralding an alienation from the natural world.

On the other hand, as Hillman (1986) points out:

> The convention informing geographical discoveries and the expansion of white consciousness over Africa continues to inform psychic geography. The topological language used by Freud for 'the unconscious' as a place below, different, timeless, primordial, libidinal and separated from consciousness, recapitulates what white reporters centuries earlier said about West Africa ... Part of psychology's myth is that the unconscious was 'discovered' as its contents are 'explored'. Even the notion of the underworld as black rather than grayish, misty or invisible bespeaks white supremacy.

> Moreover, the 'discovery' of an unconscious separate from consciousness, as a black continent separated from white penetration into it, maintains the very unconsciousness within white which the idea was invented to wound (pp. 45–46).

Both Freud and Jung relied heavily on the early anthropologists, the so-called "armchair titans" of the 19th century, such as Taylor, Haeckel and Lamarck. Taking their theories of human hierarchies, the inheritability of acquired characteristics, the assumption of European "civilisation" and the "barbarism" of the colonised, as well as Haeckel's theory that "ontology recapitulates phylogeny", both men regarded the black "primitive" as representing:

- the early stages of the development of the European,
- the "uncivilised", unrepressed id contents of the Western psyche, and
- the mind of the European infant.

The problematic evolutionary theories of 19th century anthropology are most apparent in Freud's 1913 work, *Totem and Taboo* – a treatise which has since been heavily criticised by modern day anthropologists for its ethnocentrism. For example, Freud (1913) writes:

> There are men still living who, as we believe stand very near to primitive man, far nearer than we do, and whom we therefore regard as his direct heirs and representatives. Such is our view of those whom we describe as savages or half-savages, and their mental life must have a particular interest for us if we are right in seeing in it a well-preserved picture of an early stage of our own development (p. 53).

Jung's equation between the "primitive" black other and the European repressed unconscious, led to his fear that the "civilised" consciousness of the ego was always at risk of being overwhelmed by the "savage". This he believed was a particular danger where white Europeans mix with black Africans such as in colonised Africa and the USA:

> What is more contagious than to live side by side with a rather primitive people? Go to Africa and see what happens. When it is so obvious that you stumble over it, you call it going black … It is much easier for us Europeans to be a trifle immoral, or at least a bit lax, because we do not have to maintain the moral standard against the heavy pull of primitive life. The inferior man has a tremendous pull because he fascinates the inferior layers of our psyche, which has lived through untold ages of similar conditions … He reminds us – or not so much our conscious as our unconscious mind – not only of childhood but of prehistory, which would take us back not more than about twelve hundred years so far as the Germanic races are concerned (1939, CW 10, para. 962).

In her exploration of the relationship between analytical psychology and African Americans, Jungian analyst Fanny Brewster (2013, 2017), whilst arguing for the value of many of Jung's ideas, confronts the racist Shadow in his thinking. She highlights the dubious nature of Jung's research method when he uses the dreams of 15 African Americans at St. Elizabeth's Hospital in Washington, DC to establish the idea of the universality of the collective unconscious whilst failing to take any account of the personal or cultural associations of the dreamers or of his own European cultural bias. The image provided by one dreamer was that of a man being crucified on a wheel which Jung linked to the Greek myth of Ixion. The "fact" of the dreamer being a "very uneducated Negro from the South and not particularly intelligent" (1935, CW18, para 81) who could not have known of the myth of Ixion was taken as crucial evidence of the non-racial, and therefore collective nature of the archetypal image.

Despite his own assertions that the analysis of dreams requires a careful consideration of the personal aspects of the dreamer and their associations to the dream images, despite his stating that the objective psyche can only be known by detailed examination of the context within which the image emerges, it seems that here Jung was shockingly remiss in his research methodology. Neither the name nor any personal details regarding the background of this particular dreamer were recorded. Only the motif of the burning wheel is mentioned, asserting as he did in his 1935 Tavistock lecture that the rest of the dream was irrelevant. The association with Ixion was Jung's and not the dreamer's; indeed, it seems there is no evidence at all of any enquiry into whether this individual had his own associations to the dream image.

As Brewster points out, such associations, together with a deeper understanding of the cultural and historical context of all African Americans, would have produced a more complex picture. The history of slavery in the USA included lynchings which frequently involved burning wheels – a motif of which the dreamer would have been aware. She also notes that even were we to link the dream to the myth of Ixion, the myth is itself a complex one with a number of motifs. One central theme is that of kinship and betrayal which she convincingly argues are themes relevant to the history of slavery in the USA. Such an amplification along the lines of Jung's own proclaimed method might have led to an opening of a far more intricate, more interesting interpretation of the dream. An interpretation which would include both a racial and cultural layer to the understanding of the dream, but also one which might have foregrounded a more positive reading of African American culture than the negative, potentially contaminating perspective that Jung seemed to hold. The fact that Jung used this "evidence" to assert the non-racial aspect of the collective unconscious and, therefore, its universality is troubling.

The adoption of these ideas by Freud and Jung was not inevitable. In the early part of the 20th century, there were those who criticised this way of thinking and offered alternative constructions. For example, as Andrew Samuels (2018) points out, Franz Boas, considered the father of American anthropology, was well known at the start of the century. Referencing Sonu Shamdasani (2003, pp. 277–278) Samuels writes:

> In his paper at the Clark University conference of 1909, with both Jung and Freud in attendance, Boas made it clear that there was no 'justification for (racial) hierarchies'. He also spoke against the idea that European civilisation represented the peak towards which other races and cultures were developing' (p. 6). Jung also knew the anthropologist Paul Radin who was highly critical of what he wrote about Africans.

In his paper "Jung: a racist", Farhad Dalal (1988) highlights the racist nature of Jung's thinking when theorising about non-Europeans, listing a number of quotes from his writing which are disturbing to the modern reader. Pointing out that Jung refers to his fundamental concepts of the collective unconscious and individuation when commenting on other cultures and ethnicities, Dalal raises the question of whether it is enough for post-Jungians to position him in history as a man of his time, without examining the possible racist roots of these theories.

Reading some of Jung's statements about people from Africa, the Middle East, India, Mexico can be disturbing, full as they are of Shadow material. Samuels (2018) cites the example where Jung is speaking about a bushman hunter:

> A bushman had a little son whom he loved with the tender monkey-love characteristic of primitives. Psychologically, this love is completely

auto-erotic – that is to say, the subject loves himself in the object. The object serves as a sort of erotic mirror. One day the bushman came home in a rage; he had been fishing and had caught nothing. As usual the little fellow came running to meet him, but his father seized hold of him and wrung his neck on the spot. Afterwards, of course, he mourned for the dead child with the same unthinking abandon that had brought about his death.

(1921, CW6, para. 403)

These interpretations of the bushman are breath-taking, not only in their content but also in their certitude. As Samuels points out, the anthropologist Paul Radin, author of the 1927 book *Primitive Man as Philosopher,* knew Jung. He was "a colleague of Jung's, taught at the Jung Institute, and invited Jung to write a response to his work on the Trickster. He was a Jungian, but he turned a critical Jungian" (p. 5).

Samuels (2018) then quotes what Radin wrote (in 1927) about the above quote:

No greater distortion of the facts could possibly be imagined. And yet Dr Jung obtained this example from what purported to be a first-hand account ... (it) illustrates the unconscious bias that lies at the bottom of our judgement of primitive mentality, the unconscious assumption of the lack of differentiation and integration to be found there ... That an example like the one used by Jung should in all good faith be given as representative of the normal or even the abnormal reactions of a primitive man to a given emotional situation, shows the depth of ignorance that still exists on this subject (Radin 1927, pp. 39 and 63, p. 6).

It seems that Jung's mind was made up and he took no notice of this challenge so the description remains. So be it. My concern now is how the consequent legacy has contributed to the making of our own minds.

The Shadow of Current Psychoanalytic and Jungian Thinking

Both Freud and Jung were speaking at a particular point in history within a certain cultural and social context and from linguistic assumptions that have changed. It is tempting to contend that Freud and Jung are "men of their time" and discard what is distasteful to modern ears without letting it trouble the essential concepts. Whilst I do not argue that the racist elements in earlier writings negate all the value of some remarkable and original thinking, I do believe that a too-easy blanking out of what were key assumptions within the origins of the theory risks an unwitting re-enforcement of implicit racist structures in our own minds, as well as in the minds of others.

Celia Brickman (2018) notes that within the psychoanalytic profession:

> Concern with Freud's use of evolutionary theory, where there has been any, has most often been confined to the 'antiquated' and/or unsubstantiated nature of these elements of Freud's arguments rather than the graver issues of their racist implications. To assess Totem and Taboo as peripheral to the main concerns of psychoanalysis is to avoid reckoning with its foundational status as the origin myth of psychoanalysis and the resultant paradigmatic status of its narrative for Freud's work as a whole; and it is thus to avoid reckoning with the implications of the racial assumptions of Totem and Taboo for all of psychoanalysis (p. 79).

> She also suggests that linking the unconscious to a developmental framework is itself problematic and we might be well served by loosening the tie between the two, a tie which is so connected to the distorted historic evolutionary ideas that underpin our current theories ... by disengaging the unconscious from an evolutionary/ developmental framework, psychoanalysis can begin to shed its racist baggage and use its performative abilities in the service of its ever powerful potential for the alleviation of mental suffering (p. 233).

The term "primitive" continues to be used widely within the psychoanalytic discourse without any exploration of its roots, the possible racist implications for our thinking today and the impact on people of colour reading such material. Whilst the term is etymologically neutral, its colonial pedigree means it carries troubling connotations. I recall no point in my training or in all the years attending clinical and theoretical seminars, that anyone – including myself – raised any concerns about its historic undertones. In a recent discussion with colleagues, we discovered there were a variety of perspectives on the meaning of the word including "original", "primal", "instinctive", "regressed", "violent" even "unconscious".

It will not do to dismiss the implications of such a word that appears so frequently and with such authority in the writings of our founding fathers, both of whom were fully aware of its connections to non-European peoples and the colonial attitudes of their time. Their use of the term was intended to carry a comparative imagery for the better understanding of the European individual. This forms an important part of what we as post-Freudians and post-Jungians have inherited. Given the propensity for racist thinking in the white liberal mind, to continue to use the term without proper thought means we risk perpetuating what at least consciously, we now see as the error of their ways. Stephen Frosh (2017) writes:

> Under the conditions that prevailed in these great moments of formation of seminal psychoanalytic theories – and that still exert significant

influence today – the idea of primitive thinking slips easily into the figure of the primitive, who by virtue of precisely this primitivity (irrationality, impulsivity etc.) becomes other to the civilized (p. 43).

Referring to the primitive-civilised binary, Frosh goes on to say "… the point is that psychoanalysis carries over the traces of this binary as it moves into this postcolonial era. Unconsciously, it reproduces them even when used in the decolonizing movement" (p. 44).

Warren Colman (2016) has a similar warning:

> While no psychoanalyst today would associate themselves with the idea of the primitive as a racial or cultural notion, it remains deeply embedded in psychoanalytic thought and, in this way, is likely to subtly entrench out-of-awareness racist attitudes amongst the psychoanalytic community. Perhaps this is one of the reasons why our record on diversity is so poor (p. 205).

Hillman (1986) argues that the Jungian theory of opposites keeps us pinned to a perspective of the world that is inevitably racist:

> 'White casts its own white shadow'. The conclusion may be bettered to say, 'white sees its own shadow in black', not because they are inherently opposite but it is archetypally given to whiteness to imagine in oppositions. To say it again: *the supremacy of white depends on oppositional imagining* (p. 42, italics in original).

Hillman's challenge to the notion of opposites which is a key idea within Jungian theory is important. The term implies opposition, adversity, hostility and often (perhaps always) confuses itself with the less antagonistic, more interesting concept of "difference". "Male" may be different from but is not *opposite* to "female", "night" not opposite to "day", "hate" not opposite to "love". These pairings are complementary qualities of the balance of aspects of the world we inhabit and of human nature. "Black" may be different from "white" but why should they be placed in opposition?

> If inherent to white is supremacy and if supremacy maintains itself by denying shadow, then it is 'only natural' to white consciousness to think and feel in opposites, to take them as ontologically fundamental, that is literally …. Give up the opposites, and you can move beyond white supremacy (p. 50).

Taken seriously, such challenges unsettle and disturb. But they can also stimulate by jangling the mind and shaking us up and questioning taken-for-granted ways of thinking. It's a question of whether we have sufficient confidence in the robustness of the core principles of psychoanalytic and Jungian analytic theory to trust that they can withstand some rattling. If we can loosen our transference to our founding fathers and let them rest in their own era, we can acknowledge their flaws and allow the possibility of re-visioning and re-energising our theoretical base.

The Shadow of Our Profession

Black, Asian and Minority Ethnic people who have grown up in Britain will have suffered from racism in some form or another; it will have been – and continues to be – a dimension of their personal and social life which needs acknowledgement and understanding. However, it is often reported by black psychotherapy students that their predominantly white analysts, supervisors and trainers mostly fail to recognise the reality of the problem. The consequence is, at best, significant concerns and personal experiences are not thought about and understood within the ordinary analytic endeavour, or, at worst, previous trauma is repeated and reinforced.

What emerges from research (Ciclitira and Foster 2012, and unpublished BPC Internal Survey, 2014) into the experience of black and minority ethnic individuals who seek to enter this profession is how hard it is for the black individual to get through a training in psychotherapy. The pressures are subtle but wearing. Many spoke of raising questions and concerns in seminars about theoretical and clinical material from the point of view of diversity, racial difference, cultural variation, racism, etc. which were ignored or dismissed by teachers and peers who were clearly uncomfortable in speaking freely about the issues. Many were told explicitly or implicitly that because this was depth, analytic work, the difference in "race" and colour was irrelevant. This leaves the black trainee in an invidious position. If they raise the issue, they can be seen as being "difficult" in bringing such uncomfortable matters into the room or failing to be sufficiently "analytic" by focussing on so-called "outer world" concerns. But if they don't speak then they collude with what amounts to a whitewash. Very few could recall times when the subject was raised by white seminar leaders, supervisors or colleagues.

Taken as a whole, the research reveals a climate of colour-blindness where trainers, supervisors and analysts take the position that differences in colour are not noticed and not relevant to in-depth, analytic work; we are assumed to all be the same. This denial of the reality of the impact of racism and power differentials means the black trainee is required to disregard important aspects of her or his experience and put aside their "blackness"if they are to survive.

Frank Lowe (2006) is a British black psychoanalytic psychotherapist who has been writing and speaking on this subject for many years. He says:

> I haven't met a black therapist or trainee therapist who has been
> satisfied with their training organization's handling of race issues or

feels confident that the profession is addressing the problem. I have explored how colour blindness or race avoidance can occur as a defence against fear and helplessness and I believe it also operates at an institutional level as a mechanism to maintain power, i.e. the status quo with its traditional power relations, authority and control (p. 56).

He goes on to quote from a number of black colleagues about their experience of training:

'Whenever I raise issues about race and culture, I am told this course is about the internal world not social issues' (Trainee child psychotherapist)

'During my interview I was asked about working with white patients but none of my fellow white trainees were asked about their ability to work with black patients'. (Adult psychotherapist)

'I feel isolated with my experience of the training and I do not feel confident that I will get support if I talk about my experience and views as a black person. I think it's probably best to just keep my head down and get through the training'. (Black trainee adult psychotherapist).

(ibid., pp. 56–57)

Eugene Ellis is the founder and Director of the Black and Asian Therapy Network (BAATN) in the UK. In an interview (2013), he points out:

What tends to happen with Black trainees is that they enter into the spirit of enquiry that is encouraged on any counselling or psychotherapy training course, but when they do so in the area of their culture and their race, there is all this silence and it's like you've just opened a huge hole in the floor. Somehow it becomes your fault. You can then choose either to say nothing, because it's too painful, and focus on just getting your qualification, or you insist that your voice is heard, get labelled as the troublemaker, and risk not making it to the end because you're worn out by the fighting. It's so sad to see this happen and I have heard this from so many Black and Asian students. It all goes on under the surface. Just naming what's going on becomes almost impossible and everyone gets defensive and blaming. It's normally the student of colour who gets the rougher end of things because that's how oppression works. What then happens is that students have to go outside their training to get what they need to develop as therapists within the profession (p. 16).

Farhad Dalal's challenge to the Jungian profession, "Jung: a racist" was first printed in the *British Journal of Psychotherapy* in 1988. It took 30 years until, in 2018, an open letter was published in the same journal (Baird et al. 2018) signed by 35 Jungian analysts and academics formally responding to

Dalal. The letter calls on all involved in analytical psychology to critique and revision theories that harm people of colour and to apologise for actual damage done. The letter has received mixed response within the international Jungian community. A critique of the arguments against it are summarised and challenged by Andrew Samuels in his 2018 article, "Jung and 'Africans': a critical and contemporary review of some of the issues".

Adrienne Harris (2019) writes:

> What is ironic and infuriating to many contemporary people of colour writing about racism is that the revelations and analysis of continuing racism by people of colour is not leading to work within the white community. I use the word 'work' deliberately to mean the hard but necessary intellectual and emotional labour that will be essential to transform and unpack racism as it is lived and enacted among white persons. This is a way of suggesting that reparations, forgiveness, work across racial lines requires first work within white communities and individuals (p. 311).

When we white folk choose to stay blind, deaf and silent concerning our own privilege and its impact on the black "Other", we are opting to remain unconscious of a crucial aspect of our lives and of ourselves. This part of our shadow has been whitewashed out of view, but then what colours, what potential, what depth might we be missing?

As Kovel (1988) writes:

> Racism, which diminishes its object to non-human status, also diminishes its perpetrator: all are losers by its terms. It does so, in the final analysis, by diminishing life, by reducing it to an abstraction, the better to manage it historically. And racism thereby becomes part of the wider problem of man's compact with the natural world in which he finds himself (ibid., p. 233).

Note

1 Parts of this chapter are taken from Morgan (2021).

References

Adams, M. V. (1996) *The Multi-cultural Imagination: 'Race', Colour and the Unconscious*. London: Routledge.

Alcoff, L. M. (2015) *The Future of Whiteness*. Cambridge: Polity Press.

Baird, D. *et al.* (2018) Open letter from a group of Jungians on the question of Jung's writings on and theories about Africans. *British Journal of Psychotherapy* 34: 4673–4678.

Boyd, H. (1991) *African History for Beginners*. New York: Writers and Readers Publishing Inc.

Brewster, F. (2013) Wheel of fire: the African American dreamer and cultural unconsciousness. *Jung Journal: Culture and Psyche* 7(1): 70–87.

Brewster, F. (2017) *African Americans and Jungian Psychology: Leaving the Shadows*. London: Routledge.

Brickman. C. (2018) *Race in Psychoanalysis. Aboriginal Populations in the Mind*. Oxon and New York: Routledge.

Ciclitira, K. & Foster, N. (2012) Attention to culture and diversity in psychoanalytic trainings. *British Journal of Psychotherapy* 28(3): 353–373.

Colman, W. (2016) *Act and Image. The Emergence of Symbolic Imagination*. New Orleans, Louisiana: Spring Journal Inc.

Dalal, F. (1988) Jung: a racist. *British Journal of Psychotherapy* 4(3): 263–279.

Dalal, F. (2002) *Race, Colour and the Process of Racialization: New Perspectives from Group Analysis, Psychoanalysis and Sociology*. Hove, East Sussex: Brunner Routledge.

Davids, F. (2011) *Internal Racism, a Psychoanalytic Approach to Race and Difference*. Hampshire: Palgrave Macmillan.

Ellis, E. (2013) Silenced: *The Black Student Experience*. www.therapytoday.net, Therapy Today December.

Fanon, F. (1986) *Black Skin, White Masks*. London: Pluto Press. (First published 1952 Editions de Seuil.)

Freud, S. (1913) Totem and Taboo: some points of agreement between the mental lives of savages and neurotics: Vol. 13. *The Origin of Religion: Totem and Taboo, Moses and Monotheoism and Other Works*. London: Penguin Books.

Frosh, S. (2017) Primitivity and violence: traces of the unconscious in psycho-analysis. *Journal of Theoretical and Philosophical Psychology* 37(1): 34–47.

Harris, A. (2012) The house of difference, or white silence. *Studies in Gender and Sexuality* 13(3): 197–216.

Harris, A. (2019) The perverse pact: racism and white privilege. *American Imago* 76(3): 309–333.

Hillman, J. (1986) Notes on white supremacy. Essaying an archetypal account of historical events. *Spring Publications*, 29–58.

Jung, C. G. (1921) The type problem in poetry. In *The Collected Works of C. G. Jung: Vol. 6. Psychological Types*.

Jung, C. G. (1935) *The Symbolic Life*. Collected Works 18.

Jung, C. G. (1939) The dreamlike world of India. *Civilization in Transition*. Collected Works 10.

Kipling, R (1899) *The White Man's Burden* Kipling, R. (1899). "The White Man's Burden: The United States and the Philippine Islands". New York: Doubleday, 1929.

Kovel, J. (1988) *White Racism. A Psychohistory*. London: Free Association Books.

Lowe, F. (2006) Racism as a borderline issue: the avoidance and marginalization of race in psychotherapy. *Difference: An Avoided Topic in Practice* (Ed. Foster et al.). London: Karnac.

Morgan, H. (2021) *The Work of Whiteness. A Psychoanalytic Perspective*. Oxford: Routledge.

Radin, P. (1927) *Primitive Man as Philosopher*. Reprinted by New York Review of Books (2017).

Samuels, A. (2018) Jung and 'Africans': a critical and contemporary review of the issues. *International Journal of Jungian Studies* 10(2): 122–134.

Shamdasani, S. (2003) *Jung and the Making of Modern Psychology. The Dream of a Science*. Cambridge: Cambridge University Press.

Van Ausdale, D. & Feagin, J. (2001) *The First R: How Children Learn Race and Racism*. Lanham, MD: Rowman & Littlefield.

Chapter 9

The Shadow in Politics

Emilija Kiehl

Instead of analysing the Shadow of "Populism", "Trumpism", "Putinism", "Brexitierianism", Chinese human rights record, etc., which we in the psychoanalytic professional community typically do not support, this chapter attempts to explore the manifestations of the powerful resistance to shadow awareness "close to home", i.e., in the "individualistic, progressive, (neo) liberal, democratic" group, with which the majority of us tend to identify. The lens we use to analyse Others in the socio-political arena is turned within on what we cannot or are reluctant to see in the Shadow of the political system we support. Some examples will show how the use of language and image in the neoliberal discourse perpetuate Shadow projections outwardly, fostering what Gore Vidal calls "conspiracy of thinking the same way" and feeding into a form of neoliberal "populism" whose demands for compliance and attacks on differentiated thinking mirror those of its opponents. Behind the Persona of the different political parties stands the Shadow of their similarities.

The Shadow Resists Consciousness

"Look at yourself in the mirrors of others", Jung's soul says to Jung in *The Black Books* (Jung 1914/5, p. 207). Interwoven into the composition of both the negative and the positive aspects of the Shadow are elements of the powerful and ramified system of psychological resistance towards facing the Shadow personally or collectively. In its positive aspect, the tension of this resistance produces the necessary energy for the transformation and growth of the personality as the unconscious Shadow aspects become conscious. In the negative, the system keeps us unaware of our Shadow, which we continue to project outwardly, "see", hate and attack in others. The indifference to the suffering of others, including the suffering we inflict or cause, can open the door of another shadowy area in our responses to the world around us – the inclination to exploit, seek personal (or collective) advantage in others' vulnerability, with cruelty and violence. Wars provide legal justification and give full reign to these Shadow traits. They provide fertile ground for

DOI: 10.4324/9781003255819-11

understanding the place of politics in society through the lens of *Agonism*, from the Greek word *Agon*, which means struggle. Agonism implies that politics is about struggle between conflicting interests, and therefore an area of permanent conflict. Similarly, the Social Darwinists see the world as a battleground, where the "fittest" get their needs met and the rest can only hope to settle for the leftovers. Furthermore, Tom Singer says that,

> Those Social Darwinists who make the distinction between strong and weak on the basis of race, ethnicity, or gender will work covertly or overtly to ensure that the identified weaker group remains weak or gets even weaker—whether the group is Black, Jewish, Palestinian, female, gay, White, Islamic, Christian or whomever has been identified as weak.
> (Singer 2016, p. 153)

In the world currently dominated by neoliberal values, the measure for strength and weakness is money: the rich are strong, the poor are weak. Both deserve their place in society. This viewpoint is interwoven into the market forces-driven neoliberal global society almost as a "fact of life" – not something to ponder, discuss or endeavour to change – just as in the not-so-distant past, the "weakness" of the groups identified by Singer was also seen as a fact of life, a reality that we can only adjust to and accept.

And so, the "weakness" of the economically vulnerable segments of society lies open to exploitation through neoliberal political and socio-economic thinking and actions. The "might is right" attitude and concomitant categories of "superiority" and "inferiority" are thus set in the way that exists in the animal kingdom – eat or be eaten. Animals, to the extent that we are able to understand how they operate and experience life as individuals and in groups, seem to act primarily on instinct and emotion. They live under the proverbial "law of the jungle". There is currently a view that animals possess a form of consciousness, but only human consciousness has gone through the formidable process of evolution and gradually became the seat and essence of our moral being (Lawson 2010), and the question of right and wrong began to have an impact on our actions towards others. As far as we know, we are the only species which has to negotiate the demands of the moral being abiding in our consciousness with those that stem from the amoral realm of instincts.

This brings us to a different understanding of politics, which takes into account the tension between the two positions and seeks ways of reconciling their often-opposing tendencies. Aristotle believed that politics is (can be) about cooperation, not only on the level necessary for our survival but also as an expression of an evolved way of living in the world we share with others who have needs just like we do. The word Politics originates in early antiquity from the Greek word Πολιτικά (*Politica*), referring to the decision-making process in the ancient Greek city-states, (*polis*) regarding resources and distribution of power among citizens. This process laid the foundations for *democracy*, from the Greek word *Demos* – common people – which goes back to the 5th century city-state of Athens, and means "rule of the people", rather than rule by the aristocracy or, in more contemporary language, by "the elite".

However, what was referred to as "citizens" of Athens applied only to the wealthy men. Women and slaves had no place in the discussions about the resources and the distribution of power. What we understand as democracy in current times has gone through tremendous changes, over a long period of time. For instance, in the UK, women were not allowed to vote until 1918 and then only if they were older than 30 and owned property. Men over 21 could vote regardless of their material status and, if they served in the military, they could vote at 19. It was not until 1928 that the Equal Franchise Act allowed women over 21 to vote in the UK.

It was similar in the USA, where women were legally allowed to vote in 1919, but only if they were white. Black women did not get the right to vote until 1965.

Finland was the first European country to allow women's vote in 1906, and the last was Switzerland, in 1971.

Despite the steely resolve of the Women Suffragettes and their relentless battles for justice for women, today in many of the leading neoliberal democratic countries, certainly in the USA and the UK, women are still paid less than men for doing the same jobs.

The UK abolished slavery in 1833, and the USA 33 years later. "What may be less known is that the British Government of the time spent £20 million of the tax payers' money (... 40% of its budget in 1833) to buy freedom for slaves from their owners", writes Holly Williams (BBC Culture 3 July 2020), equivalent to around £20 billion today.

> ... one of the biggest ever government bailouts. The cost was so high, the vast loans the government took out to fund it were only just paid off in 2015.... but if you're thinking you can't put a price on freedom, brace yourself for bad news – the money didn't go to the slaves, but to their owners.

Williams continues.

> The British taxpayer ... was paying off debts that the government racked up in order to compensate British slave owners for their loss of 'property'. Prime Minister William Gladstone (1809–1898) helped his father claim for £106,769, around £83 million in today's money, to just a single family.

Agonism seems to see aggression as the predominant force in human be-haviour. As a healthy instinct for asserting our needs and claiming space for our survival, aggression is a necessary part of our nature. Baby announces its existence as separate from mother's with the first kick in the womb (Mizen 2019). Mizen differentiates healthy aggression and violence:

> From [the] biopsychosocial perspective, aggression is seen as a heuristic concept that encapsulates numerous interacting elements that in ordinary development integrate and serve to promote optimal organism survival: By contrast, from this perspective, in humans violence may be understood as a pathological variant of aggression (pp. 1–14).

Looking at politics as a mere battle for power and domination (often involving violence) seems to emphasise the primal stages in our individual and social evolution, or:

> ... the most basic kind of subjective, affective experience of a sentient organism as one that gives rise to a proto-sense of self, as a sense of "mineness" or "belonging to me", which confers a primitive affective, "coloring" of the world.
>
> (Northoff & Panksepp 2008, quoted in Mizen)

However, understanding politics as a process of cooperation rather than conflict fosters behaviour beyond the evolutionary stage of "mineness" or "belonging to me".

Cooperation as a way of ensuring survival is not unique to humans. Many animal species have an instinctive understanding of the benefits of and at times necessity for belonging to a group. They also have an understanding that the group needs to be organised in a form of a rudimentary social order that fosters their common interests. What can be thought of as an emergent evolutionary property particular to human consciousness is *conscience* and the question of morality, i.e., the right or wrong of our actions.

Religious and philosophical systems have been developing around this question since the dawn of our psychological and spiritual awareness of life with others. At some point in the history of civilisation, morality began to have an impact on political thinking and decisions, and became an instrumental feature in the way those in power present political causes to the masses whose lives are most affected by them. For example, in the latter part of the 20th century, the terms "just" or "humanitarian" wars entered the public discourse as a moral justification for aggression against evil *others*. One look at their history, natural resources and geopolitical positions reveals the shadowy motives behind the political leaders' decisions to "liberate" some countries or nations and not others. Behind "a moral cause" may be a simple intent on seizing power.

Those who believe in the human capacity to have their needs met through discourse and cooperation rather than violence, are sometimes called *political moralists*, because their point of departure is the ethical distinction between right and wrong. Their opponents, the so-called *political realists*, see the moralists' thinking as un-realistic, ending in *Utopia* – a perfect world where everyone cooperates and everyone's needs are considered. Like the Agonists, the political *realists* see politics as a realm of pursuit of power and, therefore, of permanent conflict. At the extreme of this political thinking, lies the famous theory of the Florentine Renaissance diplomat, Niccolo Machiavelli, that (in politics) ends justify the means. Conscience, therefore, has no role in this view of politics. As mentioned before, in modern times, many proponents of Machiavellianism want to appear as political *moralists* and present (or "sell") their actions from a moral high ground. What does not fit in the political persona hides in the Shadow of politics. Together with the public relations companies, the corporate, establishment-friendly media have been instrumental in this area of neoliberal pursuit and maintenance of power.

In the context of this chapter, we might say that if politics is to develop along with other spheres of human life such as culture, art, science and in step with (instead of controlling and dominating) the evolution of consciousness, both views on politics need to take into account the whole of human nature, particularly the Shadow. The *moralists* need to consider the Shadow's personal and collective negative, i.e., potentially destructive aspects, which stand in the way of cooperation, while the *realists* need to consider the human potential for positive, creative actions, our undiscovered talents and capabilities, which are also in the Shadow. As we grow up, we are exposed to the demands of our family, social group, culture to be a certain way in order to fit in. Our need to belong forces us to unconsciously repress aspects of ourselves that do not seem to satisfy those demands, and they become contents of our Shadow. Both the positive and the negative Shadow traits have been seen to emerge and predominate at different points in the turbulent history of our species.

The horrific fallout of the First and the Second World Wars demonstrated how dangerous the destructive power of the collective Shadow can be when it gets out of control. The post-WWII political powers seemed to agree that this formidable force must never again be unleashed. But the question was how to keep it under control and still, when needed, harness it for political and commercial goals?

In the documentary film series, *The Century of the Self*, Adam Curtis (2002) explores how the devastations of WWII, the Holocaust and other horrific atrocities, which revealed the might of the destructive force of the human Shadow, gave Freud's nephew, Edward Bernaise, the idea for Public Relations as a tool for psychological control of the masses in peace times, and in service to political powers and big corporations. Both have benefited from public relations and the creation of the 20th-century culture of mass consumerism. The profound and long-lasting impact of this culture (which has since spread across our post WWII planet) on the way we see ourselves and the world we live in, has become the subject of philosophical and psychosocial studies, dystopian novels, films and theatre plays. According to Curtis, using psychology to read, create and fulfil the public's desires, and make products and political speeches attractive to consumers and voters has been a new way for businesses and politicians to engage with and control the masses. Through "globalism", we have become the world of *market forces,* the world of sellers and consumers. Curtis refers to Stuart Ewen, American historian of public relations, who says that the political process, which used to be about engaging people's rational, conscious minds, as well as facilitating their needs as a group, is now geared towards primitive impulses with little bearing on the issues outside the narrow self-interests of a consumer society. In other words, behind the façade of political *moralism* lies hidden the Shadow of Machiavellianism, where anything goes as long as we get what we want.

Neoliberalism, the post-WWII globally predominant political and socioeconomic system, rests on the consumer society and the ensuing consumer mentality. I am referring to this currently dominant political, socioeconomic and cultural force as *neoliberal* rather than *liberal* because there is a difference. As Phelan and Dawes (2018) summarise:

> If liberalism names the political ideology aligned to the historical emergence of "free market" capitalism and Western-style representative democracy, neoliberalism signifies a particular regime of liberalism, capitalism and democracy that has been globalized since the 1970s, in the form of an active state promotion of market and competition principles that critics see as antithetical to democracy.

Note that all recent wars of the "West Against the Rest" (Peters 2007) went under the banner of defending "freedom and democracy" in the countries whose natural resources and geopolitical positions we want to control and dominate. Understanding what is actually meant by "freedom and democracy" has simultaneously drawn the line and blurred the distinction between liberalism and neoliberalism, as Phelan and Dawes further explain:

> ... socially progressive liberals criticize neoliberalism for subordinating public life to market forces and for displacing the welfare state commitments of the Keynesian era. Some on the political left collapse the distinction between liberalism and neoliberalism, seeing them as simply two ways of justifying capitalist rule. Conversely, some of those most likely to be identified as neoliberals are motivated by deep hostility to political liberals particularly in the right-wing political discourses where liberal operates as code for left-liberal, even socialist, values that are opposed to a free market identity (ibid.).

Phelan and Dawes' distinction may help explain the hostility in the neoliberal discourse and globalised media (mostly owned by neoliberal billionaires) towards liberals in the recent fight for power within the Democratic Party in the USA and Labour in the UK, where Bernie Sanders and Jeremy Corbyn were looked upon as "too left" and their campaigns were not supported by the establishment media. Furthermore, both were often covertly or overtly presented as "Communists" and, in the case of Corbyn, also as an "Anti-Semite" and even a "Russian spy". An example is the BBC, widely considered an "impartial"" presenter of political matters, where it has been very difficult, if not impossible to find a radio or TV programme where Corbyn was not presented in a negative light. To make sure that their message reached out as widely as possible, including the potentially less sophisticated thinkers among their audience, the BBC2 TV Newsnight programme (15 March 2018) went as far as to show a picture of Jeremy Corbyn wearing a hat, which was photo-shopped to look like a "Russian" fur hat. And just in case the hat does not produce the desired effect, the background behind Corbyn was a picture of the Kremlin!

Millions of people around the world have suffered immensely under neoliberal economic programmes, e.g., EU "austerity measures", which made the poor poorer and the rich richer, and Corbyn and Sanders were committed to doing something for the economically poorer segments in their very wealthy countries. Their moral response to the unstoppably rising socio-economic inequality, poverty and lack of funding for social programmes, while the military industry continued to receive astronomical amounts of money and media support for their "business", were met with unprecedented enthusiasm among the younger population on both sides of the Atlantic. However, it was mostly thanks to the much-maligned alternative and social media that what Sanders and Corbyn had to say reached out to those who wanted change. The establishment media were forced to at least occasionally refer to them, rather than ignore or even black them out, lest they lose what is left of their already fledgling younger audience. But they continued to report in favour of the figures of the establishment: Joe Biden in the USA and Boris Johnson in the UK.

In his famous dystopian novel, *Nineteen Eighty Four*, George Orwell has this to say about the power of suggestion over our unconscious responses to different levels of experience, including our perception of history, current times and our hopes and fears about the future:

> Whoever controls the image and the information of the past determines what and how the future generations will think; whoever controls the information and the images of the present determines how the same people will view the past. He who controls the past commands the future. He who commands the future conquers the past.
>
> (Orwell 1949)

This somewhat enigmatic passage offers a glimpse into our vulnerability to the power of Shadow projections. Projections can cause occurrences of collective amnesia regarding actions and motives of the political figures we put our hopes in. Jung refers to this too when he writes:

> Thanks to industrialization, large portions of the population were uprooted and were herded together in large centres. This new form of existence – with its mass psychology and social dependence on the fluctuation of markets and wages – produced an individual who was unstable, insecure, and suggestible. He was aware that his life depended on boards of directors and captains of industry, and he supposed, rightly or wrongly, that they were chiefly motivated by financial interests. He knew that, no matter how conscientiously he worked, he could still fall a victim at any moment to economic changes which were utterly beyond his control. And there was nothing else for him to rely on.
>
> (Jung, CW 10a, para. 453)

The poor do not have a voice in neoliberal democracy. Is then the political-socio-economic order we live in democracy, or is it plutocracy (the rule by the wealthy)? The poor can certainly vote, but which of the two parties fighting for power represents their interests? As Gore Vidal wittily remarks:

> There is only one party in the United States, the Property Party ... and it has two right wings: Republican and Democrat. Republicans are a bit stupider, more rigid, more doctrinaire in their laissez-faire capitalism than the Democrats, who are cuter, prettier, a bit more corrupt – until recently ... and more willing than the Republicans to make small adjustments when the poor, the black, the anti-imperialists get out of hand. But essentially, there is no difference between the two parties.
>
> ("The State of the Union", 1975)

As Corbyn's popularity continued to rise among the younger voters, a group of UK billionaires announced that if he won the election, they would leave the country. As is well known, the Conservative Party, led by Boris Johnson, achieved a land-slide victory over Labour. Meanwhile, in the USA, Bernie Sanders was ousted out of running for leadership of the Democratic Party by the supporters of Joe Biden who was seen as a stronger candidate for victory over Trump. Furthermore, Biden's past career moves were a guarantee that the status quo will not be disturbed against the interests of those who most benefit from it.

Fake News, Post-Truth, etc.

In his book *Children of the Day, A Calendar of Human History,* Eduardo Galeano (2013) has this entry:

The Martians are Coming

"In 1938 spaceships landed on the coasts of the United States

And the Martians launched their attacks. They had ferocious tentacles, enormous black eyes that shot fiery rays, and foaming, V-shaped mouths.

Many horrified citizens took to the streets wrapped in wet
Towels to protect themselves from the poison gas that the Martians

Emitted, and many more chose to shut themselves in behind locks and more locks, armed to the teeth, awaiting the final battle.

Orson Welles invented that extra-terrestrial invasion and broadcast it over the radio.

The invasion was a lie but the fear was real.

And the fear continued: the Martians turned into Russians, Koreans, Vietnamese, Cubans, Nicaraguans, Afghanis, Iraqis, Iranians ..."

The terms fake news and post-truth have been ascribed to Trump and his time in the Office, as though we have forgotten the stark examples of lying and deceiving by the leaders before him. Being "economical with the truth" as the American General, Oliver North famously described the untruths he said when questioned about his role in the Iran Contra Affair,[1] has not been an infrequent response to public inquiries by Trump's recent predecessors e.g., the well-known Bill Clinton statement: "I did not have sex with that woman" referring to his affair with the then young White House intern, Monica Lewinsky. Or his wife, Senator Hilary Clinton's tale of having to run for her life from sniper fire when in 1996, as the first lady, she visited Bosnia with her daughter, Chelsea. The tale was proved untrue by CBS film footage showing Clinton and daughter stroll down the tarmac, greeted by high officials and a child, forcing Clinton to admit that she "misspoke" in her account of the event. (Patrick Healy and Katharine Q. Seelye, The New York Times, 25 March 2008).

Being "economical with the truth" and "misspeaking" on the UK side of the neoliberal fold by Tony Blair led to the devastating USA/UK war in Iraq. Blair's infamous false claim about Saddam Hussein's "weapons of mass destruction" sold the war to the British public with lasting consequences for peace not only in Iraq but also in the whole of the Middle East. Apart from defending "the free world" from the imaginary weapons of mass destruction, this war was presented as a "moral" cause too: we were there to protect the Kurdish population in Iraq. The plight of the Kurds in Turkey, who were also being persecuted and killed at the same time, did not merit much media coverage, no moral outrage was generated, and no action was taken against Turkey, who happens to be our NATO ally.

That war in Iraq was precipitated by the 1990s USA/UK led war with Iraq following the Iraqi invasion of Kuwait. It was also based on a fabricated story, that time by a woman who told the Congress that Iraqi soldiers had taken babies from incubators in Kuwait City and left them on the floor to die. As The Christian Science Monitor writes, the Kuwait government had been looking for ways to "sell the war" to the American public, with the help of the American PR firm Hill & Knowlton, whose president had been chief of staff during George Bush's vice presidency.

As soon as the story about the babies in incubators broke out, Hill and Knowlton sent it to newsrooms across the USA. There were no attempts to verify the story or the identity of the young woman who was in fact the daughter of the Kuwait's US ambassador and had not seen what she reported.

> Similar unsubstantiated stories appeared at the UN a few weeks later, where a team of "witnesses", coached by Hill & Knowlton, gave "testimony" (although no oath was ever taken) about atrocities in Iraq. It was later learned that the seven witnesses used false names and even identities in one case. In an unprecedented move, the US was allowed to present a video created by Hill & Knowlton to the entire security council.
>
> (Tom Regan, The Christian Science Monitor, 6 September 2002)[2]

This is hardly an unusual example of the PR companies and the news media providing a formidable tool for manipulating public opinion in favour of the decisions the political establishments make on our behalf, often in the interest of small groups of their beneficiaries (including the military) and against the interest of the general public who funds them with tax money.

In more recent times, neoliberal media have been rife with reports and articles on the evils of "Populism", Trumpism", etc., but the ills of the neoliberal socio-economic, political and cultural activities and their powerful effect on the life of our planet and all its creatures are reported mostly on the non-mainstream media outlets. A torrent of articles and books has been written about Trump's lies, his racism, sexism, the "post-truth" world that, apparently, Trump has created, as though the collective memory no longer contains the recently fabricated stories by his predecessors (viz Lee 2017). We seem to have forgotten Bush and Blair famously indicating that God gave them permission to attack Iraq, but we hate and ridicule Trump's displays of narcissism, as though he represents something previously unseen on the stage of contemporary political acts and actors. In other words, Trump has been a suitable repository for negative Shadow projections – an epitome of *all* the wrongs in the society we have created.

Keeping It in the Family

The manipulation of public opinion exists on all sides of the political divides and media follow the line that favours the side that funds them. Some forms of this manipulation are easier to see, especially on the *other* side, while others are more sophisticated. A plethora of "conspiracy theories" arises from the glimpses into the more sophisticated forms of manipulation of opinion leading to the narrative about a special group of wealthy power-driven individuals who "pull the strings" of our minds on the global scale. In the Shadow of the unconscious power over our conscious minds lie hidden our unacknowledged unattractive features intertwined with the need to feel good about ourselves. This need makes us vulnerable to manipulation. It can prevent us from facing our Shadow and integrating it into a deeper understanding of ourselves. The tension between the truth of who we are and the image of ourselves that we want to preserve can pull us into unconsciously complying with the Shadow rather than facing it. In Jung's model of the psyche, facing the Shadow is instrumental in our psychological growth and development. On the collective level, compliance with the Shadow may lead to "the conspiracy of thinking the same way", meaning that we do not question the integrity of what we support and with which we comply. In this "conspiracy", we are not under power of a group of malevolent individuals but of our individual or collective Shadow view of the world and the concomitant hostility towards those who think differently. Although it may be expressed in different ways, this "conspiracy" seems to apply equally to the neoliberal and populist discourse and their media: the negative Shadow always lives on the *other* side. *Our* candidates for power are and must be presented as Shadow-less. This attitude creates a problem for our individual and collective development because, Jung writes:

> What is commonly called "self-knowledge" is therefore a very limited knowledge, most of it dependent on social factors, of what goes on in the human psyche. Hence one is always coming up against the prejudice that such and such a thing does not happen "with us" or "in our family" or among our friends and acquaintances. On the other hand, one meets with equally illusory assumptions about the alleged presence of qualities which merely serve to cover up the true facts of the case.
>
> (Jung CW 10b, para. 492)

Moreover, Jung continues,

In this broad belt of unconsciousness, which is immune to conscious criticism and control, we stand defenceless, open to all kinds of influences and psychic infections.

(ibid., (c) para. 493)

A case in point is the recent event that forced the investigative journalist and co-founder of the independent media outlet, *The Intercept*, Glen Greenwald to leave and form another internet portal. It took place during the US Presidential election, with Shadow projections running wild on both sides. In the neoliberal media, Biden was presented as "a decent man", an attribute often repeated in private conversations among the neoliberals. Biden was the recipient of the positive Shadow projections and his virtues were not to be questioned. Meanwhile Trump, in one of his numerous attempts to smear the reputation of his opponent, revealed some of the shady financial dealings by Biden and his son, Hunter Biden, in China and Ukraine. The allegations were denied by the Bidens, but the question of Hunter Biden's highly paid position on the Board of the major Ukrainian natural gas trading company, Burisma, wouldn't go away. It turned into an interesting example of Shadow work: not only that the neoliberals were not enraged at Biden and his son, but they did not even question their integrity ("decency") in the matter. Their rage was instead directed towards Trump and the Republican-leaning media for exposing it as a proof of how despicably low *they* are prepared to sink just to get Trump into the Office.

When Glen Greenwald wrote an article about this in *The Intercept,* his Biden-supporting colleagues demanded that he censored his article – Biden must not be shown in a negative light. Greenwald, who is by no means a supporter of Trump, became well known in 2013, as a US team journalist of the Guardian, when he first published the findings of the whistle-blower, Edward Snowden, who exposed the global surveillance programmes frequently run by the NSA and with the cooperation of telecommunication companies and European governments. Greenwald later left the Guardian to create *The Intercept,* only to encounter the sharp edge of censorship from his co-founding colleagues, who refused to publish his article unless he removed all sections critical of Joe Biden and his son. Greenwald refused to be part of this "conspiracy of thinking the same way" and left.

What has been said so far will not come as a surprise to a discerning reader. Why are then so many otherwise sophisticated and "progressively"-minded neoliberals such willing consumers of political propaganda, so gullibly ready to buy into politicians' false morality tales about "good and bad" to the point of supporting wars in faraway lands with enormous amounts of money, which could instead be spent on health, education and other notoriously underfunded social problems at home? And not only that, why would "decent", educated and well-informed members of society choose to actively participate in the shadowy activities of their governments? The mesmerising shadow power-drive holds the answer to this question.

An example of shadow-compliance going too far can be found in Robert Jay Lifton's Foreword to the book *The Dangerous Case of Donald Trump,* 2017, entitled "Our Witness to Malignant Normality". "Malignant normality", Lifton writes is "to do with the social actuality with which we are presented as normal, all-encompassing and unalterable". He explains that:

> ... we start with an assumption that all societies, at various levels of consciousness, put forward ways of viewing, thinking and behaving that are considered desirable or 'normal'. Yet, these criteria for normality can be much affected by the political and military currents of a particular era. Such requirements may be fairly benign but they can also be destructive to the point of evil.

Lifton came to the idea of malignant normality studying Nazi doctors and arrived at a more recent, albeit certainly less extreme example of malignant normality "close to home": this was the revelation of the participation in torture by American medical doctors, psychiatrists, psychologists and other medical and psychological personnel.

> This reached its most extreme manifestation when two psychologists were revealed to be among the architects of the CIA's torture protocol. Moreover, than that, this malignant normality was essentially supported by the American Psychological Association in its defence of the participation of psychologists in the so-called "enhanced interrogation" techniques that spilled over onto torture (ibid.,).

It is not too difficult to imagine that these psychologists and other professionals believed not only in the normality but also in the morality of their actions too. They might have seen themselves as warriors on the side of good against evil because in any conflict *we* are on the side of the good. However, there is a shadow side to this simplified self-representation:

> When one tries desperately to be good and wonderful and perfect, then all the more the shadow develops a definite will to be black and evil and destructive. People cannot see that; they are always striving to be marvellous, and then they discover that terrible destructive things happen which they cannot understand, and they either deny that such facts have anything to do with them, or if they admit them, they take them for natural afflictions, or they try to minimize them and to shift the responsibility elsewhere. The fact is that if one tries beyond one's capacity

to be perfect, the shadow descends into hell and becomes the devil".
(Jung, Visions: Notes of the Seminar Given in 1930–1934)

To the delight of the military industry, the war scenario is known to be capable of bringing together the otherwise bitterly adversarial political "left" and "right" into what Justin Raimondo (1951–2019) called the "war party". Their differences are smoothed into a common cause of "defending freedom and democracy", "our way of life", etc., anywhere in the world. As said before, the fact that, as a rule, this happens in parts of the world whose natural resources or geopolitical positions we want to control and dominate escapes attention and rarely comes into the neoliberal discourse. It seems that in the Shadow of the apparent belief that everyone on the planet wants to live like us lies the naïve faith in the neoliberal doctrine and market forces as a solution for all the ills in the world. That faith may be what obscures our thinking and causes collective amnesia when it comes to facing the Shadow of our political leaders and the actions they take on our behalf (and with our money).

By its nature, the Shadow resists the light of consciousness. An intricate defence system is interwoven into the fabric of the Shadow and, therefore, difficult to "see". Furthermore, glimpses into its dark corners bring up the tension, which our ego (for Jung, the centre of consciousness) struggles to manage and yet, that tension is what generates the energy necessary for psychological change and development.

In other words, our reluctance to face the Shadow, personally or collectively, works both in favour and against the natural course of the development and evolution of our personal and collective or social consciousness. This applies to all spheres of life, including politics.

Where Do We Go from Here?

According to the American political scientist, Francis Fukuyama (1992), the post-WWII rise of the Western (neo)liberal democracy and the collapse of the Soviet Union have brought about the "end of history". The Western neoliberal values have become universal and consumerism has replaced all previous political ideologies. If this assessment is correct, what are its psychosocial implications? Jung warns that:

> Western consciousness is by no means the only kind of consciousness there is: it is historically conditioned and geographically limited, and representative of only one part of mankind. The widening of consciousness ought not to proceed at the expense of the other kinds of consciousness.

(CW 13, para. 84)

In fantasy, at the helm of the evolving civilisation, the Western neoliberal leads the way to an ever more progressive society, gaining ever greater moral high ground at every step. The self-righteousness and one-sidedness of the neoliberal group complex has produced a further fantasy of a "norm" which is shared by those in its grip. From this "norm" arose a value system which, as the American linguist and cultural theorist, Richard Gray (2004) points out, can be an expression of covert racism.

> ... The manner of thought which takes the norms of its own cultural attitudes and applies them to others in order to demonstrate their inferiority is characteristic of racism in all its manifestations.
>
> (Gray, p. 129)

My presentation at the Rome 2015 Analysis & Activism conference explores the shadow of racism behind tolerance in the neoliberal cultural complex. I was inspired by this excerpt from the poem by Constantin Cavafy, "Waiting for the Barbarians".

> Why this sudden bewilderment, this confusion?
> (How serious people's faces have become.)
> Why are the streets and squares emptying so rapidly,
> everyone going home lost in thought?
> Because night has fallen and the barbarians haven't come.
> And some of our men just in from the border say
> there are no barbarians any longer.
> And now, what's going to happen to us without barbarians?
> Those people were a kind of solution.

Rabbit Angstrom, John Updike's famous character, comes to mind when he wonders what is the point of being an American if the cold war is over (1990).

It seems that the unconscious impact of the cold war mentality never ceased to linger in the collective Shadow, ready to be used by political powers on both sides. Not so long ago, a colleague contacted me to ask if I had a vacancy for a new patient. She told me a little bit about this person who came from Russia, and I said "Ok, please give them my telephone number". "Are you sure you want to work with her ... even though she is Russian?" My colleague asked. Taken aback by this unexpected question, I exclaimed, "What *do* you mean!?" An uneasy pause followed and my colleague said: "... I am sorry, I forgot that you didn't grow up during the cold war". "I did grow up during the cold war", I said, "only not in the UK".

For the first time in many decades, I felt like a foreigner in my London home-town.

As it happens, I have been living in the UK for most of my life, but I was born in Yugoslavia, one of the founding members of the post-WWII

Non-Aligned Movement, comprising of the developing countries, which were not in either of the two power blocks: NATO or Warsaw Pact. As a result, in the Warsaw Pact countries Yugoslavia was seen as "Western" and in the West it was imagined "behind the Iron Curtain". When in the 70s I first came to London as a young student, I was surprised to find that proportionally, many more young people went to university in Yugoslavia than in the UK. Education seemed to be more valued in the "East" than in the "West", the latter giving more importance to material wealth. I still remember meeting a British university student who seemed curious about the fact that I came from Yugoslavia. "How did you arrive here?" he asked. "By plane, from Belgrade" I said. "Oh, so you have airplanes in Yugoslavia?!" he commented, not hiding a disdainful smile. This surprised me as much as my colleague's question if I would work with a Russian many years later. The late 60s' progressive (r)evolutionary movements for socio-political change, the anti-war and Civil Rights movement in the USA and the student demonstrations across the world capital cities, including Belgrade, were still felt in the mid-70s. My generation were "citizens of the world" and, with the Beatles and the Rolling Stones, London was *our* capital. But for this young man, I was somebody who emerged from behind the Iron Curtain – he and I were not the citizens of the same world. I was one of "them" or worse, the enemy, for, "As long as men remain unconscious of their personal and collective shadow, they will always need to make enemies" (Odajnyk 1976).

"Politics in many Western countries is broken and in a mess: we urgently need new ideas and approaches", writes Andrew Samuels in his book *Politics on the Couch* (2001). Two decades later, not much has changed in how we view and do politics. The potentially catastrophic environmental factors and the coronavirus pandemic have exposed multiple levels of the dangerous impact of socio-economic inequality, now rampant across the planet, and affecting us all. The need for new ideas and approaches became even more urgent when the pandemic revealed the multilevelled inadequacies of those in political power.

> Today's politicians leave most of us with a sense of deep despair and disgust. They lack integrity, imagination, and new ideas. Across the globe, a search is on to remodel politics (ibid.).

We live in extraordinary times. The formidable advance of technology has brought about the previously unthinkable opportunities for further development or destruction of all that has been achieved throughout the history of our species. We find ourselves on the precipice of major change in the way we live and see ourselves and the world we have created. The question is, can the political establishment in our pay be remodelled so that it works in the service of the development of our creative capacities and potentials instead of exploiting our negative Shadow traits?

As we have seen, the Shadow can cause a strange psycho-perceptual phenomenon whereby something so present in the camp of our adversaries, becomes obscured, to the point of being invisible, or even appearing in reverse when it's at home: what we do not like in ourselves, we see and hate in others. And *others* are those who threaten, or in any way stand in the way of what we want for ourselves, including how we want to see ourselves. The neoliberals believe that *we* have got it right and the rest of humanity needs to catch up with us and our achievements. However, "none of us stands outside humanity's black collective shadow" (Odajnyk, p. 71) and for as long as we believe in our one-sided perception of the world, we present danger to further development of our species.

> The integration of unconscious contents is an individual act of realization, of understanding, and moral evaluation. It is a most difficult task, demanding a high degree of ethical responsibility. Only relatively few individuals can be expected to be capable of such an achievement, and they are not the political but the moral leaders of mankind.
>
> (Jung, CW 10d para. 451)

Furthermore, it seems clear that if we continue to look at politics through the lens of conflict rather than cooperation, we will risk not only our own, but the survival of other creatures who share this planet with us. Jung warned us about this as far back as in 1946:

> The destructive power of our weapons has increased beyond all measure, and this forces a psychological question on mankind: Is the mental and moral condition of the men who decide on the use of these weapons equal to the enormity of the possible consequences?
>
> (Jung, CW 10e, para. 457)

Jung believed that any positive socio-political change can come only through the psychological development of the individual rather than through the power of the masses. Psychotherapy has shown that by facing our Shadow, i.e., the "enemy" within, we become less prone to seeing the enemy in others. However, as Hillman and Ventura (1993) point out in their book, *We Have Had a Hundred Years of Psychotherapy and the World Is Getting Worse,* looking only into the inner psyche (the classical approach in psychotherapy), without considering external socio-economic and political factors is not enough to affect the change in the world around us. Exploration of the Shadow in ourselves and in politics can help us understand the hidden, unconscious motives behind our positive or negative projections on political figures, thus enabling us to take more responsibility for our contributions to their actions.

So, what now? "What will the future bring?" asks Jung.

> From time immemorial this question has occupied men's minds, though not always to the same degree. Historically, it is chiefly in times of physical, political, economic, and spiritual distress that men's eyes turn with anxious hope to the future, and when anticipations, utopias, and apocalyptic visions multiply.
>
> (Jung, CW 10 f, para. 488)

We certainly are living in a time of distress on all levels of experience. The road ahead merges into a cloud of uncertainty. From this uneasy position, I end this chapter with concluding remarks in Thomas Lawson's book, *Carl Jung, Darwin of the Mind:*

> [Our] hope rests in the wonderous capacity of *consciousness* to evolve, and depends on our ability to bring about ... evolution at a pace sufficient to keep abreast of our capacity for destruction.
>
> (2010, p. 213)

Notes

1 North came into the public spotlight for his participation in the Iran–Contra affair during the Reagan administration. He was partially responsible for the sale of weapons to Iran. The profits went to the Contras in Nicaragua. Source: Wikipedia.
2 From The Christian Science Monitor. © 2002 by Christian Science Monitor. All rights reserved. Used under license. Christian Science Monitor – CSMonitor.com.

References

Cavafy, C. P. (1975/1990) *Collected Poems*. London: Chatto & Windus Ltd.

Curtis, A. (2002) The Century of the Self. BBC TV Documentary Series.

Fukuyama, F. (1992) The End of History? *The National Interest, Summer 1989.*

Galeano, E. (2013) *Children of the Days: A Calendar of Human History*. London: Penguin Group. Allen Lane.

Gray, R. (2004) *About Face: German Physiognomic Thought from Lavater to Auschwitz*. Detroit: Wayne State University Press.

Hillman J. and Ventura, M. (1993) *We've Had a Hundred Years of Psychotherapy and the World's Getting Worse*. San Francisco: Harper.

Jung, C. G. (1914/2020) Black Book 5, p. 207. *The Black Books*. New York: WW Norton & Company.

Jung, C. G. (1946/1970) Civilization in Transition (CW 10a, par. 453; b, par.492; c, par. 493; d, par. 451; e, par.457; f, par 488). London: Routledge Taylor & Francis.

Jung, C. G. (1968) Alchemical Studies (*CW 13*, Para 84). London: Routledge Taylor & Francis.

Lawson, T. (2010) *Carl Jung, Darwin of the Mind*. London: Karnac.

Lee, B. V. (2017) *The Dangerous Case of Donald Trump*. New York: St. Martin's Press.

Mizen, R. (2019) The affective basis of violence. *Infant Mental Health Journal*, 40, 113–128. doi:10.1002/imhj.21755

Northoff, G. and Panksepp, J. (2008) The trans-species concept of self and the subcortical–cortical midline system. *Trends in Cognitive Sciences*, 12, 259–264. doi:10.1016/j.tics.2008.04.007

Odajnyk, V. (1976) *Jung and Politics. The Political and Social Ideas of C.G. Jung*. New York: New York University Press.

Orwell, G. (1949) *Nineteen Eighty Four*. London: Secker & Warburg.

Peters, S. (2007) The 'West' against the 'Rest': Geopolitics after the end of the cold war. doi:10.1080/14650049908407654

Phelan S. and Dawes S. (2018) Liberalism and Neoliberalism. doi:10.1093/acrefore/9780190228613.013.176

Samuels, A. (2001) *Politics on the Couch. Citizenship and the Internal Life*. London: Karnac Books.

Singer, T. (2016) *Analysis & Activism, Social and political Contributions of Jungian Psychology* (Eds. Kiehl, E., Saban, M., and Samuels, A.). London: Routledge.

The Christian Science Monitor. © 2002 by Christian Science Monitor. All rights reserved. Used under license. Christian Science Monitor – CSMonitor.com.

Updike, J. (1990) *Rabbit at Rest*. New York: Alfred A. Knopf.

Chapter 10

Shadow and Earth: Eco-Psychology and the Future of the Planet

Mary-Jayne Rust

Introduction

Nature Is Shouting to Us at the Top of Her Voice. Are We Willing to Listen?

We are in the midst of major change – or transformation. Old ways of dominating Nature are falling apart. We are in liminal space, a time of great uncertainty, of chaos and suffering. The birth of the new is emerging but its shape cannot yet be seen. Part of our *psychological* task at this time is to face our ecological Shadow in all its many dimensions. This parallels, and intersects with, the psychological work of other oppressions such as racism, sexism and more.

I will begin this chapter by offering some stories to illuminate Shadow and earth, past and present. Part Two focuses on our relationship with the more-than-human world. Why do we still see ourselves as separate from, and superior to, Nature? How do we come to terms with ourselves as animals? Arguably these questions lie at the heart of our ecological crises.

In Part Three, I explore our responses to ecological crisis. The Shadow can hamper effective action: we see it in our resistance to change, in our projections onto the green movement, in the dangers of Eco-fascism. Pushing our feelings into the Shadow can lead to apathy and paralysis of action. How and where do we come together to share our pain for the world and the generations of *all* life who might follow us?

The ecological Shadow is complex and has arisen over centuries, if not millennia. It is difficult and painful to face into what we have disowned; naturally, it rouses our defences. In psychotherapy we rely on forming a trusting relationship in a safe, contained space before approaching this difficult work. *How* we face our collective Shadow in society is a crucial question. I will offer some inspiring as well as challenging stories of change. When successful this work can bring deep renewal. It offers us a chance to re-vision ourselves as humans, to recover our ancient and intimate connection with the rest of life, vitality itself.

DOI: 10.4324/9781003255819-12

I begin with a Greek myth which offers a stark mirror for the place we find ourselves in now.

Part One: The Story of King Erysichthon

Erysichthon was a vain and boastful man: He paid little attention to what other people said or thought. He paid even less attention to the gods and always did exactly as he pleased. One day he and his servants went into the woods to look for firewood. In the middle of a small grove, he spotted a fine, strong oak tree. "That's the tree I want!" Erysichthon shouted. He turned to his servants. "Cut it down right now!" But the servants would not go near the oak. "Master, we cannot cut that tree," one of them said. "It belongs to the Goddess Demeter."[1] Erysichthon laughed at them. "Give me that axe! We will see who's afraid of Demeter!"

Erysichthon picked up the axe and made a deep cut in the trunk of the oak. As he pulled the axe out of the tree bright red blood was pouring from the cut. But he ignored the strange blood, continued swinging his axe and carried the blood-soaked wood home with him. It wasn't long before Demeter found out what had happened to her favourite tree. In anger, she called upon the terrible Famine to punish Erysichthon. "Stay with Erysichthon day and night," Demeter commanded. "No matter how much he eats, it will never be enough. He will starve even as he fills himself with food." Famine did as Demeter ordered. She went to Erysichthon that very night and breathed her hunger into his body.

The next morning Erysichthon noticed that he was very hungry. The more he ate, the more he wanted but still he starved. Weeks went past and still his hunger continued. He sold everything he owned to buy food but it was never enough. In desperation, he sold his daughter to a ship's captain as a slave. With Poseidon's help she was freed, only to be sold again by her father, many times over.

Erysichthon grew weaker and weaker. He ate all day but he was starving to death. One day all the food in the house was gone. Erysichthon began to go insane with hunger. In desperation, he turned upon his own body. He chewed hungrily at his arms and legs until at last Death freed him from his torture (Mandelbaum 1993).

Reflections on the Story

This story reflects our current situation despite being written over two thousand years ago. Erysichthon (meaning "tearer of the earth") is oblivious to the bleeding of the tree; he has no awareness of Nature as sacred. He stands for the uncaring culture we inhabit which ignores the many warning signs from Nature to change our ways. Mostly we continue with business as usual: for example, 10,000 acres of rainforest are currently lost every day (Heacox 2021). No wonder Demeter is so full of rage. Her punishment is familiar to many of us in consumer culture: trying to fill emotional or soul hunger with food or material "stuff."

Erisychthon resorts to selling his daughter, symbolic of his most precious feminine self, to fund his craving. This echoes what we see in our world: what is most precious to us – such as beauty, time or the integrity of the natural world – is often sacrificed for material gain. The "other" is treated as a resource to be used with no attention to *relationship* or *reciprocity*. This is a King who has been corrupted by power. He stands for many who have reached the top only to find an empty life. But he refuses to face his Shadow so cannot find any way out of his suffering.

It is easy to feel angry with this King. But, if Erysichthon were my patient, I would be wondering what has led him to such a disconnected place where he cannot feel the suffering of others. What is he so hungry for? Equally, we might ask, what has led our culture to become so uncaring and to destroy the hand that feeds? What are we hungry for?

The Myth of Progress

Some call the story of our modern culture The Myth of Progress (Wessels 2013) in which Erysichthon could be the central character. This is familiar to all those who have experienced a western education. It describes how humans have made an epic, heroic journey from a primitive, dark world of ignorance to a brighter world of ever-increasing knowledge, freedom and well-being. This progress was made possible by the birth of human reason and the modern mind (Tarnas 2007, p. 12), driven by aspiration, ambition and power dynamic. Modern humans now see themselves as the apex of creation, separate from, and superior to, the rest of Nature. "Civilised" life and its values (in particular, white, western, rational, middle-class, urban values) are prized as success. This story sees humans as omnipotent, capable of fixing any problem through the brilliance of science and technology.

The Shadow of the Myth of Progress

What our education did not include was the Shadow side of this myth. In the early years of our species, humans enjoyed an intimate relationship with the rest of nature, often with richly sophisticated earth-based cosmologies. During our history, we gradually learned how to manipulate the world around us in search of a safer life; but this has gradually become a desire to dominate nature, creating a hierarchy of life. Those supposedly "under-neath" are treated as resources to use as we please – land, creatures, as well as people. Nature is seen as wild, brutal and out of control, at worst declared to have no soul, incapable of feeling. Certain groups of humans are branded as being closer to the earth, having a "lower", more animal nature; for some this justifies their domination and abuse. The genocide of Indigenous cultures, trans-Atlantic slavery and the oppression of women are three examples of this.

Tragically we have lost our intimate connection with the other-than-human world, a primary source of teaching and spiritual nourishment. This, together with a view that individuals exist in some kind of disconnected vacuum, is a worldview which leaves many isolated, hungry for meaning and purpose, with nothing to temper the insistent voices of "I, me and mine".

Using a depth psychology lens, we might say we are in the grip of the young male hero archetype, fighting to free ourselves from the terrible mother earth, forgetting that the earth is also the good mother who provides for all our needs. Our dominant culture displays the behaviours of an adolescent: "we" (collectively) don't clear up our mess; we are arrogant with little gratitude or thought for mothers' needs; we like total freedom with no recourse to "the other"; we think "mother" is unlimited and continue to make endless "cash" withdrawals and deposits of waste; we believe we are omnipotent and deny our dependency and vulnerability.

The truth is we are interdependent initiates learning to see in the dark, rather than superior beings.

The Myth of the Fall

Some writers (e.g. Baring and Cashford 1991; Tarnas 2007) suggest that this Shadow side of the Myth of Progress is reflected in the Myth of the Fall. The story of how Adam and Eve were expelled from the Garden of Eden can be read as a description of our withdrawal from Nature. But the traditional interpretation leaves us with unending and misguided guilt for the original sin of eating from the tree of knowledge. We are told we must atone for our flawed nature and there is no way back to the garden.

At this critical point in human history, we need a myth to live by which is about living as *part of* nature, rather than fighting it. We need to rethink where we have fallen, and what it means to progress to a life which benefits the whole earth community, rather than the privileged few.

Where we find ourselves, then, is between stories (Berry 1978, p. 77), in a liminal space, a place of great turbulence. The therapeutic task for industrial growth culture in this space of transition is to face into our collective Shadow, to understand how these myths still shape our internal worlds, our language and our defences against change, as well as to see our own part in the oppression of others. Through shedding light on these Shadows we might ask how we find renewal: what does it mean, individually and collectively, to return to The Garden?

The Clash of Two Worldviews

In his book *Edge of the Sacred* author and public intellectual David Tacey draws on Jung's thinking (Jung 1938/40, p. 140) to describe three stages of apprehending the world. In stage one, the land is sacred and spirits of the earth are seen as real forces in the world. In stage two (where we are now), these forces are seen as irrational and mere projections of the mind upon inanimate phenomena "usually to be traced back to hysterical ideas or unruly emotions" (Tacey 2009, p. 26).

While much has been achieved with the scientific, analytic mind, Tacey sees stage two thinking as responsible for the ecological crisis and calls for a stage three thinking in which the world is once again sacred. He writes: "Stage two thinking lands us in a spiritual and emotional wasteland, in which reason and science have cleansed the world of all projections, leaving nothing left in the world for us to relate to, or form spiritual bonds with. No longer sacred, it becomes real estate or "natural resource" to be used to satisfy egotistical desires" (ibid., p. 27). As we enter into stage three thinking, Tacey suggests we are becoming open again to the transpersonal forces of the earth and world but we need cosmologies appropriate to modern times.

Stage two thinking has emerged out of The Myth of Progress. It is tied into our ideas of success where everything must be faster, bigger, newer, cleaner, more international. The aspirations of the Green movement stand in contrast: slowing down growth and de-cluttering of material goods, down-sizing, investing in everything local. These values rub up against the heroic glamour of celebrity, consumer culture making the green movement a natural hook for Shadow projections. I will explore this further in section three.

In Part Two, I will explore how our collective Shadow is cast on the more-than-human world and what it means to recover our intimate connection with Nature – within and without – in our modern world.

Part Two: Shadow and the More-Than-Human World

Are there animals you fear or feel disgusted by such as snakes, slugs or cockroaches? How do you feel about yourself as an animal? How comfortable are you with sinking your bare hands into earth or spending time in wild places? Exploring these questions leads us into the Shadow territory of our relationship with earth.

"I love nature" is a commonly heard phrase: many people adore their animal companions or gardens; charismatic megafaunas, such as dolphins, whales and polar bears, capture our hearts. But do we love Covid-19? The movie "Jaws" plays on our fear of sharks. However, statistics show that around ten humans are killed by sharks every year while one hundred million sharks are killed by humans. Snakes and spiders very rarely harm humans in the UK; our fear of these animals may be ancestral or related to how they slither silently along the earth, scuttle about in dark places or suddenly emerge out of the sea.

There are many other creatures who receive our Shadow projections. "Greedy pig" is one of many expressions embedded in our language. Yet we might ask, which is the greediest animal on earth right now? "Behaving like animals" is a phrase often used to describe humans who are aggressive or behaving badly. All animals are aggressive at times when they need to defend themselves – that includes ourselves. As far as we know, humans are the only creatures on earth who are capable of calculated destruction. This phrase is, then, a good example of casting the worst of our human nature onto our nonhuman relatives.

Despite our proclaimed love for nature there remains a thick dividing line between humans and the nonhuman world. This is conveyed from our earliest experience; we are taught that nonhuman animals do not feel as we do, they do not have our superior intelligence. These beliefs give us license to continue cruel practices of factory farming, incarcerating animals for medical experiments or mining mountains because the earth is apparently dead: "it" has become an object which has no soul.

Yet when faced with these cruel practices many people are horrified. They continue, in large part, because the destruction embedded in our culture is hidden from view. We are disconnected from the source of things: buying neatly packaged meat from the supermarket shows no trace of the cruelty involved in its production; it is even illegal in the USA to photograph inside a factory farm. The production of palm oil (in so many foods and products) entails the clear-cutting forests to make way for palm oil plantations; this degrades the land and displaces Indigenous peoples as well as wildlife. Our smartphones do not reveal the child labour in the mining of rare minerals. Seeing the horror behind what we consume requires us to do some research.

The way we see wild nature is also polarised. Wilderness has been feared as dark and dangerous, a place to be tamed or civilised; it is also seen as "empty space" to be "developed" or mined for resources. In recent years it has become idealised as pristine, pure, a place of divinity; white, wealthy tourists fly there for a "nature experience", to detox from the stresses and poisons of consumer culture, ironically damaging the earth on the way.

Holding the Tension of Opposites

Looking back at our history we see times when the tension between opposites has been held. The symbol for modern medicine is an image of a snake wrapped around the staff of the Greek physician Asclepius: the snake's venom has the capacity to heal, poison or expand consciousness. In western Astrology, Aries (the Ram), Capricorn (the Goat), Cancer (the Crab) are neither idealised nor denigrated but valued for their many qualities, acting as symbols which enable us to get to know the many-sided human self.

In his paper "The Eagle and the Serpent", Jungian Analyst Roderick Peters describes how the eagle and serpent, who stand for archetypal polarities, have always been engaged in an age-old struggle, appearing in stories through the ages as well as in our dreams. He describes "Eagle mind" as an experience of flying above things, getting an objective overview, with piercing, focused vision, a place of transcendence, more separate from the earth, associated with the elements of fire, air and spirit. "Serpent mind" is an experience of being close to, or inside, the dark earth, a piercing and paralysing power of a deep and inward kind, a subjective, participatory experience associated with water and earth. He suggests that serpent mind is to be found through going "down and down through the evolutionary layers within our bodily nature and so feel a sense of linking up with the dimmest and deepest roots of life. Through it we can know renewal, as if we have touched vitality itself. The descent feels full of dangers because we know we have gone into the power of the old serpent ... The 'I' [of our conscious experience] ... is all but submerged in feelings of oneness, oceanic feelings, feelings of isolation, abandonment, eternity, infinity, fear, love, hatred, rage; all the passions in fact" (Peters 1987, p. 373).

This is a fine description of our deep fears in relation to earth. The "I" is terrified of losing itself into the boundlessness of the Great Mystery, becoming one with Nature. Yet, as Indigenous peoples have known for thousands of years, when we are able to surrender to this experience of oneness there is potential for deep healing, for becoming whole.

According to Peters, in Norse mythology the eagle and the serpent are to be found *in relationship* in the world tree, the eagle perched on the branches and the snake curled at the roots. As time went on, the eagle gradually became the victor while the snake carried our Shadow projections, paralleling the move towards a transcendent spirituality and a rising fear of earth, embodiment and darkness. For example, in many Christian churches today the eagle is on the lectern carrying the Bible, and the snake is held firmly by its claws, or absent altogether (ibid., pp. 361–364). In the Judeo-Christian Myth of the Fall, the snake has become an evil creature tempting Eve to eat the forbidden fruit from the Tree of Knowledge.

Our increasing fear of body and earth has taken centuries to evolve. There is a fear of regressing down the evolutionary scale into something "primitive" and losing what we believe to be our special human qualities; a fear of being swallowed by something so much larger and more powerful than ourselves, a fear of experiences we cannot explain with the rational mind; a fear of being taken over by the senses, "led up the garden path" unable to think. These fears underlie many polarisations between body and mind, earth and sky, ancient and modern, emotion and thought, *eros* and *logos*,[2] matter and spirit.

It is these unconscious fears that might block our willingness to re-unite with the earth. How do we address those fears and begin to integrate what has been disowned? I will give some examples of ways in which our Shadow projections onto the more-than-human world are coming to light and bringing change to our modern lives.

Animals Are Sentient

Primatologist Jane Goodall has devoted her life to studying the social life of chimpanzees. In a public talk I attended she described how she regularly visits chimps being used in medical research. On one visit she met Billy-Jo, a chimp living in a cage measuring 5′ × 5′, with no light and simply a car tyre; he had lived in this cage for ten years. When she met his gaze, she saw how happy he was that someone had relieved the grinding monotony of the day for the only time he had any stimulation was when he was taken out to have liver biopsies or other tests. Tears welled up in her eyes and started to trickle down her face at the sight of this animal so deprived of his freedom and dignity. Billy-Jo then reached out through the bars and caught the tear on Jane's cheek while he carried on grooming her wrist (Goodall 1999).

This story describes the unbearable suffering of intelligent animals in the hands of medical research. It also shows Billy-Jo's capacity to "feel with" as he gently catches Jane's tear.[3] This may surprise many readers for it reveals how much dignity, resilience, care and feeling this animal is capable of, standing in stark contrast to King Erysichthon and the inhumanity of mainstream culture today.

Jane Goodall's storytelling touches the hearts of millions around the world and her research contributes to the changing views about our closest relatives. She is one of an increasing number of people who bring emotional intelligence into the world of science. One outcome of this work is that animals are soon to be recognised as sentient in UK domestic law.

A Growing Respect for Wild Nature

Isabella Tree's book *Wilding: The Return of Nature to a British Farm* describes her inspiring re-wilding project with her husband on their 3,500-acre Knepp estate just 45 miles from central London. Seeing the deterioration of their land and soil they stopped intensive farming in 2002. Using grazing animals as the drivers of habitat creation, the project has seen extraordinary increases in wildlife. This shows how quickly Nature can restore herself given the right conditions. This has received a great deal of media attention in recent years and inspired many others to re-wild land around the UK.

At the core of this vision is the trust in the intelligence of wild nature which has its own order. This counters our centuries-old view that nature must be controlled and dominated by "man." Tree describes the resistance they met from their local community to their proposals in the early days: "It was an affront to the efforts of every self-respecting farmer, (seen as) an immoral waste of land, an assault on Britishness itself" (Tree 2018, p. 98).

Alongside the re-wilding movement there is a move towards enshrining the rights of nature in law. In March 2017 New Zealand granted rights of personhood to the Whanganui River which flows across the North Island; that means the river has legal standing and can act as a person in a court of law. In 2008, Ecuador became the first country to recognise Rights of Nature in its Constitution. Rather than treating nature as property under the law, Rights for Nature articles acknowledge that nature in all its life forms has the right to exist, persist, maintain and regenerate its vital cycles (Siddique 2008). There are many complications with putting these laws into practice but the statements show an important step in the direction of respect for Nature, away from human domination.

Re-Wilding Humans?

The majority of modern humans suffer both physically and psychologically from being over-domesticated. Just as we have gradually withdrawn from an intimate relationship with the rest of nature, so we have withdrawn from inhabiting our bodies – to the point where many see the body as a biological vehicle for their minds to get from one meeting to another! We "forget" we are animals, primates, mammals; calling someone an ape, or an animal, is very insulting. Our animal nature is commonly seen as the instinctual part of the self: aggressive, disinhibited, the Mr Hyde of Dr Jekyll, the Shadow of our rational selves. Re-wilding the self is about re-claiming our animal nature as a vital source of energy, guidance and wisdom, offering a great deal more than instinct.

Many people suffer great inner conflict between their rational and embodied selves. I have seen this in my work with women with eating problems over several decades. One client, whom I shall call Emma, brought dreams of a terrifying alien creature with rows of teeth, bursting out of the stomach, reminiscent of "The Alien" in sci-fi horror films. This image personified her regular binge eating: she was so alienated from her needs they now appeared in monstrous form, as if separate from her, having been feared and pushed away for so long.

Part of the therapeutic work was to help Emma re-inhabit her body. As she slowly began to listen to, trust and follow her body it then became an ally. This was a very difficult, long and painful process for her as she was frequently in the grip of a severe analytic, rational part of the self who had no time for feelings or vulnerability, who viewed intuition with deep suspicion and feelings as time-wasting. In fact, this part of herself was against the whole project of psychotherapy so it was astounding she managed to come to therapy each week. Her attitude had been internalised from both parents. The other part of her, whom she called her "body-soul," was drawn to paint and to spend time walking by her local river often accompanied by her friend's dog. Her body-soul found the work of therapy invaluable yet was frequently silenced by the rational self and this would often take her to a very empty and depressed place in between sessions.

Gradually she began to see that, in fact, the rational self was *afraid* of her body-soul with its messiness, unpredictable feelings, its fluid way of being in the world, with no facts or measurements for reference. It was painstaking work to gradually facilitate a conversation between these two parts of the self. One of the many things that supported Emma to reconnect with her intuition, her sensual world and her feelings was her relationship with her animal companion, her local river and particular trees. It was clear that Emma's inner world was shaped by both parental influences and cultural forces.

The Jungian map of the self identifies four functions or capacities: thinking, feeling, sensing and intuiting. We live in an overly rational culture which values the intellect and is often at odds with the other three functions which are rooted in the body. Intuition is frequently distrusted and mocked by the rational self and, as a result, may remain hidden even though we may rely on it regularly. As a result of history, intuition can carry great fear, especially for women; Janet Horne was the last woman burned at the stake for witchcraft in Sutherland, UK in 1722 (Neill 1923). The senses may be feared as seductive, leading us astray from our capacity to think; yet it is through our sensing bodies that we come into relationship with the earth. Emotional intelligence is still treated with some caution in our "stiff upper lip" culture of Britain. But thankfully it is now possible for many to speak out in our culture, without shame, about the hardships of mental illness and the benefits of talking about our feelings. One hundred years of psychotherapy have helped to facilitate this culture change.

In his book *Wild Therapy: Undomesticating Inner and Outer Worlds*, Nick Totton suggests that wild therapy is a corresponding form of re-wilding humans and human culture (Totton 2011). Some forms of psychotherapy, including Jungian, recognise the unconscious as the wild part of the self. In bringing the unconscious to light are we trying to tame or control our wild natures? Or are we exploring the unknown parts of the self in order to live with the diverse aspects of ourselves more easily? These are two very different intentions.

In recent years some therapists have been offering sessions outdoors in various forms of what is known as ecotherapy. Of course, we are part of nature and in nature all of the time but when we are outdoors, it is easier to feel more connected with the nonhuman world. There are ways in which the more-than-human world offers rich metaphors for the relational and inner work of therapy. Creatures may visit at synchronous moments bringing with them meaning and sometimes numinous experiences, as if in a dream. I have written more about this, and other forms of ecotherapy, elsewhere (Rust 2020, chs. 1, 2 & 4).

If we want to deepen any relationship and get to know "the other" we must spend time together; the same is true of our relationship with the more-than-human world. The danger in our modern world is that we learn about nature through the screen; some of this is reliable information but much of it is not. For example, Jungian psychologist and wilderness guide Ian McCallum writes: "Recently, while guiding a group of international participants attending a conference at a South African game lodge, one of the delegates on a first-time visit to Africa announced that she did not want to see any hyenas or vultures. I asked her, 'Why not?' and she answered, 'Well … there's something evil about them … you can't trust them … and hyenas are cowardly aren't they?' 'Where did you get that information?' I protested. 'From the movie *The Lion King*,' she replied awkwardly" (McCallum 2008, p. 52). This exchange shows how our attitudes towards the rest of nature are shaped by the culture we inhabit from an early age.

The recent swing from denigration to idealisation of wilderness runs parallel to the recent idealisation of everything "natural." But just as our rational selves distrust our embodied capacities, we see that many in the "everything natural" tribe distrust science and everything "rational." This is an unhelpful split which has especially come to light during the Covid pandemic where two sides of the vaccination debate have become polarised according to belief and identity. This polarisation and confusion that we see in our relationship with the rest of nature is inevitably part of bringing to light what is in our Shadow.

Shadow Projections onto People Associated with Nature

My client, Gloria, who I had been seeing for a long time, arrived very distressed; on her way to therapy some white youths had leaned out of a car and shouted "Monkey, monkey" at her, making some insulting gestures. Naturally she was profoundly shocked and so was I. It was some years since she had been on the receiving end of such blatant racism although as a black woman she was used to frequent and demeaning micro-incidents of racism, which can easily go unnoticed by white people. After she talked about her experiences of racism at length, and the session was nearing an end, she smiled as she reflected further on this incident. "The funny thing is," she said, "I love monkeys and the great apes. They're often seen as stupid animals but actually they're intelligent and quite beautiful. I guess those young, working-class, white guys are often made to feel stupid; maybe they were using me, as a black woman, to get rid of their feelings of shame – shame of feeling less than others, or even of feeling less than human." By making this move she stepped out of identifying with the racist *and* anthropocentric (and possibly sexist!) pro-jection cast onto her (Rust 2020, p. 98).

Many people of colour, including indigenous peoples, are seen as "animal" or "wild"; this is part of the appalling racism and cultural genocide they have suffered during centuries of colonisation. Women have also been closely associated with Nature, seen as hysterical, incapable of the highly prized rational thought. Cultural healing includes facing Shadow projec-tions: the oppressor must re-own what s/he has cast out and the oppressed must loosen their identification with what they have internalised – as Gloria managed to do. But this is not a straightforward process. For example, acknowledging my own white racism, as well as my own oppression of Nature, is not easy: there is deep shame in uncovering the ways in which my white privilege operates. Sometimes the different forms of oppression intersect, as we see in the above example.

Arguably, our confused and ambivalent relationship with Nature is one of the main threads that has led to our current ecological crises. Witnessing the slow increase in awareness of racism (white supremacy), sexism (male supremacy) and other oppressions offers a chink of light to the work of transforming anthropocentrism (human supremacy).

Part Three: Facing Our Shadow in the Struggle for Change

So far, I have looked at the many ways we cast our Shadow onto Nature. Now I will explore the Shadow and our responses to ecological crises.

Rachel Carson published Silent Spring in 1962; since then a host of en-vironmentalists, scientists, ecologists and others have worked tirelessly to protect the earth. Sadly, relatively little has changed, although at least we now have global agreement that we have an ecological crisis! It is hardly surprising that many activists are left feeling frustrated and angry; but anger can become explosive when it remains in the Shadow, as we see in the fol-lowing example.

Some years ago a small, green NGO released a short campaign film about reducing carbon emissions. It shows several scenarios (eg school classroom, football coaching, company staff meeting) in which audiences are asked who will take part in action for the earth. Most put up their hands enthusiastically; the few who say no are told "It's fine, that's your own choice, no pressure" but they are then blown to pieces, spat-tering blood everywhere. This was supposed to be funny in an edgy, Monty-Python style.

The film was pulled just hours after being released after much strong criticism along with damning reports in the media. Showing green activists as terrorists was a terrible mistake; yet there are many interesting things to learn from this short film.

Firstly, I can imagine how satisfying it must have been for the campaigners to release their pent-up rage with mainstream culture through film and turn it into dark humour. However, while the film may have been therapeutic for the campaigners, this is not the way to get people on side. Rather, it shows how activists deserve support to process their feelings in this very difficult work otherwise they risk blowing up their campaigns or suffering burn-out – or both!

Secondly, people's lack of action or apathy is often seen as lack of care. In fact, the great majority of people do care very much about the earth and our future but many are paralysed by intense feelings they are unable to process (Lertzman 2015). This is not helped by receiving more alarming facts, using fear to try and shake people awake; this may well be traumatising rather than awakening. Many people are now suffering from overwhelm or simply struggling to cope with daily life. Recently, ecopsychologist Zhiwa Woodbury suggested that climate change would better be described as "climate trauma" due to receiving more and more alarming news of this apocalyptic crisis unfolding in our world (Woodbury 2019).

Furthermore, there has been a great deal of misinformation spread by those invested in fossil fuels. This has been a major cause of climate change denial (Hamilton 2010). Threats to the lives of activists and journalists reporting on this subject make this work unsafe; according to Global Witness, 227 activists working to protect the environment and land rights were murdered in 2020 (www.globalwitness.org). If we are to *communicate* climate change effectively, we must understand our fearful and zombie-like mainstream culture. It's important to note, here, that many methods have been tried over the years, such as presenting a vision of a positive green future. There is no one method that will persuade all: diversity is key.

Thirdly, this film portrays green activists as fascist. The history of ecofascism has left an indelible link in peoples' minds between the Green Party and extreme social control. Many suggest the bringing together of fascism and environmentalism began with the Nazis (Biehl & Staudenmaier 1996). They passed laws including a ban on vivisection, animal trapping, the use of animals in films or any public event causing damage to their health or well-being, and the slaughter of animals without anaesthetic. Animal protection was to be part of school education. The Reich Nature Protection Law, passed in 1935, had the aim of preventing damage to the environment in undeveloped areas, protecting forests and animals and reducing air pollution. These policies sound excellent. However, when Göring announced an end to the "unbearable torture and suffering in animal experiments" he added "those who still think they can continue to treat animals as inanimate property will be sent to concentration camps" (Arluke & Sanders 1996, p. 133). Animals were to be treated as subjects while Jews and other groups of humans were relegated to objects. More recent versions of ecofascism include removing indigenous peoples from their lands to create "pristine" wilderness.

Rage with Humans

In the past decade I've been hearing expressions such as "the earth would be better off without us," "human extinction would be good for nature," or "humans are a cancer or virus on the earth." This is another version of clearing humans for the sake of nature. While I sympathise with the intention to protect the earth, I also see it as apocalyptic thinking: reaching a point of utter frustration where erasing everything to start afresh seems easier than staying with the complexity of our mess. How difficult it is to stay with our remorse and shame, to own our part in the situation, to remain in connection with the demonised "other" – finding compassion for them even. Holding the tension between polarised views is very challenging at this time when there is a strong tendency to collapse into black-and-white thinking.

Further, not all humans are responsible for this chaos. For example, the carbon emissions of the world's richest 1% are double the amount of the world's poorest 50% (Gore 2020). While this is only one measure of the many forms of ecocide, we know it is the wealthiest countries that are responsible for the climate crisis.

The Need for Psychological Understanding

As I witness the increasing turbulence of climate change and the horrors of ecocide, I notice a range of feelings: fear, anger, guilt, grief or despair – especially for future generations (of all life on earth) who will face increasing chaos in the coming decades. It is often difficult to stay with "the trouble." I notice the temptation to push my feelings into the Shadow and "return to normal" – a wish that has been strongly voiced as we have journeyed through the recent pandemic. But pushing my feelings away may impede my capacity to harness my energy for environmental action (Randall, 2005).

The scale and complexity of the crisis is overwhelming. But effective action will not happen on a large enough scale until enough people *feel* the emergency. As powerful storms, floods and wildfires cause havoc in many parts of the world people *are* waking up to the seriousness of ecocide. As a result, there has been a huge rise in reports of "eco-anxiety" in adults as well as in children. Eco-anxiety is a relatively new term which covers a range of feelings; is not something to be "treated" (unless the individual can't cope) but rather a healthy response to an extremely worrying situation.

We cannot face this alone. Those who have sought help from psychotherapy know the value of having someone experienced to accompany them on their journey into the depths. Confronting the Shadow is not something you can do in the first meeting! We need to form a therapeutic alliance so the client can feel safely contained. Where are those safe containers in our society to face our collective Shadow?

Grief in the Shadow

Buddhist scholar and deep ecologist Joanna Macy was one of the first to suggest that we need to "honour our pain for the world" within community. She emphasises that our emotional responses are part of a healthy response-ability to a catastrophic eco-crisis. Allowing the feelings to flow means that we can move from a state of numbness and apathy to feeling empowered to act – in her words "from despair to empowerment." She has developed a set of practices known as "The Work that Reconnects" (Macy & Young Brown 1998).

In 1992, she offered a series of workshops to people living in areas contaminated by the nuclear disaster of Chernobyl, Russia. They describe themselves as "people of the forest" and yet, because of contamination, the only contact they had with trees was the forest wallpaper inside their homes. The effects of the disaster included a range of physical illnesses, as well as explosive anger and grief. Yet the group was reluctant to talk about this; they'd had enough pain and wanted to move on. "Why have you done this to us?" one woman cried out. "I'd be willing to feel the sorrow, all the sorrow in the world, if it could save my daughters from cancer. Can my tears protect them? What good are my tears if they can't?" Joanna responded with "I have no wisdom to meet your grief. But I can share this with you: after the war which almost destroyed their country, the German people determined that they would do anything to spare their children the suffering they had known. They worked hard to give them a rich and safe life. They created an economic miracle. They gave their children everything - except for one thing. They did not give them their broken hearts."

The following morning everyone returned to the workshop. The first to speak was the above-mentioned woman who said: "It feels like my heart is breaking open. Maybe it will keep breaking again and again every day, I don't know. But somehow, I can't explain, it feels right. This breaking connects me to everything and everyone, as if we were all branches of the same tree." One by one they said that it had been very hard, but now they were beginning to feel cleansed, uncontaminated, for the first time (Macy 2000, pp. 7–8).

This moving story shows the value of releasing stuck grief within a community suffering from traumatic events. As climate change and ecocide worsen, we need community containers for this kind of psychological work. We need emotional education to understand the stages of grief, how to work with explosive rage or soften the stuckness of despair. Therapists have an important role to play in society to hold safe spaces for citizens who need to share and work through their thoughts and feelings about collective events. Besides The Work That Reconnects Network (founded by Joanna Macy) there are numerous other initiatives such as climate cafes (see Climate Psychology Alliance), Active Hope groups and Grief Tending Communities.

The Clash between Two Different Worldviews

Here is an example of a successful Scottish campaign that highlights the clash between two worldviews: earth as utility and earth as sacred. This case is interesting because it brings attention to the Shadow without directly confronting it, which – as we know – can arouse our defences in an unhelpful way.

In the early 1990s a concrete manufacturing company called Lafarge proposed building a super-quarry in a mountain on the Isle of Harris, a National Scenic area of NW Scotland. Scottish activist and Human Ecologist Alastair McIntosh campaigned against this proposal for the biggest road-stone quarry in the world, despite it having 90% informal backing from the local community initially. He believed that our relationship with place is central to a sustainable livelihood (McIntosh 1996).

McIntosh invited two witnesses from very different backgrounds to support him in this case: Rev Professor Donald Macleod, a native Gaelic preacher, and Stone Eagle, a Native American warrior chief, who had been involved in campaigning against a super-quarry in his homeland of Nova Scotia. Both men argued that the land should be shown reverence because it is sacred; it would be an act of desecration to mine the mountain. This caught the imagination of the general public and soon there were newspaper articles and radio programmes about this campaign which then became international news. After a very long and protracted fight, the plans for the quarry were rejected. Part of that success was due to the voices of those who articulated to the community a different narrative, counteracting the idea that land is mere utility.

The idea that land is sacred, that it nourishes the soul, is a difficult case to argue. Frequently this voice is either absent altogether or drowned out by the argument that "development" is economically beneficial to the community and therefore the necessary route. While this campaign was successful in the tight-knit community of a Scottish Isle, I wonder whether it would work in other communities who are less in touch with land as sacred.

Final Reflections

To summarise, becoming aware of our Shadow is an arduous journey. Confronting parts of the self we would rather not own may arouse strong feelings such as disgust, shame, grief or anger; at times this can feel like being lost at sea with no clear sense of who one is anymore as our identity is re-visioned. As we face our ecological Shadow, our *human* identity is challenged for it is defined, in part, by denying our animality and believing we are the "special" species. Rather, we are one species among many who all have unique qualities and intelligence.

While the psychological work of owning the Shadow involves loss and surrender, it can also bring profound renewal. Climbing down off the plinth of human superiority may feel humiliating; yet humiliation comes from the Latin *humiliare* which means "to humble" and *humus* which means "earth". Coming down to earth is coming to our senses; we sorely need to be grounded during times of crisis. We have literally been grounded during the recent pandemic and, despite the difficulties of lockdown, many have welcomed the time spent getting to know their local environment. Being stopped in our tracks, like grounded teenagers, has perhaps opened the door to further reflect on our part in the growing climate crisis.

Being an embodied part of Nature will always be painful and scary – but it is also the source of vitality. Spending time in wilderness can be brutal but it is also a place of deep, spiritual connection. Inhabiting our creatureliness puts us back in touch with vital instinct, intuition, our senses and our feelings. When these different capacities work together with our thinking minds there is a chance or wisdom to emerge, a chance to move from *homo industrialis destructivensis* to *homo sapiens*, wise person.

In this chapter I have given examples of the ways in which this change is underway: recognising the sentience of the animal and plant kingdoms is growing; the re-wilding and regenerative agriculture movements are seeing the fruits of working with, and learning from, Nature. There is a move away from control and domination of Nature towards respecting the intelligence of Nature. I have also described the value of working with difficult emotional states in community building and activism. Psychological reflection is a vital part of activism.

However, this growing awareness is still dwarfed by those who wish to maintain "business as usual". Capitalism relies on using the earth as a set of resources to create wealth. We are living well beyond the limits of our mother body, so it is hard to imagine how we might achieve enough systemic change in time to contain global temperature rise. As a result, many people are predicting collapse or, at worst, extinction in the coming century – reflecting the story of Erysichthon. Perhaps the certainty of collapse is strangely more comforting than tolerating uncertainty? In a system so complex as the web of life on earth, we can never be certain of what will unfold. Unlikely though it seems at present, something may be born out of this time of evolutionary intensity that we cannot imagine with our current ways of seeing and thinking.

In many ways the various future predictions become a distraction from the healing that is always possible in the present moment. The vital work of facing our personal and collective Shadow is about truth, repair and reconciliation. If we listen to, observe and attend to Nature, within *and* without, we will discover our next steps. Healing ourselves and our culture, coming back into relationship with the more-than-human world, depends on how far we dare to come out of our comfort zones.

Notes

1 Demeter is the Greek goddess of the harvest and fertility; she also presided over the cycle of life and death.
2 Eros is the principle of relatedness and the desire for wholeness. Although this may initially take the form of passionate love, it is a desire for interconnection and interaction with other sentient beings. The antithesis of Eros is Logos, the Greek term for rationality, which is about dividing, reasoning, judging, discriminating and reasoning.
3 After being in captivity for entertainment, then medical research during which time he endured 300 medical procedures, Billy-Jo was finally rescued into a sanctuary. You can read his full story here: https://releasechimps.org/chimpanzees/their-stories/billy-jo

References

Arluke, A. & Sanders, C. (1996). *Regarding Animals*. PA: Temple University Press.

Baring, A. & Cashford, J. (1991). *The Myth of the Goddess: Evolution of an Image*. London: Penguin.

Berry, T. (1978). The New Story: Comments on the Origin, Identification and Transmission of Values. *Teilhard Studies, 1* (Winter), 77–88.

Biehl, J. & Staudenmaier, P. (1996). *Ecofascism Revisited: Lessons from the German Experience*. Norway: New Compass Press.

Carson, R. (1962). *Silent Spring*. Boston: Houghton Mifflin.

Goodall, J. (1999). Lecture at Conference 'For the Love of Nature' Findhorn Foundation, Scotland, June 1999.

Gore, T. (2020). Confronting Carbon Inequality. *Oxfam Briefing Paper* 21 Sept 2020. https://www.oxfam.org/en/research/confronting-carbon-inequality

Hamilton, C. (2010). *Requiem for a Species*. New York: Earthscan.

Heacox, K. (2021) The Amazon Rainforest is Losing about 10,000 acres per day. Guardian 7 Oct 2021. https://www.theguardian.com/commentisfree/2021/oct/07/the-amazon-rain-forest-is-losing-200000-acres-a-day-soon-it-will-be-too-late

Jung, C.G. (1938/1940). Psychology and Religion. *CW* 11. 1958/1969.

Lertzman, R. (2015). *Environmental Melancholia*. New York: Routledge.

Macy, J. (2000). *The Elm Dance*. Pub. Joanna Macy.

Macy, J. & Young Brown, M. (1998). *Coming Back to Life: Practices to Reconnect Our Lives, Our World*. Gabriola Island: New Society.

Mandelbaum, A. (1993) trans. *The Metamorphoses of Ovid*. Book V111. New York: Harcourt Brace.

McCallum, I. (2008). *Ecological Intelligence: Rediscovering Ourselves in Nature*. CO: Fulcrum Pub.

McIntosh, A. (1996). Theology, Rocks, Superquarry Project. *Ailing Magazine Issue 19*.

Neill, W. N. (1923). The Last Execution for Witchcraft in Scotland, 1722. *Scottish Historical Review, 20* (79), 218–221.

Peters, R. (1987). The Eagle and the Serpent. *Journal of Analytical Psychology, 32*, 359–381.

Randall, R. (2005). A New Climate for Psychotherapy? In *Psychotherapy and Politics International Issue 3, 3*, 165–179.

Rust, M-J. (2020). *Towards an Ecopsychotherapy*. London: Confer Books.

Siddique, H. (2008) Ecuador Referendum Endorses New Socialist Constitution. (Guardian, 29 Sept, 2008. Retrieved from https://www.theguardian.com/global/2008/sep/29/ecuador).

Tacey, D. (2009). *Edge of the Sacred: Jung, Psyche, Earth*. Einseidein: Daimon Verlag.

Tarnas, R. (2007). *Cosmos and Psyche*. New York: Penguin.

Totton, N. (2011). *Wild Therapy: Undomesticating Inner and Outer Worlds*. Ross-on-Wye: PCCS Books.

Tree, I. (2018). *Wilding: The Return of Nature to a British Farm*. London: Picador.

Wessels, T. (2013) *The Myth of Progress*. University Press of New England.

Woodbury, Z. (2022). *Climate Trauma, Reconciliation & Recovery: Coming into Proper Relationship with Mother Earth*. Independently published.

Chapter 11

"Existential Threat" and Large Group Anxiety

Coline Covington

In March 2019, Sir James Bevan, chief executive of the Environment Agency, predicted that in 20–25 years England would be in "the jaws of death" without enough water to supply our needs.

For many of us, our expectation of continuing growth and prosperity and limitless natural resources is no longer sustainable. We are having to manage loss on a large scale: loss of resources, loss of industries, and loss of traditional social structures. Globalisation has created radical shifts in the world economy, resulting in increasing inequality, immigration, and erosion of national identities. These shifts are deeply affecting our identity both as individuals and as members of communities.

Climate change is especially threatening because it confronts us with the fact that we cannot control the most elemental forces of nature nor can we stop the earth from its trajectory towards extinction. Every time the weather surprises us with unseasonal extremes, we are reminded of not just our human mortality but the earth's mortality. Paradoxically, the fact that climate change threatens our very existence makes it harder to take seriously.

Change by its very nature is difficult for most of us to manage even in the best of circumstances. But climate change also challenges our world view that we can rely on a relatively homeostatic environment, albeit subject to the occasional vagaries of hurricanes and plagues of locusts. Galileo's demonstrations that the earth moves around the sun created huge resistance as did Einstein's theory of relativity. Both theories challenged the world view of the time and, as Thomas Kuhn was to argue in the 1960s,[1] they also debunked the scientific paradigm based on the notion that scientific progress is based on "development-by-accumulation." These revolutions in scientific thought call into question our most basic assumptions about how we perceive and understand our world. They radically undermine the idea that knowledge is a conscious and logical process that provides us with some sense of predictability and security, along with our belief that we are the centre of the universe and can shape and control our future.

DOI: 10.4324/9781003255819-13

Climate change fundamentally challenges our ability to predict what is going to happen in the future. Blake Suttle, a climate change scientist at University of California, Berkeley, comments:

> "We're likely to encounter climate regimes that there is no precedent for in modern times of observation (and where there is no past analog data for) .... Another (difficulty) is that biological systems don't tend to behave linearly.... no individual population or organisms or species experiences climate change in a vacuum. Instead, any given species is experiencing climate change amidst all of the surrounding community members that are also experiencing climate change. So what we see are changes in interactions up and down the food web that can really drive predictions into disarray." (Interview with Blake Suttle, in "Predicting Biodiversity" by Julie Gould, January 18, 2013.)

It is increasingly evident that, because of the diverse nature of ecosystems, we have only a relatively limited ability to predict the future and some change is happening faster than we anticipated. We are already experiencing the dramatic effects of climate change in floods, droughts, fires, and the extinction of certain species. In 2016, the US government awarded $48.3 million to the residents of Isle de Jean Charles in Louisiana to relocate due to rising waters to a safer, planned community. They were the first "climate refugees" to be given aid by the government. In 2020, the US estimated there were 1.2 million climate refugees within its borders and rising. But, if this is any consolation, earth has experienced climate change in the past – e.g., between 10–11 thousand years ago, in the Pleistocene epoch, all of the megafauna in the US went extinct within the span of a few hundred to a thousand years and yet new species evolved. What Suttle describes as the disarray of predictions opens up the possibility of new forms of life just as much as it foretells the destruction of life as we know it. Whether our own species will survive is another matter – and the real issue as far as we're concerned.

There is nevertheless a prevailing optimism that we will figure out new solutions to our changing environment in the future, as, e.g., when new energy sources are found and developed. Despite our optimism, we still need to remember that the earth is on a trajectory that will absolutely and with certainty end in its death, albeit in multi-billions of years' time, coinciding with the sun's implosion. The exploration of planets that may sustain other forms of life in our universe is certainly driven by some collective, semi-conscious awareness that, just as we discovered the New World in 1492, we will most likely need to move on to colonize greener pastures at some point in the future.

The debate about climate change can be viewed as a conflict about control – how much control we have over our environment and how we negotiate this politically and economically. Territorial power lies at the heart of the conflict with all its attendant anxieties about the survival of the group. The preeminent concern is not so much about the destruction of resources as about who owns what and where – who has control over Mother Earth. Climate change deniers can be criticized as living under the narcissistic illusion that the earth is our possession, to be used as we wish, and that, like mother's breast, it will always be available to us without running dry. This is a view of omnipotent control that banishes the anxiety of loss and impotence.

At the other extreme are those who argue that we are the culprits who are single-handedly destroying the breast – this argument, unfortunately, views humans as more powerful than we really are. It is similar to the child's egocentric idea that when mother is in a bad mood, it must be because of something she has done. Although humans can have a destructive impact on Mother Nature, she has a life of her own. When we are frightened of changes that are to some extent beyond our control, we tend to either deny the changes – to wish them away – or to take full responsibility for them in the illusion that we are in total control – e.g., the idea that we can "save the planet." The reality is somewhere in-between and produces in our psyches what in psycho-jargon we call "depressive anxiety." This means that we are aware of our own destructiveness and our own limits – a state of mind that for most of us is hard to tolerate.

In the Extinction Rebellion protest in London in April 2019, protestors argued that saving the planet is more important than Brexit and should be given pride of place amongst the woes affecting our lives. As school girl Greta Thunberg, protesting about climate change, dramatically declared outside the Swedish parliament, "Why should we go to school when there's no future?" On the other hand, some onlookers in London disagreed with the protest, claiming that Brexit and knife crime are more important issues than climate change. What was so striking about these seemingly disparate views is that they come from the same emotional experience of fear and impotence. The zeitgeist in most developed countries is, "everything is changing, nothing can be relied on, there is more competition than ever before, basic survival is not as assured as it seemed to be 50 years ago, the rich are getting richer and the poor are getting poorer, and even if you have all the advantages on offer, there is no guarantee of a good life." At heart the question is, "What kind of future is there for us?" and, even more fundamentally, "*Is* there a future for us?"

It is no coincidence that climate change deniers are allied with populist movements. But what is the psychology behind this and how is it culture specific?

When immediate economic and political survival is threatened, the issue of climate change needs to be understood through the lens of large group behaviour and the particular anxieties that affect group identity and cohesion and how identity has been shaped historically. A case in point is the US Tea Party position against climate change that followed in the wake of the 2001 twin towers attack and economic recession. The US was militarily invaded for the first time since its independence and this effectively marked a turning point in the American view of itself as an invincible world power. The recession, starting in 2007 that led to the collapse of Bear Stearns and Lehman Brothers the following year, only underscored the vulnerability of the US in relation to the rest of the world. The Tea Party response was to revert to the frontier myth of a rich wilderness offering unlimited resources. Sarah Palin was photographed with her bearskin trophies as the "new" frontier woman. This was the Party's way of trying to restore some illusion of control and omnipotence through the regressive belief the group could once again possess a wilderness with endless boundaries, like an ever-flowing breast. In this way, a segment of the US population tried to regain a sense of identity and security. Trump's subsequent ascension to power and his mantra, "Make America Great Again!" is a response to the wish to turn back the clock to a time when change was not associated with loss but with prosperity.

A similar political dynamic was apparent with the call for Brexit in the UK rising from a sense of disempowerment linked to global economic change and the erosion of traditional social structures. Harking back to a time of greatness, the Empire, and viewing dependency on outsiders as more of a restriction than a help is part of a natural response in the face of loss. We can see very clearly in both the US and the UK (and across Europe) that anxiety about loss of identity is managed by defence mechanisms of splitting and projection. The threat is located outside the group. In this way, the group strengthens its moral superiority and identity while demonizing outsiders or those who disagree – creating a destructive and polarized impasse.

Another large group response to instability and loss of identity is to identify with the powerful aggressor. The Democratic Republic of Congo is a tragic example of this where, following Belgium's colonisation and over a hundred years of theft of the country's rich resources, recent governments continue to collude with corrupt practices as a way of scrambling their way out of poverty and disempowerment. The entrenched levels of government corruption that are directly impacting on the region's environment can be viewed as a form of large-scale identification with the aggressor that serves to bolster an insecure group identity.

These examples illustrate how the historical and political contexts within different countries have an essential bearing on their views of climate change and their policy-making. Nowhere is this more evident as it is in contemporary China, where the commitment to climate change mitigation has made it a leading global force, underscoring its ambition for world supremacy. While it is important to acknowledge the basic psychological dynamics of denial and destructiveness that are present in every human interaction, the specific external reality within which these dynamics are played out is also essential to our deeper understanding. As in the case of individuals, group identity carries with it a collective and historical consciousness that profoundly affects our relation to the world around us.

When reality threatens the way we live, our expectations of the future, and how we identify ourselves within the world, then, as I have argued, we try to protect ourselves from loss through psychological defences such as regression and denial. And we look for leaders who promise to restore our illusion of omnipotence – and identity – by assuring us that they will take care of us no matter what. We seek the fantasised security of early childhood in which "mother" will take care of everything and we do not have to be aware of the injustices of the world, of inequality, and of changes which we cannot control.

The political scientist, Ronald Inglehart, describes a "tipping point" in democratic societies in which social and economic inequality reaches an intolerable level and creates a backlash that paves the way for authoritarian governance. Although climate change is not usually named as part of this process, it is an important factor. It is the poor who can't afford rising costs in food, oil, and housing. It is the poor who are vulnerable to becoming climate refugees. It is the poor who can't escape the path of the hurricane and, if they manage to, can't rebuild their demolished houses. It is also the poor and for that matter the middle class who will turn to populist leaders who acknowledge their need for a better life. But populism comes with the cost of de-regulation along with the dismantling of legal structures, due process, and checks and balances. And, of course, it is not just democratic institutions that are attacked, it is reality itself in the form of climate change. As climate change affects us more and more, large group anxiety is bound to intensify and, from our experience so far, this is likely to provoke greater authoritarianism. We can, for example, anticipate an increase in migration due to dwindling habitable land mass. If we are not quick in developing alternative methods of food production, due to climate change and isolationist trade policies, we can also expect much greater competition for food and rising starvation. If we consider these conditions together, they constitute many of the factors that have led in the past to war and genocide – as a means of maintaining group identity in the threat of extinction. In our omnipotent backlash, will we destroy ourselves before the climate does?

Just as extreme economic and social inequalities create fertile ground for the rise of authoritarianism, existential threats to our lives also feed into evangelism – both sell the illusion of omnipotence that is the Shadow cast by profound, uncontainable anxiety. Thunberg has become the most powerful figurehead of the climate change movement, assuming the role of the archetypal child saviour fighting to save Mother Earth. Thunberg, like all evangelists, enlists us into the conflict between good and evil and depicts a binary world of corrupt politicians and corporate leaders versus the innocent next generation who will be the ones to suffer. We enter into a simplistic, moralistic world where blame and responsibility are clear with the implicit message that climate change is primarily if not wholly due to man's destructiveness and can therefore be halted altogether. Mother Earth is also portrayed as the benign victim of human aggression and greed. The Shadow side of the Devouring Mother is repressed.

Evangelists, like populist leaders, foster political divides that are dangerous for our future. At a recent landmark US congressional hearing investigating oil companies' deliberate attempts to lie about the climate emergency, one oil company representative was asked, "Do you believe that climate change is manmade?" The representative dutifully replied, "Yes, I do." While our omnipotent belief that climate change is entirely manmade may serve a positive purpose in spurring us to recognize the urgency of what is happening and to act in mitigating further damage, there is a Shadow aspect to omnipotence that is less immediately apparent. The question, "Do you believe that climate change is manmade?" sounds eerily like the basis for a witch hunt based on a set of beliefs that, if taken at face value, distorts reality. We are in danger of failing to acknowledge the much less palatable reality that Mother Earth will in the end devour what she has borne and be devoured – the uroboros[2] incarnate; we can only do our best to mitigate this. Better to believe we've caused it all so at least we can control it rather than to face the unthinkable as the end of our world draws ever closer.

Beware extremes and beware omnipotent thinking. In the meantime, hop onto the next intergalactic space shuttle.

Notes

1 See Kuhn, Thomas S. (1962) *The Structure of Scientific Revolutions*. 1st edition. Chicago: University of Chicago Press. 1962.
2 Uroboros is the Greek term for the snake that devours its own tail, symbolizing nature's cycle of destruction and rebirth. It is also a symbol of infinity; in this respect, while the earth is doomed to be annihilated, its death may bring about new life in another form in a timeless infinity.

Chapter 12

The Impact of AI and IT in the 21st Century

Alison George

Nothing gives away the age of the 1987 movie *Wall Street* quite like the cellphone belonging to the financier Gordon Gekko. The Motorola DynaTAC 8000X was a $4,000 brick that took 10 hours to charge for just 30 minutes of calls and could store just 30 numbers.

Back then, it would have been impossible to envisage today's smartphones, which function as TV screens, gaming devices and chatrooms connecting to people all over the world, a source of money and a navigation aid. They can predict what we are going to write or say next and know our voice and face.

This digital revolution has taken us to a world which, not so long ago, was the realm of science fiction. The pace of change is furious. Yet our brains really are still caught in the Stone age. They evolved to cope with the social complexities of living in small family groups, in a hunter-gatherer lifestyle. So, it is no wonder that this brave new world unsettles us and there are widespread concerns about the toll that today's immersive and all-pervasive digital devices could be taking on our mental well-being. But should we be so worried?

Unlike many of the contributors to this book, I don't have a background in psychology or psychotherapy. I started out as a biochemist, but for the last two decades have been a science journalist, where one of my specialisations is the deep history of our species and how it evolved. I have also written extensively about neuroscience and cognition and talked to a number of the technologists who have shaped our digital world. I want to use this perspective to explore our fears about technology, computers and social media and to investigate whether they are unfounded or not. I also want to take a look back to where all this started – to take a long view of technology and its implications for humanity.

Today, surrounded by computers, phones and all the smart technologies that humans have invented, it's easy to think of technology as a modern phenomenon. However, technological innovation is something that's been going on for more than three million years. This first stone tools that we know of were made some 3.3 million years ago in Kenya by a hominid that

DOI: 10.4324/9781003255819-14

pre-dates the earliest humans. These sharp-edge flakes, hammers and anvils might not look sophisticated, but they set us off on a path that eventually led to today's supercomputers, nuclear reactors and spacecraft.

While we know very little about the hominids who designed the earliest stone tools, it's likely that these tools could have given their makers an edge when it came to survival, by allowing them to cut up carcasses more effectively. And this is speculation, but perhaps this new technology caused unease to neighbouring groups who didn't make these tools and were still tearing off meat with their hands or teeth. Humanity's love–hate relationship with technology likely has long roots.

With time, new species of hominids evolved, and new, more sophisticated tools were developed such as arrowheads to use as spear points and the multipurpose hand axe. Eventually, our ancestors mastered fire and made clothing.

Some even made it out of Africa and conquered the colder climate of Eurasia. And here, the relationship between humans and their inventions became even more embedded, because without the ability to make fires, shelters and clothing, they wouldn't have been able to survive the cold winters. The inventiveness of these humans allowed them to inhabit areas for which their physiology was not suited.

The rest, as they say, is history – with more complex inventions appearing over time, along with art, farming and writing. On the whole, these innovations gave power to those who had them. The hunter-gatherers who occupied Europe some 10,000 years ago were swept aside by incoming populations of farmers (Spinney 2020), for example.[1]

Later, as Jared Diamond argued so eloquently in his 1997 book *Guns, Germs and Steel*, technological advantages allowed people of Eurasian origin to dominate many parts of the world. Often it was quite literally an arms race, with the society who could muster the most resources and weapons wiping out others.

So technology has simultaneously been essential to our survival and destroyed many human populations or their way of life too.

The drive to invent new things eventually led to the first industrial revolution, beginning in Britain in the 1760s when steam and water-powered machines superseded the manufacture of goods by hand, particularly for the production of textiles. This industrialisation brought about huge social change, with increasing urbanisation and a population explosion.

By the 1810s, a group of disgruntled textile workers known as the Luddites began a rebellion against this mechanisation, destroying a textile factory in the process. Their protests proved to be as effective as King Canute trying to stop the waves, and today "Luddite" has become a derogatory term for people who are opposed to new technologies. However, at heart, the Luddites were fighting for their way of life. And even today, there are a few people who are proudly fighting the Luddite cause. In 2011,

I interviewed one of these "neo-Luddites[2] (George 2011)," the American writer Kirkpatrick Sale, who argues that Luddites rightfully question the hold that technology has over our lives and that we need to be mindful of its serious long-term effects. He also made the case that the situation today is far worse than it was back in the 1800s because technology is so entwined with our lives; hence, the companies who control it are even more powerful.

By the late 1800s, a second industrial revolution was underway with a rise in industrialisation in the United Kingdom, United States, Germany and other European countries, increasing globalisation due to rail and telegraph networks and more widespread use of electricity and fossil fuels for mass production. Machines were now increasingly taking over the physical labour of humans.

But our inventions don't just augment our physical capabilities. They assist our minds and cognition too. This process started out a long time in the past too – at least 40,000 years ago – with notches etched on bone which seems to be some kind of counting system and paintings drawn on cave walls. At first glance, these might not appear to be such sophisticated developments but they demonstrate the ability to represent information in a permanent form and meant that two people did not have to be in the same place at the same time for information to be transmitted between them.

This ability for abstract thought is one of the few capabilities that separate us from all other animals. It would eventually lead to the development of writing and sophisticated mathematical systems and, ultimately, to the third industrial revolution – also known as the digital revolution. Starting in the 1950s, this introduced semiconductors, mainframe computers and then the internet to our daily lives. We could now outsource some of our cognitive efforts to machines too.

Today is the dawn of the fourth industrial revolution (Schwab 2016) – a fusion of digital, biological and physical technologies that promises to change the way we live once again. This new revolution is characterised by nanotechnology, quantum computing and 3D printing. It is also the era of the Internet of Things, in which devices such as heating systems and washing machines are connected to the internet so they can be switched on from your phone from the other side of the world, and of artificial intelligence (AI).

The power of AI means that more and more cognitive tasks can be carried out by machines rather than our own minds. The first computers were essential instruments that could perform complex calculations far faster than our brains. They were clever enough to beat a grandmaster at chess, for example, like IBM's Deep Blue computer did back in 1997. But impressive though this feat is, Deep Blue was no match for the "general intelligence" of the human mind, with its effortless ability to recognise faces and emotions and to make decisions in messy real-life situations. However, this too is changing, with the advances in AI, in which computer software imitates types of human intelligence. You might not be aware of it but AIs are already part of our lives, carrying out checks on banking transactions and making recommendations of what to watch next online. They can now carry out some incredible feats. For instance, in 2019, a major milestone in machine intelligence was reached when an AI called AlphaStar, developed by Google's Deep Mind, beat top-ranked human players in the complex real-time strategy video game *StarCraft II.*

The key to the success of AI is not to give it detailed instructions on how to carry out a task but to enable it to learn for itself by examining multiple examples. For this, the more data that the AI can scan, the better it can learn. To translate from one language to another, for example, computer scientists and linguists initially tried to teach a computer the rules of each language but this approach was not very successful. Translation proved to be far more accurate when an AI could access huge amounts of real-life texts in different languages and work out the rules for itself. This is the kind of technology behind Google Translate, the system that instantly (and with increasing accuracy) decodes that German website you visited into English.

This is an amazing tool that we all can access, for free. It does, however, come at a price. The adage "if you're not paying for the product, then you are the product" has been around in various guises since the 1970s and is particularly apt for today's digital world. Google and other tech giants have access to the information that we input through their services and use this not only to train AI systems but to understand our individual preferences and behaviours.

So if you ever had any fears about a shadowy overlord watching your every move … well, this, in a sense, is what happens every time you send an email or make an internet search. This information is also used to direct our online journey – making recommendations for the next video you should watch or displaying adverts on your screen that relate to a search you just made.

This opaque situation, where invisible algorithms are tuning in to our lives and directing our online experience, is at the same time incredibly useful yet rather alarming. In fact, Cambridge University anthropologist Beth Singler, who studies our relationship with AI and robotics, has discovered that this lack of transparency about the role of AI in our online activities has led some people to elevate AI to a mysterious deity (Bates 2022).

A light was shone onto the dark side of the digital world in the 2020 Netflix *The Social Dilemma* documentary about the outsize impact of social networks and smartphones on our lives. After watching this, a Google search or quick scroll on Facebook will never be the same: "Unplug and run" was the verdict of the New York Times review.

The Social Dilemma features former tech executives who have had a crisis of conscience about the tactics that their previous employers used to keep us hooked on our devices. One of them is Tristan Harris, an ex designer for Google, who describes how tech platforms make their users have thoughts they wouldn't otherwise have had. "Never before in history have 50 designers – 20 to 35-year-old white guys in California – made decisions that would have an impact on two billion people," he says.

Clearly, these issues will play into many people's existential fears. But what about the other, more routine concerns that plague our day-to-day use of smartphones and computers?

Before I take a look at these, I want to question whether there really are any differences between spending time on a smartphone and, say, getting lost in a good book? A look back in history shows that there is a panic every time a new format is devised, whether this is writing, novels or the radio.

The Ancient Greek philosopher Plato, quoting his mentor, Socrates, wrote: "If men learn [writing], it will implant forgetfulness in their souls. They will cease to exercise memory because they rely on that which is written, calling things to remembrance no longer from within themselves, but by means of external marks."

Nearly 2,000 years later, in 1935, an article in the Annals of the American Academy of Political and Social Science titled "Radio and the child (Gruenberg 1935)" stated that "radio appears as but the latest of cultural emergents to invade the putative privacy of the home" and that "in some respects radio finds the parents more helpless than the 'movies' or 'funnies,' for no locks will keep this intruder out." How wholesome would it seem to many parents today if their children put down their computer or phone and tuned in to a radio programme?

Then in 1941, the paediatrician Mary Preston reported the results of her study of 200 young people aged between 6 and 16 (Preston 1941), after being "startled" by the effects on children of listening to radio crime dramas or watching scary movies. She classed 153 of them as having a "severe addiction," reporting that "in the case of unhappy children, most of them utilise the addiction as an escape from reality, much as a chronic alcoholic does drink."

All this has led Amy Orben, a psychologist at the University of Cambridge, to conclude that throughout history, there have been repeated concerns about new technologies – whether these are novels, radios or smartphones. She dubs this process the "Sisyphean cycle of technology panics" (Orben 2020) after the Greek myth of Sisyphus, who is condemned by the gods to roll a boulder up a hill in the underworld for all eternity. Each time he reaches the summit, the rock rolls to the bottom and he has to start the whole cycle again.

Still, there are some key differences between a smartphone and, say, a book. One is the fact that the book has a definite boundary (the ending and the back cover), whereas the content available through a smartphone is limitless. Once you have finished watching one cat video online, the system automatically channels you towards another, then another. (However, it's interesting that when books become "addictive" this is seen as a positive. The ultimate success of a book is when you can't put it down and feel compelled to keep on reading, whereas being "addicted" to your phone or device does not have these positive connotations.)

And as Harris has pointed out, social media isn't just a tool like, say, a bicycle, because it has its own goals and its own means of pursuing them.

But one common factor of spending time in front of a screen or reading a paperback is that both are sedentary. And sedentariness is a big concern for our health and well-being – both physical and mental. Today, we are far more sedentary than previous generations. Only around half of adults in the UK and US meet government targets for aerobic exercise, increasing the risk of heart problems and obesity. Some of this is down to the use of cars, labour-saving devices and changes in work practices, but, intuitively, it seems likely that screen time plays a part.

This is a particular concern for children, who, possibly through rose-tinted spectacles, we imagine would be out playing with their friends if only their IPad or Xbox wasn't keeping them inside and on the sofa.

However, the picture here isn't as clear-cut as you might think. Some studies do find a link between low levels of physical activity and high amounts of screen time, but others do not. For example, a study of nearly 2000 children in Germany aged between 4 and 17 during the first COVID-19 lockdown found that screen time and physical activity were not mutually exclusive and an increase in the former didn't lead to a decrease in the latter (all, 2020).[3]

So where does this leave us? It seems that, like much about digital technology, it's easy to jump to conclusions, but the evidence might not be there to support them.

Of course, it's a human trait to be scared of new things, and often, with familiarity, these fears die down. One event that sticks in my mind is when my daughter went tenpin bowling with some classmates to celebrate her 10th birthday. One of her friends pulled out a mobile phone (none of the other children owned one then) and my heart sank when the children showed far more interest in the phone than the bowling. However, a year later, at her next birthday celebration at the same bowling alley, most of the children did have phones, and their phones were now part of the action, used for taking photos and videos of the party – augmenting rather than dominating the experience.

We now spend a third of our waking time on mobile apps, according to a survey across many countries such as India, Turkey, the United States, Japan and Canada (Research 2022).[4] About two and a half hours of this is spent on social media apps, with Facebook, YouTube and Snapchat being the most popular. It goes without saying that there are a number of positives to this connectivity such as being able to connect with distant friends and relatives and collaborating with people all over the world without having to physically be in the same room, but what about the less positive aspects?

Many parents are concerned about the impact these online lives are having on their children – and perhaps also worried about their own screen use too.

Whether social media and screen use are actually harmful is controversial, and very much depends on the context. There is a big difference between connecting online with classmates to carry out a collaborative school project, for instance, and accessing violent and degrading imagery into the night. "Screen time" has become a catchall phrase, but computers, smartphones and tablets do not just act as TV screens but as photo albums, chatrooms, banks and shops.

One thing that's not in doubt is the huge problem that social media has with misogynistic and racist abuse. This is fuelled by the ability of online trolls to remain anonymous which the providers seem unable (or unwilling) to control. To stem the tide of vitriol, the Australian government is attempting to introduce new anti-trolling laws which would force providers to disclose the real identity of trolls making defamatory comments. The idea is that when an online post is attached to someone's real name, this will reduce abuse. However, many are pessimistic that these steps will reduce the toxicity of social media (Morris 2021). For a start, the goal of many platforms is to maximise engagement of their users and inflammatory and derogatory content is a surefire way to grab attention.

Another concern is fake news – false stories masquerading as news stories and spread online. In some ways, fake news is nothing new (think of all the propaganda during wartime) but the difference today is the way this is spread, via friends and contacts rather than through traditional gatekeepers such as newspapers and TV news channels. There are now serious concerns that social media platforms could sway voters in national elections. Fake TikTok accounts supposedly belonging to German politicians and political institutions were a concern ahead of the 2021 German federal election, for instance.

This process is fuelled by "funnelling" in which the algorithms behind online tech platforms connect us with like-minded people. This leads to us becoming unwittingly enmeshed in social media "bubbles" where everyone we are interacting with shares our opinions on, say, politics/conspiracy theories/climate change, leading to polarisation and sometimes extremism.

For some, the most insidious thing about the tech giants is their power to subtly and imperceptibly change our behaviour. As the US technologist Jaron Lanier outlined in *The Social Dilemma*, the "product" for these companies is the "gradual, slight, imperceptible change in your own behaviour and perception."

His is a particularly damning view: "We've created a world in which online connection has become primary, especially for younger generations. And yet, in that world, any time two people connect, the only way it's financed is through a sneaky third person who's paying to manipulate those two people. So, we've created an entire global generation of people who are raised within a context where the very meaning of communication, the very meaning of culture, is manipulation. We've put deceit and sneakiness at the absolute centre of everything we do."

This can be illustrated by the fact that the outcome of a Google search will be different depending on where you live and what the system already knows about. This could make the difference between Google auto-completing the phrase "Climate change is ..." with the words "destroying nature" or "a hoax."

These tricks are a bid to compete for our attention and to keep our eyeballs on our devices. Other such methods are the ways that pulling down on a screen to refresh it leads to a new set of information on display. Harris argues that this is similar to the mechanism of slot machines. "It has the same kind of addictive qualities that keep people in Las Vegas hooked," said Harris in a US Senate enquiry.

This tactic is based on a foible of the human mind known as positive intermittent reinforcement. Positive reinforcement can be regarded as a reward resulting from a particular behaviour. Surprisingly, the effect is greater when the reward is intermittent rather than consistent, so the desire to engage in the behaviour is bigger if it only sometimes generates the rewards.

Harris described the methods to command our attention used by companies such as Twitter and Facebook as a "race to the bottom of your brainstem."

Though this means it is easy to get sucked into your smartphone and spend many hours a day on it, the question of whether you can become truly addicted to your devices is a controversial one. Addiction has a precise definition, entailing compulsive and escalating use resulting in a damaging and long-term impact on our life. Choosing to spend seven hours of your day online tends to be regarded as a hard-to-crack habit rather than a true addiction, though this is matter of intense debate. Although internet addiction is not a recognised disorder by the Diagnostic and Statistical Manual of Mental Disorders or the World Health Organisation, gaming disorder – the problematic and compulsive use of video games which causes major impact on a person's everyday life – has been recognised by some authorities.

Another concern about social media is that it fuels our need for validation – that we're becoming hooked on the number of people following us and retweets. In his testimony to the US Senate in 2018, Harris made the case that the internet has created a culture of mass narcissism.

Statements like these are alarming and also broadly believed in part due to popular books such as *iGen* by Jean Twenge, a psychologist at San Diego State University. This makes the case that digital technology is causing great harm to a generation of young people. The difficulty with this view is that data generated in studies can be interpreted in different ways (Twenge 2017).

One of the most comprehensive studies into the effects of screen use on the well-being of adolescents is a 2019 study *Screens, Teens and Psychological Well-Being*, carried out by Orben (Orben 2019).[5] In this paper, she and co-author Andrew Przbulski wrote that "the notion that digital-screen engagement decreases adolescent well-being has become a recurring feature in public, political and scientific conversation. The current level of psychological evidence, however, is far removed from the certainty voiced by many commentators. There is little clear-cut evidence that screen time decreases adolescent well-being, and most psychological results are based on single-country, exploratory studies that rely on inaccurate but popular self-report measures of digital-screen engagement."

To address this, their study included more the 17,000 young people from Ireland, the United States and the United Kingdom and found no substantial negative link between technology use and well-being, even when devices were used before bedtime.

However, not everyone agrees with this conclusion. The US psychologist, Jonathan Haidt, argues that social media is particularly harmful to teenage girls. "Much more than for boys, adolescence typically heightens girls' self-consciousness about their changing body and amplifies insecurities about where they fit in their social network," he wrote in November 2021 in The Atlantic. "Social media – particularly Instagram, which displaces other forms of interaction among teens, puts the size of their friend group on public display and subjects their physical appearance to the hard metrics of likes and comment counts – takes the worst parts of middle school and glossy women's magazines and intensifies them."

Data he has compiled along with psychologist Twenge shows that "something terrible has happened to Gen Z, the generation born after 1996," he says, with rates of depression, self-harm and anxiety soaring, especially for adolescent girls, along with an increased suicide rate for both genders. The same patterns are seen in Canada and the United Kingdom. Although these trends coincide with the rise of social media, correlation doesn't mean causation. Haidt, however, argues that many studies lump all screen-based activities together, such as watching movies and texting friends, and research that focuses solely on social media shows a stronger relationship between time spent on these platforms and poor mental health. Instagram seems to be particularly harmful for mental health, he says, perhaps due to the high levels of social comparisons on this platform compared to others (viz. Steffen et al 2020; Wakefield, 2022).

However, we don't know for sure the cause of the poor mental health of Gen Z adolescents, so Haidt thinks we are in the midst of a massive social experiment. "Social media platforms were not initially designed for children, but children have nevertheless been the subject of a gigantic national experiment testing the effects of those platforms," he writes.

So where does this leave us? At the moment, it is not clear whether concerns about the harmful effects of digital technology are just another example of the technopanic that inevitably accompanies the advent of any new invention or an insidious experiment that will scar the lives of the younger generation in particular.

Today's uber-connectivity, however, will one day seem pedestrian compared to what is coming.

In October 2021, Facebook rebranded itself as "Meta" in response to its ambition to create an immersive virtual reality world. In this "metaverse," we will work, entertain ourselves and connect with others in a virtual reality world rather than a physical one (Stokel-Walker 2022). If this sounds like something from a science fiction novel, that's because it is. The term metaverse was coined in Neal Stephenson's 1992 science fiction novel *Snow Crash*.

It is easy to see the advantages to companies like Facebook and others who are investing in the metaverse. The more of our lives we spend online, the more money they can make out of us through advertising. This immersive new world will have a virtual physical reality which our digital avatar will experience. So, for example, through virtual reality, you might meet with your colleagues in the meeting room at your virtual workplace. But it is questionable what advantage this offers to us, aside from avoiding the need to commute to the office or to travel to a conference.

However, in future, will our jobs actually exist? Employment is yet another concern about the impact of AI and the digital world on our lives. At one time, robots were only adept at carrying out the same repetitive tasks, but now they can adapt, learn and respond to a changing environment, making them a viable alternative to employing people. Even therapists are being replaced by computers such as the Woebot, a "fully automated conversational agent" which is proving to be surprisingly effective.

A 2021 World Economic Forum report[6] predicted that robots and AI could replace 85 million jobs by 2025, but would create 97 million new ones, mainly in the care system, content creation and, somewhat ironically, developing more AI (The Future of Jobs World Economic Forum Report, 2020). Already call centres, banking and legal roles have been replaced by automated systems. AIs are even edging their way into the more creative industries which were once seen as the bastion of human talents, creating impressive artworks and musical compositions.

But there are other, more apocalyptic concerns about AI. One is that we will one day create intelligences that are far superior to ours in every way. While this has the potential for many good things – like finding cures for diseases and developing new medicines – some thinkers argue that these superintelligent machines pose the greatest existential threat to humanity. Nick Bostrom of the University of Oxford's Future of Humanity Institute, for example, argued in his 2014 book *Superintelligence* that these machines were more likely to cause our species to go extinct than a pandemic, climate change or nuclear war. He makes the case that the first machine that far outperforms all biological intelligence will become very powerful and will shape the future of life according to itself (Bostrom 2014).

Stephen Hawking too warned that AI is "our biggest existential threat," arguing that humans are limited by biological evolution, which happens at a glacially slow pace, and hence would be superseded.

Another concern is the use of AI in autonomous weapons, which can make their own decision. So worrying is that trend that in 2015, more than a thousand AI experts and leading researchers, including Stephen Hawking and Elon Musk, signed an open letter warning of a "military AI arms race" as the third revolution in warfare, after gunpowder and nuclear arms. The letter warned that although AI can make warfare safer for military personnel, offensive weapons that operate autonomously would lower the threshold of going to war and ultimately lead to greater loss of human life.

If this brave new world worries you, then perhaps you should not read any further.

The pace of technological change isn't linear but exponential, and this has led futurists such as the US inventor Ray Kurzweil to predict that sometime in the next few decades we will reach what is known as The Singularity: A time when speed of technological change will be so fast and its impact so strong that human life will be irreversibly transformed. We will have the capability to reprogramme our biology and ultimately transcend it. The outcome will be a union of ourselves and the technology we have created.

Quite when The Singularity will occur (indeed, if it ever will) is much debated. Kurzweil predicted that by the mid-2040s, our brains would be artificially enhanced, with the non-biological portion of our intelligence billions of times more capable than the biological portion. However, a 2017 survey of nearly a thousand AI experts predicted that it would happen further in the future – by 2060 (Dilmegani 2017).

If this day ever comes, then surely we will look back on today's concerns about technology with a rosy glow of nostalgia for simpler times?

New technology simultaneously intrigues and scares us, tapping many primal fears: Of not being in control of our lives, of being watched and judged by a shadowy entity, of being made redundant or wiped out of existence entirely. Although fears about new inventions might have been with us since before our species evolved, the furious pace of change today and the increasing intelligence of machines mean that these fears are at the forefront like never before.

Notes

1 https://www.scientificamerican.com/article/when-the-first-farmers-arrived-in-europe-inequality-evolved/

2 https://www.newscientist.com/article/mg21228440-400-im-a-neo-luddite-and-anti-technology/
3 https://www.nature.com/articles/s41598-020-78438-4
4 https://www.bbc.co.uk/news/technology-59952557
5 https://journals.sagepub.com/doi/full/10.1177/0956797619830329
6 https://www.weforum.org/press/2020/10/recession-and-automation-changes-our-future-of-work-but-there-are-jobs-coming-report-says-52c5162fce/

References

Bates, E. (2022). Beth Singler interview: the dangers of treating AI like a god. New Scientist.
Bostrom, N. (2014). Superintelligence: paths, dangers, strategies.
Dilmegani, C. (2017). When will singularity happen? 995 experts' opinions on AGI. AI Multiple.
George, A. (2011, December 20). I'm a neo-Luddite and anti-technology. New Scientist.
Gruenberg, S. M. (1935). Radio and the child. Annals of the American Academy of Political and Social Science.
Morris, S. (2021). Ending online anonymity won't make social media less toxic. The Conversation.
Orben, A. P. (2019). Screens, teens, and psychological well-being: evidence from three time-use-diary studies. Psychological Science.
Orben, A. (2020). The Sisyphean cycle of technology panics. Perspectives of Psychological Science.
Preston, M. (1941). Children's reactions to movie horrors and radio crime. The Journal of Pediatrics, 19(2), 147–168.
Research, d. (2022). The state of mobile in 2022: how to succeed in a mobile-first world as consumers spend 3.8 trillion hours on mobile devices. data.ai.
Schwab, K. (2016). The fourth industrial revolution: what it means, how to respond. World Economic Forum.
Spinney, L. (2020, July 1). When the first farmers arrived in Europe, inequality evolved. Scientific American.
Steffen C. E., Schmidt, B. A., Burchartz, A., Eichsteller, A., Kolb, S., Nigg, C., Niessner, C., Oriwol, D., Worth, A. & Woll, A. (2020). Physical activity and screen time of children and adolescents before and during the COVID-19 lockdown in Germany: a natural experiment. Scientific Reports.
Stokel-Walker, C. (2022). The metaverse: what is it, will it work, and does anyone want it? New Scientist.
Twenge, J. (2017). iGen.
Wakefield, J. (2022). People devote third of waking time to mobile apps. BBC News.

Chapter 13

Fundamentalism, Terrorism, and Mindlessness: The Shadow of Thinking

Malcolm Rushton

A quote from Jung: "*the devaluation of the psyche is based on fear – on panic fear of the discoveries that might be made in the realm of the unconscious. These fears troubled the originator of psychoanalysis himself, who confessed to me that it was necessary to make a dogma of his sexual theory because this was the sole bulwark of reason against a possible 'eruption of the black flood' of 'occultism'. In these words, Freud was expressing his conviction that the unconscious still harboured many things that might lend themselves to 'occult' interpretation. It is this fear of the unconscious psyche which not only impedes self-knowledge but is the gravest obstacle to a wider understanding and knowledge of psychology. Often the fear is so great that one dares not admit it even to oneself*" (Jung 1964, para. 530). Jung is talking about the terrifying nature of the individual and collective Shadow which underlies fundamentalism, terrorism, and mindlessness.

These three – fundamentalism, terrorism, and mindlessness – are rife in human society. They are inextricably linked, and constantly confront our world, emerging in myriad guises. I would like to explore some thoughts about how this state originates, and how it may be thought about in both individual and collective realms, often seeming extremely intractable. In the 2011 film version of John le Carré's 1974 novel "*Tinker, Tailor, Soldier, Spy*", George Smiley declares that he knows Karla, his Kremlin adversary, can be beaten because "*The fanatic is always concealing a secret doubt*". This "*doubt*" is our very slim window of hope.

The Problem

"I was not thinking my thoughts. I was not myself" (Maysa).

– (Burke, 2015)

The Guardian ran a story of a young Muslim girl in Brussels who they called Maysa. Her grandparents had come to Europe fifty years ago from Morocco, and her parents had built their careers and a home for

DOI: 10.4324/9781003255819-15

their children. There was no family extremism but contact with young radicalised Muslims through social media gradually drew Maysa into an ISIL net, which almost led to her going to Syria to join them. The heading of the article speaks volumes. Maysa was in a psychological state where *"she was not thinking her thoughts and was not herself"*. We're not told what had led her to that place, why her sense of self had become quite fragile, and why she was so easily influenced by radicals.

An organisation called *"Educate against Hate"* lists what they consider the key factors making a person susceptible to radicalisation:

- Struggling with a sense of identity,
- Becoming distanced from their cultural or religious background,
- Questioning their place in society,
- Family issues,
- Experiencing a traumatic event,
- Experiencing racism or discrimination,
- Difficulty in interacting socially and lacking empathy,
- Difficulty in understanding the consequences of their actions,
- Low self-esteem.

Underlying all these factors is likely to be a child's experience of not feeling loved, not wanted for themselves as a unique individual, but shaped by the needs of others. The feeling underlying this psychological state is almost certainly *terror*, the terror of not knowing who one is and not living one's own unique life.

I remember the feeling of *terror* throughout my childhood for these reasons and see it in a number of my patients, both reported historically and experienced directly in the consulting room; terror brought about by those who believe a child's life is not to be lived according to their own instincts, but moulded by adult fantasies, often imposed down the generations and brought into a very immediate experience in the present. This leaves a child or an adult profoundly disorientated, empty, and with an existential crisis. They may be able to find ways of functioning in life fairly normally, compliantly, and in a dissociated manner until something happens to tip the balance, often in their teens when first facing adult life without any sense of a clear identity of their own, and the *terror* of very early traumatic experience returns. An extreme organisation at this point may provide a window through which to project their terror and a way to become a *terrorist*. By stirring up hate, they may tap into the hate at feeling controlled and "not able to be themselves", from which the individual had previously dissociated.

One further thought about what provokes Muslims in the West to become radicalised, usually to the absolute dismay of their parents. Parents come to Western countries, carrying the collective norms of their cultures, and are faced with a hugely difficult internal conflict. How can they preserve their cultural roots that the West has undermined and at the same time have gratitude for Western society's benefits that they have chosen? In this struggle, their anger about the loss of their diminishing cultural identity may lead to a deep psychological split. This needs to be consigned to their Shadow and remain unacknowledged until their children pick up one side of the split and act out this repressed hatred towards the West. The unconscious dilemmas of the fathers are visited on the children to the third and fourth generations. The living out of a transgenerational trauma will indeed be a massive shock to immigrant parents and Western citizens alike.

Some time ago, I saw a television documentary, "A Child of our Time", made by Professor Robert Winston (2014). He studied a number of white Caucasian babies who had only been exposed to people of their own ethnicity and, at a very young age, were shown pictures of people of that same ethnicity. This was repeated with pictures of people of two different ethnicities and then with pictures of a group of meerkats. The astonishing thing was that all the babies could clearly distinguish each individual in all of the groups. The experiment was then repeated when the children were slightly older, and remarkably, they had largely lost the capacity to distinguish individual meerkats and individuals of an ethnicity other than their own. My conclusion was that, just as muscles atrophy through lack of use, so do visual capacities of discrimination. We are born with many resources which are easily lost.

I want to suggest that this phenomenon may be more far-reaching. I see quite a few patients who have come from homes where I would describe their way of relating as along a power axis, in the power of another, and not able to live their own lives. My sense is that when exposure to an alternative axis, a love axis, is denied them over many years, this "muscle" atrophies and they become less able to recognise the love alternative and lose a sense of their own identity. The power axis is omnipresent and is driven by terror. *"I was not thinking my thoughts. I was not myself".*

The two are mutually exclusive. A quote from Jung: *"where love reigns, there is no will to power, and where the will to power is paramount, love is lacking. The one is the Shadow of the other"*. (Jung 1917, para.78). With a love axis an individual exists, comes *to know their own thoughts* which they can reflect on, rather than being trapped in a fundamentalist mindset following the dictates of another.

This is very related to another axis that a baby has to negotiate: a fantasy axis in opposition to a reality axis. Parents, extended family, historical beliefs of past generations, and rigid community tribal norms may be imposed on children and reinforced with psychological or physical power. This will have profound psychological effects on children, who grow up to be adults with similar conviction and little chance of "knowing their own thoughts or becoming themselves".

A baby's initial experience of reaching out to another, who is caught in power, fantasy, and control, is to meet a psychotic space where the experience encountered does not accord with any reality that the baby expects. This psychotic space means an experience of terror and a rapid withdrawal of the baby's true self to a place of dissociation where the baby is simply concerned with survival. This is a defence against the meaninglessness of psychosis, where the incompatible mental worlds of the self and the other clash irreconcilably. This space mimics the space the parents inhabit, in their own lives and transgenerationally, losing touch with both love and reality.

Another way of describing this fundamental trauma is the sense of not being wanted/rejected when we come into the world. This leads to a withdrawal from normal ego development and consequently a traumatised state where the Self takes precedence. This results in a terror of the outer world of ego/social/group/unfamiliar activities with an unhealthy focus on one's inner world. Difference and reality are much harder to cope with and narcissism and borderline personality states with the predominance of primary process thinking are dashes to safety. Dialogue with another is a profound threat and a deep splitting in the psyche ensues.

The Individual

I have had a succession of patients who have been locked into a power and fantasy dynamic all their lives. With a number of them, as a precursor to *thinking* and moving to an axis shaped by love and reality, an important step has been for them to move away from victimhood and mimic the omnipotent *perpetrator* world of those who had shaped them. This is known territory and the *untested* option. This has often felt, in Jung's terms, "purposive". When a relationship begins to feel safer, this is the only option that the patient can envisage, when wanting to pull away from a victim stance. I see this as their holding onto a fragile omnipotent Self, supported by the analyst, which can be a first attempt at holding onto their own identity, "*thinking their own thoughts*", an attempted "reboot". The baby comes into the world with archetypal expectations and an omnipotent belief that the abundant breast will be on tap. To return to this infantile ruthlessness, largely at odds with their adult experience, can be an attempt to return to the beginning. This is a profound challenge for the analyst to respond in a neutral way to sometimes serious aggression and totally unrealistic demands until weaning and concern for the other can begin. It may feel anything but purposive. This is the patient's reality. The analyst's role is to dive deep *with them* into their perpetrator and fantasy dynamic and to keep one foot on firm ground.

As we risk a dalliance with the underlying psychotic space, the patient will usually start to feel some safety and security from being met in their madness, often for the first time. What is paramount in this process is an absence of control. To try to control the patient's omnipotence would reinforce a feeling of rejection and a belief that the old pattern is being repeated with the toxic parent once more projecting poison. If the analyst can stay with the perpetrator dynamic undeterred, there is the possibility of the beginnings of the breakdown of defences and we may get glimpses of the patient *"thinking their own thoughts and becoming themselves"*. Thinking can begin, and *terror* needs no longer be projected. Maysa had enough security to face this and to experience being herself. The "muscles" of the love and reality axes could begin to be re-engaged.

There is no way that a patient and analyst can embrace this option without profound disorientation and the analyst embodying the love axis over some considerable time. The mother's role in relation to the baby is to have a mind until the baby can begin to become aware of, and then begin to inhabit, the reflective space of love and reality axes. In severe trauma, any potential for *thinking* is on life support. Resuscitation is extremely precarious and can only come about through patient and analyst experiencing the terror of the underlying psychosis. This can be a profound and very uncertain search for a new start.

The Group

It is possible, though difficult, to make headway in analysis with highly traumatised individuals, but when it comes to a group, the forces against change rise exponentially. I witnessed an incident where a lesbian couple were holding hands about twenty yards in front of me. A van full of a dozen policemen drew up beside them, rolled down their windows, and hurled abuse. I was deeply shocked at their collective impulse to immediately act as one in an extremely destructive and unthinking way. To change such a perpetrator/fantasy-driven culture is a much bigger ask. With twelve psyches in unison, egging each other on, the result was not in doubt. Anything purposive was not on offer. It was simply a mindless act of misogyny.

Any difference – sexual, racial, economic, class, or political difference – is ruthlessly attacked in society. This was writ large recently in America with the killing of innocent black people by police officers, born out of fantasy perpetrator/victim dynamics and evoked powerful reactions across the world, focussed in the "Black Lives Matter" movement. The fires of hatred had been stoked in opposing communities, where the power axis underlying so many individuals' early traumatic experiences has been fanned into flame in a group arena. The test comes in the ability of those inhabiting the love axis to maintain an "analytic" openhearted stance.

The Sexual Divide

ISIL is avowedly a patriarchal society. Stories emerge of women being used as sex objects, allocated to the leadership for this purpose. An American woman, since murdered, was reputedly used in this way by the overall leader of the group. The Taliban has an antagonism to the education of women and their holding significant roles in society. This form of patriarchal tribalism has been a part of the culture in the Middle East down the centuries, expressed in practices like temple prostitution in Biblical times. Western "democracy", feminism, and equality would be seen as at odds with the beliefs of extremist groups who are the carriers of the collective cultural norms passed from previous generations. A patient I see recounted some thoughts about a Madonna concert he attended. One of his reflections was that Madonna liked sex, and she was very explicit about this, yet not as the object but as the subject. By this, he meant that she didn't place herself as the object of a man's desire but wanted sex unashamedly from a place of her own appetite and feminine power. He also said that he was interested in the makeup of the audience. He said he felt there were many gay men and lesbians and a lot of heterosexual women but a great dearth of heterosexual men. We thought about this together as possibly reflecting a largely heterosexual male culture in the UK being frightened of a woman who espoused a tribal culture where women took their power. Madonna was espousing an alternative to some UK tribal norms. The culture of ISIL is one of unashamedly undiluted patriarchal power where women have to cover themselves, are subservient, and there to be used by men; but this is not limited to the Middle East. The secularism of French society, preventing Muslim women from wearing a head covering, may have increased the likelihood of extremist attacks, by being seen as a challenge to the whole patriarchal culture. A particular form of tribalism is at the core of all that ISIL stands for, and any assault on its values, particularly the value of the feminine emerging from the Shadow, will almost inevitably end in conflict. Maybe this too, ISIL have imbibed from French and British colonialism of the 19th century. This is another dimension to the power axis which is terrified of the psychosis that might ensue if the feminine – the receptive rather than the penetrative – is given its head.

The Internet

Although the internet has brought much richness to life, it is two-edged. It has had a role in amplifying power dynamics – for individuals, groups, and nations. An interesting phenomenon has emerged in the United Kingdom and American Universities. In the name of emotional well-being, students are increasingly demanding protection from words and ideas which would give offence. Pressure is brought to bear on teaching staff not to say things such as teaching rape law or using words like "violate". Scott Fitzgerald's book, "The Great Gatsby" has been criticised for portraying misogyny and physical abuse. Professors are being asked to put out what have been called "trigger warnings" to alert students to anything that might cause the reactivation of past trauma. It seems that emotional well-being is being equated with a ruthless determination to ensure that nothing which normally resides in a person's Shadow ever sees the light of day. It is not coincidental that this is the first generation who have grown up immersed in social media, where it's simple to join crusades, express solidarity, show outrage, and shun traitors. The use of this media is having significant impact on the pressure to project the Shadow onto and into offending "baddies" – the university staff as surrogate parents.

Social media has become a trap where the fantasy perpetrator/victim axis is reinforced. Children are being bullied by each other, hate is being disseminated, sometimes ending in death threats and even death, and dating sites can become vehicles for power games, sexual dominance, and entrapment.

This can happen on a much larger platform too. The internet has been exploited by more and more power-hungry politicians, as much from Western democracies as dictatorships, to feather their own nests and attack other politicians or political systems. Even when the internet was used by victims in repressive societies to orchestrate their campaigns, express their longings for an "Arab Spring", the backlash from the powerful has left many countries in a far worse situation with huge loss of life. An irresistible force clashed with an immovable object and the *non-thinking* treadmill continues. The incredibly rapid rate of change in the world, a feature that the internet has intensified, means that a measured *evolution* is rarely possible. Both sides operate from a one-person power dynamic, in touch only with the beliefs and needs of their own particular tribe. The internet plays its part in shrinking the possibility of reflective space emerging.

Another area of change is the growth of often quite violent computer games for the under thirties eclipsing television. Facebook, Instagram, and Twitter are based on the growing voyeuristic and exhibitionistic trends in society. Real-life engagement is distressing for victims of trauma and a dissociated fantasy world is a welcome substitute on the power axis. This fantasy existence is often infused with a great deal of split off violence, which, once played out on the computer screen, can sometimes move on to enactment in the real world. ISIL's activities in Syria, Iraq, and many other countries became the incarnated fantasy equivalent with enacted video atrocities watched by millions of voyeurs. Many of ISIL's recruits have been traumatised young people deprived of a childhood, suffering from catastrophic loss, desperately enacting an unfulfilled need for attention, and not knowing what is reality and what is fantasy. *"I was not thinking my thoughts. I was not myself"*.

With most of the current world power bases totally unable to hear the view of those with whom they disagree, there is a near zero search for the "unknowable" love axis, and a large-scale reversal is hard to see. Some suggest that a reversal will happen through the increasing pain of the current world traumas such as Covid-19 or climate warming. This may however simply increase the threat of psychosis and drive the powerful to hang onto a more precarious powerbase, leaving the powerless to fruitlessly fight. More retraumatisation seems inevitable. We see this with the short sightedness of denying the poorer nations access to Covid-19 vaccinations which ultimately shoots the richer nations in the foot.

The Middle East

Let's move more determinedly onto the world stage. Fundamentalism and terrorism are playing out in stark relief throughout our world. The Middle East, the cradle of civilisation, is central in this dynamic and has been historical. The conflict between Sunni and Shia Muslims is a powder keg, stirred up by the interventions of first Russia and then the West in Iraq, Syria, and Iran. Power struggles with the Taliban in Afghanistan and assorted proxy wars between America and Russia in countries such as Yemen and Syria all highlight the victim/perpetrator dynamic. The layers of violent conflict in this region are rife, with the goal of greedy access to the natural resources such as oil and global influence. Little reflective space is left.

ISIL has been a particularly gruesome example, of the extreme and very visible tactics used, to undermine their enemies. This is, however, far from unique in the region but perhaps striking in its focus on individual victims and on the publicity sought. What we would often expect to be found in the *Shadow* has not been hidden but flagrantly paraded to the world. The feelings we would expect to be cherished, like love and affection, are not in evidence. They occupy ISIL's *Shadow*. This seems an attempt to express a new order where the perpetrator/victim axis is the new normal.

The Tribe

Ancient and modern tribes are dominated by *fear* – fear of wild animals, disease, starvation, neighbouring tribes, and above all death. Much of their energy was taken up in trying to control their environment to ensure their survival in a power-driven collective. Tribalism is the root from which modern society has emerged, and the separation of the individual from the tribal collective is a very recent evolutionary step in the sweep of world history. This has been the precursor to any democratic political system. In Western countries, the emergence of the individual can be linked to the rise of what have often been termed the middle classes from the binary system of the tribal "aristocracy" and "working classes". This has been facilitated by the breakdown of the extended and transgenerational family, the rise of the nuclear family, and greater mobility.

Fear has the powerful effect of binding a tribe together with a vice-like grip. The tribal members huddle together for warmth against the all-encompassing icy wind, perceived as coming from the threatening other. In this exclusive "huddle", fear leads to contraction of the potential for change, an inward-looking perspective on life, circularity, stagnation, and paralysis. All thoughts and feelings are obsessed with the threat. Yet little are ISIL, and other similar tribal groups, aware of the extent, to which they have constructed this threat, through the projection of their own Shadow onto the world at large. Their Shadow is everything in their lives which makes them uncomfortable, particularly their aggression, hate, and murderousness, which they evoke in the enemy, so that when this enemy attacks them, they can feel they have the moral high ground and can justifiably react against the "infidel". But equally, they are uncomfortable with their own vulnerability and fragility, and this too is projected striking fear into their enemies through posting beheadings and other gruesome enactments. This has also led to them attempting to wipe out some vulnerable groups such as the Yazidi Christians – an attempt to destroy the parts of themselves they abhor. Love also resides in their Shadow and is not accessible to consciousness. They have dissociated from or projected so much of their own unwanted feeling into the world, leaving an emotional vacuum in their *inner* world. *"I was not thinking my thoughts. I was not myself"*.

The perceived threat becomes a self-fulfilling prophecy, turning up the heat, binding the tight knit tribe ever closer together in hate for their persecutors, and becoming a more and more exclusive group. Each air strike increases their belief in the righteousness of their cause and that all bad feelings and intentions belong elsewhere. There is no linear development, purposiveness, thought, or feeling. There are no boundaries, no borders. Their omnipotence simply grew … until it was crushed by the might of others, leaving more resentment and the prospect of more terrorism, fuelled yet again by fundamentalism and omnipotence.

The West

So why did ISIL emerge in this grotesque form? Robert Fisk in the Independent Newspaper (2014) pointed back to an earlier omnipotent erosion of borders, alluded to in one of the earliest of ISIL's videos. It showed a bulldozer pushing down a mound of sand that had marked the border between Iraq and Syria. The camera then moved to a handwritten poster, lying on the ground saying, "End of Sykes-Picot". Mark Sykes, a British diplomat, and Francois Picot, a French diplomat, drew up new borders in the Middle East during World War I, giving Syria, Mount Lebanon, and Northern Iraq to the French and Palestine, Transjordan, and the rest of Iraq to the British. This act of neo-colonialism, known to all in the region, brutally divided tribes and families and was seen as a cancer that the region had had to live with painfully for a century. ISIL was reversing, in a stroke and at lightning speed, what many Arabs had struggled to achieve for several generations, unravelling these falsely imposed borders, set up in the name of democracy. But a new cancer was replacing the old with ISIL setting up its "Caliphate" across Syria and Iraq and attempting to draw into the fold Libya, Algeria, Tunisia, Afghanistan, Egypt, Yemen, Nigeria, and many more countries. They have had a powerful role model given to them by their colonial masters.

Saddam Hussein drives his tanks across the border with Kuwait and is bemused by the hostile stance that America takes. Isn't he doing just what the West taught him – remove boundaries which don't suit? Syrian refugees marched across Europe, with no acknowledgement of borders, carrying a few cancer cells from the "Caliphate" to set up new tumours far from home. We got some of our own Western medicine and we didn't like it. It was unpalatable to trace this sadistic power dynamic back to that hallowed holy grail, Western Democracy; but the Trump era, if we needed more evidence, has so clearly shown that the West has deep cracks in its facade. We will do what we like and call it "alternative truth". As my earlier example showed, the police can be the Shadow side of criminality.

The thirst for oil has been an added factor in the interference by the West in countries like Iraq under the guise of a moral imperative to liberate the world from a tribal dictator and tyrant, little knowing that a tribal dictator is the norm. To remove one tribal dictator is a very limited goal as, in tribal society, they will simply be replaced by the next in line. ISIL is a perfectly predictable outcome from the removal of Saddam Hussein or the tribal power vacuum in Syria. However much people disliked Saddam Hussein, a large contingent would say "What right have you to invade our country?". How would we feel if another nation invaded the United Kingdom with concomitant disturbance to our way of life and huge loss of life? Many in Iraq and Afghanistan resent terribly the huge arrogance of the West believing they know better and leaving untold chaos in their wake. Many, in fact, miss the basic *security* that the tyrannical prison of Saddam Hussein brought. Their prison was familiar. Before the power struggles between America and Russia in Syria, the population, whilst still horribly oppressed, was not engulfed by a blood bath. The contact with the West, that many in these countries had, provoked envy, particularly in the young, and had become a signal for the West to jump in with both feet. This goes back and back to Vietnam and far beyond.

The end result has been that the West, far from acting under the auspices of democracy, has reignited its own tribal agendas, has made alliances with other tribes, and entered into the fray of an intertribal war, thus abdicating its fragile hold on democracy and individuality. This has, paradoxically, led to the West being taken over by the enemy's tribal Shadow so that both sides live out the hate and the murderousness. Far from the West converting the "natives" to democracy, the "natives" have succeeded in reversing the West's tentative evolutionary step towards the importance of the individual and pulled them more full bloodedly into a collective tribal way of life. The power axis can overturn the love axis so easily. Terror is a marker of the tribal way of life and is a powerful aspect of the tribe's disowned Shadow, which it seeks to project into the enemy, from the painting of faces with woad down to the belt of the suicide bomber and the West's power grab for oil. Terror is passed backwards and forwards with "shock and awe".

I was interested by an interview with someone present at the Stade de France on the night of the Paris atrocities who said that he was standing in a toilet next to a man who was sweating profusely, obviously very anxious, only to find a few minutes later that he had blown himself up. Both tribes are terrified and terrorised. It has also been postulated that one of the reputed Paris bombers on the run was in an extremely difficult position, sandwiched between the authorities in Belgium and France and ISIL of whom he had fallen foul, through becoming a traitor to the cause by not detonating his suicide belt and killing more of the "infidels". His brother publicly imploring him to give himself up to the Belgian and French authorities sensing that, on balance, he might be more likely to survive if he surrendered. Power versus power and no niche for love.

The Leaders

Abu Bakr al Baghdadi, the leader of ISIL, prompted by the US invasion of Iraq, helped found an Islamic group which attacked US troops. In 2004, Baghdadi was detained by US troops in the city of Falluja and taken to a detention centre, Camp Bucca. This camp has been described as "a university for the future leaders of ISIL" with inmates becoming radicalised and developing networks. Baghdadi was not seen as a great threat by the Americans and was released after ten months but this experience hardened him and a number of others to form ISIL as a successor to al-Qaeda. He inherited an organisation that US commanders believed to be on the verge of a strategic defeat but with the help of several Saddam-era military and intelligence officers, among them fellow former Camp Bucca inmates, he gradually rebuilt ISIL. The power dynamic was powerfully fuelled by the imperative to seek revenge against the invaders. Leaders form in reaction to the power of others.

Perhaps we need to consider whether democracy has really deeply penetrated our society or whether there is a superficial lip service given to the notion which caves in when our own economic "wants" are under threat. As well as economic considerations, I think we also need to think if there are psychological imperatives. The United States, and many Western countries, seem to need to paint themselves as having the "moral high ground", as being the "good guys", and that then presupposes there are "bad guys" and the love axis of dialogue again disappears. This is nothing new. We see this played out in America in the fifties, sixties, and seventies, with the huge number of cowboy and Indian films, where the "savages" are tamed. The Indians became the receptacle, by projection, for the feelings that white Americans did not want to own. The tribal Indians are no longer kosher scapegoats, nor are the victims of European colonialism. Perhaps the leaders in the West need to create a new series of tribal scapegoats at a good distance across the world, with Iraq and Afghanistan as good candidates replacing Vietnam and the Empire, as an excuse to call in the cavalry and project their aggression. One capsule that the United States has created for its Shadow is Guantanamo Bay, a safe distance from its own shores, out of sight, out of mind. Obama attempted to close Guantanamo without success. He was prevented by the overwhelming need in his electorate to retain this receptacle for a tribal/national aggression. The leaders are pawns in a game with somewhat limited mobility.

It is very dangerous to see the problem of ISIL in isolation, as the "goodies versus the baddies". To do so is again to enter an endless game of pass the parcel where the music never stops and bodies litter the streets. The "baddies" are no longer solely over there, but in terms of terror and mass immigration, as a friend put it, "metastases are cropping up all over Europe, and how effective surgery will be, remains to be seen". I remember reading an article about "the troubles" in Ireland, where the writer was bemoaning the fact that both sides needed to enact their anger in violence rather than articulating it. To have negotiation means that the leaders, who are partially pawns in the game, have a changed mandate and an arena can open up, where there is the possibility that everyone is at least confronted with owning their "bad bits". The door is open to some integration of their respective Shadows. This normally only happens when both sides are totally depleted financially and in body counts. Taking back the Shadow is the only possible route to the emergence of a collective love axis. I think that the image I mentioned earlier, of metastases, is an interesting one. Cancer knows no borders in our bodies. It leads to chaos and death. Some cancers do heal. There are situations in the world where we see glimmerings of a love axis, but sadly they are few. The cards do seem stacked against us.

Tom Stevenson in his review of Simon Akam's recent book, "The Changing of the Guard" (2021) says "The invasion of Iraq was a generational disaster, but its effects will endure far longer. American and British armies descended in 2003, initiating the kind of cataclysm that registers in the fossil record.

The war left hundreds of thousands of Iraqi dead, most of them civilians. The war's survivors were forced into violence or flight. A polity that had already endured a decade of genocidal sanctions suffered total collapse. The subsequent occupation was upheld through the use of torture. Most former champions of the war accept that it led to an increase in global Jihadist activity culminating in the rise of Islamic State. To speak of individual war crimes is to ignore the fact that the war itself was a terrible crime. Its purpose was to reinforce US domination of the Middle East after the challenge mounted by al-Qaida was clear. The intelligence services knew, as the senior MI6 officer for the Middle East later admitted, that Weapons of Mass Destruction were a 'vehicle' for going to war. The British government didn't hold its nose and accept that it had to join the invasion in order to retain its position in the US global order. In certain circles, enthusiasm for the war was high". What right have we to invade another's country because we don't like the way they operate? What right have we to form an empire? How on earth could we expect any other response than for this to stoke up the fires of the power axis and lead to more and more hatred and retaliation?

Tom Stevenson further says, "After seeing its terrible consequences, one might have expected the countries responsible to reflect on what had happened. But the UK has continued to evade scrutiny. Every Prime Minister since Blair has supported Britain's involvement; none has paid for it politically. No convincing account of the British role in the war has yet been written. The Chilcott Report was delayed until it was so overshadowed by Brexit that the parliamentary debate on its findings was attended by only a handful of MPs". The Ministry of Defence tried to prevent the publication of Simon Akam's book, not wanting a close examination of a string of catastrophes, and the original publisher, Penguin Random House, decided to pull out.

One further quote from Stevenson:

"A country that claims having soldiers in 46 countries is necessary to keep its citizens safe.

A country where professing a willingness to use nuclear weapons is considered a precondition for political office.

A country that passes legislation to protect itself from prosecution for torture and war crimes.

A country that has an undercover domestic police force to spy on and interfere with anti-war activists".

This shows me unequivocally what a devastating force the power axis is. In so many situations, even in the "benign" West, the love axis, in a collective frame of reference, stands little chance of really prevailing.

The Military

Returning to Simon Akam's book "The Changing of the Guard", (p. 566) he says, "Desperate to put bums on seats at Sandhurst, forty-eight candidates who had previously failed, some failing assessments as many as four times, [were sent back for reassessment]. They were not promising material and all had even spent six weeks at Sandhurst on a remedial development course attempting to get marginal candidates to pass. Despite this, most of the candidates' original flaws were still evident, including some who would still panic and become irrational under stress. They ran them through the tests again; they eventually decided that twenty-five of the forty-eight could – just – be passed. That was not enough for the system, though; the trainers were told to go back and scrape the barrel, to look at even those they had failed. They managed to justify passing another ten or so. Sandhurst, desperate for manpower, finally took all but the eight worst of the forty-eight". To go to these lengths surely underlines the blatant fundamentalism that is driving our military, stirring up comparable fundamentalism in retaliation across the world.

The Intractability

The West is reaping what it sowed in the Middle East. The rapid withdrawal from Afghanistan shockingly showed how little had changed as a result of twenty years of war. The improved lot of women is being reversed as the Taliban return to power stoked up by twenty years of fury. There is a real cost of interfering in other people's countries. The Afghan war has left a staggering fourteen percent of the population disabled, over one million people. President Biden is making noises about America no longer taking on the role of world policeman. But I think the die may well have been cast as we see the next actor, China, stepping in for a power grab in Afghanistan.

Writing this in many ways feels very depressing. It is hard to see any easy, or indeed any *hard*, solutions. The love axis is fragile and easily undermined, while the power axis is easily reinforced. It is an incredibly uphill struggle but vital we find small ways to play our part in the greatest battles the world faces.

"I am writing this on the 20th anniversary of 9/11", Stephen Wertheim, a senior fellow at the Carnegie Endowment for International Peace, writes in Prospect Magazine (2021). *"For all the solemn odes to the day's significance that will be heard on its looming 20th anniversary, the truth remains: September 11 did not, as it turned out, inaugurate a new age of massive terrorist attacks in the United States. Even the initially unimaginable scale of the attacks themselves has slowly come to look less shocking. The 2,977 souls lost now rank alongside the successive tolls of Hurricane Katrina and the coronavirus pandemic. The latter has claimed well over half a million American lives [as I write, over 800,000] already. According to official statistics, on 38 individual days of the pandemic, more Americans died from Covid-19 than perished on 9/11.*

Nor was September 11, lest we forget, what sent the US military into the Middle East. A full decade earlier, in the wake of its first war against Iraq to liberate Kuwait, the United States had already begun to station tens of thousands of troops in the region – a grievance cited by Osama bin Laden when he declared war on America in 1996. America's pursuit of military dominance – dividing the region into friends and enemies – would have happened regardless of 9/11, albeit probably to less deadly effect".

He sees America's intervention as power in search of a purpose and quotes Madeleine Albright, the then Secretary of State, proclaiming America to be the world's "indispensable nation". She did so on *The Today Show* in 1998 while explaining why her government, regretting its earlier caution, was gearing up to bomb Iraq. She said: "If we have to use force, it is because we are America; we are the indispensable nation. We stand tall and we see further than other countries into the future, and we see the danger here to all of us". George Bush too framed the attack as proof of the centrality of America to world affairs. An unambiguous power axis.

The Progress

What's to be done about all this? A man in London asks an Irishman how to get to Dublin. He gets the response "if I were going to Dublin, I wouldn't start from here"! Each step that the West takes in aggression compounds the problem. If we were in a pre-Iraq war situation, then our destructive enmeshment would be considerably less, and the problem for the West much much simpler. We cannot, by force, change another person, much less a nation. It would serve us well to attempt to find a more creative response, rather than a kneejerk, and equally violent, reaction. The only person we can change is ourselves. By concentrating on our own evolution, on the integration of our own Shadows, the increasing of our own awareness of our part in the quagmire, the less we are likely to project our hatred and our power dynamics into others who will only want to hand it back immediately in reaction.

There are lots of attempts to counteract the power axis. George Floyd is killed by a policeman in the US. "Black Lives Matter" is visible across the world. Harvey Weinstein is outed for his gross abuse of women and the "#MeToo" movement is galvanised. Greta Thunberg leads a powerful crusade for climate change and "Extinction Rebellion" rises up. Many other movements too are fighting for change in a largely peaceful way and achieving much. One possible problem though is that the power axis is still in the ascendancy. Power meets power; action meets reaction. It is hard to win over perpetrators.

And Yet ... and Yet, We Have Examples of Progress

On September 17, 1978 at Camp David, President Jimmy Carter was involved in forging a peace treaty between the Israeli Prime Minister, Menachem Begin, and the Egyptian President, Anwar Sadat, which came into effect the following year. This was the first such treaty between Israel and any of its foreign neighbours and was known as *"Framework for Peace in the Middle East"*. The process began when Sadat made a dramatic visit to Israel and spoke to the Israeli parliament. Later followed a fraught and secret summit with no press interference which Carter convened and which lasted thirteen days. Egypt and Israel had been at war for many years and the chemistry between the leaders was not at all easy.

Begin, always formal in dress and manner, was extremely detail-oriented and careful about the possible ramifications of any agreements. He was pessimistic about what he believed could be achieved at Camp David, insisting that the objective be limited to developing an agenda for future meetings. By contrast, Sadat wore fashionable sports clothes, was relaxed and forthcoming, and was willing to join in comprehensive negotiations aimed at settling all controversial issues during the few days of the summit. After three days, the negotiations reached an impasse, becoming so heated that Carter had to shuttle between them rather than having a direct dialogue. Talks on quite a few occasions almost broke down, with Sadat threatening to leave and Carter preparing to return to the White House. Primarily due to the extraordinary efforts of Carter, a third in this equation, a *"Framework for Peace in the Middle East"*, was agreed which included:

1   Palestinian self-government in the West Bank and Gaza,
2   A peace treaty between Egypt and Israel ending a state of war between the two countries,
3   A framework for peace between Israel and its other neighbours.

There was resistance. The UN and the PLO rejected the Accord, and most Arab countries ostracised Egypt. Nonetheless, it was an advance to be built on by the Oslo Accord signed by Israel and the PLO in 1993 with the help of Bill Clinton.

I was interested that the Camp David agreement could only happen by shuttle diplomacy where Carter was able to meet the protagonists alone and I imagine do what I described in analysis of individuals trapped in power/ fantasy axes – immersing himself in their power fantasy worlds so that they felt understood enough and safe enough to tentatively take incremental steps towards a love/reality axis.

We can add to this the Good Friday agreement, with which initially Sir John Major and later Tony Blair were involved, the removal of apartheid in South Africa spearheaded by Nelson Mandela, and many other important changes for the better in the world. These changes involve key third parties bringing "power" players together outside of the public gaze.

Another factor making change possible is pressure building up in the collective that is opposed to warfare, so many people suffering, too much money being spent, and too much energy is being invested. And this happens at a Kairos moment, when conditions are right for the accomplishment of crucial actions. Then, there is a tiny questioning of the power treadmill, a slight awareness that says, *"I was not thinking my thoughts. I was not myself"*, and there is a glimpse into futility, into a terrifying psychotic space that pulls leaders, communities, groups, and tribes back from the brink and opens the door a crack to thinking, to the loosening of the hold of fundamentalism. This sometimes has the glimmerings of the love axis we saw in the individual. Warfare however seems to have to go so far down the line before there is any possibility of dialogue and the hard-won changes are so fragile and potentially reversible through collective pressure.

I return to where I started, the quote from the film *"Tinker, Tailor, Soldier, Spy* (2011): *"The fanatic is always concealing a secret doubt"*. There is always a vestige of the traumatised person, an archetypal residue in the individual, group, community, or nation where humanity lurks to find a true free existence and to rediscover the atrophied "muscle" of living an authentic life. Jung would see this as more accessible in the second half of life, driven by mortality, the great leveller on the horizon.

References

Akam, S. (2021). "The Changing of the Guard: The British Army Since 9/11".

Burke, J. (2015 – 26th November). The Guardian Newspaper. "The Story of a Radicalisation".

Educate Against Hate Website. Resources for Parents, Teachers and Schoolchildren. https://educageagainsthate.com

Fisk, R. (2014, 13th June). Independent Newspaper. "The Old Partition of the Middle East Is Dead".

Jung, C. G. (1917). The Psychology of the Unconscious. CW7. London: Routledge & Kegan Paul.

Jung, C. G. (1964). Civilisation in Transition. CW10. London: Routledge & Kegan Paul.

Le Carré, J. (2011). Film Version of "Tinker, Tailor, Soldier, Spy".

Stevenson, T. (2021, 1st July). London Review of Books. "The Most Corrupt Idea of Modern Times".

Wertheim, S. (2021, 11th September). Prospect Magazine.

Winston, R. (2014). BBC Documentary, "A Child of Our Time".

Chapter 14

Imago Diaboli

The Devil and Its Manifestations in C. G. Jung's *Black Books* and *Liber Novus*

Tomasso Priviero

Satan crawls out of a dark hole with horns and tail, I pull him out by the hands. [...]

Satan: 'What do you want from me? I don't need you, impertinent fellow.'

I: 'It's a good thing we have you. [...] You're the liveliest and most interesting thing in the whole dogma.'

Jung (Black Book 4)

If ever you have the rare opportunity to speak with the devil, then do not forget to confront him in all seriousness. He is your devil after all.

Jung (Liber Novus)

Introduction

Readers who are not particularly familiar with the works of Carl Gustav Jung may be amazed by how seriously this world-renowned psychiatrist and analyst, who for his entire life advocated the status of being an "empiricist" and "man of science", took the figure of the devil. It is safe to say that no other comparable major psychologist of the 20th century investigated in such depth and in many ways the symbolism of Lucifer. Only a brief look at Jung's personal library in Küsnacht, Zurich, reveals an astonishing list of classics on the topic, among which: *Faust's Life, Deeds, and Journey to Hell in Five Books* (1907), Wilhelm Bousset's *The Antichrist Legend* (1895), Karl August von Eschenmayer's *Conflict between Heaven and Hell* (1837), Joseph Kroll's *God and Hell: the Myth of the Descensus Fight* (1932), Selma Lagerlöf's romance *The Miracles of Antichrist* (1911), Victor Maag's *The Antichrist as a Symbol of Evil* (1961), Riwkah Schärf's *The Figure of Satan in the Old Testament* (1947), Friedrich Alfred Schmid Noerr's *Demons, Gods, and Conscience* (1938), Raphael Judah Zwi Werblowsky's *Lucifer and Prometheus: A Study of Milton's Satan* (1952), Paul Wiegler's *The Antichrist: A Chronicle of the 13th Century* (1928), Giovanni Papini's *The Devil: Notes for a Future Diabology* (1955), and others. If not a proper

DOI: 10.4324/9781003255819-16

"sympathy for the devil", Jung certainly guessed his name with pleasure and ease, to quote the Rolling Stones. The fact that already as a fifteen-year-old boy, he remained so profoundly impressed by Goethe's *Faust*, and particularly by the character of Mephistopheles, was the harbinger of what was to become a growing source of interest in the years ahead.

However, readers who are more familiar with the ideas of Jung hasten to explain such concern with the devil by juxtaposing it with one of his most popular "archetypes" – the "Shadow". The devil, they say, is one of the many names and manifestations, albeit a very powerful one, of the *Shadow*, i.e., those rejected, undesirable, unknown, and obscure aspects of the psyche which trouble us in all possible manners at a personal and collective level. Toni Wolff, Jung's patient and soulmate, thus called the Shadow our "*dunkle Bruder*" ("dark brother") or the "*Andere in Uns*" ("other in ourselves") and Jung himself gave numberless illustrations of the Shadow image, deeming it the first fundamental step of one's encounter with one's deeper self, or "unconscious". The course of Western literature and mythology is so imbued with the motif of "dark brothers" and "sisters" that Marco Innamorati suggested that, more than Oedipus, we should think of the *doppelgänger* as the real representative psychic complex of the West (personal communication). In addition to the works of Fyodor Dostoyevsky and E.T.A. Hoffmann, Mario Trevi has pointed out (Trevi 2009, p. 49) one example for all of the classical Shadow story: Joseph Conrad's short novel *The Secret Sharer* (1910), which narrates, a long time before Brexit, the dark odyssey of the captain of a British vessel escorting his alter ego, an unexpected guest with a murderous past, to a place of security and freedom. Nevertheless, reading Jung's multifaceted confrontation with the devil through the lens of the "Shadow" archetype, however completely legitimate in a Jungian sense, does not satisfy the scope of the present discussion. Firstly, the successful formulation of the "Shadow" archetype inevitably risks turning the powerfully evocative image of the devil into an abstraction. But the symbol of the devil substantially remains a more instinctive and unpredictable fact than what the psychological "Shadow" aims to circumscribe. Secondly, Jung's encounter with the frightful image of Satan historically *precedes*, and indeed transcends, the scientific conceptualisation of the "Shadow" vocabulary. Therefore, instead of framing the problematic of Jung and the devil in strictly "Shadow" terms, this chapter will go to the roots of his confrontation with this living image, the *imago diaboli*, upon which the later formulation of the "Shadow" concept is based: the *Black Books* and *Liber Novus*.

Dia-ballein ("To Separate")

In all European languages, the devil is a "him", a masculine word, which quite significantly evokes the patriarchal atmosphere in which the legacy of this figure blossomed, alongside his more fortunate counterpart, God, the *imago dei*. Richard Lowe Thomson (1929), in his classic *History of the Devil,* identifies the archetypal ancestor of all forms of the devil, including the pre-Christian ones, in the image of the "Horned God of the West", which he traces as far back as to the most ancient cave paintings of Stone Age man.

Descriptors such as *devil, dev'l, deofol, diable, diablo, diavolo* share the ancient Greek root *diábolos*, from *dia-ballein*, a Greek verb meaning "to throw across", "to separate", "to slander", which are some the most traditional features of the devil. The opposite of *dia-ballein*, in Greek, is *sym-ballein*, "to unify", "to reconcile", "to put things together", from which, clearly, the word "symbol". The symbol unites, one might say, what the devil divides. One language is dogmatic (*dia-ballein*), the other is enigmatic (*sym-ballein*). Or in other words, as Erich Neumann pointed out in *Depth Psychology and a New Ethic*, "whatever leads to splitting" in our consciousness may be seen as "evil", "whatever leads to wholeness" may be seen as "good" (Neumann 1969 [1949], p. 126). It is precisely around the nature of this splitting, that the horned image of the devil has evolved in the West. The Greeks were deeply acquainted with the moral ambivalence of gods and demons. Thus, Heraclitus beautifully observed (Heraclitus 1889, DK B67): "The god is day and night, winter and summer, war and peace, surfeit and anger; but he takes various shapes, just as fire, when it is mingled with spices, is named according to the savor of each".

The Pre-Socratic Greeks observed the play of opposites in nature, hence in man, and thus were generally inclined not to take seriously absolute claims about the separation of good and evil, peace and war, sanity and insanity. Many centuries after, Friedrich Nietzsche lamented, at the beginning of *On the Genealogy of Morality* (1887), that while the ancient man instinctively recognised in madness a grain of wisdom and genius, we immediately search for a grain of insanity wherever there is genius, having banned fragmentation, multiplicity, and ambivalence from our psyche. Similarly, in a ground-breaking study on possession and the "demoniacal other", the psychologist of religion Traugott Konstantin Oesterreich (1930) noted how frantically, in the development of modern Western culture, all benevolent or positive ideas of "being possessed" (for example, by the Muses, by Eros, or by Dionysos) gradually turned into something sick or diabolical after the historical affirmation of the Christian Era. In the Middle Ages, *"the split which speaks by the mouth of a possessed person should always be a demon, a devil"* (Oesterreich 2014 [1930], p. 186). For Luther, "all mental affections" were essentially demoniacal possessions, a common bias which lasted for long, while the plight of witch-hunting was darkening the history of Europe. The demoniacal "brother" within us truly rose to the status of "an ancient and astute adversary, strong and exceedingly evil" *(antiquo et arturo hoste, forti et nequissimo)*, a traditional formula for addressing Lucifer during exorcisms, should the reader need.

On the one hand, this process somehow gave more dignity to the status of the devil, against the one-sidedness of the Biblical view which confined him to the subsidiary role of "rebellious angel". On the other hand, Philip C. Almond has noticed that the process of "diabolisation" of the gods in the political wake of Satan in the West fostered even more the idea of a "cosmic dualism", which saw the devil as the adversary of God in a battle for the triumph of "goodness", which hierarchically came first (Almond 2014, p. 19). This cosmological splitting, in Jung's view, created many problems to the troubled Western mind. Little help was brought by the spirit of the Enlightenment and the progressive decline of the religious belief in the devil. What was once called the devil, he noted (Jung 1933/1934, para. 309), "today we call it a neurosis". Though the language has changed, the substance has not, for what we continue to be obsessed by, as he puts it, is a *"monotheism of consciousness", "coupled with a fanatical denial of the existence of fragmentary autonomous systems"* (Jung 1929, para. 51). This religion of consciousness was common to both Western science and religion, since the two shared a similar process of *dia-ballein*, a splitting between man and nature. Beyond the only apparent opposition, the theological truth hypostasised nature as the creation of "God", just as the anthropo-logical truth regarded the "Ego", by designing nature as the house of man's technical progress. For Jung, the origins of this anti-natural "cult of consciousness" had a fundamental connection with the theological doctrine of the *privatio boni* ("absence of the good"), which originated with Origen, continued with Augustine, and was systematised by Thomas Aquinas. The core of this view is summarised in a militant Augustinean expression: *Omne bonum a deo, omne malum ab homini* ("All good from God, all evil from man"). "Evil", according to this vision, cannot be a reality in itself, the legitimate counterpart of "good", but only the *"absence of good"*, a sort of rebellious guilt subordinated to an original "absolute goodness" which conforms to the Christian values. But while this view assigned the *summum bonum* (the "highest good") to the Almighty and the *infimum malum* (the "worst of evil") to the vulnerability of man, it ironically also reserved for man, as told since the *Book of Genesis*, the fate of having dominion over animals, earth and nature. However, for Jung, the denial of evil in the name of a godlike consciousness was not only a theological paradox, but also and especially a psychological impossibility which was at odds with the uninterrupted flux of opposites, visions, and autonomous complexes which animate the psyche and far escape the control of "conscious will" or intentional "goodness". As opposed to the Greeks and the Romans, the truncated image of divinity in the Christian world provoked, in Jung's vision, four fundamental "exclusions" within man's modern mind: sexuality, animality, creative imagination, and, indeed, the *"inferior man"* within us, what is under-developed and undervalued (another name for the "shadow") (Jung 1923, p. 74).

The Experiment

The *Black Books* and *Liber Novus* convey a Dante-esque journey of radical self-transformation, which lasted for more than sixteen years and was based on a technique of deep introversion and visioning. Like in Dante's adventures, the odyssey of Jung's visionary experiences entailed a movement in darkness, a descent into Hell, and a return to light, a process of inner rebirth, which was fundamentally facilitated by the presence of Toni Wolff by his side, and by the stability provided by his wife, Emma Rauschenbach, his family, and his work.

And just as Dante went on his epical search for Beatrice in the underworld, so Jung described his book of visions in terms of sending "letters to the soul", the *anima*, to which he said he came *"like a tired wanderer who had sought nothing in the world apart from her"* (Jung 2009 [circa 1915], p. 233). In many occurrences in this experiment, particularly at the beginning, the author evoked the threatening autonomous power of the visions and the dangerous risk of being mentally overwhelmed by the experience he embarked on. This darker side of the journey was often described as a katabasis ("descent"), a *nekyia* ("evocation of the dead or ghosts", "necromancy"), a "descent into Hell", an infernal visit to the blackest regions of the mind. In a place of this sort, meeting the devil cannot be a surprise. So did it happen to Jung, or better yet, Jung's "I", the narrator of *Liber Novus.*

The voices of the devil in the course of the *Black Books* and *Liber Novus* are at least as various as the ways in which the author named him throughout his notebooks: Devil, Satanas, Satan, Serpent, Antichrist, the "terrible worm", God's dark side, the Horned God, the "Red One", the black one, the "fourth one", the tempter of Christ, the destroyer, the devourer, the "frightful" one, the "shadow of beauty", the "one who dwells behind the night". Altogether, the references to the devil in *Liber Novus* outnumber two hundred. Not only are the references to the devil so numerous, but they are also scattered across the entire spectrum of Jung's experiment, from the start to the latest entries. We can recognise at least five crucial thematic appearances: (1) the devil in the desert (temptations), (2) the motif of the Antichrist, (3) the "Red One", (4) the devil in the "Magician" section, (5) the appearance of Abraxas in "Scrutinies". Although it is difficult to summarise such a controversial figure, one may say that the role of the devil in *Liber Novus* shows the two main properties of the fire element, with which he is commonly associated: *"to destroy"* and *"to create anew"*. He is, on the one hand, the "devourer", i.e., the mind intoxicated with the obsession of "understanding" and "grasping", the "quintessence of the personal" (ego-clinging), the sinister messenger of death, chaos, and suffering. On the other hand, he bears the torch of his Luciferian nature, in the capacity of bringer of light and instinctual energy, without which, Jung always argued, no self-transformation or psychological purification would be possible. In other words, as he later commented in the seminar on Christiana Morgan's visions (1930–1934), the devilish fire is the burst of passion that burns up all rubbish and makes possible to see that "*in the ashes a molten drop of gold will appear*" (Jung 1997 [1930–1934], p. 1055). Around the search for a balance between the destructive and the creative aspects of the *imago diaboli* essentially revolves Jung's encounter with the devil in the *Black Books* and *Liber Novus*; an encounter which, however dreadful and unpleasant, resulted in a fundamental cathartic experience of transformation.

"The Desert"

Just a few nights after the commencement of his experiment, on the 28th of November 1913, the "soul" leads the "I" "away from mankind" and into a mental "desert". A "*barren, hot desert, dusty, and without drink*" (Jung, 2009 [1913], p. 141). In an eerie wasteland of this kind, the protagonist is in a state of complete bewilderment and, like Dante in the *Inferno*, he really has no clue how to behave. The desert compels to "wait": a hopeless state of suspension and psychic immobility. Yet the longer one waits in the desert without shade, the more one's back is scorched by the heat of the midday sun. Thus midday, noontide, which Nietzsche called "*a death with waking eyes*" (Nietzsche 2004 [1878], p. 350), is the time of the day when the sun begins to invert its course and a shadow appears on the ground: demons and ghosts reveal their presence. In a brilliant study on the topic, Roger Caillois observed that in Latin cultures midday is the magical and religious time par excellence, the sacred and dangerous hour "well known by magicians and exorcists" (Caillois 1991 [1936], p. 91), as the favourite time in which, traditionally, the living are granted access to Hades. In a similar ghostly "desert", the name of the devil makes his first significant appearance in Jung's notebooks, as one can read in *Black Book 2*: "*I think of Christianity in the desert. Physically, those ancients went into the desert. Did they also enter into the desert of their own self? Or was their self not as barren and desolate as mine? There they wrestled with the devil. I wrestle with waiting. It seems to me not less since it is truly a hot hell*" (Jung 2020 [1913], v. 2 p. 35). This entry evokes the devil's frequent visits to the monks who lived and meditated in the desert in the early centuries of Christianity, often referred to as "desert Fathers": Antonius, Pachomius, Arsenius the Great, Macarius, Moses the Black, and many unknown others who all went to the deserts of the Middle East to experience physical solitude and inner awakening. Introversion in the desert, according to Jean Chevalier and Alain Gheerbrant, entails two essential symbolical features: "*Primordial undifferentiated state, or [...] superficially sterile crust under which Reality must be sought*" (Chevalier, Gheerbrant 1994 [1969], p. 285). In a Christian context, the ambivalence of this symbol is strong. For Matthew (12:43), the desert is the abode of demons and temptations. For Richard of St. Victor and other Christian mystics, it is the centre of the heart and spiritual elevation. Echoing these motifs, Jung describes his own "desert" as a space of extreme solitude and spiritual concentration. A place in which, like an ancient shade crawling out of a cave, the devil shows his horns again.

Shortly after, in a new section entitled "Splitting of the Spirit", Jung's "I" cries: "*To journey to Hell means to become Hell oneself. It is all frightfully muddled and interwoven*" (Jung 2009 [1913], p. 240). The monstrous visions brought forth by the "soul" are hard to digest. "*On this desert, there is not just glowing sand, but also horrible tangled invisible beings who live in the desert*" (*ibidem*). Experiencing deep techniques of introversion leading to one's inner "desert" is no child's play. Yet Jung notes that at this point of his self-explorations there was no chance for him to go backward whence he started. He could only go forward by learning how to increasingly let things happen psychically. Thus, he turns again to the "soul", his inner counterpart, and invites her: "*Come close, I am ready. Ready, my soul, you who are a devil, to wrestle with you too. You donned the mask of a God, and I worshiped you. Now you wear the mask of a devil, a frightful one, the mask of the banal, of eternal mediocrity!*" (ibid., p. 241). The passage epitomises the "splitting" Jung comes to grip within this section, by providing an unsettling prelude to a central motif of the whole devil conundrum: the ambivalent forces of the soul-image.

The "Antichrist"

Confronted with the powerful emergence of a new stream of visions, Jung writes in his notebooks in January 1914: "*This is really Good Friday, upon which the Lord died and descended into Hell and completed the mysteries*" (Jung 2009 [1914], p. 304). What this cryptic mention refers to is the *Apostles' Creed*, which succinctly claims that after his death Christ "Descended into Hell". The third day He arose again from the Dead (Cross & Livingstone 2005, p. 90). He elaborates further on the reference and notes in more detail:

> After his death Christ had to journey to Hell, otherwise the ascent to Heaven would have become impossible for him. Christ first had to become his Antichrist, his underworldly brother.
>
> No one knows what happened during the three days Christ was in Hell. I have experienced it.
>
> (Jung 2009 [circa 1915], p. 243)

In an emphatic Christian vibe, these lines convey the core of Jung's confrontation with Hell and the devil motif. First of all, Hell is described as a Bardo *experience* of challenging self-transformation: an in-between place of contact with the deepest and darkest grounds of oneself. This experience is identified as a startling journey to the "other side", a frightful encounter with "the dark brother", death, the Antichrist, the opposite of everything acceptable, meaningful, and valuable for oneself. Most importantly, this encounter harbours a substantial movement forward of inner regeneration, which would have not been possible otherwise. In his writings on alchemy, Jung refers to Christ's descent into Hades as a process of purification into the flames of Hell, out of which the New Fire rises again (Jung 1937, para. 440, 451). Later, he comments on the meaning of this event as follows:

> The three days descent into Hell during death describes the sinking of the vanished value into the unconscious, where, by conquering the power of darkness, it establishes a new order, and then rises up to heaven again, that is, attains supreme clarity of consciousness.
>
> (Jung 1938/1940, para. 149)

As to the problematics presented by Christ's venture to a place like this, theologians since Thomas Aquinas (*Summa Theologiae,* Questio 52, Pars 3) have answered with the hypostasis of "Christ's harrowing of Hell". That is, Christ descends to the land of the Dead and triumphantly conquers the power of evil. The theological reading of the passage opts for a distinction between *Inferno* (Hell), which supposedly indicates the eternal destiny of those condemned at the Final Judgment, and *inferos* (hell, from *locus inferos,* the "place beneath"), such as the Hell of the Old Testament, the Hebrew Sheol, the Greek Hades, the underworld of Odysseus, Aeneas and the heroes of European literature up to Dante. It follows that *inferos,* rather than *Inferno,* would be the place into which Christ descends for three days. However, in the apocryphal literature, Christ's journey to Hell is described in more detail, particularly in the *Gospel of Nicodemus* and the *Apocalypse of Peter,* an early apocalyptic Christian text (c. 150 AD) which conveys the earliest extant paleo-Christian description of Hell (Elliott 1993, p. 595). Jung certainly did not spare himself the curiosity of consulting these texts, since the apocryphal works were a crucial abiding topic in his psychological interests concerning the historical significance of Christianity. References to apocryphal pieces are scattered all through his works. Relevant to the current discussion, Jung considered the apocryphal Christ an alternative and a completion at once of the canonical story of the Harrowing of Hell. The dogmatic vision for which Jesus, as the son of a God of absolute goodness and almighty power, could only go to Hell to descend there as triumphant would essentially confirm the Christian splitting between goodness and evil, as this view coalesced in the doctrine of *privatio boni*:

> This classic formula [*privatio boni*] robs evil of absolute existence and makes it a shadow that has only a relative existence dependent on light.

Good, on the other hand, is credited with a positive substantiality. But, as psychological experience shows, 'good' and 'evil' are opposite poles of a moral judgment which, as such, originates in man. A judgment can be made about a thing if its opposite is equally real and possible. The opposite of a seeming evil can only be a seeming good, and an evil that lacks substance can only be contrasted with a good that is equally non-substantial.

(Jung 1942/1948, para. 247)

On the contrary, the apocryphal version presents a different account of Hell, a significantly more balanced story, in which Christ and his "brother from the underworld", the Antichrist, have to come to terms. If the splitting of good and evil, or the separation of the opposites, naturally leads to a one-sided vision of *staying in* Hell as the place of a permanent exile, the rapprochement of the opposites, as conveyed by the apocryphal descent to Hell, triggers a dynamic conception of *traversing* Hell in terms of a potential transformative condition. This view is deeply reflected in *Liber Novus*, in which Hell entails no fixed moral connotation, but a place of suspension and radical confusion which takes the mental traveller, the "I" (the ego), to the roots of self-deceptions. As Dante must come to a compromise with Lucifer, the *"emperor of the despondent kingdom"* (*Inferno*, XXXIV, 28; Dante Alighieri 1987, p. 334) in order to regain his freedom, so the "I" announces in *Liber Novus* that Christ (or the hero) must first acknowledge the Antichrist (the anti-hero or dragon), in order to make the advancement in the journey possible. Later on, as pointed out before, he ascribed this process to the integration of the "Shadow" archetype (Jung 1917, para. 103n; Jung 1951, para. 13–19).

The "Red One"

Far from being exhausted with the dramatic appearance of the Antichrist, the *imago diaboli* in *Liber Novus* changes again, as unpredictable and multifaceted as only the *"Father of All Tricksters"* (Jung 1952, para. 620) could be. If the visions which have been mentioned thus far mostly gave voice to the apocalyptic side of Lucifer, another chapter of *Liber Novus*, explicitly dedicated to Him and entitled "The Red One" (December 26, 1913), presents the devil from a very different angle: an exuberant, eccentric, and humoresque spirit with a markedly pagan connotation and a red appearance. If the devil appears in red he is of a *"passionate"* and *"fiery"* nature, Jung later noted in the *Children's Dreams* seminar (Jung 2010 [1936–1940], p. 174).

The author observes himself, i.e., his "I", standing on the highest tower of a castle, far back in time, in a medieval atmosphere, when he suddenly sees a red figure coming out of a forest and directing himself toward the castle.

As the unknown wanderer approaches, he reveals himself to be the "Red One", a horseman wholly shrouded in red, with red garments shining like red "growing iron". At this sight, without further ado, the "I" jumps to this amusing conclusion: "*In the end, he will turn out to be the devil*" (Jung 2009 [1913], p. 259). A dialogue between the two takes place. The "Red One" is a somewhat erratic and unconventional figure, a proper trickster, with a sneering sense of humour. He is the exact counter-type of a saint-like figure whom the "I" will encounter a bit later, in another vision: Ammonius, the anchorite of the desert. The "Red One" has reached the castle to bring the "I" "something pagan", a radiant sense of joy and communion with nature, a certain lightness of being, and a heartfelt disposition to laugh and play. In a surely Nietzschean spirit, he also brings the "I" the precious warning that "life doesn't require any seriousness", and against the "spirit of gravity" through which "all things are ruined", one should learn instead how to dance through life, by saying "Yes!" to everything she sets forth for us (*ibidem*).

By contrast with the joyful style of the "Red One", one is struck by the moral rigidity of Jung's "I", who even labels his guest as an adept of the "black school of Salerno", an old alchemical school in South Italy, "*whose pernicious arts are taught by pagans and the descendants of pagans*" (*ibidem*). Due to such stubbornness and solemnity, almost "smelling of fanaticism", the red knight has a difficult time while conversing with the "I", and thus he points out (and one could hardly agree more with the devil in this occasion): "*If you're no saint, I really don't see why you have to be so solemn. You wholly spoil the fun. What the devil is troubling you? Only Christianity with its mournful escape from the world can make people so ponderous and sullen*" (ibid., p. 260). At this point, before the amazed stupor of the "I", who tries once again to intellectualise what he has just heard, the devil doffs his mask and finally claims: "*Don't you recognise me, brother? I am joy!*" (*Ibidem*). Altogether, although a "toned-down" type of the devil motif (as the anchorite Ammonius calls him), the scene with the "Red One" contains some important points of reflection for the present discussion: (1) it is the part of *Liber Novus* in which the name of the devil is used most frequently and explicitly by Jung; (2) it suitably depicts how, for Jung, the devil essentially works by *compensation*. The "Red One", the fiery and passionate devil, is the forgotten half of the one-sidedness of the "I", and strives in all ways to make the latter not forget that he is, after all, his "*brother*"; (3) it is a particularly enjoyable section, characterised by a quasi-comical and humorous tone which aptly balances the more prophetic, at times exaggeratedly serious, language with which the author tackles the devil motif elsewhere. Thus, in a layer of commentary added later, Jung writes in remarkably positive and honest terms of his new encounter with the devil, calling him a "*warm southerly wind*" bearing "*self-forgetting*" (ibid. [circa 1915], p. 260). He then completes these observations by offering a description of the devil which could not portray in better terms the psychological function of the "Shadow", the "dark brother" inside, the "other side" of one's habitual or customary self:

> The devil as the adversary is your own other standpoint; he tempts you and sets a stone in your path where you least want it.

> Taking the devil seriously does not mean going over to his side, or else one becomes the devil. Rather it means coming to an understanding. Thereby you accept your other standpoint. With that the devil fundamentally loses ground, and so do you. And that may be well and good. [...]

> Through my coming to terms with the devil, he accepted some of my seriousness, and I accepted some of his joy. This gave me courage.
>
> (Ibid., p. 261)

The "Magician"

Shortly after the encounter with the "Red One", the *imago diaboli* changes his skin again, like the most characteristic of the devil's animals, the serpent. The period of January 1914, in the records of Jung's visions, seems particularly flourishing for the number of references to the devil motif. In one mention, the fundamental compensatory force of the symbol of Satan occurs: "*You locked Satan in the abyss for a millennium and when the millennium had passed, you laughed at him, since he had become a children's fairy tale. But if the dreadful great one raises his head, the world winces. The most extreme coldness draws near*" (Jung 2009 [1914], pp. 265–266). A few days after, the "I" encounters the "Red One" again, this time while he wanders in company of the anchorite of the desert, Ammonius. The two form a couple of antithetical opposites, Christian asceticism and pagan hedonism, exemplifying the ongoing process of dis-identification of the "I" from both extremes, and the search for a middle way. A few nights after, it is the devil again, in a new section entitled "*Hell*": "*The devil knows what is beautiful, and hence he is the shadow of beauty and follows it everywhere, awaiting the moment when the beautiful, writhing great with child, seeks to give life to the God*" (ibid. [1914], pp. 316–317). In another series of visions with an atmosphere à la David Lynch, the "I" is in a "madhouse", and the "soul" invites him to understand and welcome the divine gifts of "madness" ("Divine Folly"):

> Words, words, do not make too many words. Be silent and listen: have you recognized your madness, and do you admit it? Have you noticed

that all your foundations are completely mired in madness? Do you not want to recognize your madness and welcome it in a friendly manner? You wanted to accept everything. So, accept madness too.

(Ibid. [1914], p. 298)

This time, against this view, is a small fat professor, a grotesque caricature of psychiatric and scholarly misuse, to convey the word of the devil, by personifying the scientific prejudice against the divisions and contradictions inherent in the human psyche – a bias against which Jung notoriously spent many years of his life and work, and which acted at the very heart of the inner struggle experienced at the commencement of *Liber Novus*.

Overall, these multiple references to the devil throughout January 1914 prepare a fundamental part of the experiment, entitled "The Magician". In this chapter, the various threads illustrated so far concerning the devil come together in novel and challenging ways. The protagonist of the "Magician" is no less than *Philemon*, the leading voice and inner character of Jung's entire visionary journey. This central figure of *Liber Novus* encapsulates knowledge, insight, superior wisdom. He represents the "guru", the "master", the "guide" into the unknown, the "psychopomp", that is, in ancient Greek mythology, the deity or figure that escorts the descent of the souls in their journeys to the underworld. As such, Philemon is the hermetic "instructor of the demons", the crucial point of conjunction that allows the communication between "above" and "below", lower and upper realms of the mind, spirit and earth, "good" and "evil". Thus, Philemon also enables a fundamental intercession between the "I" and the image of the devil, which through the intervention of the "Magician" is more clearly raised to the function of a force of balance operating toward the reconciliation of the opposites. (ibid., pp. 207–208).

In addition to this, and most importantly for the scope of the present discussion, the magician Philemon is described by Jung, in the pages of *Memories, Dreams, Reflections* (/1983), as a "*pagan*" who "brought with him an Egypto-Hellenistic atmosphere with a Gnostic coloration" (*ibidem*). In *Liber Novus*, the "I", after a long search, encounters Philemon in a small house "*fronted by a large bed of tulips*" (Jung 2009 [1914], p. 312). The "I" has come to learn the secret arts of magic, given that no books or professors "know anything more" in the field. Philemon is puzzled by the incomprehensible request of his visitor and frankly tells him that "there is nothing to learn" about magic. Despite this reluctance, the "I" insists to hear something else – a path to follow, a rule to learn, a model to imitate. "*Comical fellow, how stubborn you are!*", Philemon exclaims (ibid., p. 313). A long enigmatic discussion between the two follows, about the nature of magical operations. Against the background of this encounter in the magician's garden, Philemon's words reveal, since the first moment of his appearance, that the "wise old man", in Jung's mind, decidedly shows more than one "pagan" trace. One should remember that Jung's account of Philemon is partly based on the story of this figure appearing in Ovid's *Metamorphoses* and Goethe's *Faust*. His appearance, as Jung asserts in *Psychological Types* while discussing the Goethean vision of Faust, brings forth the unmistakable signs of a "*primordial paganism*" (Jung 1921, para. 316), which essentially evokes in this context what Jung describes as the "daemonic energy" of psychic opposites underlying psychic activity. The wise guru or psychopomp embodies the particular capacity to lead the student or hero into the difficult process of reconciliation with the other side, the unknown and rejected pole of the mind, which is so often religiously associated with the image of Satan or the Horned God. The psychopomp, in other words, guides the subject in their coming to terms with devilish or demonic complexes, while inspiring them to unleash the psychic energy potentially contained in such images. The devil, in this sense, is no longer the great architect of the *dia-ballein*, the dualistic splitting between man and nature, but on the contrary, he is the Promethean catalyst of self-transformation, the necessary counterpart or "other half" of the equilibrium of opposites that rules psychic life. The psychopomp or wise old man helps the novice to experience the complex and controversial stages of this transformation. Analogously, following the appearance of Philemon in the records of *Liber Novus*, the image of the devil evolves in highly significant terms. As Philemon brings to the "I" the radical novelty of his teachings, the "I" alarmingly turns to the "soul": "*How will it be, now that God and the devil have become one?*" (Jung 2009 [1914], p. 318).

A little later, in search for an answer to this question, the "I" has the idea of summoning Satan himself, by pulling him by horns and tail, to his utter annoyance. The "I" sees nothing less than the throne of God and the trinity ascending to Heaven, and the Dark one with them, unwillingly invited. The "I" explains that the meaning of his call resides in the attempt of unifying the opposites and overcoming dualistic views (in the proper sense of *dia-ballein*), by integrating the dark side of the devil motif with the lightness of life, through the powerful image of the trinity. Although the theme is proverbially associated with later texts once more the reader should recognise that the theme is first tackled by Jung in the form of this first-hand encounter with the *imago diaboli*, at the core of his meditational endeavours.

As soon as the devil crawls back into his hole, almost for a process of automatic regeneration, another vision of demonic proportions immediately follows in the section "The Magician": the "Cabiri" (ibid. [circa 1914–1915], pp. 320–322). As noted by Sonu Shamdasani, the vision of the Cabiri, which is interestingly not mentioned in *Black Book 4*, appears in the *Handwritten Draf*, and thus it has most likely been written prior to the summer of 1915 (Shamdasani 2009, p. 425, n310). This confirms how vividly and fascinatingly the author dealt with the symbolism of demons and devils during the phase of his experiment which followed the encounter with Philemon.

The Cabiri, who also appear in Goethe's *Faust*, are ancient Greek deities of the underworld mostly associated with fertility and navigation. They are the sons of Hephaestus, the god of fire and blacksmiths, and a nymph of the sea, Cabeirus. Though later defined as *"mysterious creative powers"* and *"gnomes who work under the earth"* (Jung 1942/1948, para. 244), the Cabiri of *Liber Novus* are directly presented as the *"sons of the devil"*, which indicates the birth of a "hidden treasure", a new generative force springing from the creative confrontation with the devil image, the Horned God. They are really the gnomes of the furnace of the devil, *"animal faces/of the human body"*, *"foolishly sweet, uncanny, primordial, and earthly"* (*ibidem*). They challenge the "I" with radical paradoxes and especially with one of the most intriguingly enigmatic scenes of *Liber Novus*. In the manner of the role they fulfilled for their father Hephaestus, they present in fact the "I" with a magical flashing "sword", a secret weapon, with which he should firmly cut off the *"skillfully twined knot that locks and seals you"* (ibid., p. 321). One may find a parallel in this scene with the symbolic function of the *phurba* in Tibetan Buddhism, a three-sided knife which is used in rituals to control demonic forces and entails the power to sever all worldly ties or attachments. The terrible "knot" Jung is entangled within the encounter with the Cabiri is his own *"brain"*: the danger of identification with the deceitful powers of ego-thinking. Thus, the mysterious earth spirits compel the "I" to acknowledge that while his attachment to the brain fosters "madness", the magical sword they provide represents "the overcoming of madness" (*ibidem*). Only an act of courage from the "I" can secure a successful strike.

   In conclusion, following the intervention of the Cabiri, "offsprings of the devil", Jung notes down something remarkable about the meaning of serpenthood, which once again signals the continuous transformation of the *imago diaboli* through *Liber Novus*:

> If I had not become like the serpent, the devil, the quintessence of everything serpentlike, would have held this bit of power. This would have given the devil a grip and he would have forced me to make a pact with him just as he also cunningly deceived Faust. But I forestalled him by uniting myself with the serpent, just as a man unites with a woman.

> So, I took away from the devil the possibility of influence, which only ever passes through one's own serpenthood, which one commonly assigns to the devil instead of oneself. Mephistopheles is Satan, taken with my serpenthood. Satan himself is the quintessence of evil, naked and therefore without seduction, not even clever, but pure negation without convincing force. Thus, I resisted his destructive influence and grasped him and fettered him firmly. His descendants served me and I sacrificed them with the sword.

> (Ibid., pp. 322–323)

Scrutinies

To sum up what has been observed thus far, the devil in the records of Jung's Hell is the dark and threatening side of a deep process of self-transformation. It is the core of everything we do not desire in ourselves, yet which we have to face in order to go beyond ourselves. It is a *"roaring lion"* (1 Peter 5:8), the quintessential image of chaotic energy, the receptacle of the instinctual and the animal. It is the overthrowing of moral codes and deceptive beliefs, of the stagnation of life into one-sided, dogmatic truths. *"Expect Poison from the Standing Water"*, Blake writes in one of the Proverbs of Hell (Blake 1974 [1790–1793], p. 152). The devil is a call for change. It is Christ's neglected brother from the underworld, which is re-claimed by the apocryphal writers. In a different guise, it is a pagan spirit, an exuberant and eccentric "Red" demon bringing joy and irony to the gravitas of the ego. It is an element of primordial magic and wisdom in the teachings of the "wise old man" Philemon. It is the other and opposite half of the godhead, the chthonic aspect of the deity that makes Jung observe, in the company of Nietzsche and Emanuel Swedenborg, that while the crown of a tree reaches Heaven, its roots always simultaneously touch the bottom of Hell. (Jung 2009, pp. 244).

The motif of the union of Heaven and Hell finds its culmination in *Liber Novus* in the context of Philemon's "Seven Sermons to the Dead" The "Sermons" are the part of *Liber Novus* in which Jung's profound interest in Gnostic symbolism is most manifestly revealed. For our present concerns, what should be highlighted is that Gnosticism funda-mentally provides Jung with a more balanced view of the relationship between God and the devil. Everything that has been evidenced until now about the *imago diaboli* finds its sublimation in the appearance of the *"God who is difficult to grasp"*, the "terrible Abraxas", the illustrious hidden protagonist of this book, the deity of Gnostic roots that unifies all opposites and compensates for the one-sidedness of the Christian image of God. Abraxas is the non-dualistic mind. In the author's own words, he is *"splendid as the lion in the instant he strikes down his victim"*, *"as beautiful as a spring day"*, *"Priapos"*, *"the hermaphrodite of the earliest beginnings"*, the *"holy begetting"*, *"love and its murder"*, *"the saint and his betrayer"*, the Lord that reconciles the *"brightest light of day"* with *"the darkest night of madness"* (Jung 2009 [1916], p. 350). Before such a tre-mendous appearance, Jung's "I" can only turn to Philemon, in dismay: *"How, oh my father, should I understand this God?"*, to which follows the answer: *"My son, why do you want to understand him? This God is to be known but not understood. If you understand him, then you can say that he is this or that and this and not that. [...] The God whom I know is this and that and just as much this other and that other"* (ibidem).

Conclusion

Many years after *Liber Novus*, Jung wrote in "Attempt at a psychological interpretation of the dogma of the trinity" that the Lucifer legend should be essentially interpreted in terms of a *"therapeutic myth"* (Jung 1942/1948, para. 291). The type of therapy the devil would offer, and certainly not on a low-fee scheme, is thus explained: *"We naturally boggle at the thought that good and evil are both contained in God, and we think God could not possibly want such a thing. [...] Evil is a relative thing, partly avoidable, partly fate—just as virtue is, and often one does not know which is worse. Think of the fate of a woman married to a recognized saint!"* (*Ibidem*).

Although the Greeks would have not boggled at all at the thought that "good and evil" are equally present in the gods, for that was in their view the nature of things, we certainly do, and most likely to an extent of which we remain largely unaware. Thus Jung emphasised the importance and therapeutic power of the Lucifer symbol, a necessary stage in re-adjusting our one-sidedness towards a more balanced attitude of mind. "Life", he continued in a more Blakean vein than ever, "being an energetic process needs the opposites, for without the opposition, there is no energy" (*ibidem*). As one can easily guess, the integration of the *imago diaboli* is never intended in this context as anything particularly satanic or crazy. Rather, the confrontation with the *imago diaboli* means coming to terms with the complex process of healing man's split from nature. When man becomes aware that the same process of continuous transformation that nature uninterruptedly unveils is contained in themselves too (what Buddhists call the law of "impermanence"), then therapy has for the most part already succeeded. Just like the fire that Prometheus subtracts from the gods, the devil within us provides us with the energy and the source of light for acknowledging this process of reconciliation with nature. It fosters, as a healing myth, our fully coming to consciousness through the realisation of everything we have missed and rejected until that moment, in the name of our deceptive attachment to personal truths and hopes. And although none likes the intrusive, destructive, and disturbing methods of the devil, there is possibly no stronger call for change, wake, and growth than that which is offered by his unwelcome and unsettling presence. In time, we may want to thank the demon to have dissipated long-cherished dreams and values which, in themselves, were symptoms of a delusional adaptation to reality. The devil mask, in other words, reminds us, like the Eastern symbol of yin and yang, that the seed of whiteness grows at the core of the deepest blackness (and vice-versa), and seemingly opposite forces may actually be complementary and interdependent poles of being. On the basis of this intuition, later on, Jung extensively elaborated on the concept of the "Shadow" and wrote on the reality of evil in the controversial *Answer to Job*, reaching a point of no return in his dialogue with the contemporary theologians, especially Father

Victor White. It was not an abstraction or a scientific theorisation: it was a direct cathartic encounter with the demoniacal "otherness". Accordingly, the critical lens of this study has been placed as close as possible to the language of Jung's experiment, by limiting the use of secondary or subsidiary commentaries and allowing in this way a significant degree of creative reflections upon the devil motif. This symbol, in short, was as profoundly *red* as the color of the huge leather cover of *Liber Novus*, the *Red Book*, the colour of *"creative passion"*, as Jung describes his experiment in the protocols of *Memories* (Jung *Protocols*, p. 1004), and the fiery nature of the devil. By understanding and *transforming* the fundamental energy of this living image, he joined the party of other illustrious travellers to the underworld such as Dante, Swedenborg, John Milton, Nietzsche, and William Blake, who magnificently encapsulated this idea in the opening image of the *Marriage of Heaven and Hell*:

> Without Contraries is no progression. Attraction and Repulsion, Reason and Energy, Love and Hate, are necessary to human existence.
>
> From these contraries spring what the religious call Good & Evil. Good is the passive that obeys Reason. Evil is the active springing from Energy.
>
> Good is Heaven. Evil is Hell.
>
> (Blake 1974 [1790–1793], p. 149)

References

Alighieri, D. (1987). *The Divine Comedy (Commedia)*. Milano: Garzanti.

Almond, P. C. (2014). *The Devil: A New Biography*. London/New York: Tauris.

Blake, W. (1974). *Complete Writings*. Oxford: Oxford University Press.

Caillois, R. (1991). *The Demons of Midday (Les démons de midi)*. Saint Clément de Rivière: Fata Morgana.

Chevalier, J., Gheerbrant, A. (1994). *Dictionary of Symbols*. London: Penguin.

Cross, F. L., Livingstone, E. A. (ed.), (2005). 'Apostles' Creed', *Dictionary of the Christian Church*. Oxford: Oxford University Press.

Elliott, J. K. (1993). *The Apocryphal New Testament*. Oxford: Oxford University Press.

Heraclitus. *Protocols of Aniela Jaffé's Interviews with Jung for 'Memories, Dreams, Reflections'*. Washington, D.C.: Library of Congress.

Heraclitus. (1889). *Fragments*. Baltimore: N. Murray, C. G. Jung, H. Read, M. Fordham, G. Adler (ed.), Hull, R. F. C. (tr.) (1953–1983). *The Collected Works of C. G. Jung*. Princeton: Princeton University Press. (CW).

Jung C. G. (1929). 'Commentary on the "Secret of the Golden Flower"'. CW13.

Jung, C. G. (1917). *The Psychology of the Unconscious Processes*. London: Routledge & Kegan Paul.

Jung, C. G. (1923). *Polzeath Seminar* (unpublished). Thanks to Sonu Shamdasani for allowing me consultation.

Jung, C. G. (1937). Religious Ideas in Alchemy. CW12. London: Routledge & Kegan Paul.

Jung, C. G. (1938/1940). Psychology and Religion. CW 11. London: Routledge & Kegan Paul.

Jung, C. G. (1942/1948). Attempt at a Psychological Interpretation of the Dogma of the Trinity. CW11. London: Routledge & Kegan Paul.

Jung, C. G. (1952). *Answer to Job*. CW11. London: Routledge & Kegan Paul.

Jung, C. G. (1997). *Visions: Notes of the Seminar given in 1930–1934 by C. G. Jung*. Princeton: Princeton University Press.

Jung, C. G. (2009). *The Red Book 1913–1959: Liber Novus*. In Shamdasani, S. (ed.) New York/London: W. W. Norton & Company.

Jung, C. G. (2010). *Children's Dreams: Notes from the Seminar Given in 1936–1940*. Princeton: Princeton University Press.

Jung, C. G. (2020). *The Black Books 1930–1932: Notebooks of Transformation*, 7 vols. In Shamdasani, S. (ed.) New York/London: W. W. Norton & Company.

Jung, C. G. (1921). *Psychological Types*. CW6. London: Routledge & Kegan Paul.

Jung, C. G. (1933). The Meaning of Psychology for Modern Man. London: Routledge & Kegan Paul.

Jung, C. G. (1951). *Aion*. CW9ii. London: Routledge & Kegan Paul.

Neumann, E. (1969). *Depth Psychology and a New Ethic*. New York: Harper and Row.

Nietzsche, F. (1887). *On the Genealogy of Morality (Zur Genealogie der Moral: Eine Streitschrift)*. Leipzig: F. N. Erstdruck.

Nietzsche, F. (2004). *Human, All too Human (Menschliches, Allzumenschliches, II)*. London: Penguin Classics.

Oesterreich, T. K. (2014). *Possession: Demoniacal and Other*. London: Routledge.

Shamdasani, S. (2009). 'Introduction', in C. G. Jung, *The Red Book 1913–1959: Liber novus*. New York/London: W. W. Norton & Company.

Thomson, R. L. (1929). *The History of the Devil: The Horned God of the West*. London: Kegan Paul.

Trevi, M., Romano, A. (2009). *Essays on the Shadow (Studi sull'ombra)*. Milano: Raffaello Cortina Editore.

Chapter 15

Five Perspectives on Evil: Buddhism, Christianity, Hinduism, Islam and Judaism

Nigel Wellings, Stephen Bushell, Raj Balkaran, Sheikh Ahmed Haneef, and Yoram Inspector

Buddhism
Nigel Wellings

> It is a man's own mind, not his enemy or foe, that lures him to evil ways.
>
> Shakyamuni Buddha

On the surface there seems to be quite a lot about evil in Buddhism. Open a book on the Dharma and you will read how on the eve of the Buddha's enlightenment, the tempter, Māra, and his army, appeared. First come the enticing "dancing ladies" and when these fail, his whole host of monsters brandishing weapons and firing their arrows. But the Buddha is neither disturbed nor afraid; seated firmly beneath the Bodhi Tree, he turns their darts of desire and fear into a rain of flowers that fall upon the earth.

In the same book there may also be something on Buddhist cosmology. Here, we will find a description of the six realms of existence, including the hells in which beings suffer the consequences of their past karmic misdeeds. Hieronymus Bosch-like, the denizens of these infernal regions are portrayed as suffering the intolerable torments of extreme heat and cold while being dragged and prodded by the fiends and demons who work there.

More satanic still are the tantric Buddhist yogis who meet within terrifying cremation grounds by the side of rivers. In the dead of night, they practice antinomian rites in which they consume and consummate all that is taboo within their society – alcohol, the five forbidden meats including that of the dead, semen and menstrual blood. Singing and dancing, locked in ecstatic union with their consorts, they demonstrate that within ultimate reality, all are of one taste.

And finally, anyone who finds themselves within a Tibetan Buddhist Temple may be forgiven for thinking that it is a religion populated by devils. Upon the walls, wreathed in flames, fearsome male and female ogres romp and sway singly or as *yab* and *yum*. Rolling eyes, fanged roaring mouths, adorned with gold and bone ornaments, the skins of

DOI: 10.4324/9781003255819-17

flayed animals and freshly severed human heads, they pummel ignorance beneath their gyrating feet.

Given all this, it may then come as a surprise that Buddhism does not have a concept of evil; nor is there any one Satanic being who is responsible for the suffering of the world. That beneath all the razzmatazz, Buddhism is more like a psychology of perception that seeks to save us from our palpable woes. What Buddhism is most concerned with is knowing how things really are. It believes that by knowing the truth of things, by ending ignorance, suffering may be brought to an end forever.

The historical Buddha Shakyamuni taught almost two thousand years ago that we live within an interconnected universe where each and every mental and physical event exists or occurs only because of the causes and conditions that created it. This is called "Dependent Arising", *paticcasa-mupada*. As the Buddha put it:

> That being, this comes to be; from the arising of that, this arises; that being absent, this is not; and from the cessation of that, this ceases.[1]

Such a universe is sustained solely by the natural law of cause and effect. This happens at all levels from the sub-atomic to the cosmic and also, on the level of morality or ethics. What we do, say and think has karmic consequences that we will experience at some point or another. Karma may not be instant, but unless diverted by purification, it is inevitable. Because we live in a contingent universe there is no place in Buddhist thought for either an ultimate Creator God or its opposite, a force of evil that is responsible for humankind's fallen, sinful nature. The only ones responsible for that, Buddhism suggests, is ourselves.

How does this work? The Buddha and most subsequent Buddhist writers have observed that, one way or another, what we perceive is distorted by our previous karma. Good karma creates heavenly experiences while bad, hellish. Put more psychologically, we do not experience the present because the mind cloaks it with the residue of previous experiences. Quite simply we make a lot of stuff up without even knowing it. The Buddha describes this at length. He observed how deep habitual patterns, saturated with the three root poisons of ignorance, greed and aversion, keep us in an endless cycle of suffering that is only brought to an end by the dawning of Nirvāna. He called these bad habits by different names: the ten fetters, the underlying tendencies and the three types of influx. Basically, all the ways we obscure experiencing something – everything – in a fresh and open way. Ways we occlude, with our thoughts and emotions, the "brilliantly shining mind" that the Buddha had fully discovered in the depth of his being at the moment of awakening. Later Buddhist writers describe this obscuration in different ways. It is misperceiving reality as something made up of discrete and truly existing parts rather than recognising an ever-changing interdependent process that is more like a single seamless cloth. It is a delusion that mis-perceives our personality as a separate or true self, which we then fearfully cling to, when it is no more than transient habitual patterns. It is an igno-rance that does not know that everything is ultimately mirrored like non-dual awareness and that within this awareness everything comes into and goes out of being.

Whatever way this is formulated what emerges is the clear message that we ultimately are the source of our own discontent and that only by taking full responsibility for ourselves, for our delusional misperceptions, can we begin to make a difference. But how exactly are we to do this? Buddhadharma has had ample time to come up with a variety of strategies but there are some common themes that run throughout them. One found in early Buddhism concerns a combination of generosity, *dāna*, moral virtue, *sīla* and the cultivation of mindfulness, *bhāvanā*. These combined actions create "merit" which is a translation of the Pali word *puñña* and the Sanskrit *puṇya*. Each of these points to what is auspicious, fortunate, fruitful, what thrives, flourishes and prospers. They also contain the meaning of making clean, pure and bright.[2] Merit then is what is karmically fruitful – what creates a good life and prepares the ground for enlightenment. It is like a seed that enables a fruit. And this leads us back to evil again. The opposite to *puñña* is *apuñña* – that which produces undesirable karmic fruits or *pāpa*, which is frequently translated as evil, bad, infertile, barren, harmful and bringing ill fortune. Note, while we are back with the Christian themes of fruit and the knowledge of what is good and evil, there is no God or Satan here and the fruit is to be eaten. What is being stressed is that we have the means within ourselves to achieve our own salvation. The Buddha may show us the path but it is we who must tread it. It is we who, using our mindfulness, must recognise which things within us are unwholesome, fruitless, and which are wholesome and fruitful. Which things to let go of and which to encourage. Not repressing nor projecting the dark and driven aspects of our characters but rather seeing we have a choice in each moment and knowing what we choose to be important – mindfully making conscious choices guided by kindness and wisdom in a way that does not create a war within ourselves.

Later Mahayana Buddhism picked up the Buddha's recognition of the brightly shining mind and reworked it into the concept of the buddha-nature, *tathāgatagarbha* – the awakened mind that may be found within each of us. Sometimes conceived as a seed that required the kind of culti-vation we looked at above and sometimes as something already perfectly existing, requiring nothing more from us other than we uncover it from behind the veils of conflicted emotions and delusional thoughts that hide it. The buddha-nature speaks of our inherent divinity. We are not flawed from the beginning but entirely the opposite. Our true nature is the awakened mind, primordially pure, eternally blissful, full of enlightened qualities, a non-dual awareness that is without limits. It is a beautiful vision of our potentiality and who we have always been. Having such a nature comes with its responsibilities. Mahayana Buddhism also developed the notion of the Bodhisattva – one who delays their own awakening so that they may first save all sentient beings from *samsara*, the endless cycle of birth, old age, sickness and death. We could say this is our buddha-nature in action. What is awakening for? It is to bring suffering to an end, not only for ourselves but everyone else as well.

So finally, what are we to make of the demons and demonic practices that we met at the start of this piece? We already know that Māra and his army represent that which entraps us – the craving that, along with ignorance, the Buddha identified as one of the two roots of suffering. The hellish fiends who prod and push beings in hell may be understood as self-persecution and self-loathing or unwholesome, insistent painful desires and behaviours that are resistant to change. The Tantric yogis demonstrate that within the sky-like awakened mind all is already primordially pure as it spontaneously manifests. And last of all, the dancing wrathful deities are none other than the fierce expressions of our awakened nature – an intrinsic, naked aware-ness that demands it be recognised. Cutting through everything that serves to hide it, they shout, "Wake up!".

A Christian Perspective on Evil

Stephen Bushell

The perspective on evil offered here cannot be representative of any church and certainly cannot represent Christianity as there is no monolithic Christian viewpoint on this issue. There are at least as many "Christian" viewpoints on evil as there are church denominations. I attempt to offer a perspective from the general theological background to the issue of evil as culturally inherited in the West from the Judaeo-Christian framework. To this I will add some reflections from personal and professional experience.

In the creation myths offered in Genesis 1–3, Adam and Eve in the par-adisal garden of Eden are warned by God not to eat the fruit from the tree of the knowledge of good and evil; if they do they will die. Eden is paradig-matic of a unitive, non-dual state in which there is no separation of oppo-sites like good and evil, life and death. Knowledge is needed to know this. This mythic[3] state comes to an end when Adam, having eaten the fruit, perceives his separation from God. He becomes a knower and the world becomes the known. And in the known world, the world beyond Eden, there is suffering, indeed both Adam and Eve are told by God how much they will inevitably suffer.[4]

This knowing of good and evil has exercised theologians and philosophers down the ages with the core question: if God is wholly good, how is it that there is evil in the world?[5] In the 5th century, St Augustine argued that evil is essentially a privation of good (the *privatio boni* argument) and thus, does not refer to something existent in itself. In the 12th century, this was elaborated further by St Thomas Aquinas, sealing this as a core doctrine in the Western Church. Jung came into conflict with theologians of his day by noting that psychologically there is a dark side of the god image in the psyche (as in images of Satan or antichrist) and went on to argue that from this we might well infer an existent evil.[6]

The *privatio boni* could help to explain natural and human atrocities but does not help to explain the theological conundrum of how a good God could create such a world that came to be so flawed. According to the churches, this is made good in the incarnation of God in Jesus, whose sinless life and obedience to God atone for the original sin afflicted on humanity by Adam. This is summarised by St Paul's statement, "*As in Adam all die, so in Christ shall all be made alive*".[7] But does that really resolve the problem? There are just as many atrocities in the world as ever there have been, if not more. A major question for the churches remains, just what has the coming of Christ done to restore the so-called sin of Adam?

Let's step back from theology for a moment and ask a philosophical question: Does "evil" grammatically operate as a name of an entity or is it a descriptor?[8] There are many instances of acts of violence that could be pointed to as examples of evil: abduction, rape, murder, genocide. We could say that these are referred to as evil because calling them "bad" does not state the appropriate level of feeling they bring about. This includes the desire that these never happen again and that it is not possible for the perpetrator to make amends. Natural events such as earthquakes, cyclones, tsunamis, have been considered theologically as "natural evil".[9] I sense however that this view is changing as we begin to review the ways we see and relate to the planet so I will discard this from the discussion.

When I point to a lone gunman shooting and killing school children as an example of evil, does "evil" operate in ways other than as an expression of horror, revulsion, a way of saying that such things ought not to happen and a hope that there will be no repetition? With psychoanalytic theories being embraced more generally, it is now common to assume that such a murderer will have had a particular life history to bring him to act in such a way, such that evil is located in a life narrative. In Jungian terms, we could say that there is an acting out of the personal or collective Shadow. And beyond that? Is there an ontologically existent evil that intentionally possess a person in such instances? Is there a cosmic enmity between a force of good and a force of evil (in Christian terms between Christ and Satan)? Some Christian denominations answer "yes", others "no".[10] What we do know is that when there are great atrocities, it is hard to contain such violence within the scope of the human psyche and to project onto an external agency can bring relief.

With these questions in mind, I turn to a more personal narrative. I came upon a sense of evil by way of a childhood dream that still causes a shudder when I recount it. I grew up in the suburbs of London and my walk to junior school was shortened by taking the alleyway. This path had a sharp bend halfway along at a point where it crossed a small stream. At age eight or nine, I dreamed that having crossed the stream, I saw a dark, terrifying force coming towards me that I knew would kill me. I took out a crucifix, held it up in front of me and repeated the words, "I banish you in the name of Jesus Christ". I could only share that dream some 30 years later when I was in analysis. I did not come from a religious family and knew nothing of the rite of exorcism until I was ordained a priest. The disturbing element of this tale though is that two years later, a girl of my age was brutally murdered in that alleyway. Was my dream somehow "knowing" of an existence of some evil presence in this place? Or was it prescient of what was to occur? It is such images that informed Jung of the presence of evil in the objective psyche.

For some years I was a member of a Diocesan Ministry of Deliverance team. This was a "specialist" group who would be assigned cases of paranormal occurrences referred by parish priests. The cases I worked on nearly always, to my mind, had a psychic explanation in the unconscious projection of Shadow material. This was effectively dealt with by discussing unexpressed emotion and the offer of prayer as a way of stabilising and bringing into balance situations that had become destabilised due to difficulty to contain Shadow material. In five years of this work, I never met a situation where I found it relevant to use the term "evil" as a referent to an external causal agency; so there was never a thing (other than the fear of the persons witnessing the events – usually objects moving, or unidentified sounds in the building) that needed to be delivered ("exorcised" in the old terminology). I resigned from the team when some colleagues were overly keen to attribute external "evil" causation to events and would want to use a service for expulsion of evil. As I remarked at the time, what is there to expel and where did they consider it will be expelled to?

In my psychiatric chaplaincy experience, I noticed that patients who had been through psychosis often wanted to talk about evil as an external reality acting upon them as a way of making sense of the intensity of the experience they had undergone. This always seemed significant to me and to them; if there was a way of reflecting on the experience this helped adaptation towards a recovery. I will share one account of a patient who died of natural causes many years ago as it illustrates the questions I have been raising. John, as I will call him, a churchgoer, had been diagnosed with schizophrenia some years before I met him in hospital. During Lent, his agitation and dissociative behaviours intensified as Holy Week drew close. He told me that each year he underwent the experience of being one of the soldiers at the arrest, trial and crucifixion of Christ. He would break down telling me how this was on account of the devil who made him go through this agony. If he could bear it, come Easter Sunday he would find relief. On one occasion, John told me of a recent ward round where he had pleaded with the psychiatrist to retract his comment that all this was in John's mind as this was impossible for him to contemplate; John being sure that his Lenten suffering was the work of the (external) devil. For John, attributing agency to an external entity made his suffering bearable and meaningful.[11] Whose version of meaning do we go along with: John's, that he was afflicted by the devil; analytical psychology, that this was an irruption from the collective unconscious; medical psychiatry, that this is essentially simply an imbalance of chemicals; or the *privatio boni* doctrine, that John was experiencing the absence of good?

Mother of Shadow, Mother of Light Demons of the Unconscious in Indian Myth

Raj Balkaran

The Sanskrit narrative text *Devī Māhāmtya* ("The Greatness of the Goddess"), crafted some 15 centuries ago, presents a radically different vision of divinity than seen before in the Hindu world, one venerating supreme divinity as feminine. The Devī Māhātmya (hereon referred as DM) indeed constitutes a profound anomaly in the known history of world religions insofar as it posits a cosmos governed by a Great Goddess. Minor goddesses such as Uṣas (the goddess of the dawn) and Rātri (the goddess of night) have graced India's sacred Sanskrit texts since ancient Vedic times circa 1500 BCE, but never before – and in no other cultural context – was "God on high" presented as Goddess supreme. Beyond the heavenly pantheon of Vedic gods, and beyond even the Hindu triumvirate of cosmic creator (Brahmā), sustainer (Viṣṇu) and destroyer (Śiva), lies the great Goddess, support of all things. And yet, she immanently dwells within all beings, readily summoned in times of need. The Devī Māhātmya presents us with a Goddess who engages in great martial feats to quell the forces of evil, restoring heaven's throne to Indra, its rightful ruler and securing the welfare of the world. She actually does so on two occasions which comprise two of the DM's three Episodes. How do we interpret the Goddess' battle with the demons to restore sovereignty to the gods? While these Episodes dominate the DM (occupying 11 of the work's 13 chapters, chapters 2–12), it is to the first and final chapter to which we must turn to properly contextualise the feats of the Goddess. It is in looking to the narrative frame of the text (chapters 1 and 13) that we rightly regard the monumental feats of the Goddess as an interplay between Shadow and Light, indeed emblematic of the journey into the unconscious to confront the demons therein.

The DM begins with a mighty and noble king, Suratha, whose territories are conquered by his enemies. He retreats to his capital city to rule his home province, but there too, evil forces (in the form of his corrupt ministers) seize his army and treasury. Bewildered and bereft of power, the deposed king mounts his horse and rides into the deep dark forest. This opening frame of the DM itself readily signals a turn from the ordered light of the conscious, rational realm where king reigns supreme to the unconscious, occult realm of the forest – home of animal and spiritual impulses alike. The king soon encounters a hermitage in the forest run by so spiritually elevated a sage that the wild beasts of the wilderness are tamed by his very presence. He takes great solace there, but after some time, he laments, reflecting on his lost throne, his lost possessions, and his lost treasury. Just at that moment, as if an externalisation of his inner life, along comes a merchant, equally dejected due to the treachery of his family who cast him out, coveting and appropriating his riches.[12] Disenfranchised and displaced, the king and merchant both approach the wise sage, emblematic of the Self, for counsel on the nature of their suffering.

The sage explains that all creatures – even the wise – are deluded by the occlusive presence of the Great Goddess whose very body is this manifest universe. Elucidating the extent to which corporeal creatures are pushed and pulled by objects of senses, the sage indicates that some are blind by day, while others blind by night and yet there are others still who see equally well by day and night (DM 1.35). The sage goes on to explain that the Goddess grants not only the phenomenal delusion we experience as individual beings but she also grants liberation from the cycle of rebirth: she is both darkness and supreme light. The sage then proceeds to tell the tale of the Goddess' crucial important role at the dawn of time.

One should note that, in the Hindu worldview, the cosmos ceaselessly passes from creation to maintenance to destruction, and then to creation anew. These cycles of creation operate ad infinitum, literally without beginning and without end.

At the beginning of any given creation, the god Viṣṇu (the all-pervasive principle of cosmic consciousness) enters his deep yogic sleep sprawled out upon his serpent couch upon the cosmic oceanic abyss. From the navel of the sleeping Viṣṇu, emerges Brahmā, the Creator-born anew to usher in a new cycle of Creation. The sage explains to the king that at the beginning of this current cycle of creation, something unexpected occurs: two demons emerge from the ears of the sleeping Viṣṇu. Intent on destruction, they approach the lotus-born Brahmā. If the Creator himself is only newly born, where could they have come from? They come from Viṣṇu himself, more specifically from his unconscious. Terrified at the impending doom, Brahmā collects himself and calls upon the divine mother for aid. In his luscious Sanskrit praise, Brahmā hails the Goddess as the primordial power being all things, which even he and the rest of the gods harness for their aims. He hails her as Great Goddess and Great Demoness alike, as mother of both Shadow and Light:

> You are the great knowledge *(mahāvidyā)*, the great illusion *(mahāmāyā)*,
> the great insight *(mahāmedhā)*, the great memory (mahāsmṛtī),
> And the great delusion, the great Goddess *(mahādevī)*,
> the great demoness *(mahāsurī)*. (DM 1.58)

The purpose of his praise is to petition the Goddess to release her occlusive grasp on Viṣṇu so that he may become awakened. Pleased by his praise, the Goddess brings Viṣṇu out of his yogic slumber so that he may combat the demons from his unconscious.

The battle between Viṣṇu and the demons proceeds for five thousand years with neither making any headway. So, the Goddess leverages her occlusive power to tip the hand of destiny in Viṣṇu's favour. Enveloping the two demons in her occlusive field, they are deluded into thinking themselves powerful. By virtue of this delusion, they mockingly offer Viṣṇu a boon in order to show their power. The Goddess of our text represents cosmic power (śakti) itself, power which can be harnessed for good and ill alike. It is power lust, which lies in their Shadow, brought to the fore by the Goddess' delusive grace. Moreover, they themselves can be said to represent the destructive impulses innate to Viṣṇu's own Shadow, that is, the Shadow of creation itself. Seeing clearly the demons of his unconscious, Viṣṇu isn't triggered by their insolence but merely accepts their boon and asks that he should be able to kill them. Fancying themselves too clever to be cornered by Viṣṇu, the demons agree to be killed anywhere in the cosmic ocean where there is no water. So, Viṣṇu scoops them up upon his lap and dismembers them. By the grace of the Goddess, Viṣṇu is victorious, successfully confronting the demons of Shadow.

The opening frame of the *Devī Māhāmtya* is crucial in contextualising the psychospiritual power of the text. Myth communicates unconsciously what psychology does consciously. Such as the likes of Jung would have found natural conversation partners in the mythmakers of old. In invoking the Goddess, one calls upon a cosmic searchlight, so to speak, turned towards the inner recesses of one's being. For is it there one finds the demons usurping one's power. The Goddess' empowerment cannot possibly occur without the pacification of those parts of self which steal our power. The scene at the dawn of time readily represents the human entirety of the complex whose unconscious threatened the ability to manifest the life one desires (personified by Brahma born anew from Viṣṇu's navel). Only through the Grace of the Goddess can we become empowered to fruitfully confront the demons of our unconscious. As such, the subsequent episodes of the *Devī Māhāmtya* which depict the Goddess battling demon after demon in order to restore the throne of heaven can also readily be read as emblematic of – and inextricable from – the work to be done in the inner life, as one battles one's demons to regain one's sovereignty.

Upon hearing the acts of the Great Goddess (Chapters 2–12), the merchant and king take leave of the sage in order to seek the Goddess' grace themselves. They settle down upon a riverbank and engage in austere devotion to the divine mother. After three long years, she appears before them and grants them a boon of their choosing. The king wishes for his kingdom back. It is telling that the Goddess does not merely snap her fingers and restore his power. Rather, like any good mother, mentor or coach, she blesses him with the strength to combat his enemy on his own and regain his sovereignty. She promises that his kingdom will be his for the rest of his days and moreover, blesses him to be reborn as the Sun's son to rule Manu in his next life. Hers is the work of kings,[13] confronting evil for the welfare of the world and she begins within it. The merchant, on the other hand, wishes for enlightenment which the Goddess also grants. Encoding complexities as only narrative can, the *Devī Māhāmtya* therefore presents us with a vision of the Supreme which, to be supreme, must encompass both shadow and light, consciousness and unconsciousness, occasioning enlightenment and delusion alike. As such this work affords profound meditation on the mechanics of personal and spiritual growth, and the indispensability of Shadow to point the way towards the light.

Works Cited – Balkaran, Raj. *The Goddess and the King in Indian Myth: Ring Composition, Royal Power, and the Dharmic Double Helix*. London: Routledge, 2019.

The Metaphysical Necessity of the Shadow in Islam
Sheikh Ahmed Haneef

In Islam, there is a concept called the *ghayb*, usually translated as the Unseen. It ranges from what we are unaware of in the physical world to other existences beyond the reach of our senses, imagination and intellect. The Unseen is always real. It does not include wayward imaginations. A blindfolded person might touch an elephant's leg and think it is a tree but the Unseen is the fact that the object was the foot.

Belief in *the Ghayb* is an essential aspect of the faith of the Muslim, for it includes such things as angels, heaven, hell and purgatory. At the beginning of the second chapter, or Sura of the Qur'an, it says,

> Alif, Lam Meem,
> This is the Book, there is no doubt in it,
> A guidance to the Godwary,
> Who believe in the Unseen
> And maintain the prayer.
> (Qur'an: Sura 2, vs 1)

The Unseen is not seen as dark but it includes dark things, for it encompasses all that is unseen. It ranges from levels where we don't know something or know nothing about our own true selves to realities in the outward world that we may mistakenly interpret, and thus not see; but it also continues outward to include the angels and the Empyrean of God.

But what is our true self? Like many of the other great religions of the world, this true self is exemplified in the life and teachings of their great founders, thinkers and saints. With this as a core, it acts as a central reference point around which the personality is formed and evaluated.

The knowledge of the life, conduct and teachings of the Prophet of Islam are still comparatively historically fresh. That his personality and habits became developed into the discipline of *Akhlaq* or The Science of Character Development is fundamental. This deals with treating or perfecting both the personal and the social states of the human being.

The concept of darkness does exist in Islam and is used to describe negative states, or tendencies and behaviours of human beings. In Islam, being or existence is light; and nonbeing is darkness; thus wrongdoing is an action that is oriented towards darkness and nonexistence. The word for darkness in Arabic is *ʐulm*, which also means oppression. The concept of oppression in Islam is not restricted to unjust actions being imposed upon a separate other. It has a wider frame of reference, wherein a human being suppresses or denies the right of any living being to live and seek their natural self-realisation in accordance to their own particular needs. Thus, a person can be an oppressor of himself, for example, when he does not choose to get an education or chooses to go against the natural law.

The reason why we oppress ourselves and others is explained in Islamic mystical psychology as occurring when our imagination deludes us from correctly arriving at the truth about the realities we confront. In Islamic psychology this state is called *wahm* or the delusive imagination. *Wahm* usually is driven by the id, which is called *nafs*, that sees the satisfaction of the base desires of the self as the central principle for all value. *Wahm* becomes more dominant as a force the more emotional the subject's relationship to the presenting reality may be. It can get so strong that it can supersede the intellect and proper reasoning by the subject imposing his inaccurate idea of the reality as the basis for his reasoning.

Deluded imaginations have fuelled the most destructive mass movements in history such as Nazism, racism and colonialism. Thus, from the Islamic perspective, evil comes forth from the outward activities of a mind deluded by *wahm*.

So evil comes about only at the hands of humans in their encounter with reality who distort it. In distorting reality, they in effect turn away from the light of being towards the darkness of non-being.

According to the arguments of Islamic theodicy, there are two kinds of evil: the first is what we have described above as the moral sins that emerge from the mind of the deluded; and the other is completely relativistic and is not evil per se. This is due to the individual's negative encounters with natural phenomena such as sickness, earthquakes and death which are not evil in themselves but essential to balance and equilibrium in the world. These phenomena are seen in Islamic philosophy as the limitations of being in the physical world. No life in the physical world is immortal, so all living things face death. No human being has absolute knowledge, so all knowledge of human beings is circumscribed by ignorance. It is our negative experience of these limitations that make us think of them as evil and that spurs us on to eliminate or alleviate their negative effects.

In Islamic psychology and the science of character development, the hidden tendencies that lie buried in the *nafs* which are synonymous with the id (in Freudian psychology) and the negative unconscious are exposed. The prophetic character is used as the reference point against which the tendencies of the self are compared, and their true value ascertained.

The Unseen is not only those realities that are inaccessible to our senses, but also the misunderstanding of those realities that we experience. When that misunderstanding or ignorance is of the self, it can be manifested as mental illness or evil behaviour from the egotistical or narcissistic depths within ourselves.

Uncovering the higher Unseen realities is the goal of all religions but, to do so first requires that the searcher be in command of the *nafs* and the *nafs* not be in command of the seeker. In this way the transcendent intellect is freed which can then guide the seeker to wisdom and liberation.

Evil and Judaism
Yoram Inspector

The idea of Evil emerges in Judaism very early, immediately after God completes the creation. "*Thus, the heavens and the earth were finished and all the host of them*". Already in Genesis (2:1-3) the first book of the Old Testament – The Jewish Bible, God plants a garden in Eden where, among all the vegetation, he grows also a special tree, that of the Knowledge of Good and Evil. God then "*took the man and put him into the Garden of Eden to dress it and to keep it*" and commanded him: "*Of every tree of the garden you may freely eat, but of the tree of the Knowledge of Good and Evil, thou shalt not eat (2:15-170)*". God threatened humankind with death for disobedience.

As we know, Eve could not resist the tempting Serpent which offered her the fruit of the Tree of Good and Evil. She ate it and offered it to Adam who ate it too. This was, one may argue, the first visceral incorporation and embodiment of Good and of Evil. Both went straight into our bloodstream. As death is also a symbol of transformation, man did indeed die as God warned: he was transformed from an innocent, unaware creature to one capable of choosing between doing Good or Evil.

The catalogue of **Evil** acts, such as murder, theft, incest, deception and betrayal that follow the disobedience, in the Bible and during the history of mankind ever since is endless. I chose therefore to focus only on one of its manifestations: The Holocaust, – the planned, systematically organised massacre of 6 million Jews by the Nazis; and to ask two questions:

What happened to the Jewish faith after such a collective horrific Trauma?

If you belong to the Jewish tribe, what does facing the ultimate evil do to your relationship with your God?

I would like to approach these through my very personal lenses, those of a son of two Holocaust survivors:

> My mother Eva and her parents, Ervin and Esther, lived in Trnava, a beautiful historic town in Slovakia which was also called the "Slovak Rome" because of its many churches and as it was the site of a Roman Catholic Archbishopric in the 17th century. There were two old synagogues in Trnava that served the Jewish community, most of whom perished in Auschwitz Death Camp, including my grandmother's four sisters, their husbands and their little children.

My mother and my grandparents miraculously survived.

At first, they naively tried to save themselves by converting to Roman Catholicism. My mother used to look back with laughter at the irony of her having to confess her sins to the Catholic priest, in the midst of the Evil madness hovering around humanity at the time.

As a 15-year-old girl (and in fact, in all her 87 years on this earth) she did not have any Evil sins to confess. Anxiously she approached the priest, dreading that she will have nothing to say to him and he might be angry with her. She didn't want to make up some random sin as she was an honest person. In her despair she prayed to God to remind her of a sin she committed. She suddenly remembered that she read Gustav Flaubert's Madame Bovary – the story about the adultery committed by Emma Bovary. She was overjoyed with relief that she now had a "very good evil sin to report". She secretly thanked God for saving her from a possible disappointed suspicious priest.

Then it became too risky to remain Catholics and my mother and her parents found refuge in the attic of Slovak peasants who risked their own lives to save them, especially as in the same house, two Nazis forcefully occupied a room for nearly a year. These Nazis came to the house only late at night everyday so my mother and her parents could spend the day outside the attic on the first floor.

One morning, when they were out of their hiding, my mother started to cry for no apparent reason and told my grandparents that they all needed to run immediately and hide in the attic as the Nazis would be coming back to drink water. My grandfather, who was a relentless optimist, told her not to worry. She insisted and continued to cry so that finally he agreed. Five minutes later the Nazis came, not only did they come for the first time in the morning, but they were also heard one saying to the other "Where is the water, I am so thirsty?"

After the war the chief Rabbi of Trnava who survived Auschwitz told my mother who was a student in his school before the war: "After what I saw in Auschwitz, I can tell you God does not exist". My mother did not care about belonging to any formal religious group, be it Jewish, Christian or any other organised religion, but she always kept contact with her personal God: the one who helped her remember Madame Bovary before the confession; the same one who connected her through her intuition to the level of the psyche C.G. Jung called the Psychoid (the relationship between our internal world and the material world outside of us), which enabled her to have the pre-vision that saved her family. Interestingly, her father before and after the Holocaust was an admirer of the Jewish Philosopher Baruch Spinoza (1632–1677) who was cast out from the orthodox Jewish Community of Amsterdam because he argued that everything in the universe is God and the manifestation of God, but that God is neither related to reward or punishment nor to Good and Evil.

My father, Abraham, was deeply connected to the Jewish culture and humour but had serious problems with the Jewish God. On the most holy day in the Jewish calendar – The Day of Atonement – "Yom Kippur", when believers are requested to fast and ask God to forgive them for all their sins, he often committed a triple sin: he ate bread with butter and Ham. It is a triple sin because you are forbidden to: eat, eat dairy products with meat, eat pork. All three are violations of the fast and Kosher rules.

He used to accompany this rebellious ritual by citing from the depth of his soul in Hebrew, all the lines of the poem of one of Israel's most unique poets – Nathan Alterman – entitled: "From All the Nations" which was written in 1942 in Israel in the midst of the Holocaust.[14]

The poem is a tantalising, bitter ironic cry, confronting God and the idea of the Jews being "The Chosen People". The love of God for his "Chosen Nation" is juxtaposed with the murder of 1,000,000 Jewish children by the Nazis and their helpers.

Towards the end, the poet focuses on the eyes of those children who are on their way to the gas chambers and describes what he sees. In their eyes he feels their unconditional gratitude to their God who chose them to be his wanted and loved children even though they are about to be slaughtered. They feel privileged to be killed in front of his "chair of honour", and they are thankful for the intimate way in which he handles their blood: He collects it in special jars, smells it "like flowers", and gathers it in his handkerchief.

At the same time the poet sees in the children's eyes their plea for revenge – that God will claim back their blood from the murderers and from the ones who witnessed the horror in silence and did not do anything to save them.

This unspeakable paradox is the heart of the poem by which my father chose to communicate with God on "Yom-Kippur".

I could deeply relate to and understand my father's ritual.

His mother – Zipporah, father – Yitzhak, his brothers – Josef, Haim, Moshe and Lova, and his sisters – Rachel, Genia and Golda were all murdered by the Nazis.

He never spoke about a murderous revenge against this Evil. He preached for having a good, happy fulfilling life. His revenge against the Nazis was that my brother Michael and I were having fun, playing on the sunny Mediterranean beach of Tel-Aviv.

He constantly made the distinction between the Germans and the Nazis and went to teach for a year in a high school in Germany. He believed that the young generation in Germany also needed help to cope with the fact that their grandparents had supported the Nazi regime.

His grievance was against God – how could He permit such a thing? Does He exist? Is He indifferent to Evil?

My father's open unanswered questions echo the question: "God, who created Auschwitz?" which the author Yehiel De-Nur, also known by his pen name Ka-Tsetnik 135633 (the number tattooed on his arm in the concentration camp) asks in his book "SHIVITTI".[15] It is a documentation of psychedelic visions, some of which containing images from Kabalistic mysticism he experienced during a psychiatric treatment with L.S.D. given to him by the Dutch Professor Jan Bastiaans. This treatment redeemed him from the intensity of his Post Traumatic Stress Disorder symptoms, resulting from his imprisonment for two years in Auschwitz.

He embarked on this treatment following the evidence he gave in Adolf Eichmann's trial in Jerusalem in 1961, during which he repeated that Auschwitz was "Another Planet". In his L.S.D visions he saw himself in a truck with a tired Nazi officer. For the first time in his life he felt he could have been this Nazi Officer. Speaking about this vision in a TV Interview, he said: "It became clear that Auschwitz was not another planet I thought it was. Auschwitz was not created by the Devil or by God. It was created by Man. Hitler was not Satan. You could enter a nursery and among 50 children will be one child named Adolf Hitler. In the Bible it is said: "*I offered you Life and Death, the Blessing and the Curse and you should choose Life*" (Deuteronomy, 30:19)".

Both my dear mother and father would have warmly embraced these words.

Notes

1 Saṃyutta Nikāya 11.28.
2 Harvey, Peter 2013, *An Introduction To Buddhism, Teachings, History and Practices.* Second Edition. Cambridge University Press.
3 For more on the mythic see Jung et al. Man and His Symbols, Eliade, The Myth of the Eternal Return, Campbell, The Hero with a thousand faces.
4 Genesis 3:16.17.
5 Often called "The problem of Evil"; see Hick, John Evil and the God of Love for a good overview.
6 See the Jung-White letters and Answer to Job.
7 1 Corinthians 15:22; elaborated further in Romans 5:12ff.
8 Ludwig Wittgenstein was the most creative philosopher of language and could have great impact on theology see for example, Kerr, F, Theology after Wittgenstein.
9 See Hick.
10 See Satan (religioustolerance.org) for examples.
11 Jung commented that what is meaningful is bearable.
12 Raj Balkaran, *The Goddess and the King in Indian Myth: Ring Composition, Royal Power, and the Dharmic Double Helix* (London: Routledge, 2019), 95.
13 Balkaran, 117.
14 Nathan Alterman, "From All the Nations" first published in Hatur Hashvi'I (The Seventh Column) 1942 in "Davar" Newspaper, Israel. It can also be found now in "Hatur Hashvi'I" by Hakibbutz Hameuchad, Publishing House Ltd, Tel-Aviv, Printed in Israel 2003.
15 Ka-Tzetnik 135633, SHIVITTI-A VISION, Harper &Row, Publishers Inc., 1989.

Chapter 16

Sexual Boundary Violation: Betrayal and the Shadow of Therapy

Christopher Perry

> *The psychotherapist learns little or nothing from his successes, for they chiefly confirm him in his mistakes. But failures are priceless experiences, because they not only open the way to a better truth, but force us to modify our views and methods*
>
> (Jung 1954 CW 16 para. 73)

Can therapists learn from the experiences of their mistakes and transgressions?

Much of our daily work, as therapists, is about learning to be in the presence of another whilst keeping our heart and mind open to the vicissitudes of the ever-evolving therapeutic relationship and to the patterns and habits that have proved unhelpful to the patient, who may consciously want to discard them. To help us grow and extend our knowledge, every week or fortnight we review our relationship with our professional selves and explore our strengths, weaknesses, "areas for development", and mistakes. During this process, carried out both in self-reflective solitude and with a peer group or supervisor, we will undoubtedly experience a range of feelings: gratitude, joy, sadness, regret, disappointment, dread, defeat, and guilt about mistakes – even shame.

It is this last affect, shame, which so often reminds us painfully of something I call "slippage", or, to use a sailing analogy, unwisely slipping the moorings of our internal ethic, our ethical attitude to each patient, and our professional Code of Ethics. We know that much slippage is unconscious; I will return to this later. But some slippage, although often unconsciously motivated, is planned, like secretly slipping moorings in the dead of night. The therapist ignores and overrides the Shipping Forecast with excitement and fear: "Sea of Ethics: Wind – Gale Force 8 increasing to Force 9: Visibility – poor: Sea – turbulent". I am referring primarily to sexual boundary transgressions, which are usually experienced by the victim-patient as utterly traumatic violations with long-lasting effects (Jones 2010; Wiener 2010).

DOI: 10.4324/9781003255819-18

In this chapter, I will try to elucidate the following:

1   The "helping personality" and the "Wounded-Healer".
2   The therapeutic relationship and process.
3   Some of the dynamics of the transgressive process.
4   Institutional/societal responses to sexual transgression.
5   Advice to patients who become concerned about their therapist and their therapeutic relationship.

The "Helping Personality" and the "Wounded-Healer" [1]

The analyst must go on learning endlessly ... it is his own hurt that gives the measure of his power to heal. This, and nothing else, is the meaning of the Greek myth of the wounded physician.

(Jung 1954 CW16 para. 239)

Jung was not orphaned, but in his early years, his mother's disturbance and preoccupation with ghosts and apparitions meant that she secluded herself away in her bedroom (not shared with her husband) and had to be away in hospital for months at a time. Her absence led him to form the opinion that women were by nature unreliable. With his mother coming and going, Jung developed anxiety, an "avoidant attachment" (Bowlby 1969), and distanced himself from her, never knowing when the next separation was going to take place.

Both Chiron and Jung started life with experiences of profound loss, which is the singular cause of most of us seeking therapy because the loss either has not been acknowledged or has not been fully grieved and mourned, leaving the bereaved person stuck. These may include the **loss** of:

*   Early positive attachment possibilities because of caregivers being very disturbed, inconsistent, or emotionally unavailable and unable to bond with the infant/child.
*   A relationship through separation, severance, abandonment, betrayal (through emotional, physical, and sexual abuse), suicide, and death.
*   Psychosomatic health – the senses; mental, physical, and sexual capacities.
*   Deep contact with the inner self – the inner world of feeling, fantasy, dreams, impulses, aspirations, and values.
*   Hope of being understood.
*   Feeling alive, embodied, and grounded on the Earth.
*   Direction, purpose, and meaning.
*   Vocation – in terms of burn-out, redundancy, incapacity, or retirement.
*   An unlived life.

- An ideal or ideology.
- Country, extended family, and cultural context.
- Work, home, and financial security.
- Positive mirroring as offered by a partner, family, or work setting.
- Self-esteem.

People who train as therapists are not, of course, immune to loss and the catastrophic effect it can have when not given full expression and the time and space to work through it. Barr (2006) investigated the significance of wounding experiences as a determinant of career choice in a sample of 253 counsellors and psychotherapists. She found that about 74% of the sample had suffered from one or more of the following wounding experiences: abuse, other early trauma, bereavement, parents with disabling/life-threatening illnesses, and mental ill-health in the family, all of which are congruent with my notion of loss as a unifying reason for seeking therapy and becoming a therapist.

In addition to shared developmental deficits and wounds, there are personality profiles quite common amongst therapists. One is based on the Myers–Brigg Personality Type Indicator (Myers 1962), which evolved out of Jung's explication of "Psychological Types" (Jung 1921), which was his attempt to make some sense of his differences with Freud. (For an excellent overview see Williams 2019). The Indicator has been used extensively by organisations as an aid to fitting personality with role. A huge proportion of therapists tend to fall into the INFJ type – introverted, intuitive, feeling (guided by internal values and beliefs), and judging (clear evaluations and decisions). They tend to be conscientious, or rather conscience driven, with an inclination to seek meaning in relationships, events, and ideas. Their mission is to deepen their understanding of themselves and others. They see difficulties as giving them scope to participate in carving out creative paths forward.

A rather more helpful and realistic profile has developed from the ideas of the psychoanalyst, Karen Horney, whom some see as the founder of feminist psychology. She suggests that we all have ten basic neurotic needs, divided into three groups:

1   Needs that move us towards others (compliance).
2   Needs that move us against others (aggression).
3   Needs that move us away from people (withdrawal) (Horney 1942).

The "helping personality" tends to belong to the first group. Such people are partly motivated by the need to be loving and loveable and to please others. Sometimes this is based on an inflated *idealised self-image* to compensate for deep feelings of being unlovable arising from "… *direct or indirect domination, indifference, erratic behaviour, lack of respect for the child's needs, lack of real guidance, disparaging attitudes, too much admiration or the*

absence of it, lack of reliable warmth, having to take sides in parental argu-
ments, too much or too little responsibility, overprotection, isolation from other
children, injustice, discrimination, unkept promises, hostile atmosphere
..." (Horney 1946). The danger of this idealised self-image is that its
opposite tends to be split off and relegated to the Shadow, where it will
cause trouble. The conscious motivation – "I want to be patient, compassionate, full of loving-kindness, tolerant of difference, responsible, and
conscientious" – is too one-sided and is supported by a list of fearsome
moral strictures – "I must not be selfish, irritable, impatient, angry,
dependent, or demanding of others".

What happens? The unacceptable and disclaimed qualities and behaviours
sent packing into the unconscious do not embark on a pleasurable cruise
along the River Lethe – the river of forgetfulness and oblivion in Greek
mythology. Like Jacks-in-boxes, they leap out as projections onto "an
other": figures in dreams; physical symptoms – e.g. headaches, back problems; constipation restricting flow of movement; a partner/family member/
friend/organisations in an effort to get themselves invited back into the
unifying community of selves where acceptance and integration enable us
to individuate. In using that term, I am evoking Jung's definition: "*... the*
process by which a person becomes an 'individual', that is, a separate,
indivisible unity or 'whole'" (Jung 1921, para. 490).

I am going to introduce an adaptation (Groesbeck 1975) of Jung's gate
diagram of the therapeutic relationship with special reference to the archetypal (universal) image of the "Wounded-Healer" – which is so prevalent in
cultures where shamanism is felt to be a vital part of everyday life. Shamans
are often traumatised individuals who have had a breakdown or broke down
during their initiation. Boundaries with their unconscious are permeable,
and they have access to realms of awareness- beyond the ken of lay people.

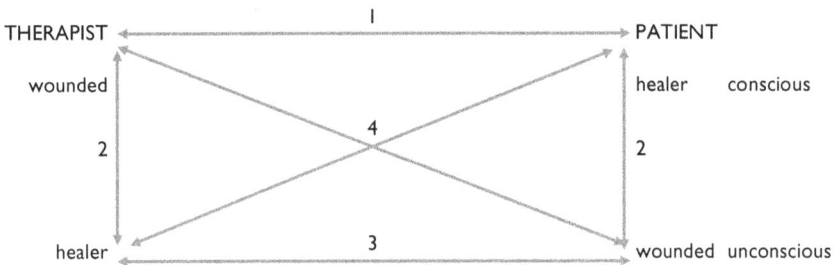

Line 1 is the conscious relationship between therapist and patient based
mainly on explicit communication and the creation of a containing frame in
which the therapeutic endeavour can develop.

Lines 2 are the highways between each party's conscious awareness and
unconsciousness. Both have border-crossing points where goods from the

dark regions of the unconscious (such as slips of the tongue, dreams, fantasies, and impulses) are allowed to pass into the light of consciousness where they can be pondered and examined. Because of a training in therapy, the therapist's border crossing tends to be more open.

Line 3 is the unconscious relationship between the two people, where communication is more implicit, often non-verbal (as in shared dream motifs or psychosomatic sensations, incidents when past patterns get enacted by both, for example, abandonment).

Lines 4 are the pathways of understanding between the unconscious of one person and the conscious of the other, not infrequently an empathic connection and one sometimes based on "hunch" and intuition.

This diagram can be used to think about any relationship, as I will show later. For now, I will use a personal experience to illustrate.

Some years ago, after a restless, breathless night, I took a plane to a foreign city for a teaching assignment, one in a series. I was sweating and breathless, but neglected my internal messengers and battled my way onto the plane. By lunchtime, I was feeling worse. At the end of the day, I returned to the hotel, showered, and went out for supper.

Within minutes of returning, I became seriously breathless and phoned a psychiatrist (one of the "students") whom I knew had a room two floors above me. She came down immediately to be with me as we waited for the ambulance. I became more and more terrified and aware that, without medical help, I was going to die. As is customary in that country, in serious cases, a doctor arrived with the ambulance crew, gave me an injection and oxygen – and I knew that I would live.

In the emergency room, what seemed like a very young female junior registrar confirmed the ambulance doctor's diagnosis of double pneumonia. But she had a hunch, later proved by tests, that I had a potentially lethal illness – myocardial endocarditis, which, in my case, was serious partly because it had gone undetected and therefore untreated.

I was transferred to a specialist cardiac centre and placed on the "critical list" where I remained, although ambulant, for ten days before the treatment kicked in.

By the time I arrived, extensive tests had been done. Usually, this infection comes into the body through various points of entry. None could be found. The conclusion, which I accepted, was that something puzzling had been taking place at a deeply psychosomatic level, way beyond my awareness. Would I be prepared to explore this possibility with my key nurse, Anna, over twelve forty-minute sessions, three times per week?

Empowered by the Unit's philosophy and approach, I structured each day and week around tests, x-rays, meals, and the counselling with Anna. My partner and the family came in relays and stayed in the very modestly low-priced hospital hotel. I had plenty of internal work to do both in terms of my room-mate, by whom I felt challenged on every level, and of the process and content of my sessions with Anna.

As the sessions progressed, we came to the realisation that the seeds of my illness had been sown nine months earlier. I had felt massively betrayed at that time but had denied to myself the degree of dejection and fury the re-traumatisation had engendered and had soldiered on. It was this denial that manifested itself so suddenly and dramatically.

Significantly, as we drew close to the heart of the matter in the middle of the second week and my resistance softened as my trust deepened, the barrage of daily tests showed a marked improvement. Recovery had begun!

In the third week, Anna was trying to teach me how to inject into my stomach, something I would have to do for a couple of months back at home. After about half an hour of my dithering, she said sharply: "For Heaven's sake, Christopher, just do it. You are not my only patient". It was a relief to see and experience that side of her. Furthermore, she "forgot" my last session, thereby re-enacting the betrayal and abandonment we had been exploring in our work. I found her tending another patient. She glimpsed me out of the corner of her eye, gasped, and promised to be with me shortly. It was difficult to hold in my cupped hands that mixture of anger, disap-pointment, grief, and profound gratitude for how the "Wounded-Healer" had constellated between us so movingly and meaningfully. Supported, contained, and emotionally held by *the setting and our relationship*, I could surf the huge wave of emotions whipped up by her unwitting "forgetting" and travel back safely through the rocks of betrayal and abandonment to the shore of my own inner being.

Now, contrast my experience with that of a patient with whom I worked some years ago and, after long consideration, has given permission for me to write about our work. To protect confidentiality, I have changed any details that could identify her.

Lindsay, a sculptor, was 44 when she first consulted me. She was seeking therapy after a serious cycle accident, which had smashed her left arm – her hammering arm – and broken her left hip, leg, and ankle. The left side of her face had also been badly damaged, leaving her scarred and feeling robbed of her former beauty. The accident had occurred almost a year to the day after the death of her partner, who had been her therapist and whom she had nursed to a painful demise from a virulent and accelerated form of cancer. After the accident, Lindsay herself had spent some months in hospital, undergoing a series of demanding operations, mostly suc-cessful but nonetheless leaving her with an awkward gait and "my mon-strous face". I thought that the accident was suicidal and needed to be taken with the utmost seriousness despite her brush off – "At least I am still alive".

She told me her story in a surprisingly colourless way for someone so aware of shades of nuance. But it was a story that chilled me to the bone, thus alerting me to a frozen state within herself with which she had habitually dealt by living life at the edge. This was something that was confirmed for me quite vividly when, during the course of our work, she announced that she had to stop sculpting for fear of going mad.

She was born six weeks prematurely to post-graduate students and spent that time in the inhospitable and painful environment of an incubator, unable to bond with a mother who did not want her and deprived of all that infants need to form secure attachments to their caregivers. Her father, naturally maternal, stepped into the void left by his wife but was mainly preoccupied with his research. Later, a brother was born and became the much beloved son of his mother. Lindsay seemed to become her mother's shadow, and her individuality and giftedness came under constant attack. She felt blamed for things going wrong in the family and was frequently physically chastised by her father at the behest of her mother.

Between the ages of 13 and 16, Lindsay and her brother were deposited for three successive summers in the care and under the supervision of the eldest daughter (who had a younger sister and brother) of family friends, whilst the four parents spent six weeks in their shared holiday home in Italy. It was in that totally anarchic, unsupervised, neglectful, and abusive setting that Lindsay had her first experience of drugs, alcohol, gay and heterosexual sex, and incest. And those explorations included frightening but exciting sadomasochistic scenarios. The whole situation was analogous with that portrayed by William Golding (1954) in his novel "Lord of the Flies". The five swore each other to secrecy, an oath Lindsay kept until she started work with her first therapist.

Having left home and gone to university with an unerring eye for violent men and women, she slept around a great deal and suffered much violation, some of it of a very dangerous kind, always living on the edge. Intense relationships with men and women were short-lived, frantic, and broke up as one partner after the other used and abused her and threw her on the rubbish tip.

She had just landed a deal with a major gallery when a violent ex-lover broke into her flat, physically attacked, and brutalised her before raping her and leaving her unconscious. The Police were not helpful because she had not immediately reported the assault, and there were no medical records or any witness statements to support her case. Friends persuaded her to prosecute, but her case was thrown out. She decided to kill herself using an overdose of pills. Her brother, who, along with their parents, knew nothing of this horrendous trauma, had a key to her flat, where he used to stay occasionally. He was passing and decided to visit on the off chance that she would be at home. She was found by him, admitted, pumped out, and assessed by a psychiatrist, who referred her to a psychiatric colleague who had just qualified as a therapist.

The therapist was male, in his early forties, and turned out to be single. His idols, as he later told Lindsay, were Otto Gross[2] and Christiana Morgan,[3] an unholy internal alliance of highly gifted and self-destructive therapists. Gross died from pneumonia and drug abuse at the age of 42 after he was found freezing and starving on a street in Berlin. Morgan drowned in very shallow water close to the beach, possibly due to alcohol.

Lindsay embarked on twice weekly therapy with her therapist, whom I will call Nick. She took up residence in a flat her parents owned, found a new studio in a community of artists, and began to produce work that externalised her trauma so that she could relate to it rather than be over-whelmed by it. She found the rhythm and structure of her sessions sus-taining, and increasingly she felt understood.

She told me that, it was at the point when she was exploring in therapy whether or not to talk with her new, gentle, kind boyfriend (a painter from within the community) about what she calls the "'Lord of the Flies' Summers", she felt a deep visceral shift within herself and Nick which inexplicably saddened her. At the next session, she perceived him as a bit detached, almost disinterested, and chilly. She developed a belief that he was jealous, and she closed down, remaining virtually silent for several weeks and feeling that he had left her "chewing ashes". I was very struck by the phrase, which, with hindsight, was astutely portentous. Her grief leaked into the relationship with her boyfriend, who withdrew to give her space. Once he was safely out of the way, Nick came back to life. He began to drip-feed Lindsay with compliments and positive affirmation; sometimes he would reveal that he, too, had once been in a dilemma similar to the one she was describing. And, as far as she could remember, Lindsay began to be curious about this kind man who understood her so well [and, of course, had harvested a huge knowledge of her, giving him a lot of power].

It was not long before this new intimacy became tactile – the odd pat on the shoulder, a hug at the end of a difficult session, the offer of a lift to the station on a rainy night – and longed for by Lindsay. "It was so different from my incubator mother", she said to me, "but I didn't really feel OK about it". But, not really trusting herself, she repeatedly obliterated that unease and, on his declaring undying love for her, accepted his invitation to move in with him at the beginning of the summer break. Unaware that this was the beginning of the end, she was soon married to him.

Lindsay found herself trapped in a master–servant relationship. The newlyweds had moved to another town, making access to her friends and artistic community problematic. Inspiration for her work drained away. She found employment as a cashier, but spent most of her time in the waiting room of life, many of her gifts and qualities refrigerated. She was back in the world of physical punishment, emotional withdrawal, and relentless criticism and shaming. After two terrible years, she resolved to leave, return to her home town, and try to re-establish her life; but, she felt defeated on learning of Nick's diagnosis of terminal cancer and felt morally unable to abandon him. Her "nursing him to death" enticed her sadism and cruelty out of the dark deep recesses of her psyche. At a primitive level, she felt that her accident was a punishment both for that and for her surviving him.

The Therapeutic Relationship and Process

We all know that the first duty of a therapist is to do no harm. And, reading Lindsay's story, all of us can quickly slide into condemnation of Nick and a similar attitude to Lindsay, much as some people do in relation to rape victims. Compassionate curiosity tends then to be extinguished. It may help if, aware of the UK's fascination with "Downton Abbey" and relations between "upstairs" and "downstairs", we realise that within each of us there is the potential to incarnate and behave from within either pole of the Nick–Lindsay dyad of master–slave. Jung's diagram may assist us.

Replacing the therapist–patient dyad with the master–slave (dominant–submissive) dyad we arrive at this:

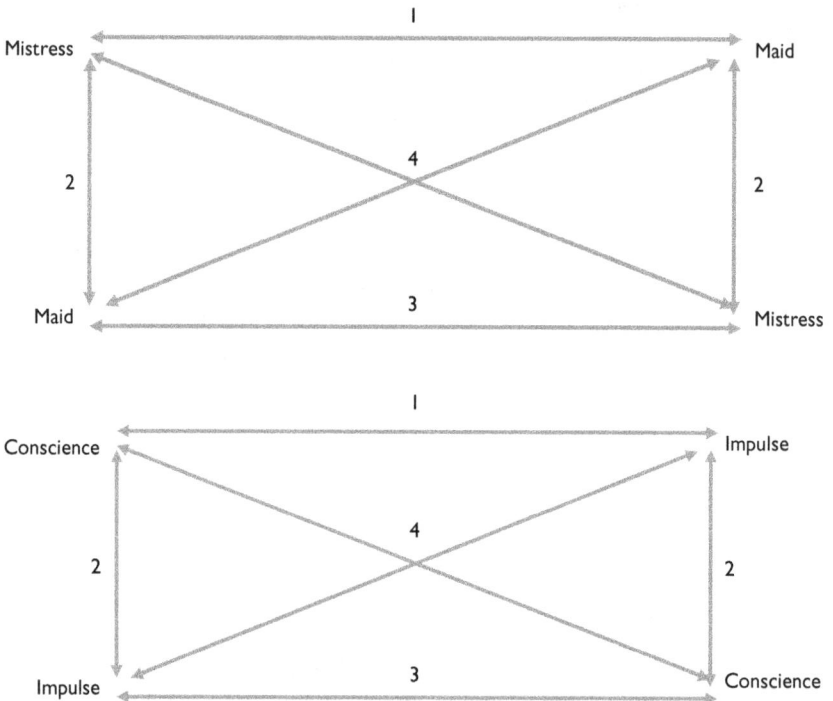

We can use this diagram to explore all the typical dyadic relationships in which we get involved through life: parent–child, teacher–pupil;

doctor–patient; policeman–criminal; lawyer–client; priest–parishioner; shop-proprietor–customer; manager–employee; political party–member, etc.

And, by taking the lift down to our depths, we can use it to try to explore our internal world, where we may find the dyads: strict conscience - unruly fantasy/impulse; neglectful parent - resentful child; idealised self - denigrated self. Like a conductor, we can invite the voices of each sub-personality into our internal choir of selves.

This is not so possible for Lindsay and the several people with whom I have worked through my career as a Jungian analyst, including both therapists who have crossed the line and patients whose boundaries have been transgressed. The latter have been seeking deeper understanding and sometimes tussling with the agonies of making a formal complaint. Two such patients in that process were told by senior members of the professional organisations, to which the offending therapists belonged, that such a complaint would ruin the therapists' careers!

People like Lindsay typically present with fear, pain, confusion, and utter bewilderment about their betrayal. That is on the surface. Below lie deep shame, self-loathing, and quasi-delusional beliefs about their bodies, which, internally may have become the **objects** of contempt. The natural expression of their selves and their sexuality has been syphoned out into a black hole devoid of love and compassion. They are imprisoned in a permafrost where nothing can grow, blossom, or come to fruition despite a capacity to adapt, which, of course, was in one way their undoing. They have become psy-chically guillotined in the sense that their intellect, rather than their emo-tional intelligence, enables them to skate through life on the ice of their permafrost without any relationship with the soles of their feet. Because trauma impels the brain to process events at lightning speed and in a state of organismic hyperarousal, verbalising pathways are bypassed. Instead, violations are encoded and retrieved by the survivor as non-verbal, often highly disorganised feelings, somatic eruptions, flashbacks, nightmares, and dangerous behaviour. The victim is plunged back into the prison of the past where s/he and others dissolve in confusion.

What the therapist's transgressive behaviour has done, despite the best of conscious intentions, is to destroy what we call the "transference". This is the world of the imaginal and the symbolic, usefully expressed in the phrase "as if". I would not use these exact words with a patient; but, I may say something like: "When you arrived late again today, I could see from your facial expression that you were expecting me to be cross **as if** I were your teacher when you arrived late for school". Such an intervention opens a space between past and present, a space for mutual reflection between therapist and patient. It brings into the open between us a habit, a pattern of relating to figures in "authority". And, it expands the patient's area of conscious choice. "Will I/won't I be late again?". This is not about beha-vioural change or conformity *per se*. It is about travelling up and down together along the spiral of the patient's inner world and the therapeutic relationship, constantly re-visiting points or moments in order to find deeper meaning and understanding. We call this "working-through": it's like patiently unpicking a tapestry where warp and weft are out of kilter and have become skewed and misaligned. We have to start again and again …

If, on the other hand, I do not process, reflect on, and take to supervision my feeling that "her story chilled me to the bone", heart-breakingly moved as I was at the time, I may short-circuit my internal ethic, my training, and my experience. Infected and consumed by her distress, which had set alight a bonfire of my own complexes, I may decide to slip my moorings, give her a hug, and (un)consciously ensnare her. The hug uncouples the space in the middle of "as if", like a fireman uncoupling a steam engine from its tender of coal or an internet provider cutting the connection with the network. A severance has taken place, precluding both re-connection and healthy separation. Flow is reduced to despairing stagnation in both parties.

From my decades of experience, I know that a long-term effective therapy will often embrace an erotic charge, which I call a "phase of enchantment", akin to those between mother and son and father and daughter. My view is that this needs to be internally acknowledged by the therapist, renounced, and mourned, leading to deeper mutual trust and individuation (Perry 1997). This phase has to be taken to supervision because its territory is hazardous and very demanding of therapists. This enchantment is so very different from an eroticised mutual attraction/ attachment between therapist and patient, which always conceals from both parties their unmet dependency needs, unless the therapist has feet on the ground.

Research suggests that the mutual satisfaction of therapeutic endeavour is based on:

1   Congruence between the patient's and therapist's goals as a result of **listening** to the patient.
2   The therapist's positive regard for and capacity to empathise with the patient.
3   The therapist's flexibility in terms of not imposing on the patient a methodology or "dogmatic" approach.
4   The development of deep trust, enhanced by a mutual commitment to agreed confidentiality.
5   The therapist's faith in the process of the therapeutic endeavour despite expected times of adversity.
6   The therapist's self-awareness (Madeson 2012).

So, what of the therapists whose work has gone badly wrong?

Some of the Dynamics of the Transgressive Process

Let's now have a look at the profiles of transgressors and seek some deeper understanding of them, knowing, as we now do, that "S/he that is without sin among you, let that person cast the first stone ..." (John 1611, 8.7).

In this section, I draw extensively on the work of Andrea Celenza (2007) and Andrea Celenza and Glen Gabbard (2003) who, at the time of writing that paper, had evaluated, treated, or consulted with 350 transgressive therapists between them as well as a similar number of clergy. They continue to work in this very specialised area.

Once they had been assured that their responses would be anonymous, about 6% of therapists who took part in a survey reported having had sex with a patient, with males outnumbering females.

Celenza and Gabbard divide this population into two types: the predators (people that the public may think of as psychopathic) and the love-sick. Fewer than 25% were predators and multiple transgressors. Most (75%) were one-time transgressors who had participated in a long-term sexual relationship.

Most, but not all, of the predators often denied the transgression in a highly defensive way, frequently claiming that it was in the patient's interest and supporting this claim by asserting that they tended to work in unorthodox ways in order to meet the patient's needs and love them back to health. They are not motivated to explore their behaviour and what might have led up to it, and they show no remorse or wish to make reparation to the patient-victim. The rehabilitation of such transgressors is not possible until they take full responsibility for what they have done.

In the love-sick group, it is not uncommon for sexual misconduct to take place in an otherwise ethically sound practice with the other patients saying that they are satisfied with their therapist and the work they are doing. The therapist in this group who commits a major boundary transgression may be in a mid-life crisis, recently divorced, in a lifeless partnership, living with illness/death in the family, dealing with the effects of a patient's suicide, facing bankruptcy, or a malpractice litigation. The sexual relationship is experienced by both therapist and patient as an intense love affair in which they both become convinced that they understand each other better than anyone else and are the only people who can meet each other's needs. They co-create a fantasy of rescuing one another, the therapist supporting this with rationalisations. The therapist self-discloses, thus reversing roles, and invokes famous analysts such as Ferenczi or Jung to justify his position.

The sexual relationship, because it is transgressive, is fuelled by unconscious aggression in the therapist often taking the form of revenge against a person in childhood who was abusive and traumatising. It is perverse in the sense of being "an expression of unconscious aggression in the form of revenge against a person, who, in early childhood made some sort of threat to the child's gender identity in the form of overt trauma ..." (Stoller 1979). Other elements of sexual excitement that cluster around that hostility include the following: (i) risk (of harming the patient, the therapist and family); (ii) secrecy; (iii) reversal of passive into active (what was done to us, we do to others); (iv) the dissolution of the symbolic (the shift from "as if" to lived reality); (v) the creation of illusion, and (vi) depersonalisation (whereby, in deep fantasy, a person is turned into a thing). When the creation of mutual understanding has reached an impasse, the penis, rationalised as a bridge of love, is actually used as a weapon of destruction of the other and self.

The love-sick share some intrapsychic factors. Males often have unconscious guilt possibly stemming back to feeling responsible for their mother's unhappiness and distress, which, in turn, may have deprived them of positive mirroring. Some manifest a compensatory identification with a heroic and idealised self-representation – a figure such as Gandhi, for example. Most find aggression and conflict very threatening because neither was accepted, tolerated, or even acknowledged in the childhood family of the therapist. This can become very problematic with an attacking and challenging patient whom the therapist can turn into a "bad" mother. The therapeutic relationship becomes too arousing, too depriving, and totally forbidden. The patient's hostility feels insufferable because it induces in the therapist the despair he felt in relation to his mother. The patient escalates the attack; the therapist gets caught in the futility of masochistic surrender and resorts to the lie of love for the patient as a way out of the dilemma.

What about the patient-victim? Once the transgressive relationship has come to the misery of its conclusion, there is a real danger that the patient (female or male) may become suicidal. She may have thoughts, feelings, fantasies, and impulses to kill herself as a way of dealing with unsustainable guilt, self-blame, abandoning herself, and being abandoned by her therapist. The defence of "never again" erected after her childhood trauma has been undermined by her realisation of "There I went again", and it may seem as if there is nowhere to go with this other than oblivion. The violation has destabilised the equilibrium of the therapeutic relationship, re-creating betrayal and abandonment and setting the stage for suicidal ideation (Campbell & Hale 2017). Grieving is complicated by an unbearable conflict between gratitude for the good work done and rage with the damage inflicted.

Institutional/Societal Responses to Boundary Violation

Neither Freud nor Jung – the founders of psychoanalytic psychotherapy – was analysed. As pioneers in "the talking cure", which focuses both on unconscious processes in the patient and unconscious processes between therapist and patient, they were flying by the seats of their pants across new territory, and both made mistakes and transgressed boundaries in ways now totally unacceptable.

As groups of Freudian psychoanalysts and Jungian analytical psychologists spawned through Europe and the USA (later in other countries), it became apparent that, along with the professions of medicine and law, etc., the public needed to be protected from malpractice and to have clear grounds on which to make complaints. Also, therapists needed clear guidelines, enshrined in Codes of Ethics, to be created in response to serious mistakes and boundary violations committed by therapists. Such codes, with a range of sanctions, were to be complemented by the development within each therapist of an ethical attitude (Allphin 2005) – the therapist's inner authority, based on empathy, compassion, and a devotion to putting the needs of the patient always in front of those of the therapist.

Several, but not all, training institutes insisted on people wanting to train as therapists embarking on a "training therapy" with senior members of the institutes. These senior members had at least five years of experience (often more), and some had the status of "training therapist". This training therapy would continue at least until qualification.

Despite what I believe to be the best of intentions, in hindsight, several things went a bit awry.

1 **Confidentiality:** This has become a *sine qua non* of every therapeutic relationship and lays one of the foundations for trust and safety. In the early days of some of the training institutes, training therapists were required to report to Training Committees on the process of trainees' therapy; such people had the power to hold back trainees at various stages. I think this practice no longer pertains. Looking back, it is clear to see that this very extended idea of confidentiality militated against trainees expressing negative feelings about their therapists (what in the jargon is called the "negative transference") because of the power dynamic involved and a fear of retaliation.

2 **Incestuous patterns:** In some institutes, younger members will have been in therapy with older colleagues and may well later meet their therapists on committees or socially. This situation creates very strong bonds of allegiance and loyalty as well as very complex dynamics which include the difficulty that trainee and therapist do not separate in the way that a patient and therapist in the NHS or private practice would do. These bonds act like an invisible glue holding together dynastic lines with muted sibling rivalry murmuring away and unconscious competition between dynasties. The organisation can become one run on a system of patronage and nepotism with a good deal of idealisation thrown in for good measure. It comes, therefore, as a great shock to such organisations when one of the members is found guilty of breaking the incest

taboo – the boundary between therapist and patient – which is the kernel of sexual violation and transgression (Margolis 1997).

3   **Charisma and certainty:** People who found therapeutic institutes tend to be very gifted and charismatic. They have a keen intellect and a strong interest in human development, psychopathology, theory, and its relation to practice. They generate new ideas and, in doing so, attract initially a small group of therapists who espouse them, and they build up a following, sometimes of an unquestioning nature. They tend not to like conflict and disagreement to the extent that dissenters are shown the door. This is true of Freud, for example, in relation to Wilhelm Stekel, Sandor Ferenczi, and Otto Gross, and we know that some Jungian groups have succumbed to schisms, particularly when they contain two powerful personalities, each vigorously adhering to their own theoretical position. Members of these groups not only find themselves in a conflict of loyalties; they also often feel caught between an (un)conscious pressure to uphold an orthodoxy, and a desire to dwell in "negative capability" – "when a man is capable of being in uncertainties, mysteries, doubts without any irritable reaching after fact or reason" (Keats 1817), which is also at the core of the ethical attitude. This capacity is one that is fostered in many psychotherapy trainings and is the opposite of

4   **Institutional denial and splitting:** it takes the most enormous amount of courage and internal work for a patient-victim of sexual boundary violation to file a complaint against their therapist. From my experience of working with such people, s/he needs to work through a period of mourning; to move from a place of vengeance and hatred to one of the deepest respect for herself to find the energy from her own ethical attitude to re-instate herself as a person of worth with a commitment to extend her self-compassion to that for others, which may include members of the public as well as trainee therapists, supervisees and tutees of her therapist.

The fear of reporting sexual boundary violation has much in common with that of rape victims seeking the help of the police and victims of child physical and sexual abuse. There is searing shame, a fear of not being believed, a terror of being blamed ("Why did you consent?"), and acute anxiety about the matter becoming public and drawing in family and friends.

The patient's internal shock waves roll onto the shores of her therapist's institute where they are often rebuffed by denial and splitting even though it is often the case that rumours have been circulating for some time about the perpetrator-therapist's laxness about boundaries.[4]

As Coline Covington has pointed out:

"The therapist who succumbs to the erotic transference (*loving/sexual feelings from the patient towards the therapist*) and breaks the incest barrier is then repeating the past by using the patient for his or her own narcissistic needs rather than being able to resist the incestuous pull and think about what the patient actually needs in order to grow and become independent, and to enable the patient to understand the ways in which his or her own incestuous longings act as an attack against the need to be able to differentiate between hate and love".

(Covington 2003)

Returning to denial and splitting: We now know that some perpetrator-therapists, like Carl Jung and the psychoanalyst Masud Khan (Sandler & Godley 2004) (who was struck off), were experienced by their patients as people with an unusual knack of diving below their patients' defences and very quickly arriving at "the heart of the matter". This is, of course, a gift – an amalgam of their own childhood, their profound intuition, their openness to the psyche of others, their deep understanding of theory and practice, and their conscious desire to understand their patients and witness their "individuation". But this gift has a highly seductive quality which, if (un)consciously exploited by the therapist, can aid and abet the sexualisation of longings in the patient and therapist for deep intimacy.

So, when therapeutic organisations feel the shock waves of a complaint being made against one of their members (often highly esteemed), their predictable response, along with that of many other professional groups and families of abused children, is "this cannot be true". Despite rumours circulating as gossip (which is a symptom of a lack of clarity about information – like Chinese Whispers), members turn "a blind eye", and look away into a dreamy, nostalgic past where everything was so new, so exciting, so inspirational, so devoid of the sordid world of incest.

And then, the cracks and fault lines within the organisation begin to admit the light of realisation before further tectonic plates shift and a "splitting" occurs. Splitting means that I bisect a person, and consciously see them as wonderful, whilst unconsciously denigrating them or vice versa. So, members congregate, form factions, and fight; each faction acting like a fundamentalist sect so certain of its convictions and going to extremes of collective institutional behaviour.

Of course, every complaint arouses acute anxiety, fear, and shame in members. Most therapists have been enticed at one time or another into incestuous longings. Some have sought further therapy; others have taken these complex issues to supervision; some have done both. Others have been sanctioned or struck off, or have left the profession.

Sadly, it is my experience that patient-victims, like relatives and friends of those who commit suicide, or victims of both child abuse and rape, need a very long, spacious time to recover. As one patient-victim told me towards the end of several years of our working together: "It is the first thing that comes to my mind every day when I wake up. It fades, but it never goes away. How could such a betrayal occur?". We therapists have to awaken to an understanding that forgiveness can never be an idealised goal of our therapeutic strivings; some things are, perhaps, beyond forgiveness? They can be accepted and integrated, but may forever remind us that we are all capable of doing great harm given the "right" frame of mind and circumstances which can suck us into mindlessness.

Advice to the Public

All the evidence we have to date suggests that it is the **quality** of the therapeutic relationship, rather than any specific method or theoretical orientation, that is healing and fosters the process of individuation.

It is therefore important that anyone seeking therapy intuitively senses the possibility of a "good fit" between patient and therapist.

Once in therapy, it may help to distinguish between mistakes and transgressions.

Mistakes by the therapist:

- Forgetting a patient's name.
- Giving the wrong invoice.
- Going to sleep.
- Missing a session.
- Repeatedly getting hold of the wrong end of the stick.
- Changing the time of a session, and then forgetting the change, etc.

These can be helpfully explored and potentially understood.

Transgressions by the therapist:

- Patting the patient.
- Putting arms around the patient.
- Providing tea/coffee as a "comfort".
- Offering "lifts" in inclement weather.
- Sending unnecessary texts out of session times.
- Being inappropriately dressed.
- Encouraging idealisation.
- Making the patient feel "special".
- Inappropriately self-disclosing.
- Sexually violating the patient in any way, verbally or physically.

In any and all of these instances, the patient needs to seek advice from a third party. The next chapter will give guidance about this.

Conclusion

Replying to Jung's concerns about boundary transgressions in his work with Sabina Spielrein, Freud wrote:

> "Such experiences, though painful, are necessary and hard to avoid. Without them we cannot really know life and what we are dealing with. I myself have never been taken in quite so badly, but I have come very close to it a number of times and had a narrow escape. [These experiences] help us to develop the thick skin we need to dominate 'countertransference' which is after all a permanent problem for us; they teach us to displace our own affects to best advantage. They are a *'blessing in disguise'*...".
>
> (McGuire 1974: p. 230)

The difference between the two men lies in both professional practice and language. Jung was the first analyst to insist that aspiring therapists needed personal therapy before and through their training in order to enable them to understand their countertransference – complicated feelings, fantasies, thoughts, and impulses about and towards patients. This is very different from "dominating" all of those, something which is likely to contribute to sexual boundary violation, because these things do not go away, as I have tried to explain, and will erupt at some time or other.

Secondly, Jung used the Greek word "*eros*" not in an erotic sense; rather, he was writing about a capacity to make loving, creative connections between me, my shadow, and sub-personalities (Wounded-Healer, for example), and the otherness of difference, which is the cause of so much terrible distress and suffering within ourselves and between ourselves and those that we love and hate, our international community, and our planet and universe.

Whilst I firmly believe and know that the community of therapists needs to improve the way it responds to complainants and defendants, I think we can return to the quote from Jung at the beginning of this chapter and ask the question: Can we, as a profession, learn from our mistakes and failures?

Notes

1 Note: I am using the generic terms "therapy" and "therapist" to denote those in the "helping professions" who are dedicated to the "talking therapies".

  Jung is referring to the wise centaur, Chiron. His father was the Titan, Cronos, who consorted with the nymph, Philyra, in the guise of a stallion, and then left her. When Chiron was born, she was so disgusted and appalled by his appearance that she abandoned him out of shame. As an orphan, he was later found and adopted by Apollo who taught him music and medicine. Chiron died as a result of being accidentally shot in the thigh by Heracles with a poisoned arrow. Unable to cure himself, despite his great skills in medicine, he gave up his immortality, passing it on to Prometheus, and was placed in the stars as the constellation Centaurus.

2 Otto Gross (1877–1920) was a disciple of Freud, but was cast out of the psychoanalytic community because of his extremist and non-conformist views on analysis. He was committed by his father, because of misbehaviour and drug addiction, to the Burgholzi Hospital, where he and Jung analysed each other.
3 Christiana Morgan (1897–1967) was an artist, writer, psychoanalyst, and co-author with Henry Murray of the Thematic Apperception Test. Her analysis with Jung went awry. Fighting his own attraction to her, he encouraged her to be a *femme inspiratrice* for her lover, Henry Murray.
4 For the purpose of this case, we are assuming the victim was female and use the feminine pronouns.

References

Allphin, C. (2005). An Ethical Attitude in the Analytic Relationship. *J. Anal. Psychol.*, 50 (4): 451–468.
Barr, A. (2006). An Investigation Into the Extent to Which Psychological Wounds Inspire Counsellors and Psychotherapists to Become Wounded-Healers, the Significance of These Wounds on Their Career Choice, the Causes of These Wounds, and the Overall Influence of Demographic Factors. (http://www. thegreenrooms.net/wounded healer).
Bollas, C. & Sundelson, D. (1995). *The New Informants: Betrayal of Confidentiality in Psychoanalysis and Psychotherapy*. London: Karnac
Bowlby, J. (1969). Attachment and Loss. London: The Hogarth Press and the Institute of Psycho-Analysis.
Campbell, D. & Hale, R. (2017). *Working in the Dark: Understanding the Pre-Suicide State of Mind*. Oxon: Routledge.
Celenza, A. & Gabbard, G.O. (2003). Analysts Who Commit Sexual Boundary Violations. *J. Amer. Psychoanal. Assn.*, 51 (2): 617–636.
Celenza, A. (2007). *Sexual Boundary Violations: Therapeutic, Supervisory, and Academic Contexts*. Maryland: Jason Aronson.
Covington, C. (2003). Incest in Jung's Work. *J. Anal. Psychol.*, 48 (2): 255–262.
Golding, W. (1954). Lord of the Flies. London: Faber and Faber.
Groesbeck, C. (1975). The Archetypal Image of the Wounded-Healer. *J. Anal. Psychol.*, 20 (2): 122–145.
Horney, K. (1942). *Self Analysis*. London: Routledge.
Horney, K. (1946). *Our Inner Conflicts: A Constructive Theory of Neurosis*. London: Kegan Paul & Co.
John the Evangelist. (1611). Chapter 8. Verse 7. King James Version of the Bible.
Jones, S. (2010). A Survivor's Account of Sexual Exploitation by a Jungian Analyst. *J. Anal. Psychol.*, 55 (5): 650–660.
Jones, S. (2010). Reply to Jan Wiener. *J. Anal. Psychol.*, 55 (5): 670–671.
Jung, C. G. (1954). Fundamental Questions of Psychotherapy. CW16. London: Routledge & Kegan Paul.
Jung, C. G. (1954). The Aims of Psychotherapy. CW16. London: Routledge & Kegan Paul.
Jung, C.G. (1921). Psychological Types. CW6. (1939) para 490 CW16 paras 73 & 239.

Keats, J. (1817). Letter to his brothers, George and Thomas, 22nd December, 1817.

Madeson, M. (2012). Characteristics of Effective Counselling and Counsellors. PositivePsychology.com.

Margolis, M. (1997). Analyst-Patient Sexual Involvement: Clinical Experiences and Institutional Responses. *Psychoanal. Inq.*, 17: 348–387.

McGuire, W. (1974). *The Freud-Jung Letters*. Princeton: Princeton University Press.

Myers, I. (1962). *The Myers-Briggs Type Indicator*. Palo Alto: Consulting Psychologists Press.

Perry, C. (1997). Transference and Countertransference. In Young-Eisendrath, P. & Dawson, T. (Eds), *The Cambridge Companion to Jung*. Cambridge: Cambridge University Press.

Sandler, A. & Godley, W. (2004). Institutional Responses to Boundary Violations. *Int. J. Psycho-Anal.*, 85 (1): 27–42.

Stoller, R. (1979). *Sexual Excitement: Dynamics of Erotic Life*. New York: Pantheon.

Wiener, J. (2010). Response to 'Susan Jones'. *J. Anal. Psychol.*, 55 (5): 661–669

Williams, R. (2019). *C.G.Jung: The Basics*. Oxon: Routledge.

Chapter 17

Bringing the Shadow Towards Light: Approaches to Assimilating the Shadow

Marilyn and David Mathew

> *One does not become enlightened by imagining figures of light, but by making the darkness conscious. The latter procedure, however, is disagreeable and therefore not popular.*
>
> (C G Jung, CW13, para. 335)

Having come to this last chapter, the question arises: can we afford to ignore the Shadow? And more than that – will the Shadow allow us to ignore it?

Change begins with ourselves, but can ripple out into the wider world. Here are some ideas about how to discover and engage with our Shadow personally and organisationally in the hope of unlocking potential and integrating its silver linings.

The Personal Shadow

Sciophobia, the fear of Shadows, is completely understandable – what terrors lurk in places where light doesn't shine? Which of us as little children were not afraid of the dark? Instead of allowing time for our sight to adjust, human beings can become remarkably adept at denying, evading and projecting our Shadow – but doing that can mean sacrificing the authenticity of wholeness; living a colourless "half-life", splashing around in the shallows rather than engaging in the depths required for what the Jungian analyst, James Hillman (1997), calls "soul-making".

How can we locate and face our own personal Shadow?

Personal good, bad or ugly daemons/daimons/demons can shift their shapes, Trickster-like in matter and/or spirit, plaguing the body or psyche. Sometimes we have to go hunting Shadow creatures in the uncharted continents of our blinding darkness, but sometimes our Shadow erupts, laying its pelt before us, offering us – if we have the mind – the chance to explore their encoded meanings.

Some light can be shed through exercises of imagination, but to really travel into Hades it is advised to be accompanied by a companion.

DOI: 10.4324/9781003255819-19

All analysts and psychotherapists will have visited their own personal rings of Hell (as much as they possibly could). They know that individuation may necessitate enduring the crucifying torments of the "Transcendent Function" (Jung CW7 & 8) at work. They may not have trodden your path, but they will have acquired faith in the analytic process. A companion's experience can certainly help, but no one goes into analysis or psychotherapy for a joyride – although that's not to say that we don't find an immense amount of joy in the process.

Diving into a Personal Darkness

Here is a story about how the Shadow of the Self demanded to be taken seriously; how an alarming dream was followed by a conjunction of nightmares and illness, and how, out of darkness emerged a path towards wholeness.

Years ago, at a crossroads in my life, I dreamed:

> I am walking down a path through a beautiful deciduous woodland full of dappled sunlight and birdsong. I meet a friend, a paediatric anaesthetist, who tells me, "You don't have to go that way you know ...". He gestures to the left, indicating a vast and rather ominous coniferous forest of which I had been completely oblivious. There are no tracks through the tall huddled tree trunks and no sign of light through their apparently endless gloom. There is no vegetation, only needles carpeting the forest floor. It is as still and silent as the grave.

A terrible thought came to me as I continued to think about this dream. Maybe, when maternity leave ended, I wouldn't, as planned, walk the sunlit path back to the job I thought I loved in kid's television ... Maybe I should take a turn into the unknown ... Maybe I should train as a counsellor?

But then a nightmare erupted:

> I see, through my living windows, that a madman is trying to break into my house in the dead of night. Quick, quick, quick, I must lock all the doors and windows! But I turn round in the hall to find he is already inside, his eyes boring into me, laser-like.

This nightmare came with intense urgency. I knew in an instant what it was about, and why it had come now. The madman's eyes reminded me of the os of a cervix; I had been waiting for the results of a smear test ... I knew there would be bad news.

Was there more to it? "Why this part of my body?", I wondered. To me the cervix represented the entrance to my most creative symbolic interior, the gateway to my/the underworld. "Why now?", I wondered as well.

This nightmare seemed to amplify the previous dream of the deep dark forest, pointing out a scary alternative path to the one I'd been contemplating. But it was only when coming round from the anaesthetic after surgery that the final unthinkable Shadow-voice spoke: "You must train as a Jungian analyst".

Thence ensued a ferocious battle between my conscious "sane" mind and the "mad" Shadow-voice within: "You must be joking!", I raged, "Absolutely NO way! I'm just not clever enough. We simply can't afford it!". My excruciating fear of failure, being thought of as stupid or lazy because, however hard I tried, I couldn't spell (I now know I'm dyslexic), meant I'd become ill for every single set of important exams I'd ever taken apart from my Art "A" level. Now, instead of saving me, my unconscious had thrown up a monstrous Shadow to torture me.

The fight went on for months. My dreaming self bombarded me night after night with dream after dream to the extent that eventually I gave in, "OK, OK – you win", I told my Shadow-voice, "I'll find myself an analyst. I'll apply. They won't have me and that will show you!" Well, the Shadow won, and the rest is history. I'm doing what I was born to do, thanks to the determination of my relentless Shadow.

Toolkit for Exploring the Land of the Shadow

Dare we "boldly go" venturing behind our socially polished persona to risk viewing the naked truth underneath the mask of a false self?

Facing our Shadow means dismantling years worth of carefully erected defences; they will have been constructed for good reason, but often remain rigidly ensconced long after they are needed. Inevitably, once our armour begins to crack, the new skin underneath can feel intensely vulnerable – we may encounter blistering shame, acute embarrassment, appalling guilt, atrocious humiliation and unforgivable regret. In addition there is the danger of getting stuck in a masochistic swamp of self-flagellatory self-criticism. However, if we don't find any of those uncomfortable feelings, perhaps we are looking in the wrong territory or have yet to remove the rose-tinted spectacles?

"Why bother descending into a hellish underworld?", you may well ask.

What does this heroic task require?

As well as an attitude of imaginative curiosity, we will need to allow ourselves to be courageously vulnerable, brutally honest and generously compassionate. Being able to hold our monstrous self in mind, to walk around it, to try to step into its shoes and "feel into" its experience is not an easy task. As those who have really explored their own racism will have found to their dismay, dig deep enough and there it will be. We need to remember we are only human.

Dreams and Nightmares

> Knowing your own darkness is the best method for dealing with the darkness's of other people. One does not become enlightened by imagining figures of light, but by making the darkness conscious. The most terrifying thing is to accept oneself completely. Your visions will become clear only when you can look into your own heart. Who looks outside, dreams; who looks inside, awakes.
>
> (Jung 1973, p.33)

For some, our dreamlife may have been a reliable companion or a faithful storyteller. Whether in the form of snapshot, story or series, they can deliver the relief of an alternative reality or the wisdom of a guiding light.

Nightmares, however, are another thing. I was always intensely relieved to wake up from their terror, and as far as I was concerned, the faster they burned up, like vampires in sunlight, the better. Why do nightmares have an annoying habit of recurring? What if, rather than persecutors, they were Psyche's alarms?

I am constantly amazed at Psyche's healing power through dreams and nightmares; how persistently small creatures beaver away in the Shadows; how the slightest shift in the central axis of the Self can result in the most extraordinary change in our whole world.

So let us proceed with the idea that nightmares are our friends (Mathew 2021) challenging us to listen to, engage with and learn from our Shadow. We can't always dialogue directly with an "inner voice", but there are other ways to interact with our dreams.

Ideas for Working with the Shadow in Dreams and Nightmares

- Record your dreams. The most effective way to stimulate a dreamlife is to wish for it.
- Think about the feelings in the dream, and how you feel on waking. Pay special attention to dreams that insist on staying with you – dreams that linger will have undiscovered layers, sometimes only revealing their deepest aspects after decades.
- Free association can be helpful. It means opening your mind to all kinds of imaginative links.
- Amplification can be interesting – is it useful to know that, e.g. copper is the metal associated with Venus?
- Who is the "you" in the dream? Usually, but not always, all the characters can be viewed as aspects of ourselves.
- Where are we in time? Is that meaningful? Are memories breaking out?
- What about the pattern, map, or landscape of the dream? Does it take you on a journey? Horizontally, vertically? In/out, coiling in spirals, circles, paths, mazes?

- Are there people in the dream? Who are they? Known or unknown? Mythological or every-day? Try to capture their fine details and even their back-story. Sometimes it's possible to ask your dream characters to tell you about themselves.
- Which elements are present? Air, Fire. Water. Earth? They will all have their personal as well as archetypal associations with alchemical processes e.g. *solutio, coniunctio/separatio, mortificatio, etc.* (Edinger 1991)
- Some dreams will have a dominant colour, texture or smell that might be useful. This invites us to be forensic – exactly what kind of green? Like what?
- Active imagination, "Dreaming the dream forward". Sometimes a dream will unfold further if we give it space. Don't be scared to have a go at this; they have an integrity of their own and cannot be forced.
- What is the Shadow this nightmare wants to bring to my attention? Have I cast out something out like the "bad fairy" in "*Sleeping Beauty*" that needs understanding or integrating?

The Body

> What men call the Shadow of the body is not the Shadow of the body, but is the body of the soul.
>
> (Oscar Wilde 1891)

We begin life as highly sensitive psychosomatic creatures. Psyche and soma, mind and body, are the two poles of spirit and matter that come together to form us as conscious, animated stardust. Gradually our minds develop a degree of separation from our physical selves, but the link remains.

Emotions can be written, painted, danced, played or spoken. Bodily idioms pepper our language: b*utterflies in the tummy, a pain in the neck, chin up, etc.* Emotions, truths and history are also encoded in the body (Van der Kolk 2015).

Bodies speak their own language through gesture, action, accidents and illness. Patterns of illness can scar our timelines. If an idea or an emotion cannot be felt or named, and cannot be dreamed, how can it come to light? Might it be written on the skin, erupting through it, or buried deep inside it?

Very many people today are still dealing with the long-lasting effects of intergenerational trauma when historic taboos are cast into a family dungeon of unspeakable shame. What was previously shut away (often literally, in a "mad room" or lunatic asylum) can surface later down the line for children or even grandchildren to deal with. Ann Karpf (1999) writes about how the unspoken trauma of her parents' experiences in Nazi Germany wrote itself over her skin in eczema.

Ideas for Drawing out the Shadow

"Drawing", in this sense, is not about how artistic we are, it's about drawing on our imaginations, pulling out wisps of Shadows, to access verbal as well as non-verbal expression.

- On big pieces of paper, make two big outlines of your body, front and back. Which parts feel OK and which do not? Use colours, textures, symbols etc to indicate how you feel about different areas. Think about the skin and what lies under it. What is the story behind any part that is not OK? What does it need to feel better about itself?

Mandalas

Jung described the Self as being "*not only the centre but also the whole circumference which embraces both conscious and unconscious ...*"(Jung CW12 para. 44)

Mandalas are circular, often geometric drawings that symbolically represent the universe of our inner world. At certain points in his life, Jung made a practice of creating mandalas as a way of externalising and tracking the shifts in himself.

- Mark a central point on a piece of paper and draw a circle. Empty your mind and let your hands dance. Does it help to work with eyes closed? Or to use the non-dominant hand?
- Repeating this exercise enables movement and direction to emerge. Are there symbols recurring, or changing, or colours morphing? Is it meaningful?

Painting Hell

The third panel of Hieronymus Bosch's *The Garden of Earthly Delights* (1505) presents us with a grotesque vision. There are many other examples from the world of art – Andy Warhol's *Electric Chair (1967)*, Salvador Dali's *The Face of War* (1940). More horrific, perhaps come from photojournalism – *Nick Ut's The Terror of War: Napalm Girl* (1972) or images of concentration camp survivors. Trawling through depictions of humanity's Shadow might be revolting, even traumatising.

How do images like these make you feel? Could empathy mean they are unbearable? Can you draw your own hell?

Ideas for Playing with the Shadow in the Theatre of the Mind

Scenes can be set in the theatre of our minds full of Shadow characters; a chorus or a single voice telling us exactly what they think of us. Are they ever complimentary? Mostly they are undermining and critical saboteurs of confidence, like an inner *"Trunchbull"* (Dahl 1988) or a cluster of hideous *"Harpies"* (Pullman 2007).

It's worth exploring the relationships of all the characters to see how they interact. It may be possible to visualise, but sometimes there are only intrusive voices. Journalling can be useful. If we record the Shadow-voice, it's possible to shed some light by cross-examining it.

- Choose two characters – an aggressor and a victim. Describe their personalities and appearances. What about their back-stories – how did they become who they are?
- Is there a dialogue, or is someone mute? It might be important for them to be helped to find their voice – how can that happen?
- Stand in the shoes of the bully. How does it feel? Is there anything good about it?
- And the one who is being lambasted? How do they feel? What are they lacking? How does that feel?
- What is it like for you to witness this scene?

Now introduce a third, wise observer.

- What are their qualities? How are they different from the other two? What can they say or do to improve the situation? Can they see the Shadow in both? Can they see the potential in both?
- Is it possible to see how this scenario became established? Does it reflect a personal myth? Is it still relevant? Would it be worth holding on to any Shadow elements?
- What kind of scene would be better?

Projections

All around us we can see the projections and personification of Shadow characters. In families, neighbourhoods, at work, in newspapers, social media, and politics, in plays, TV, novels, films, etc.

How often do we condemn and demonise rather than attempt to understand?

It's all to do with point of view. Might the "idiot" hurtling down the motorway be selfishly enjoying the thrill of speed – or rushing a child to hospital? Might the "rude" person shoving another out of the way be having a bad day – or saving someone from falling debris?

Some of us will do everything they can to trample on rivals to grab hold of power. How frequently absolute power in public or private life corrupts absolutely, and what grotesque fun there is in condemning or applauding them.

There is also a habit we have, certainly as a society, of elevating people to the status of celebrity, raising them on pedestals before scanning for the tiniest slip, mistake, bad hair day. Trolls creep out from under their bridges and attack in the most vicious ways, anonymously on social media.

Ideas for Revisiting Projections

- Who do I despise, hate, loathe most? What is it about them that is so dreadful? When have I found myself acting or thinking like them? Have they hurt me personally? Have I hurt them?
- Is there anything about them to be envied? (Envy is a nasty green-eyed monster but it can also tell us what we need more of ourselves.) Who do we delight in slagging off? Who would rate as our "Desert Island Nightmare" companions? What might it be like to stand in their shoes? Where is the shame? Do they make us feel self-righteously pristine by slinging mud?
- Who makes me feel uncomfortable enough to avoid? The homeless guy on the street? What about the pick-pocket or scammer? Are they steeped in avarice or starving?
- How do we relate to sadism or masochism? How to we feel about the misery of others, smugness of possessions, badmouthing a colleague, spinning falsehoods, scapegoating, spoiling innocence, abusing trust, not speaking out? Is there a sexual thrill?
- When have I really failed? What were the negative consequences – and the positive ones?
- What triggers self-destructive behaviour? Who is really being punished? Why?

The Shadow of Love

Love comes in many different hues and tones – it can be tender, passionate, adoring, erotic, unconditional, enduring. From another pole it can be possessive, idealising, nationalistic, narcissistic. The Shadow of love can be manipulative, obsessive, controlling, perverted, predatory or sadomasochistic. There's one thing it's really famous for – being blind.

Many social injustices and inequalities exist about what was considered at the time to be "correct" and consequently "loveable". With hindsight we can look back in horror or anger at the way things were and how we may have colluded with them. On the receiving end of being "unacceptable", if we don't fit inside the socially constructed battlements of gender, race, physical appearance, mental "normality" or sexual preference, we are cast out to live in the borderlands. Then the division can be inverted and what was considered "right" can be flipped into "wrong". As soon as there is a divide there will be a Shadow, and Shadows breed counter-Shadows.

One of the hardest Shadows to face is the one that comes with mother-hood. The arrival of a baby might give birth to the most intense protective love we ever feel or it might not. The crippling shame and the courage it takes to admit to not loving, even hating or feeling indifferent towards our own baby is unthinkable; yet not at all uncommon. The real tragedy is that motherhood is endowed with the status of a gilded icon and anything less deemed unacceptable.

There is, however, another twist on this fiercest kind of love which inevitably interweaves it with the Shadow. This is to do with the potential for hurting and being hurt. If we love our little ones more than ourselves, and if they suffer, we can never again protect ourselves from the worst hurt imaginable. How could that fear not be experience as hate?

Ideas for Exploring the Shadow of Love

- Think about all the songs there are about love in all its shades. Make a list of sentiments that feel uplifting and ones that produce a cringe or sense of revulsion. What might that indicate?
- On both sides of a piece of paper, draw a heart. On one side write all the positive aspects of love. Then turn it over and write down all the Shadow aspects imaginable. What are the ingredients of true love? How much is it spiritual and/or carnal – are either loaded with value?
- What is it like to be "in love"? Is it heaven or hell? Or both? Scary or empowering? What's the risk?
- When we are hurt or rejected, what does that mean? How do we react when love goes wrong? Can a heart be locked away for protection? Might we seek revenge?
- What are we doing when we repeatedly get into relationships that don't work? Do we feel free to be ourselves or are we camouflaging who we really are in the belief that nobody would be interested if they knew the truth? Are we selecting partners thinking we can change them? Or that they will change us? Are we trying to re-work a relationship from the past?
- Is there a mutual degree of respect? Where is the power? Is it balanced? Is there ever fear – of speaking out, raising a thought, violence? Aggression has a positive Shadow – it comes from the Latin "to move forward".
- How do we get our own way? Do we always capitulate? Ever manipulate, shame or bully?

It takes a good deal of time and courage to take these first steps towards working with our personal Shadow. We can also go on to observe how the Shadow operates in our culture and in the wider world of organisations.

The Organisational Shadow

A Shadow has three components: light, an object that obstructs the rays of the light, and the resulting image that is cast. Foucault (1982) develops this, breaking it into three components: the source of power, the subject and the resulting behaviour. This perspective is helpful in considering the Shadow in organisations, their leaders and their teams, their officers and employees.

The Shadows of Leadership – Power, Charisma and Responsibility

The balance of power in organisations is usually hierarchical and asymmetrical – bosses and workers are rewarded differently, in more ways than pay. Even in collectives, people will tend to emerge as leaders and followers depending on their personalities. Power differentials are a perfect setting for the Shadow to flourish, to divide people into a "them" and an "us".

This becomes particularly relevant in times of change. You could almost conjugate a verb around change: "I respond flexibly to changing circumstances" …, "You are inconsistent", "They can't make their mind up".

"Boss-watching" is an organisational sport, and a hazard for the unwary leader. People pick up on the slightest discrepancy between what the mouth says and the body does – and that's weighed up against the values a team has signed up to. Every fault or discrepancy is likely to be noted. Leaders can acquire the patina of gods.

Fifty per cent of us don't trust management or believe what they say. There is a well-researched psychological phenomenon known as "sinister attribution": basically, we are inclined to project our worst fears into others, assuming the worst motives for their bad behaviour (whereas if we behaved in the same way it would be because circumstances forced us to). Hardly fair, but it's a fact.

There is another potential dark side. When a visionary leader starts to believe success is all down to them rather than in the team effort they have been part of and helped to generate, they can easily be tempted into arrogance and hubris and begin to believe that they can succeed where others have failed, taking riskier and riskier decisions. At its worst this generates a toxic personality cult of if you're not "for us" or "against us". There is evidence that charismatic leaders often leave a trail of devastation in their wake as they "leave others to pick up the pieces" that their narcissistic personalities have bequeathed to the organisation.

Empowerment

Lack of power can breed resentment, cynicism, lethargy, hostility or irresponsibility. This Shadow of power – impotence – drains enthusiasm and diminishes confidence. How can we deal with that?

Ideas for Empowering People

- Say "thank you" and acknowledge effort.
- Celebrate success by picking out the little ways that everyone contributed.
- Encourage people to take on more responsibility and further training.
- Help people develop their careers. Dare we appoint people better than us?
- Speak constructively. Good listening is often, quite rightly, spoken of as a much needed, and absolutely non-trivial, skill to develop. "Active, constructive" speaking requires similar effort at development, to make sure that you link your conversation in an engaging way with the person you are conversing with. There's a fun and instructive exercise where you go round your team with each person saying one sentence and the next person saying "No, but ..." and continuing the thread of the conversation for one sentence. After a few rounds of the team in that way you start a new conversation with every person starting "Yes, and ...". Have a go, to see the difference between an active/constructive conversation and a passive/destructive conversation. You might even find your "natural" style improves!
- "Appreciative Inquiry" is a very helpful way to stay positive, building on team and individual strengths to build a positive direction for the future. Just focusing on what works well, rather on what is not going well – which is where a lot of problem-solving starts – improves the solutions you find. (Ng 2017)

Exercise for Conquering Disempowering Beliefs

This exercise examines unhelpful or disempowering beliefs, however true or not they are in reality.

It can also include general unhelpful patterns of thinking that you know you easily fall into – e.g. always focusing instantly on the worst thing that could happen. Psychologists call these habits "cognitive distortions". Over time, replacing disempowering beliefs with more positive ones will increase resilience and happiness.

One example of a disempowering belief for an individual might be: "I feel bullied by my boss, but there is nothing I can do about it", and the corresponding empowering belief might be, "I can do something about it". The consequence of this change might be to confidentially approach HR, or a trusted colleague.

Another example, for a team, might be: "We don't have the resources to do everything we are asked to do so we constantly feel we are performing badly", to which the counterpoint could be "Our resources are fixed so we should make some decisions on what is most important and stop blaming ourselves for not addressing the less important tasks". The consequence may be that you communicate the need to prioritise, and that your focus will be on your top three priorities.

Take some time to reflect on any beliefs that might be holding you back from reaching your full potential. You are going to work on these disempowering beliefs and try to overcome them. When you have an idea of what your particular disempowering beliefs are:

1   Divide a page into three columns: "Disempowering beliefs", "Empowering beliefs" and "Consequences".
2   Write your "disempowering beliefs", one underneath the other, in the left-hand column.
3   What might be the corresponding "empowering belief"? Write it in the middle column.
4   Now reflect on what it would be like if your "disempowering beliefs" were replaced with the empowered versions? What would be different? What would the consequences be? Note all the consequences in the right-hand column.
5   Finally, pick just one disempowering belief that you will consciously look out for over the next week. When it pops up, immediately replace it in your mind with your empowered version. As a team you can help each other: if you spot a conversation in the team that is going back over your disempowered beliefs you can flag it up and try as a team to move onto more positive ground.

Disempowering beliefs	Empowering beliefs	Consequences

Self-Empowerment Through Forgiveness

Finally, you can take back feelings of personal power in the power-based cauldron of an organisation by forgiving your boss for not being the boss you deserve. Like you and me, they are recruited from the human race and come with their own hang-ups and foibles. It may take work, but trying to step into their shoes might help your Shadow to feel less triggered by their actions. You can also try this in your mind with colleagues.

The Shadow in Teams – Dynamics and Decision-Making

Teams thrive when they can have full and informed discussion, not when there are "taboo" subjects that cannot be discussed or the same voices dominate whatever the topic. When people are regularly denied a voice, morale and team effectiveness suffer. This is one of the most common complaints in teams. But the solutions are straightforward. Which is not the same as "easy".

Spotting the Shadow When a Team Needs to Make a Decision Can Be Useful

- How often does one person jump in first and loudest with a view, often followed by one or two others who dominate the conversation?
- How often is there an illusion about knowledge that is supposedly held "in common" when actually only one or two people are in the know?
- How often do people conform because they don't want to stick their neck out in case they face hostility from others in the group? "Dissent" is known to improve decisions.

Psychological Insecurity

A supportive and accepting culture is essential for fostering a sense of inclusion and collective enterprise. Successful happy teams need to be able to provide a sense of belonging for team members, but a Shadow can readily cast a pall if:

- Mistakes cannot be discussed (and we all make them!).
- People can't say what they don't understand.
- Ideas most others seem to accept cannot be challenged.
- Individuals feel criticised personally when there are conflicting views.
- Issues bubble under the surface that no individual really wants to raise for fear of unsettling the team.

An Example: How Team Decisions Are Made

If you have worked in a few teams you may have noticed that they don't all work in the same way. In particular, some have a more collaborative, "inquiring" dialogue while others are full of robust points of view thrown onto the table to win an argument. You could call these "inquiry" and "advocacy" and they are each Shadows of the other. In fact "discordant polar opposites" are often a good way of identifying Shadows like black holes that rotate around each other.

The key to identifying quickly which kind of team you are in, if it isn't immediately obvious, is how listening works in the team. Are people listening in order to build on or include the points that are being made (inquiry), or are they listening to see, and be able to pick holes in the person's position and defeat their argument (advocacy). Both inquiry and advocacy have a place in good decision-making – although inquiry seems to win most of the time in the research – but the real challenge is for a team to be able to use both appropriately. Being able to engage constructively with the Shadow is essential.

The Shadow of Diversity and Inclusion

Diversity is good for business (Rock & Grant 2016), but the evidence shows that it's particularly the combination of diversity and inclusive practices that improve team performance, commitment, individual job satisfaction and well-being.

Teams, or team leaders, may have little control over the diversity of membership in the team, but what happens if the range of different experiences and mindsets available in the team are not encouraged?

"Everyday" discrimination or exclusion – casual and often unconscious ways in which people can undermine each other – can be more toxic to mental health and wellbeing than overt discrimination (Jones et al. 2016).

Research indicates that team leaders have a particularly important role to play in showing visible support to members of minority groups to facilitate their full contribution to a team and deal with divisions.

When the Shadow Erupts at Work

At work people should expect to be treated with respect, not talked over, not humiliated, not belittled, not passed over on the basis of protected characteristics (race, sex, disability, etc).

Unacceptable behaviour at work is not straightforward. It can be intentional or not, obvious to others or not, and range from apparently innocuous comments to criminal acts. The behaviour can be directed outwards at others, or turned inwards in terms of attitude. It can be as subtle as just causing a bad feeling in the room. Moody people worry more and feel more vulnerable. They may be impulsive and quick to anger and need more help to make a constructive contribution, but they may be your most skilled designer or surgeon.

Although often extremely challenging, the more serious the behaviour is, the more straightforward the avenue to deal with it. If it is clearly inappropriate or wrong, the route is simple – refer and take advice. The larger problem is with everything else. It's difficult because behaviours can be difficult to pin down, and often have been going on for a significant period of time without the person being called out – especially if that person is senior. The behaviour may be unacceptable but, if it has been left unchecked, may have developed into a "new normal"; it's not ok, but it's what people have come to expect.

The Un-Discussable Shadow

Sometimes people are well aware of a particular dynamic in a group. They talk about it privately but no-one is prepared to discuss it in the team or raise it with the team leader. It is un-discussable; a taboo subject. What's worse, its un-discussability is un-discussable.

Sometimes the problem is relatively minor: e.g. Carol joined the team right at the start as IT Lead but the project has changed and she doesn't have the level of specialist IT knowledge the team needs. She flies in especially from the other side of the world. Privately, people are muttering about the expense but no-one confronts it because they cannot get round the issue of hiring extra local IT expertise.

Sometimes it's more serious, and anxiety about discussing the issue amounts to fear: e.g. Fred says too much, too loudly and talks over everybody. No-one interrupts him, even when he's gone way off the point, because of his volatile temper. He may not realise the negative impact he's having.

There is understandable apprehensiveness and fear of conflict behind these silences. We can resort to a range of avoidance "tricks" – pretending the issue doesn't matter, waiting to see if anyone else raises it, etc. But these defensive routines get in the way of effective team performance, undermine openness, trust and psychological safety.

Exercise for Addressing Difficult Issues in a Team

Individually, look down the following list to see what you are confident everyone could raise and discuss openly, honestly and helpfully together. Tick the topics you are confident the whole team would be prepared to discuss and put a cross against those where some or all might find the discussion too uncomfortable.

How Comfortable Would All Team Members Be in the Following Situations:

- Discussing a recent success and what made it happen.
- Discussing a recent success for an individual and why/how it happened.
- Someone asking about something they don't understand.
- Discussing a publicly embarrassing problem the team is facing together and how to resolve it.
- Discussing a problem an individual team member is having (they are seeking advice on how to resolve it), like a sexual boundary violation.
- Raising this: an important decision that seems agreed but you know several members think may be a mistake but are not voicing their reservations.
- Raising this: one team member keeps talking too much/too little despite them agreeing they would change.

- Discussing a mistake the team made, why and how it happened, and moving on to agreement on how to do things differently next time.
- Discussing a mistake an individual team member made, that impacted the team, why and how it happened, and moving on to agreement on how to do things differently next time.
- One team member frequently lets the team down (e.g. misses deadlines or targets). The team needs the member to acknowledge and resolve the issue.

Collect the ticks (out of 10) from all team members. Is there broad agreement about what you could discuss and what you would find difficult? Which topics would be challenging for the team and why? Discuss it together and agree on what needs to happen next, with potentially a review in three months' time.

Exercise for Calling the Shadow out in an Individual

Challenging Shadow behaviour isn't unlocked with a single key. Here are five approaches you can try, depending on the kind of situation you encounter. Remember – with all of the approaches, kindness and courage are vital.

1   Raise the issue in private in a clear and candid way. Strike a respectful, enquiring tone. Defences have a tendency to fly up – anger, upset, denial – so try moving from the position of "judge" to the position of "helper". State that you're not looking to point blame, or make judgments, but trying to understand so you can help.
2   Make the space psychologically safe by introducing the issue as a learning opportunity, not a punitive one. Say that everyone has blind spots (and use an example from your own life – it really helps).
3   Ask your colleague for their perspective. People won't tend to listen if they're intimidated, humiliated or feel like they're not being heard. The goal is to understand what's going on for them. Listen, and try not to interrupt or express your own opinion.
4   Ask your colleague for their insight into the perspectives of others.
5   Ask what, if anything, needs to change. Insight is key: they need to come up with this. If you instruct them not to do something, the change will be inauthentic and/or short-lived.

Resolving Conflict

The Shadow feasts on conflict. Can you think of a time that you were involved with a disagreement or conflict at work?

Take part in this mental exercise right now: Think of a situation you've been involved in that required you to raise an uncomfortable subject with someone or engage them in a conversation you knew was going to be difficult. What feelings did that raise?

Common responses to this question are unease, anxiety, uncertainty, avoidance, unease, dread, anger, frustration, heart pounding, sweatiness, isolation. Although some people seem to thrive on conflict and seek out situations where they can be confrontational, most of us don't. At the other end of the spectrum, some of us find mild disagreement so difficult we avoid it at all costs, even though we can see the benefit of "robust debate" sometimes for good decision-making.

In the face of such powerful feelings, how can we best try to face this Shadow constructively?

Research indicates that the people who are most successful at managing conflict are those who don't welcome it, but have learnt to not shy away from dealing with it.

Commonly, in conflict, we both think we are right and the other is wrong because we are likely working from an overlapping, but different, set of facts about the issue. Assumptions (often incorrectly) get made about other people's interests and needs – we tend to think their motivations and intentions will impact us negatively: e.g. a brief email is rude rather than hurried because they were responding quickly. The intention was helpful but the impact on us was to make us feel offended.

We are aware of our own intentions and the impact others have on us, but may not be so aware of others' intentions or the impact we are having on them. Then, if in conflict, the emotional heat is turned up and it can turn into a nice feast for the Shadow.

Exercise for Resolving Conflict

1   Establish a safe conversation – one where both parties feel comfortable expressing themselves without negative ramifications or feeling threatened.

   • State that you want to work together to understand each other's perspectives and to see how best to resolve the issues and move forward – not to apportion blame.
   • Acknowledge that you consider their perspective to be legitimate, and that you hope they are able to understand your perspective too.
   • Accept that the conversation may not be easy, but that you are looking to try and make things better for everyone.

2   Listen. The other person won't start to listen until they've felt heard

3   Explore. What is really going on? How do they see the situation? Genuine curiosity goes further than "fact-finding". Don't expect to

agree but compel yourself to listen open-mindedly without interruption or judgement. (Key test: you shouldn't be doing most of the talking.)

4   Dig Deeper. Pick up on what's important. What impact is the situation having? What do you think needs to happen for us to be able to move on? What do you hope to get out of this discussion? Make sure you understand correctly by reflecting back what you've heard.

5   Common solutions can be considered when everything important to all is set out clearly. If this hasn't occurred, no-one will have felt heard, and they'll go back to "their story". The best outcome is a "win-win" not a compromise, which usually involves agreeing on the lowest common denominator causing offence, or agreeing a trade-off where one side sacrifices something it wants in return for a corresponding sacrifice.

Personality and the Shadow

We are not all the same! People come in a wide variety of psychological shapes and sizes.

Personality theories like The "Myers-Briggs Type Inventory (MBTI)" or The "Big Five" Personality Characteristics help us to understand and explain why people behave the way they do at work.

Each aspect of our personality will have a Shadow. What is crucially important is not which function is "inferior" or "superior"; ideally all are well balanced. What matters is that what we might not think of as valuable has a silver lining if it can be recognised and respected. When one aspect of personality is over-emphasised it can be problematic and can reveal a dark side. All personalities have virtues – difference does not mean better or worse.

Watch out, however, for the Shadow in the form of unhelpful behaviour dressed up as, "That's just the way I am". That will need further thought.

A team profile using Myers-Briggs is just the sum of the individual member profiles, so you can just add up e.g. the number of introverts, extraverts and say e.g. "This is an extravert type team". The more evenly balanced the team between "I" and "E", the less likely this dimension is to be problematic.

We often use this, particularly to look at

- the way the team discusses issues e.g. too little data (T), too much feeling (F) and
- the way the team communicates externally e.g. too much big strategic picture (N) and too little detailed information (S).

You can see below how ENFP and ISTJ teams are Shadows of each other but both have the value of difference.

ENFP M 6% F 10%
Futurist / Inspirer

Loves creating ideas, enthusiastic, ingenious and imaginative.

Quick with solutions, and ready to help anyone. They trust and take others at face value, and are diplomatic.

May have difficulty deciding, and rely on their ability to improvise instead of preparing advance.

Trust hunches, exuberant, spontaneous and insightful about people.

Can contribute to a team by exuding enthusiasm, empowering others and contributing creative original ideas. They understand other people, include them, and recognise and validate their contributions.

They may talk and promise too much.

ISTJ M 16% F 7%
Planner / Duty fulfiller

Pragmatic, consistent, and attentive to detail. Serious, quiet, and thorough.

Concise, focused, organised, and predictable. Reserved, conscientious, and calm.

Make-up their own minds, and work steadily regardless of distractions.

Realistic, trusting facts.

Wants structure, and makes time to be alone.

Contributes to the team by hard work, effort, and ability to classify ideas.

Is organisationally skilled, and systematic. Can be relied on to gather facts and examine their logical consequences.

May irritate team members by being too task focused.

Final Thoughts

We hope this last chapter has given you some ideas for tackling the Shadow both personally and organisationally and has inspired to you delve further into your depths.

For further information about the Teams and Leadership online platform for working in organisations see: https://www.teamsandleadership.com/

References

Dahl, R. (1988) *Matilda*, London, Puffin.

Edinger, E. (1991) *The Anatomy of the Psyche – Alchemical Symbolism in Psychotherapy*, Chicago, Open Court.

Foucault, M. (1982) *The Subject and Power, Critical Inquiry* vol 8, 4. pp. 777–795, The University of Chicago Press.

Hillman, J. (1997) *The Soul's Code: In Search of Character and Calling*, London, Bantham.

Jones, K.P., et al. (2016) Not so subtle: A meta-analytic investigation of the correlates of subtle and overt discrimination, *Journal of Management*, vol 42, 6, 1588–1613.

Jung, C. G. (1969) *CW 8. The Structure and Dynamics of the Psyche*, London, Routledge.

Jung, C. G. (1967) *CW 7. Two Essays on Analytical Psychology*, London, Routledge.

Jung, C. G., Adler, G., & Jaffé. (1973) Letter to Fanny Bowditch, Letters of C. G. Jung, vol I, 1906–1950, 33.

Karpf, A. (1999) My Weeping Skin, *Journal of the British Association of Psychotherapists*, vol 36, 3–14.

Mathew, M. A. F. (2021) Together – apart: in touch in a time of separation, *The Journal of Analytical Psychology*, vol 66, 3, 463–483.

Ng, T. W. H. (2017) Transformational leadership and performance outcomes, *The Leadership Quarterly*, vol 28, 385–417.

Pullman, P. (2007) His Dark Materials Trilogy, *The Amber Spyglass*, New York, Scholastic.

Rock, D. & Grant, H. (2016) *Why Diverse Teams Are Smarter*, Harvard Business Review.

Van der Kolk, B. (2015) *The Body Keeps the Score: Mind, Brain and Body in the Transformation of Trauma*, New York, Penguin Books.

Wilde, O. (1891)*A House of Pomegranates*, London, James Osgood McIlvanie.

Appendix

Writings on the Shadow by Toni Wolff

Edited and translated from German by
Katerina Sarafidou

The individuation process is the empirical realisation of psychic totality. Individuality is the inseparable structural unity of the individual. Individuation is the conscious realisation of this unity and the resulting integration of the ego into the totality of one's psychological conditions, i.e. into that aspect of the totality that is constellated in a given psychological moment.

Individuality exists a priori, but unconsciously. The unconscious components of psychic totality therefore appear in and through the outer object. Individuation is a process of differentiation that releases the projected psychic material from its identity with the outer object and integrates it into the subject. In this way, the individual becomes conscious of its structural wholeness.

Individuation strives for a living cooperation of all psychic factors. Its purpose is none other than to free the self from the false wrappings of the persona on the one hand and the suggestive power of unconscious images on the other.

The images of the collective unconscious were not discovered by complex psychology. On the contrary, they are evident in the form of mythical and religious symbols, from primordial times until the most differentiated religions of the present time. As such, however, they were never understood as psychological images, i.e. as images through which the life and essence of the psyche could be expressed. Even when great poets and artists draw their material from this inner world of experience, this is not seen as an experience of the objective psyche, but rather they are understood as aesthetically motivated without any reference to the creative subject within and to the universality of their content.

Complex psychology, however, brings two new facts: an experience and a recognition. On the one hand, the psychic image is experienced as a primordial phenomenon, not in a form that has been processed and fixed by consciousness, but as it emerges directly from the psyche's substance. It is therefore neither aesthetically, nor intellectually, nor in any other way differentiated – it is of iridescent form and manifold meaning.

The unconscious image is a seed, grown on the soul's primordial ground, the imagination which, before the differentiation of the psychological functions (thinking and feeling, intuition and sensation, extraversion and introversion), is brought together in a symbol which is the basis for the conscious mind in terms of substance, content, form, and idea.

On the other hand, these germinal images are not of an aesthetic or intellectual nature. Rather, they concern the human being directly. They have grown in his soul, emerged from his most subjective life, from his various personal conflicts. They are his psychological drama, they are beings from his psyche, indeed they are the essence of the psyche itself. They are the Also-I of the human being, the Other in him that makes him whole. They are the mediators who realise the autonomous life of the psyche.

Through the effect of these objective psychic contents on consciousness, a state is created in which man begins to experiment with his being, where nothing is given forever, and nothing is hopelessly fossilised. This is also a state in which there is no longer absolute certainty, but everything is in a process of becoming and is therefore more or less relative. By complementing the consciousness of the present through the integration of the collective unconscious, an expanded consciousness emerges that has historical continuity. But when ego-consciousness, as the highest peak of the spirit of the times, collides with the spirit of the collective unconscious of humanity, the latter is awakened and transformed from the shadowy and unchanging state of mere psychic being that contains its general essence, and reveals to this one individual in this one moment, through the most personal experience, the unique meaning of his life.[1]

The individuation process in this specific form has two preconditions that can set it in motion. One is psychological analysis, and the other a life situation that demands the total engagement of the human being. Both preconditions require a certain maturity in life and the necessary fulfilment of the normal responsibilities of adaptation. Common to both, however, is the indispensable criterion of the psychological relationship to another person: one who is objectively confronted with the problem, i.e. who is not himself involved in it. In the case of analysis, this is the professional psychologist, whereas in the case of a specific life situation, it is a person who has had experience of the objective psyche and therefore possesses the necessary psychological knowledge.

The relation to the Other is therefore indispensable because the Other represents the particular human reality with respect to the autonomous process of the psyche, and thereby enables the subject to grasp and differentiate its own function of human relatedness. Only by preserving the integrity of this relatedness can an objective standpoint be guaranteed vis-à-vis the collective psyche.

Jung calls the method of psychological analysis a dialectical procedure – a dialogue or a confrontation between two people. A person is, in the sense of dialectics, a psychic system which, in the case of an influence on another person, interacts with another psychic system. In the field of a dialectical procedure, the doctor must step out of his anonymity and give an account of himself, just as he himself asks the same from his patient.

The dialectical procedure alone does justice to the individuality of the individual. It is a complete renunciation of theories and practices in favour of an attitude that is as unprejudiced as possible. The therapist is no longer an acting subject, but a co-experiencer of an individual process of development. Under all circumstances, the supreme rule of a dialectical procedure is that the individuality of the patient has the same value and right to exist as that of the doctor, and therefore all individual developments in the patient are to be regarded as valid, unless they self-correct. Another source of the dialectical procedure is the fact of the multiple interpretability of the symbolic expressions of the psyche. The individuality of the patient ultimately decides the interpretation.

The individual relationship to the psychologist is the preliminary stage of the individual's attitude towards other people and the outside world in general – a task that begins with psychological analysis, but can only be solved in the real world, just as the integration of the symbols of the autonomous process of the psyche also requires full realisation in life. Psychological analysis only provides the means by which the relationship to the total psyche can be recognised and experienced. With the constellation of new problems later on, new unconscious contents will be activated, because the fullness of the human being is only lived to the end when one dies.

When the unconscious psyche is activated, its contents are projected onto a human object, through which the most difficult entanglements and most violent shocks arise. Everything that is constellated in the psyche but left in an unconscious state because of inertia, inattention, or fear acquires energetic intensity and effectiveness and, when the subject dissociates itself from it, it migrates into the environment and into those objects with which it has strongly connected, in line with the law of least resistance. As a result, other people are also affected by it and may even be forced to play the role of an aspect of the soul that has been delegated to them. Other people then suffer the effects that the subject avoids.

It is therefore clear that, when it comes to human relationships, it is paramount that the "participation mystique" with fellow human beings is eliminated as far as possible and that the psychic contents represented by the Other are integrated into the subject. Only after the object of projections has been separated from the projections themselves can it become clear whether the object was only a receptacle for subjective content or whether the projection was based on the necessity for a more complete, i.e. individual relationship. Therefore, resistance to psychological insight is often based not only on one's reluctance to see oneself clearly, but also on the fear of depriving the object of its value by withdrawing the projections. The individual meaning of the object, however, is a question of fate that is not at the discretion of the persons in question. Having a soul is a hazard of life.

The integration of the unconscious psyche that takes place through the individuation process does not produce a state of unrelatedness and impenetrable isolation – rather, it is the basis for a more unconditional connectedness than that which is possible through the mere superficial connections of the superior functions and the persona attitude. The inferior functions can only be differentiated relatively and therefore always retain the property of their relation to the collective psyche. This gives a more total and natural connection to humanity as a whole: a conscious and experienced participation, which consists both in influencing others and suffering the influence of others on one's own individual character.

The experience of the objective psyche is bound to the most banal and lowest point of passage, which involves taking seriously one's own most subjective and personal facts. The soul is only experienced by those who do not bypass themselves.

The psychic object which man first encounters in his inner world is the figure of the Shadow. The Shadow is always of the same sex as the subject but of an essentially different nature than the ego. It is the ego's dark reflection. Shadow is that which does not stand in the light of consciousness and which cannot ascend to the heights of conscious achievement because it partakes of the inadequacy, tragedy, and evil inherent in human nature. The Shadow contains all the values that stand in opposition to the values of the ego. It has a morally and spiritually inferior quality and, moreover, it does not accord to the spirit of the times as the ego does; all kinds of remnants of the near and distant past cling to the Shadow. In so far as human nature participates in universal qualities, the collective psyche contains the possibilities of all the highs and lows of humanity.

The Shadow is always on the other side, where the ego is not. It is the alter ego, the "I" which I also am, not in the world of my individual consciousness, but in the world of the total psychic reality. The Shadow is not identical in value with the ego and making it conscious does not take away any of the ego's qualities; rather, these are augmented beyond the personal and time-bound to the universally human. Just as the persona contains everything corresponding to external collective values that one wants to be and to represent toward oneself and toward others, so does the Shadow include everything that belongs to the collective human nature, but which one rejects for moral, aesthetic, intellectual, or other reasons. It contains these qualities which one does not allow to emerge because they do not correspond to conscious principles and because they appear impractical or nonsensical. For this reason, the Shadow's activity is often like a trickster that surprises and frightens one with the most unexpected and unpleasant pranks. It is at work there, where one lets oneself go, where one appears stupid, where one catches oneself being spiteful, or where one discovers to one's own horror egotistical motives in an ostensibly selfless act and petty criticism in a noble sentiment.

The Shadow is the dark brother that accompanies the ego everywhere, it is the Other in us that also wants to live with us so that we can be whole. It is always where the ego is not. If the ego is above, the Shadow is below. If the ego is capable, the Shadow is unreliable. If we are modern in temperament, the Shadow is old-fashioned. If we are conservative, it is rebellious. The Shadow does not compensate for the one-sided conscious attitude, but is complementary to our functional personality, which can only ever be a section of the collective, a particular variant of humanity. If we are one thing, the Shadow is another, it is half of our basic mirror image that lies in the background. If we are aware of this and allow it to live with us, we are able to tread the middle way and thus do justice to the paradoxical nature of the psyche. For when we give ourselves truly and unconditionally to a given situation, the Shadow is also there in everything that we are and everything that we do. And if we are tolerant enough to recognise this "neighbour" in us and to give him his necessary rights, we understand not only our own nature, but also the nature of the Other, much better than if we had elevated ourselves above him. Then, the Other does not need to assert himself violently against us. The integration of the Shadow is the beginning of a detached and objective attitude towards one's own personality.

The Shadow appears in dreams and fantasies as a socially, morally, or spiritually dark and inferior figure. It is an archetype that also plays a major role in the psychology of primitive cultures. There the Shadow is concretised as a functional, separate element of the individual personality. One should therefore not step on someone else's Shadow as this would violate the integrity of their personality, i.e. one would have a magical effect on them.

The fate of the human being who loses his Shadow and thus his humanity was symbolised by Chamisso in "Peter Schlemihl".[2] But there are also people for whom the opposite happens, i.e. the ego mistakes itself for the Shadow and then takes on the role of the Shadow in the real world. These are the unlucky ones, for whom nothing flourishes and who stumble from one misfortune to another. For some reason they have fallen into the reverse, Shadow side of the psyche and therefore have no proper relationship either to the outside world or to themselves. They blame themselves for all misfortune and are complicit in every evil act. They live in reality, what should be experienced in psychic space.

Something similar happens in the individuation process through the encounter with the Shadow. The Shadow has a personal and an impersonal side, half of which belongs to the ego and half of which is a content of the collective psyche. The two sides, however, are not separate – on the contrary, they are indistinguishably fused. Furthermore, the archetype of the Shadow is intertwined with all other archetypes that lie behind it. Only the influence of consciousness distinguishes the various figures and components of the Shadow, which in their unconscious state are experienced only in their intense effectiveness.

The differentiation of the Shadow occurs through the ego's most acute self-evaluation that allows it to become aware of its own nature. Through this process, the Shadow as an archetypal figure is delimited, but its effectiveness is not thereby nullified; rather, it can now unfold and be related to for the first time. The Shadow mediates experiences that place the ego in symbolic situations of a collective character, insofar as these lie on the actual Shadow side. They are experiences of darkness and evil, experiences of the inferior human, of the ugliest parts of humanity. It is everything that the human being also is when he is not human, but human beast. I, as a person in my conscious being, am not that, but I, as a universal human being, am that too.[3]

Through the recognition of the Shadow, the individual is confronted with his own polarity. The archetypal part of the Shadow leads the individual further into his inner opposite and thus into the oppositional nature of the unconscious in general.

When consciousness fulfils its natural function of orienting itself towards external reality, man creates an image of the world and of himself. If this image is to be in any way accurate, this will depend on whether the individual knows himself sufficiently so as not to falsify that image; for all illusions, all desires, all that is feared, all that is not assimilated into the subject, is then projected onto the world and becomes the ground not only for thought but also for action. And as long as one sees the good and the bad only on the outside and expects the necessary changes from the outside, one is not yet psychologically mature, because one does not make oneself responsible.

Psychic reality imposes itself precisely on those individuals who fulfil the standard of external conformity, competence, common sense, and awareness of things given in reality. Consequently, the compensatory function of the psyche here does not consist in accentuating these values, but in a kind of relativisation of them by demonstrating its own reality as a counterweight: the inner subjective becomes as effective as the outer objective, the unreal as convincing as the concrete, and the fantastic as illuminating as the rational.

It is precisely when consciousness carries out its function with full commitment, when it really grasps what is objectively given and actually realises what is concretely real, that it reaches its own limits, for then man engages with his whole being. The whole, however, is alien to him and must be alien to him, for it is new and sacrificial psychic life which is only beginning to become.

Thus, the way is wide open for all the subjectivism and the fantasy operation of the psyche. It is the irrational that could devour concrete reality, and it is the danger of all primeval instinctiveness. It is psychic nature that threatens to dissolve cultured consciousness. It comes to life when consciousness fulfils its own task and when it has no forms with which to grasp the operations of the psyche.

It is a psychic law that what the individual fears most or is unconsciously threatened by, becomes his fate. In that which frightens him lies his weakness, his sore spot, and perhaps also the seed of transformation.

Human strength is the psychological place where one decides and acts from his I. Human weakness is the place where one suffers and where things happen to him. In strength, one relies on himself; he is consciously differentiated from others and willingly drawn to them. In weakness, he is dependent, variable, and subject to transformation, inevitably influenced by external and internal factors. Strength and weakness together make the whole man, the man as he really is.

It is so much nobler to help the other and it is also so much more comfortable, for one can thereby bypass the Other in oneself. But now one discovers that the demand to love one's neighbour as oneself depends on a presupposition whose meaning one had taken far too superficially, for one does not love oneself at all. One is perhaps in love with oneself or with certain qualities. Love, however, is not only a feeling or an emotion but an attitude, and it presupposes the whole person, "with all my heart and with all my soul and with all my strength and with all my mind".

Christianity has brought to the awareness of Western culture the inestimable value of the inalienability and uniqueness of the human soul. But how can I appreciate and understand the soul of the other if I do not know my own soul? I am blind to both.

I must see myself as I am and stand by myself as I am. I cannot become other than what my psychic structure has marked out for me; I cannot get away from myself; I can only fulfil myself and be responsible for myself. No one can take this responsibility from me, no one can live my life, and no one can do for me what I myself must do, create and suffer. I cannot delegate to others what I want to achieve, and I cannot make others the cause of my own inadequacy. I cannot blindly love or blindly hate others, for I must know why I love or hate them and what part of myself I am imposing on them. I must know why I have this or that conviction and I must account for the fact that any conviction can only be subjective; I must know to what extent my subjectivity is legitimate and to what extent it merely contains my unacknowledged self.

This realisation does not make me any better but only a little more aware and honest, and possibly a little more tolerant of what is different and foreign. In so far as I am human towards myself, I can also be human towards others. By experiencing the deviations and aberrations of my nature, it is possible for me to trust natural development without trying to bend something into shape with a rational argument or with an instinctive defence. I have to realise that I can only overcome what

I have previously accepted, and I have to realise that the irrational and the evil also exist because I have experienced them in my own depths.

To the extent that an individual is brought by this fate to the experience of his inner chaos, he experiences the objective psychic law. Not as advice and guidance, but as an event and as a dark suggestion that must be grasped by the conscious mind and whose validity or dubiousness can only be proven through life's venture.

From the experience of psychic law comes the realisation that nothing is absolute and that everything also has its opposite side and counter-movement. The yes is followed by a no and the no by a yes, the morning by an evening, the ascent by a descent, and the downfall by a renewal. The solidity and uniformity of consciousness are just as real as the diversity and non-differentiation of psychic nature; willing and deciding are just as necessary as allowing something to grow and letting things happen. The eternal images slumbering in the soul require all our efforts to be awa-kened into redemptive form, and yet this happens not by doing and willing, but by grace.

Psychic reality is change and movement, relativity and polarity. And yet it only becomes real for me through my unequivocal commitment, only by renouncing everything provisional and inauthentic, and through the unconditional affirmation of the here and now. The smallest and most ev-eryday things are important if the greater things are to last, and only from the complete engagement with the most personal does the impersonal arise. Spirit is only generative when it permeates even the most banal everyday life, and culture is more than mere civilisation when it not only dominates nature but also contains and shapes it.

I am rooted in my own being and yet inseparable from the world and immersed in it in such a way that everything that escapes my external ex-perience of the world meets me in my inner reflection, so that I can grasp it as a whole, for only in this way can I myself become a whole. I am responsible for myself and completely on my own, and yet I experience my being as it is only in obligatory solidarity with others. The people who are the closest and most real to me and whose essence is open to me are also the bearers of a mystery and a fulness of meaning that I cannot interpret. I gain the Self only by becoming fully myself – and I can never experience myself unless I recognise that it is very little my own and that others are included in it.

Thus, the experience of psychic reality gives rise to a certain view of life. It is not philosophy, for it explains neither the world nor the spirit, and it is not religion, for it knows nothing about the metaphysical. At the most, it can be called a certain philosophical attitude based on psychic facts that have been proven reliable and valid. Alternatively, it can be called a religious attitude, insofar as the human being has experienced that the ego is not the last instance of itself, but that it is entangled in helpful and destructive powers which reach beyond its capacity and comprehension and to which it must expose itself.

The reality of the psyche is a paradox in every respect. It confronts man with the task of knowledge and experience at the same time, for neither is sufficient without the other. It shows him that his being is nature and spirit, individual and collective, present, past, and future, and that fate always happens simultaneously both outside and inside; that the individual must both intervene and let things happen; that he is I and not-I at the same time. The realisation of psychic reality leads man honestly to draw the ethical consequences of conscious insight and, thus, he gets in opposition with himself and into an endless conflict where all movement stands still, where he is crucified between his own yes and no, between his I and everything that is Also-I and yet this is the only way that life is fully lived and individuality is realised.

Notes

1 The experience of the objective psyche has always found expression in the primordial images. These are images of the "night sea voyage", of the battle with the dragon that hides the jewel, of the dangers of the soul in the underworld and in the state after death and before reincarnation, as described in the Egyptian and Tibetan Books of the Dead; they are the cosmogonic symbols of the gnostic philosophies, of the processes of alchemical transmutation, and so on. They are the images of the essential problem of humanity, the problem of becoming conscious, of the struggle of consciousness against unconsciousness, which at first confronts us as a demonic enemy, but which at the same time contains the most precious treasure: the sacrificial life of the psyche and the expansion of consciousness that is won through its integration. The expansion of consciousness consists in the reconnection of the ephemeral, rational, outward-oriented consciousness, to the eternal and vital symbols that fulfil the depths of our soul. The fullest life is only possible in harmony with them, wisdom is a return to them. It is in reality neither faith nor knowledge, but the conformity of our thinking with the archetypes of our unconscious, which are the inconceivable emitters of every thought that our consciousness is capable of grasping.

2 Translator's note: Peter Schlemihl is a novel written in 1814 by Adelbert von Chamisso, where the main character sells his shadow to the devil in exchange for inexhaustible wealth. By doing this he discovers that he has also bartered away his soul and wanders through the world searching for the peace of mind he gave up.

3 In the psychology of primitive cultures, the shadow is also called the bush soul, which is a part of the soul that is not at home in human society but is at home only in the wilderness. One encounters this shadow in the form of an animal into which one can transform under certain circumstances, usually for the purposes of black magic.

Name Index

Page numbers followed by "n" indicate a note on the corresponding page.

Subject Index

Page numbers followed by "n" indicate a note on the corresponding page.

For Product Safety Concerns and Information please contact our EU
representative GPSR@taylorandfrancis.com
Taylor & Francis Verlag GmbH, Kaufingerstraße 24, 80331 München, Germany

www.ingramcontent.com/pod-product-compliance
Lightning Source LLC
Chambersburg PA
CBHW050333270326
41926CB00016B/3430